Socratic Citizenship

Socratic Citizenship

Dana Villa

PRINCETON UNIVERSITY PRESS

PRINCETON AND OXFORD

Copyright © 2001 by Princeton University Press
Published by Princeton University Press, 41 William Street,
Princeton, New Jersey 08540
In the United Kingdom: Princeton University Press,
3 Market Place, Woodstock, Oxfordshire OX20 1SY
All Rights Reserved

Library of Congress Cataloging-in-Publication Data
Villa, Dana Richard
Socratic citizenship / Dana Villa.
p.   cm.
Includes bibliographical references and index.
ISBN 0-691-08692-3 — ISBN 0-691-08693-1 (pbk).
1. Socrates—Contributions in political science.
2. Citizenship. I. Title
JC71.S62 V56 2001
323.6'01—dc21   2001021017

This book has been composed in Janson

Printed on acid-free paper. ∞

www.pup.princeton.edu

Printed in the United States of America

1 2 3 4 5 6 7 8 9 10
1 2 3 4 5 6 7 8 9 10
(Pbk.)

TO MY MOTHER

VIRGINIA BARRETT VILLA

Contents

Preface	ix
Acknowledgments	xv
CHAPTER ONE What Is Socratic Citizenship?	1
CHAPTER TWO John Stuart Mill: Public Opinion, Moral Truth, and Citizenship	59
CHAPTER THREE Friedrich Nietzsche: Morality, Individualism, and Politics	125
CHAPTER FOUR Max Weber: Conflict, Integrity, and the Illusions of Politics	186
CHAPTER FIVE Hannah Arendt and Leo Strauss: Citizenship versus Philosophy	246
CONCLUSION	299
Notes	311
Index	355

Preface

THIS IS A BOOK about the relationship between citizenship and philosophy, on the one hand, and citizenship and moral and intellectual integrity, on the other. In it I argue that Socrates was the first to suggest (in the words and deeds reported by Plato) that citizenship must be informed by these two intimately related kinds of integrity, typically seen as the virtues of "good men" or "philosophers" but not *citizens*. With this suggestion, Socrates created an alternative conception of citizenship, one which placed the traditional civic virtues beneath the related claims of individual moral conscience and intellectual honesty. Many of his fellow citizens viewed this stance as an example of *bad* citizenship, one destructive of Athenian democracy and ultimately worthy of death.

Socrates' suggestion, though familiar, is still radical, especially when it is contrasted with the ideal of citizenship inscribed in the texts of the Western tradition of political philosophy (Aristotle, Machiavelli, and Rousseau in particular). Citizens, we are told, should be public-minded and self-sacrificing; they should have a keen sense of obligation and an eye to the "common good." They should be loyal, brave, law-abiding, and not unfamiliar with what Leo Strauss labeled the "severe virtues." They should take part in the life of their community, reserving a not insignificant part of their energies for the fulfillment of shared duties and goals. They should actively participate in deliberations concerning common matters. They should be pious, moderate, and of good moral character. They need not "love their country more than their souls" (to paraphrase Machiavelli), but they should value their political rights and obligations every bit as much as they value their families or property. For only a stable political order permits the enjoyment of such "private" pleasures, and a stable political order is built not simply on laws and institutions but (as Rousseau observed) on the character and mores of its citizens.

This line of argument has found recent and amplified echo in the writings of communitarians, "virtue theorists," and neo-Aristotelians of one stripe or another. It has also been a staple of self-styled participatory or "radical" democrats, who, influenced by the sixties, have sought to revivify the idea of citizenship in the context of a consumerist culture. While the list of "civic virtues" touted by these camps varies considerably, one finds a shared insistence on the need for commitment to something bigger than one's self, as well as the related conviction that rampant "individualism" is the root cause of the anomie and disinterest plaguing contemporary politics. Citizenship is thus offered not only as a potential vehicle for the recovery of democratic self-government but as a necessary discipline for the individual. Properly pursued, citizenship helps turn us away from the false gods of materialism and egoism toward something larger, truer, and (supposedly) more meaningful: the life of community or political engagement.

I am skeptical of such arguments, but not because I question the motives of their contemporary proponents. Often (though not always) their intentions are admirable. Many recent writers on these themes wish to combat the growing centralization and bureaucratization of political power, and to limit the disproportionate influence wielded by large economic interests (an influence which often makes a mockery of the democratic process). In light of such developments, the desire to restore the rudiments of civic virtue—to cultivate a more publically oriented form of life—is entirely understandable and, on the whole, laudable. The problem is that this desire is often presented in an overtly moralizing form, one which values community over individualism, service over dissent, belief over skepticism. It is as if the current disenchantment with politics—the enormous anomie which has descended upon the American (and other) electorates—warranted any and all strategies which might conceivably reengage people.

But suppose citizens—urged on by communitarian rhetoric, a shift in the national mood, or (more likely) events themselves, become more active, more engaged? What then? What kinds of actions and judgments will their newly rediscovered sense of political membership encourage?

In this form, the question is hypothetical and exceedingly general. Who is to say in what direction a reengaged citizenry might move? Whichever direction it is, it will be a function of issues, events, conflicts, and causes which no one can foresee. My worry is that contemporary discussions of citizenship—responding, on the whole, to the vaguely perceived "malaise" of individualism—have predisposed us to view anything which is either cause-based, group-related, or service-oriented as the core of "good citizenship," and anything which simply dissents or says "no" as of little value. To be giving of one's time and energy in the service of a "cause" (the environment), animated by the desire for recognition of the identity and rights of one's group, or simply involved in the rich associational life (churches, charities, voluntary associations of all types) that constitutes civil society: these are the current paradigms of good citizenship. Each is marked by the assurance that action is better than thought or inaction, affiliation better than alienation, belief (in one's "cause," the moral purposes of one's community, or simply the value of belonging) better than doubt or unbelief. Contemporary discussions and ideals thus reinforce the essential lesson of the tradition, namely, that "good citizenship" consists, above all, in the active service of something bigger than the self, a positive moral purpose the group pursuit of which is equated with virtue.

It is my contention that Socrates invented a form of philosophical or dissident citizenship which puts these well-worn nostrums in doubt. By any traditional account—indeed, by contemporary communitarian standards—Socrates was truly a "bad" citizen. He did not take an active part in the deliberations of the Athenian assembly, and he was ignorant of many of the procedures through which the daily business of the democracy was conducted (no small sin in a direct democracy such as Athens). He did, by all accounts, serve his country bravely in war and also served on the Council of Five Hundred, the body which set the agenda for the assembly of citizens. It was in the latter capacity that he performed one of his famous acts of dissent, vocally opposing as unconstitutional proposal to try eight victorious Athenian generals en bloc (*Apology*, 31b)—an act which clashed with overwhelming popular sentiment and ran the risk of imprisonment and even death. For the most part, however, Socrates avoided both the assembly and law courts (the places where public business was conducted and public opinion expressed) the better to pursue his philosophical calling. This made him, in the eyes of many of his fellow citizens, the archetypal philosophical good-for-nothing, someone who failed to actively contribute to the public good. In the memorable words of Callicles in Plato's *Gorgias*, Socrates evidently preferred spending his time "sunk in a corner and whispering with three or four boys" (485d), undermining the foundations of the polity through his philosophical conversations with Athenian youth.

But, as Plato's *Apology of Socrates* eloquently testifies, Socrates saw himself as performing an invaluable service to his city through this (apparently self-indulgent) behavior. This service, as I shall argue, did not consist in "making men moral," nor in urging them to standards of nobility higher than those pursued by the masses around them. It consisted in Socrates being a "gadfly," an irritating moral and intellectual conscience to his city. He did this not by standing up publicly, in the name of justice, to indict some particular policy or action of the Athenians. Rather, he did it by questioning the dominant conceptions of virtue and "good behavior," and by maintaining rigorous moral and intellectual integrity as an individual. He did it by scrambling the traditional distinction between the "good man" and the "good citizen," while avoiding homiletics or edifying clichés. He did it by undermining authorities, purging opinions, and creating a general puzzlement where previously there had been a firm faith in the soundness of "traditional values." He did it, in other words, by enacting *thinking* in conversation.

This enactment created a kind of alternative public sphere, one in which the overriding criterion was neither persuasion, decision, nor action but the application of scrupulous intellectual honesty (and irony) to the "unquestionable" grounds of his city's moral culture. What such examination revealed was not a new set of answers or definitions but the dogma and partiality that attends each and every response to the question: What is virtue? It also revealed the need of all citizens to be open to such puzzlement, lest they become the fomenters or willing instruments of the injustice inevitably generated by their city and, indeed, by every polity.

Socrates can be said to put intellectual doubt at the heart of moral reflection; he makes such doubt the duty of any conscientious citizen. Indeed, he can be described as the inventor of "conscientious citizenship." Such citizenship, I believe, is the only kind truly compatible with moral individualism—itself a phenomenon or mode of being one could say was invented by Socrates. His suggestion is radical not merely because it makes the individual—rather than tradition, the gods, or the city—the gravitational center of the moral world. It is radical because it suggests that civic virtue and morals, unaccompanied by intellectual hygiene—by a thinking which dissolves opinions rather than solidifying them—are the invariable accomplices of injustice and immorality.

The skeptical yet conscientious individualism introduced by Socrates has never been popular with proponents of civic virtue or traditional values. Yet rarely has he been denounced or directly criticized. (Nietzsche and Hannah Arendt are exceptions to this rule, but, as my discussions in chapters 3 and 5 indicate, they are beholden to Socrates even when they attack him.) Far more common are variations on the strategy first deployed by Rousseau in his *Discourse on the Sciences and the Arts*: the "gadfly" Socrates, the ironic and endlessly questioning Socrates, is converted into an exemplar of stern moral virtue or piety. This new "Spartan" Socrates is then juxtaposed with the "corruption" of an overly intellectualized, overly skeptical Athenian civic culture.

The reason for the popularity of this strategy is obvious: few in our culture want to be seen as attacking *Socratic* doubt. That would be like agreeing with the Athenians' verdict at Socrates' trial. Yet, truth be told, many *do* agree with it. Skepticism and doubt, together with individualism, are routinely singled out as the corrupting evils of our time, the things which stand in the way of a healthy (and much-needed) civic or moral reengagement. The idea that one can be skeptical *and* morally serious—that a particular form of negativity is crucial to genuine moral seriousness—is dismissed out of hand since moral seriousness is reflexively identified with the passion or conviction with which one pursues a political cause or a set of positive moral doctrines.

This study does not aim at distinguishing Socrates' true friends from his false ones. Rather, it traces the resonance of his conception of philosophical citizenship—and the relation of moral to intellectual integrity—in the works of key political thinkers of what might be termed the "late modern" age. These thinkers—John Stuart Mill, Friedrich Nietzsche, Max Weber, Hannah Arendt, and Leo Strauss—all respond to Socrates' provocation in significant ways. Most important, they offer instructively varied opinions on the possibility (and relevance) of "philosophical citizenship" in an age of mass politics. For, we must ask, how relevant to the conditions of modernity is a conception of civic and moral agency which grew up in a "face-to-face" political culture, one in which the very choice *not* to engage civic life in the normal way was bound to attract attention, to be revolutionary and subversive? As the chapters which follow recount, Socrates' shadow may be long, but—for these thinkers, at least—it seems to have lost much of its former power. With the possible exception of Mill, they tend toward the view that the idea of philosophical citizenship no longer signifies. Intellectual honesty and moral integrity—yes; philosophy and citizenship—perhaps. But none of these theorists believes that these qualities or activities can be linked in the way Socrates suggests.

The story I have to tell, then, is not the happy and edifying tale of the triumph of an ideal articulated over two thousand years ago. Yet merely tracing the growth of the conviction that a Socratic brand of citizenship has become impossible or irrelevant, a contradiction in terms, reveals just how crucial this ideal has been for thinkers concerned with the tense relations between philosophy, politics, moral individualism, and independent judgment. It is no exaggeration to state that this ideal has provided a touchstone for all serious subsequent discussions of these topics. My narrative also illuminates the alternatives posed by these self-consciously modern theorists, revealing their pronounced tendency to restrict intellectual honesty and the purging of avoidable illusion to the cultural sphere—something good for philosophers, perhaps, but not ordinary citizens.

One final note: while Socrates was a historical figure, he did not write texts, philosophical or otherwise. What we know of him is based entirely on the contradictory reports—and, no doubt, creative re-descriptions—of his contemporaries Aristophanes, Xenophon and Plato. The Socrates that looms large in the Western philosophical and moral imagination is, in many respects, a literary creation: one born not only of conflicting reports but of innumerable interpretations and reinterpretations of the Platonic dialogues, the history of philosophy, as well as Socrates' own textual silence and well-known irony. The interpretive paradoxes are many, but I will not enter into them here. They have been well treated in three recent works: Gregory Vlastos's *Socrates: Ironist and Moral Philosopher* (Cornell, 1991), Alexander Nehamas's *The Art of Living: Socratic Reflections from Plato to Foucault* (California, 1998), and Sarah Kofman's *Socrate* (Paris: Editions Galilée 1989; recently translated as *Socrates: Fictions of a Philosopher* [Ithaca: Cornell University Press, 1998]). Instead, I have limited myself to teasing out what I consider an important but relatively neglected strand of Socrates' influence as a philosopher and moral-political figure, an influence growing out of his appearance in other people's texts, interpretations, and theories.

Acknowledgments

IT IS A PLEASURE to acknowledge the generous support of two institutions: The Center for Human Values at Princeton University and the Institute for Advanced Study. I began writing this book as a Laurance S. Rockerfeller Fellow at Princeton in 1997–98, and I was able to complete a draft of the manuscript while a member of the School of Social Science at the institute in 1998–99. My sincere thanks go to Amy Gutmann and George Kateb for their collegiality and leadership of the center, and to Michael Walzer, Clifford Geertz, and Joan Scott for making the institute's School of Social Science such a stimulating and productive environment. It is rare good fortune to be able to spend a fellowship year at either of these institutions, let alone have the opportunity to pursue research and writing at both for two uninterrupted years. This book would not exist were it not for that fact, and I want to take this occasion to express my deepest gratitude to everyone at the center and the institute. I also want to thank the American Council of Learned Societies for a fellowship award, which was essential in getting this project off the ground.

I spoke to many people about Socrates and things Socratic over the years, including John Cooper, Josh Ober, Alexander Nehamas, Peter Euben, Patchen Markell, and Patrick Deneen. I had the good fortune of being able to attend Alexander Nehamas's graduate seminar "Nietzsche and Politics," which instigated many of the thoughts in chapter 3 of this book. Dennis Thompson was good enough to read and comment upon an essay which grew into chapter 4. I also own a debt of gratitude to Jim Schmidt of Boston University, whose words of informal encouragement one fall day outside the Harvard Bookstore enabled me to see, more clearly than I had, the way the individual parts of this book fit together.I would also like to thank the Fellows at the center and the institute, particularly John Kleinig and Bernard Reginster at the center, and Nancy Hirshman, Michael Mosher, Tom Flynn, and Gordon Schochet at the institute.

More thanks are due to my colleagues in the political science department at the University of California, Santa Barbara. The department has proven itself committed to promoting faculty research, and graciously allowed me to spend more time in Princeton, New Jersey, than I originally planned. Stephen Weatherford and Lorraine McDonnell have been particularly supportive and understanding, as have my colleagues in political theory, Peter Digeser and Thomas Schrock. To all many thanks.

Chapters of this book were originally presented at the Princeton Political Philosophy Colloquium, the Members' Seminar at the School of Social Science, and the Philosophy Department Colloquium at the New School for Social Research. I'd like to thank those who participated in these events, especially Richard Bernstein for his kind invitation to speak at the New School. Once again it is a pleasure to thank Charles Meier, Abby Collins, Sandy Selesky, and Anna Popiel at the Harvard Center for European Studies for providing a summer home where various chapters were rewritten and edited.

Special thanks go to Svetlana Boym, who, in her own way, is the most Socratic person I know (she certainly has the most "human wisdom," as Socrates would say). My father, Alfred Villa, was supportive in many ways during some rough patches. Finally, I wish to thank my mother, Virginia Barrett Villa, who provided, along with much else, my first model of intellectual integrity.

A small portion of chapter 4 originally appeared in *Constellations*, 6, no. 4 (Dec. 1999): 540–60, copyright Blackwell Publishers. Parts of chapter 5 originally appeared in *Political Theory*, 26, no. 2 (1998): 147–72, copyright Sage Publications.

Socratic Citizenship

What Is Socratic Citizenship?

JUDITH SHKLAR BEGINS her short book on American citizenship by observing that "there is no notion more central to politics than citizenship, and none more variable in history, or contested in theory."[1] Indeed, it is the very centrality of citizenship to politics which has made it one of the most fiercely debated ideas in the Western tradition of political theory. From Aristotle's gentlemanly possessor of practical wisdom to Machiavelli's citizen-soldier; from Hobbes's anarchy-fearing citizen-subject to Locke's government-fearing citizen-proprietor; from Rousseau's virtuous citizen-legislator to our own (inclusive) conception of a rights-bearing, interest-pursuing voter—there has been no shortage of models of citizenship to inspire, frighten, or fill us with aesthetic and moral revulsion. Given the recent spread of ostensibly representative institutions to Eastern Europe and beyond, it should come as no surprise that the debate on the nature and meaning of citizenship has intensified, with theorists on both sides of the Atlantic offering up neo-Aristotelian, neo-republican, neoliberal, and "radical democratic" formulations for both domestic and foreign consumption.

This chapter—and the present study as a whole—is devoted to retrieving a model of citizenship which has received relatively little attention of late, namely, the dissident, philosophical citizenship we find in Plato's depiction of Socrates in the *Apology*. I will argue that this Socrates is the inventor of moral individualism in the West, a thinker who presents a radically new articulation of the relation between individual moral consciousness, political authority, and one's fellow citizens. By making the avoidance of injustice the moral center of "care for one's soul" (or self), Socrates transforms both the meaning and the practice of citizenship, pushing it beyond the boundaries of the "official" public realm. To be sure, he does not collapse the distinction between public and private—a distinction which was absolutely central to the self-understanding of Athenian democracy.[2] Nor does he substitute a set of private, "philosophical" virtues for the more manly, public-oriented virtues of the Greek

1

city-state (although this is how he is often perceived, both by his contemporaries and by his latter-day interpreters). Rather, Socrates' originality is found in his introduction of moral individualism and intellectual sobriety as *the* critical standards of justice and civic obligation. With this innovation, he invents the possibility of a conscientious, moderately alienated citizenship.[3]

In both his philosophical activity and his refusal to countenance injustice, Socrates, like Thoreau, reminds us of the gravitational pull toward injustice exerted by any group, community, or state. His use of the method of questioning and refutation (*elenchus*) aims at undermining his fellow citizens' falsely confident understandings of what justice and virtue demand, understandings which promote myriad injustices, large and small. Often portrayed as an archrationalist who professes ignorance but whose irony conceals his own firm grasp of *the* moral truth, Socrates is, I shall argue, far more skeptical in temper and practice. The simple fact of the matter is that his deployment of *elenchus* and rational argumentation do not (at least in the early "Socratic" dialogues)[4] yield any positive result: the question of what, in fact, the virtues (courage, piety, justice, temperance, etc.) are is never definitively answered. Moreover, Socrates is convinced that he himself is no moral expert. Virtue may indeed be knowledge, but, if so, it is a kind of knowledge Socrates explicitly disclaims (*Apology*, 21b). He does not claim to be virtuous, let alone a teacher of virtue (33b).[5] Rather, his energies are devoted to dissolving the crust of convention and the hubristic claim to moral expertise—the two things which stand in the way of thought and real moral reflection. In the apt words of Hannah Arendt, Socrates "purged people of their 'opinions,' that is, of those unexamined prejudgments which prevent thinking by suggesting that we know where we not only don't know but cannot know, helping them, as Plato remarks, to get rid of what was bad in them, their opinions, without however making them good, giving them truth."[6]

The thinking stimulated by this dissolvent use of rationality is, as Arendt notes, a "dangerous and resultless enterprise." The dissolution of an established creed or opinion can always lead to cynicism or renewed dogmatism. Yet Socrates' hope seems to have been that the resulting perplexity would slow his fellow citizens down in their performance of injustice, which is almost always wrapped in the cloak of "virtue." Moral improvement of this sort becomes possible only when the individual recognizes that social life (which is profoundly mimetic in character) has put him or her to sleep, morally speaking. Hence the famous simile of the *Apology*: Socrates is like a "stinging fly," one who attempts to rouse a great and lazy horse, the city of Athens (31a). His essential task is to get his fellow Athenians to entertain the possibility that the demands of morality may, in fact, run counter to the established norms of the society and its conception of virtuous citizenship. If Socrates is a "connected critic" who feeds on the "shared meanings" of the community, he is a peculiarly heretical one.[7]

In emphasizing the dissolvent nature of Socratic rationality, I follow Hegel and Kierkegaard as well as Arendt. They all stress Socrates' "absolute negativity" over his apparent conviction that the moral truth (or, at least, strong rational conviction) can be reached by way of elenchic argument. This perspective runs counter to the important work of Gregory Vlastos and Terence Irwin, both of whom view *elenchus* as "a method of philosophical investigation."[8] Broadly speaking, this is certainly true. However, to call *elenchus* a "method" implies that it is pursued mainly for the sake of the positive results it yields. This, in fact, is how Vlastos interprets Socrates' philosophical practice, rejecting his own earlier presentation of a "skeptical" or "agnostic" Socrates.[9] If we take the term "skeptical" to imply a rigorously maintained suspension of judgment, then Vlastos is clearly right: the sheer intensity of Socrates' moral commitments refutes the characterization of "agnosticism." Yet one can legitimately ask whether Socrates' "method" is in the service of his moral integrity or whether his moral stance is the "product" of his method.[10]

I think Vlastos leans too far toward the latter alternative and, as a result, misses the possibility that for Socrates "moral truth" may be a more elusive and complicated affair than this phrase commonly denotes. It may be that Socratic ethics is more negative than positive, more a morality of abstention than the fulfillment of codified obligations or the exhibition of a fleshed out set of virtues (such as we find in Aristotle). It may also be that "moral truth" eludes capture in terms of any single code of conduct; that here, as elsewhere, the truth is many-sided and requires the cultivation of a certain form of perspectivism to be even minimally grasped.[11] The key point is that Socrates maintains his ignorance, his lack of wisdom about the ultimate nature of the virtues and human excellence, until the very end (23a–b). Unlike Plato or Aristotle, he never offers us a hierarchy of human lives, culminating (unsurprisingly) in the "best life" of the philosopher.[12] As Alexander Nehamas has recently noted, he has no arguments to convince people that the unexamined life is not worth living.[13] Nor does he offer any code or finalized moral doctrine. What he *does* do is try to infect his fellow citizens—indeed, aliens, freemen and slaves[14]—with his own perplexity concerning current usage and his own passion for leading a life free from injustice.

The moment thinking starts—the moment perplexity about the virtues sets in—the practical side of everyday life is suspended, at least temporarily. Rules which provided a solid foundation for action suddenly become questionable, along with the understanding of the virtues from which they derived. The Socratic attempt to throw out of gear the derivation of actions from rules and a falsely confident understanding of virtue is not a *directly* political exercise.[15] Yet it does have political implications, not least of which is that it inserts moral doubt where there had been not only complacent belief but impatience to act. The Athenians posed the greatest possible challenge to Socrates not because they were more dogmatic than other peoples (that was hardly the case) or more lawless in their behavior, but because they were the most *active* of peoples, the most restless and driven. In the words of the Corinthian delegates at a debate in Sparta prior to the beginning of the Peloponnesian War (432 B.C.): "An Athenian is always an innovator. . . . They never hesitate . . . they think the farther they go the more they will get. . . . Of them alone may it be said that they possess a thing almost as soon as they desire it, so quickly with them does action follow upon decision. . . . They are by nature incapable of either living a quiet life themselves or of allowing anyone else to do so."[16]

Of course, there is more to Socrates' philosophical activity than the desire to introduce moderation to a restlessly dynamic people. Its central target is the self-loss (manifest in passions, resentments, illusions, and shared errors) that marks *all* political and social life. This is why Socrates' relentless questioning and ferocious intellectual honesty remain essential for anyone who cares about justice, citizenship, and democratic political action. He helps us to recognize the inevitable moral distortions introduced by any creed or ideology, including that of a "post-ideological" pragmatism. He forces us to acknowledge that by far the greater part of both our activism and apathy is unexamined, no matter how well it has been "theorized" or rationalized. He is the enemy of all forms of self-righteousness, but especially of those that congeal around groups. He exposes the manifold corruptions of solidarity. His lesson for democrats is not, as some have claimed, that their "regime" needs to be ennobled, lifted up from demotic vulgarity to the pursuit of collective perfection or communal excellence. Rather, it is that the consistent avoidance of injustice demands sustained moral energy, coupled with a ruthless intellectual honesty which certainly looks, at first glance, like a relentless skepticism.

The present chapter elaborates this characterization of Socrates' activity by looking first at the ideal of Athens as articulated by Pericles, her greatest statesman. This ideal is the true subject of the Funeral Oration Pericles gave at the end of the first year of the war between Athens and Sparta. I turn to this text because it provides an image of Athens at its most noble, at the very pinnacle of its greatness. The set of values articulated by Pericles are the best democratic Athens has to offer. Yet it is against these very values that Socrates wages his indirect and subversive campaign. Taking the *Apology* as my central text, but with additional attention to the *Gorgias* and *Crito*, I show how Socrates transforms the Periclean ethos. "Transform" is perhaps an insufficiently strong word since it implies that the raw materials are basically sound. Socrates' critique, however, verges on a full-scale transvaluation of values. As Victor Ehrenberg has pointed out, its revolutionary moral implications cannot be underestimated,[17] but neither can its implications for our understanding of the nature of citizenship.

In considering the *Apology*, I will also address the question of Socrates' active practice of Athenian citizenship. This practice, which essentially consists of dissent and noncompliance, complements his activity as a philosopher-citizen, that is, as someone who devotes his entire life to engaging his fellow citizens on the question of how one should live. The model of citizenship we can elicit from these two activities—the first public, episodic, and negative; the second virtually continuous but not public in any traditional sense—is essentially critical yet not fundamentally anti-democratic (as is frequently maintained). Unlike Plato, Socrates does not believe in a moral form of expert knowledge possessed by an aristocratic few who are (by nature, character, and intelligence) fit to rule. He is, as the argument of the *Crito* shows, a *kind* of democrat. To call him a "loyal" one, however, is misleading, if only because the vocabulary of loyalty and patriotism sets severe limits to the reach of philosophical questioning and moral criticism.

5

The arguments of the *Gorgias* and the *Crito* provide support yet also pose difficulties for my characterization of Socrates. (I will discuss the dual aspect of both dialogues.) The *Crito* presents the more obvious challenge since the theory of political obligation Plato's Socrates puts into the mouth of the Laws of Athens seems to rival that of Hobbes in its demand for strict obedience to authority. It is a curiosity of the history of political theory that the originator of moral individualism should be so solicitous of the welfare of the state, and so ready to part with his life in order not to harm it (even though Socrates believes the verdict of his five hundred-man jury to be unjust). In this connection, I will consider Antigone and Thoreau as alternative models of disobedience, the better to probe the nature and limits of philosophical citizenship as a form of dissident citizenship.

Pericles' Funeral Oration: Aesthetic Monumentalism

In postwar interpretations of the history of political thought, the thematics of loss, closure, and fragmentation loom large. Thus, in her 1955 essay "Tradition and the Modern Age" Arendt writes of a tradition in ruins, destroyed not merely by the catastrophic course of historical events but also by its inability to transcend the logical possibilities created by Plato's separation of knowing and doing in the *Republic*. According to Arendt's very influential story, Plato's innovation—motivated by his desire to undermine the democratic understanding of political knowledge, action, and judgment—set the conceptual pattern for the whole of the Western tradition, a tradition which took the basic distinction between theory (*theoria*) and practice (*praxis*) for granted. Marx's and Nietzsche's inversion of this "contemplative" conceptual hierarchy brings the tradition to a close, as "labor" and "life" are set above thought.[18]

Arendt's tale is the story of a fall away from a world in which thought and action, power and intelligence, were not yet estranged from one another; in which the *bios politikos* and the *bios theoretikos* had yet to emerge as contradictory forms of life. The world we have lost, of course, is the world of Athenian democracy in the fifth century B.C.: Periclean Athens, in which thought and action, speech and deed, were in a kind of harmony we latecomers find difficult if not impossible to grasp.[19]

The chief exemplar of this original harmony is Pericles himself, as he is represented in Thucydides' *History*. In Pericles we seem to have a democratic leader who unites thought and action, power and intelligence, speech and deed. This, evidently, is how Thucydides viewed him, as the implicit contrast he draws between Pericles and his successors, Cleon and Alcibiades, makes clear. In Pericles we find a faith in the capacity of human intelligence and power to restrict the realm of chance and to impress upon a recalcitrant, hostile world a vision of a free form of life. In making this vision a reality, the Athenians create not only a great power but an "education to Hellas" and the West.[20]

This faith in the ability of human intelligence to illuminate a world seemingly hostage to fortune is reflected by the Athenian democratic practice of submitting all important matters, in both domestic and foreign affairs, to debate and decision in the citizen assembly. Pericles articulates the ethos behind this practice in the Funeral Oration, where he states: "We Athenians, in our own persons, take our decisions on policy or submit them to proper discussions: for we do not think that there is an incompatibility between words and deeds; the worst thing is to rush into action before the consequences have been properly debated."[21]

The worst thing, from both a practical and moral standpoint, is to let the passions of the moment dictate policy—an omnipresent danger for a direct democracy such as Athens. "Proper discussions" not only illuminate consequences but moderate passions. Thus, the Athenian passion for talk and speeches had the effect of filtering out the most violently emotional responses to events. This is precisely what Cleon, Pericles' successor and a man "remarkable among the Athenians for the violence of his character," chastises his fellow citizens for when they consider reversing themselves on punishing a rebellious ally, the Mytilenians, with death and enslavement. "You have become regular speech-goers," he rails, "and as for action, you merely listen to accounts of it. . . . You are simply victims of your own pleasure in listening. . . ."[22] Dismissing prolonged speeches in the assembly as mere cleverness indulged in by "intellectuals" who want to show off, Cleon repudiates the Periclean ethos of public discussion and the discursive conception of practical wisdom it implies. He is convinced, as Thucydides later remarks of the feuding parties in the Corcyrean civil war, that the "ability to understand a question from all sides meant that one was totally unfitted for action."[23] Thought and action, speech and deed, are here framed as opposites—a separation fraught with tragic implications.[24]

Pericles' personal integration of speech and deed is apparent in his exceptional foresight. This foresight is manifest in his first speech in the *History*, where he tells the Athenians that they should feel confident in achieving ultimate victory against Sparta and her allies if they resist the temptation to use the war as an opportunity to add to their empire and engage themselves in "new perils."[25] The tragedy of Athens is, to a large extent, a tragedy born of the Athenians' failure to heed this advice, allowing their desire for more to overwhelm their better judgment. But there is more to Pericles' "harmony" of thought and action than foresight or exceptional prudence. The special quality of this harmony is most compellingly present in his vision of Athens itself, a vision laid out in the Funeral Oration.

With the possible exception of the Gettysburg Address, this speech is the most celebrated piece of political oratory in the history of the West. It is remarkable for a number of reasons. It is, above all, a call to action, to emulation of the heroic deeds of those who died defending their native city. But it is also an astonishing portrait of that city, of the radically unique character of Athens both as a polity and a way of life.[26] In Pericles' words the consciousness of historical novelty and greatness become brilliantly and blindingly explicit. He takes the raw materials of an imperial democracy and fashions them into a vision one would have felt blessed to die for. Above all, he wants his fellow citizens to recognize the *beauty* of the city his words have described: "I could tell you a long story (and you know it as well as I do) about what is to be gained by beating the enemy back. What I would prefer is that you should fix your eyes every day on the greatness of Athens as she really is, and should fall in love with her. When you realize her greatness, then reflect that what made her great was men with a spirit of adventure, men who knew their duty, men who were ashamed to fall below a certain standard. . . . It is for you to try to be like them."[27] This is not merely a call to action: it is an invitation to be intoxicated by an ideal. Pericles wants his listeners to be ravished by the beauty of Athens, to give themselves up to the greatness of the city.

The problem is that so much of what Pericles describes *is* intoxicating. The Funeral Oration is no simple call to patriotic self-sacrifice. It is the articulation of democratic principles and democratic individuality, an expression of how freedom and equality can generate both power and more freedom, a freedom which extends beyond the bounds of the public realm into private life itself. In this important sense, the ethos conveyed by the Funeral Oration cannot be assimilated to the ascetic love of the *patria* or the vision of civic virtue familiar to us from the civic republican tradition. Immediately after describing the basics of a democratic political constitution, Pericles states that "just as our political life is free and open, so is our day to day life in our relations with each other. We do not get into a state with our next-door neighbor if he enjoys himself in his own way.... We are free and tolerant in our private lives, but in public affairs we keep to the law...."[28]

The pride manifest in these words—and in Pericles' subsequent contrast between Athenian bravery and the "state-induced courage" created by the Spartan educational regime—signals an awareness that no previous city has been able to match the level of individual freedom and tolerance created by the democracy (a claim confirmed by Plato's critique of democracy in book 8 of the *Republic*). Every citizen is able to enjoy not only a public realm characterized by equality and freedom but also a "private" realm where the appreciation of beauty and intellect opens up the possibility of individual self-fashioning.[29] Civic involvement and the concern for self-cultivation exist in what Pericles presents as a harmonious balance, one in which (to use Rousseau's terms) *homme* and *citoyen* are distinct but not opposed: "Here each individual is interested not only in his own affairs but in the affairs of the state as well: even those who are mostly occupied with their own business are extremely well-informed [*sic*] on general politics—this is a peculiarity of ours: we do not say that a man who takes no interest in politics is a man who minds his own business; we say that he has no business here at all."[30]

It is on the basis of this unprecedented mix of civic involvement and (relative) individual freedom that Pericles is able to declare his city "an education for Greece," citing "each single one of our citizens" as a potential model for the harmonious balance of public and private pursuits.[31] Indeed, the love of beauty and intellect he ascribes to his fellow citizens is presented as firmly bounded by an overarching public-spiritedness and willingness to sacrifice: "Our love of what is beautiful does not lead to extravagance; our love of the things of the mind does not make us soft."[32] Every Athenian citizen, in other words, has achieved a certain harmony of thought and action; every Athenian citizen is, in fact, a work of art.[33]

But Pericles does not stop there. Democratic freedom and participation, the appreciation of beauty and the life of the mind: these are perhaps goods in themselves, but they are also components of a larger artwork, that of the State. This characterization may seem an anachronism, the foisting of Hegel's and Burckhardt's nineteenth-century coinage onto the Greek world. There is no denying, however, that the terms in which Pericles casts his final appeal are heroic/aesthetic. The category of "greatness" subsumes the moral content of democracy as well as the protoindividualism it has bred:

> Athens, alone of the states we know, comes to her testing time in a greatness that surpasses what was imagined of her. In her case, and in her case alone, no invading army is ashamed at being defeated, and no subject can complain of being governed by people unfit for their responsibilities. Mighty indeed are the marks and monuments of our empire which we have left. Future ages will wonder at us, as the present age wonders at us now. We do not need the praises of a Homer, or of anyone else whose words may delight us for the moment, *but whose estimation of the facts will fall far short of what is really true.* For our adventurous spirit has forced an entry into every sea and into every land; and everywhere we have left behind us everlasting memorials of good done to our friends or suffering inflicted on our enemies.[34]

Peter Euben cites passages like this as evidence of Pericles' "visionary imperialism," contrasting it with the "weary realism" of the Athenian representatives at Melos fifteen years later, who, practicing the most brutal sort of power politics, have become numb to any distinction between honor and interest or fear.[35] Nietzsche is more pungent. In *The Genealogy of Morals* he draws our attention to the last line of this passage, emphasizing the enormous difference between a code of conduct in which "the good done to our friends and the suffering inflicted on our enemies" are of equal moral worth and a code which heeds the more "slavish" (that is, compassionate) demands of a universalist ethic.[36]

His admiration for Greek heroic values notwithstanding, Nietzsche is the better guide here. For no matter how noble the Periclean vision looks in comparison to the genocidal realpolitik of the Melian Dialogue, it is still a vision in which greatness—a fundamentally aesthetic category—trumps all moral values (although Pericles, like Machiavelli, would deny that true glory can ever be achieved through inglorious deeds). This is in keeping with the self-conscious sense of Athenian uniqueness which animates the Funeral Oration as a whole. According to Pericles, Athenian democracy and freedom have bred a daring and innovative spirit unlike any ever seen, surpassing not only contemporaries but also inheritors ("Future ages will wonder at us, as the present age wonders at us now"). Here Periclean foresight reaches truly Olympian proportions: each one of his boasts will be turned by history into an objective report of the truth. He offers the Athenians a reflected image of their own uncanniness which is itself uncanny. Yet nowhere in this picture of Athenian greatness do we find the slightest hint of moral unease about the imperial project as such, or any indication of a possible tension between the moral world of democracy and that of empire. Indeed, the *moral* dimension (if we can call it that) of the Funeral Oration consists entirely of the exhortation to live up to the virtues of those whose martial feats laid the foundation of Athenian greatness.

It might be objected that to expect anything more from a statesman in Pericles' situation—giving a speech in praise of the fallen at the end of the first year of war—would be misguided. What the Athenians need for the trials ahead is inspiration, not self-criticism. Pericles was, of course, perfectly capable of delivering harsh criticism to his fellow citizens, as his speech during the demoralized days of the plague clearly illustrates. In this, his third and final speech in the *History*, he chastises his fellow citizens for their lack of constancy and their desire to enjoy the privileges of an imperial power while evading the "burdens of empire." The chief burden is the need to preserve the empire at all costs, since its destruction will surely cost the Athenians their freedom: "Your empire is now like a tyranny: it may have been wrong to take it; it is certainly wrong to let it go."[37] In moments of severe crisis, in which private misery overwhelms the citizens' sense of their public responsibilities, the task of the political leader is to remind them of the realities and consequences of power, *not* to offer a critique of the values that created the situation in which they find themselves. These become, strictly speaking, unquestionable.[38]

The issue, however, is not whether Periclean political rhetoric can lay claim to the title of moral criticism but whether the vision set forth in the Funeral Oration can be reconciled with Socrates' radically revised conception of citizenship. On some readings it can. Yet, as I shall argue, the tragedy of Athens is found not in the breakdown of an original harmony of speech and action (a breakdown that finds symptomatic expression in the figure of Socrates himself, a thinker who withdraws from the life of action) but rather in the very vision Pericles articulates. This vision—Athens at its greatest, as the best the world has seen—already contains the worst; it makes the derivation of the worst (the Melian genocide) possible.[39] From the Socratic perspective, it ignores or is ignorant of the most important things.

This is, however, to anticipate. If we compare Pericles' steadfastness and devotion to the common good in matters of policy with the actions of his successors, we see (as Thucydides wants us to see) an unmistakable decline, a failure to marry intelligence, power, and moderation. Cleon attacks learning, intelligence, and discussion as vehicles by which clever elites undermine the common sense (and passion for revenge) of average citizens, inserting compassion and moderation where they are least needed.[40] Alcibiades, Pericles' ward and one of the leaders of the ill-fated Sicilian expedition, is universally recognized for his extraordinary ability; however, his immoderate, self-aggrandizing character arouses the fatal distrust of his fellow citizens. Nicias, his cautious elder and reluctant partner in the expedition, trusts neither intelligence nor power to achieve the city's goals; his piety and superstition are more Spartan than Athenian.[41] Finally, we have the evidence of the Melian Dialogue, which shows the degree to which the Athenians came to view themselves as mere executors of a "general and necessary law of nature," a law which dictated that one "rule whatever one can."[42] Here the space for free action guided and moderated by intelligence has disappeared. The Athenians wearily instruct the Melians, who would remain neutral, that they must either become subjects of Athens or be destroyed. The imperatives of imperial power offer no other alternative: "The strong do what they have the power to do and the weak accept what they have to accept."[43]

The decline of the Periclean ethos of civic greatness, then, is mirrored in leaders who lack at least one of the crucial elements of responsible leadership. In the case of Cleon we have rhetoric and passion without moderation or genuine intelligence. In that of Alcibiades we find intelligence and ability without devotion to the common good. In Nicias we have moderation devoid of daring and energy. The ingredients of the Periclean balance have been dispersed. Disaster follows with a seeming inevitability.

THE *APOLOGY* OF SOCRATES

The decline traced by Thucydides' depictions of Athenian leadership points not only to a degradation of character in Athens but also to a troubling estrangement of thought and action in Greek politics, an estrangement which has its apparent culmination in the trial and condemnation of Socrates in 399 B.C. (fourteen years after the defeat in Sicily; a mere five years after the second, and bloodiest, oligarchic coup endured by the Athenian democracy—this one after her defeat in the Peloponnesian War).

As an Athenian citizen, Socrates had fought in three engagements just prior to or during the war—at Potidaea, Delium, and Amphipolis—with notable bravery. But he was also the unofficial teacher of the ambitious and opportunistic Alcibiades, who was himself overtly contemptuous of the democracy, went over to the Spartan side during the war, and played a role in instigating the first oligarchic coup in 411 B.C.[44] Even worse, from a popular point of view, was the fact that Socrates exercised considerable influence over Charmides and Critias, two leaders of the Thirty Tyrants, the violently antidemocratic regime brought briefly to power by the second oligarchic coup in 404 B.C. This fact, combined with the character of his philosophical activity (which was hardly kind to the moral pretensions of Athenian elites)[45] and his long-standing reputation as a subversive sophist (promoted by Aristophanes), made it easy for his fellow citizens to suspect him of harboring antidemocratic sentiments, as well as fostering contempt for democracy in the circle of well-off young men who surrounded him.[46] Indeed, as Vlastos and others have shown, Socrates was widely perceived to be a *misodemos*, an "enemy of the people," a perception drawn from the careers of his associates and his reputed teachings.[47] His trial for "corrupting the youth" and failing to believe in the gods of the state reflected a generalized distrust of his unconventional intelligence and even more unconventional activity during a period when Athenian democracy was still struggling to recover from traumatic defeat, betrayal, and virtual civil war.[48] If we also take account of the no-holds-barred criticisms of Athenian democracy Socrates offers in the *Apology* and the *Gorgias*, the popular perception of him as a crypto-oligarch and dangerous corruptor of youth becomes eminently understandable.[49]

13

However predictable the trial and condemnation of Socrates look when put into political context, the effects of these events far outstrip their historical background, marking an epoch in the relation between thought and action, philosophy and politics, theory and practice. Arendt made the point starkly in her 1954 essay "Philosophy and Politics," where she wrote: "The gulf between philosophy and politics opened historically with the trial and condemnation of Socrates, which in the history of political thought plays the same role of a turning point that the trial and condemnation of Jesus plays in the history of religion."[50] Euben is less dramatic, but he is equally convinced that Socrates' trial represents a crossroads from which there is no turning back: "The projected estrangement of philosophy and Socrates from politics and Athens makes these dialogues [*Apology, Crito*] tragic. . . . The *Apology* is a tragedy of philosophy as well as politics or, more exactly, of the failed relationship between the two."[51] With the trial and condemnation of Socrates, the increasing disharmony between mind and action—so admirably captured by Thucydides' *History*—turns into all-out war as the philosopher's attempt to establish a new, post-Periclean relationship between the two results in a death sentence. From this point on, we are told, philosophy and (democratic) politics go their separate ways, and a unique opportunity is lost.

As I intimated earlier, this narrative of loss and fragmentation is a little too neat. Nevertheless, Plato's grand attempt (in the *Republic*) to make politics safe for philosophy by creating a tyranny of reason demonstrates how what began as a tension was transformed into a veritable chasm by Socrates' death. This estrangement has its tragic side, to be sure, just as the attempt to overcome it has created tragedies (for example, the Marxian attempt to "realize philosophy" through political action). However, to fixate, as Arendt and Euben do, on the "gulf" that opened up as a result of this traumatic event blinds us to the possibility that the *partial* estrangement of philosophy and politics, of thought and action, was a key element of Socrates' life and teaching rather than merely the unfortunate result of his death. We can, in other words, see this limited estrangement in a positive light, as initiating a new, individualist form of citizenship. In the *Apology* Socrates articulates the moral need for this estrangement, as well as the mode of conscientious citizenship it enables.

From the standpoint of political theory, the *Apology* is without doubt the most important of Plato's Socratic texts. For it is here that

Socrates directly addresses the political import of his philosophical activity, in addition to offering a defense of his own (novel) practice of citizenship. It is in the *Apology* that a new moral world is glimpsed, one whose gravitational center is the conscientious individual rather than tradition, convention, or public norms and opinion. To borrow Hegel's terminology (although not his precise meaning), with Socrates "natural morality"—the morality inscribed in creeds, customs, or a set of laws—gives way to "reflective morality," the standpoint of a "universal" (that is, semialienated) I. We need not accept Hegel's metaphysical definition of universality to see the truth of his remark that "the world here begins to change, a change which was later carried on to its completion."[52] Socratic philosophy teaches the art of estrangement. Through this art, the secular conscience—a conscience born of thought's dialogue with itself—is invented and the idea of citizenship reformed.

Before turning to the *Apology*'s account of his philosophical and civic activity, I should note Socrates' famous claim that he is "one of the very few Athenians, not to say the only one, engaged in the true political art [*alethos politike techne*], and that of the men of today I alone practice statesmanship" (*Gorgias*, 521d6–8). In the *Gorgias* this claim comes after a blistering critique of the leading Athenian statesmen of the fifth century—Themistocles, Miltiades, Cimon, and Pericles—who are all said to have failed the one true test of statesmanship, namely, whether their leadership resulted in the moral improvement of the citizens of Athens (515–19c). Real statesmanship evidently resides in a form of soul-craft of which Socrates alone is the master. The greatest political leaders of Athens only succeeded in flattering the people and (thus) in making them more "wild."

I cite this passage from the *Gorgias* because it seems, at first glance, to offer a self-understanding dramatically at odds with the one Socrates offers in the *Apology*. The Socrates of the *Gorgias* evidently thinks that there is a true political art guided by expert moral knowledge, a specialized form of craft knowledge (*techne*) analogous to that practiced by a horse trainer or physician. The difference between the true statesman and his false counterparts is that the former possesses such expert moral knowledge, while the latter lack it. As many a commentator has pointed out, the implications of this line of reasoning are radically antidemocratic: political legitimacy becomes a function of a specialized (and quite rare) form of knowledge rather than of consent or popular judgment. It therefore seems a short step from Socrates' position in the *Gorgias* to Plato's full-scale elaboration of the potently antidemocratic "royal art" (*basilike techne*) in the *Republic* and *Statesman*.

The standard interpretation of the "true political art" is also anti-individualist since it deprives us of grounds for respecting the moral capacities of the individual who lacks the *techne* in question. If the Socrates of the *Gorgias* has little regard for the leading statesmen of his time, his conception of moral knowledge implies an even lower regard for the *hoi polloi*, both individually and collectively.[53] The average individual can be morally improved, it seems, only if he or she is lucky enough to be ruled by an adept of the true political art, one who is capable of dishing out the strong medicine that *demos*-flattering politicians avoid.[54]

Like the *Gorgias*, the *Apology* contains a vehement critique of democratic practice. However, in the *Apology* Socrates eschews the categories of "statesmanship" and "the true political art." In answering the charges brought by Meletus, Lycon, and Anytus, he presents himself not only as a "citizen amongst citizens" but also as one who stands self-consciously apart, the better to pursue his philosophical mission. His place, he tells his fellow citizens (five hundred jurors plus an audience of unknown size), is neither in the assembly nor the law courts. He pursues the cross-examination of his fellow citizens in such unofficial public spaces as the agora and in more private settings, such as Callicles' home (the setting of the *Gorgias*). In part this has to do with the nature of his philosophical activity, with the fact that a genuine examination can take place only where the examined party is free to say what he or she actually believes. But it also has to do with the realities of democratic politics and the tendency of any majority to be intolerant of criticism. "Please do not be offended if I tell you the truth," Socrates chides the jurors. "No man on earth who conscientiously opposes either you or any other organized democracy, and flatly prevents a great many wrongs and illegalities from taking place in the state to which he belongs, can possibly escape with his life. The true champion of justice, if he intends to survive for even a short time, must necessarily confine himself to private life and leave politics alone" (31e–32a).[55]

This is a breathtaking indictment. Socrates presents his withdrawal from public life not simply as a choice entailed by his philosophic vocation but as a sad necessity dictated by the political domination of the multitude. The flighty, passionate, and self-righteous

16

nature of democratic majorities—well documented by Thucydides—makes it impossible for an individual of genuine moral integrity to lead a *public* life. Public speech, whether in the law courts or
the assembly, is fundamentally rhetorical and strategic in its approach to an audience. It seeks to persuade people to decide or act
in a certain way. As a result, it can be couched in "moral" terms only
when the speaker is relatively certain that the terms in question are
widely shared and (thus) are effective means for stirring the passionate and approving response of a self-righteous "we" (virtually all
appeals to patriotism are of this order). To oppose the majority on
more strictly moral grounds in the context of public debate during
times of war or civil unrest is ineffectual at best and probably suicidal. Thus, when (in Thucydides' *History*) Diodotus speaks in opposition to Cleon's murderous policy during the Mytilenian debate,
he is careful to cloak his argument in terms of utility, pointing out
that "Mytilene can be most useful to Athens" if she is treated with
moderation rather than vengefulness.[56]

The point here—Socrates' point—is not that democratic assemblies are privileged sites of irrationality (although they can be that)
but that public political speech must always appeal to common feeling and common sense if it is to avoid arousing suspicion or resentment. In the public-political world, the individual who conscientiously and vocally opposes majority policy whenever it is unjust will
be a pariah who runs the real risk of becoming a martyr. In the
political world of Athenian direct democracy this risk was greatly
enhanced; hence Socrates' withdrawal from the public realm.

But the very terms in which Socrates casts his withdrawal from
the "official" public realm make it clear that his philosophical activity has a distinctly political dimension. Were it not for the peculiarly
distorting character of the public stage, Socrates seems to be saying,
his own attempt to make his fellow citizens "as good as they can be"
could take a more conventionally political form, one which would
make his activity seem less "abnormal" in the eyes of his compatriots
(20d).

What, then, is the political dimension of Socrates' philosophical
activity, of his relentless questioning of himself and others? The first
thing one should note is the *negative* quality of Socrates' characterization of his activity. Contrary to what is implied by the *Gorgias*, he
begins his defense by explicitly disavowing the role of "expert in
perfecting human and social qualities" (20b). This was the role

claimed by the sophists, who offered to sell their moral expertise to well-born sons of Athens. In contrast to them, and to his ill-deserved popular reputation, Socrates is all too aware that he has no such expertise to sell or impart: "I should certainly plume myself and give myself airs if I understood these things"—namely, the art of "perfecting" the human and social qualities—"but in fact, gentlemen, I do not" (20c).[57] Any reading of Socrates which portrays him as reinventing statecraft as soul-craft must view this and similar professions of ignorance in the *Apology* as sheer disingenuousness.

Given the scorn Socrates heaps on the idea of groveling to save one's life (35a–b), there seems little reason to suppose that he is lying when he emphasizes his own ignorance of the correct definition of the virtues, of a *positive* account of moral truth. The sole form of wisdom he does claim is, famously, the awareness of his own *lack* of positive knowledge of the good: "I am only too conscious that I have no claim to wisdom, great or small" (20b). His radically imperfect "human wisdom" consists in knowing what he does not know, in realizing that he does not possess anything like the moral expertise claimed by the sophists, politicians, and poets (21d4–6). It is this negative wisdom—the sense of one's own relative ignorance of what virtue is and what the "best life" looks like—which serves as the basis and goad of Socrates' philosophical activity.[58] Thus, his response to Chaerephon's report that the oracle at Delphi had pronounced him the "wisest man in the world" was relentlessly to seek out and disprove the claims to expert moral knowledge being made all around him. The activity he describes himself undertaking (in *Ap.* 21c–23c) is a consistently deflationary one, consisting in the systematic refutation of others' claims to moral wisdom—an activity which made him anything but popular (21d). *Elenchus* reveals the confident claims of the "moral experts" as so many baseless illusions, but without offering the comfort of an alternative set of "moral facts." In these matters—the most important for human beings—real wisdom is, paradoxically, "the property of God," not man (23a).[59] No human being can claim to be wise when it comes to virtue.[60]

Socrates, then, turns the oracle's reply into an allegory about the illusory nature of human knowledge of the good: "It seems to me that he is not referring literally to Socrates, but has *merely taken my name as an example*, as if he would say to us, The wisest of you men is he who has realized, like Socrates, that in respect of wisdom he is really worthless" (23b, my emphasis). And it is on this basis that he conceives his philosophical mission, one framed in consistently negative terms: he does not know and commits himself to showing that those who claim to know are even more ignorant than he. He uses reason, in the form of cross-examination, to purge others of opinions parading as truth. As he describes it in the *Apology*, his philosophical activity consists essentially in the attempt to disillusion his interlocutors. This is his highest duty and sole occupation, his "service to God" (23c).

But what, one might ask, can be gained by purging alone? What *point* is there to Socrates' philosophical activity beyond the dissolution of such false claims to wisdom or moral expertise? One answer to this question has been offered by Richard Kraut, who sees Socrates' use of a dissolvent, deflationary form of rationality as the prelude to the ultimate attainment of correct definitions. It also serves as the primary means by which Socrates attempts to "convert" his interlocutors to his own unorthodox moral opinions. In this interpretation, the role of *elenchus* is not to cast conventional opinion or morality in doubt but rather to purify it by ridding it of the various false beliefs that promote injustice.[61] Thus, the perplexity induced by Socratic examination is but the first stage in a process of moral development which leads from the unreflective acceptance of the hodge-podge that is conventional morality to a more systematic and consistent (hence truer) set of moral beliefs.

A far different account is given by Arendt in her essay "Thinking and Moral Considerations" (which I consider in greater detail in chapter 5). Arendt locates the center of Socrates' philosophical activity precisely in its purgative character.[62] Such disabusing cannot be reduced to the elimination of inconsistencies and the false moral beliefs which create obstacles to moral development. It is, rather, a deeper and more radical questioning of the cognitive bases of the interlocutor's practical life. The resulting moral perplexity is not a transitional stage between the elimination of error and the steady progress toward moral truth; rather, as the precondition of *thinking*, this perplexity is itself the primary goal of Socratic purging. Only when action has ceased and words such as courage, justice, and virtue become genuinely perplexing does thinking actually begin. Plato has Socrates respond to Meno's likening of him to a kind of "stinging fish" (which paralyzes those it touches) by saying, "As for myself, if the stingray paralyzes others only through being paralyzed itself, then the comparison is just, but not otherwise. It isn't that, knowing the answers myself, I perplex other people. The truth is rather that I infect them also with the perplexity I feel myself" (*Meno*, 80c–d).

Playing on this simile and that of the gadfly in the *Apology*, Arendt notes how, in the course of Socratic examination, one is "aroused" by the gadfly, only to be "paralyzed" by the stinging fish. But what looks like paralysis from the standpoint of "the ordinary course of human affairs" is, in fact, the restless, ceaseless activity of thinking.[63] The purgative effect of Socratic questioning does not end once the "winds of thought" have been aroused and all quotidian activities interrupted. Rather, it transforms and expands itself, unfreezing "what language, the medium of thinking, has frozen into thought." Concepts, sentences, definitions, and doctrines are now put into motion. As Arendt notes, "The consequence of this peculiarity [of the "winds of thought"] is that thinking inevitably has a destructive, undermining effect on all established criteria, values, measurements for good and evil, in short, on those customs and rules of conduct we treat of in morals and ethics."[64] The "examined life" does not consist in tidying up our intellectual and moral household, ridding ourselves of those false beliefs which clutter our moral self-under-standing. Rather, it consists in the endless and seemingly circular questioning of the basic terms of our moral culture, those whose meaning seems self-evident and unarguable.[65] Questioning is an end in itself.

I think Arendt is closer to the spirit of Socrates here than Kraut, whose attempt to contextualize Socrates' disillusioning activity in terms of a broad schema of moral development is curiously Millian.[66] But Kraut is certainly right when he states that "Socrates has no wish to reject all conventional moral beliefs."[67] While the kind of thinking Socrates introduces "relentlessly dissolves and examines anew all accepted doctrines and rules [and is] equally dangerous to all creeds" without itself bringing forth any *new* creed, its goal is not to destroy the given just because it is given, nor is it to invert all (conventional) moral beliefs.[68] Rather, Socrates tries to inculcate a certain attitude in his conversational partners, one which combines high moral serious with a corrosive intellectual honesty. This atti-tude is characteristic of Socrates' own brand of moral and intellec-tual integrity, predicated as it is on an intense awareness of the way the everyday interpretation of moral norms and rules constantly draws us to (or encourages us to be acquiescent in) injustice. Indeed, the everyday interpretation frequently presents injustice *as* justice, a fact many of the dialogues (particularly the *Gorgias* and *Thrasymachus*) bear out.

As social and political beings, it is our nature to praise and blame the things "we" praise and blame. We become "moral" just as we become "social," namely, through imitation and habituation. The Socratic imperative is not that the individual reject *in toto* the stock of moral propositions he or she has come to possess in this manner but rather that the individual struggle to maintain a certain skeptical distance on all accepted definitions. Such skepticism is animated by the awareness that by presenting themselves as either the whole moral truth or as the moral fact of the matter, all "final" answers immediately become falsehoods. They may, in fact, be *part* of the truth, but the dogmatism implicit in their everydayness—the dogmatism born of mistaking the part for the whole—renders them fit subjects for elenchic dissolution.

Socrates was well aware that the audience to his philosophical activity included leisured youth inclined to derive a cynical lesson from his repeated refutations of self-proclaimed moral experts. In the *Apology* he cites the facile imitation of his elenchic art by the young as yet another potent source of his unpopularity (23c–d). The fact of the matter is that the dissolvent use of rationality lends itself to frivolous and potentially immoral use. Indeed, as Arendt reminds us, thinking itself is dangerous since it produces no positive result, offers no substitute code or credo. Yet Socrates deemed the risk inherent in thinking worth taking. He was convinced that most, if not all, injustice was the result of conventional ideas of morality or happiness thoughtlessly applied rather than any "will to prove a villain."[69] "Thoughtlessness" here does not refer to any recklessness or blindness. Rather, it refers to the essentially mimetic character of social life, to the fact that the greater part of our conduct is derived from custom, convention, and received opinion, and therefore has an automatic or intrinsically conformist quality.

This last point is reinforced if we look at the reason why Arendt—one of the great modern appreciators of the Periclean ideal—turned to Socrates as a model for thinking. It was her observation of Adolf Eichmann at his 1960 trial in Jerusalem which led her to insist on the moral and political significance of thinking. While his deeds—the transporting of millions of Jews to Nazi death camps—were monstrous, the doer was not. Indeed, as Arendt puts it, "The only specific characteristic one could detect in his past as well as in his behavior during the trial . . . was something entirely negative: it was not stupidity, but a curious, quite authentic inability to think."[70] Eichmann's reliance on clichés, stock phrases, and "conventional, standardized codes of expression" even when these were ludicrously out of place bespoke an "extraordinary shallowness." This led Arendt to ask: "Is evil-doing, not just the sins of omission but the sins of commission, possible in the absence not merely of 'base motives' (as the law calls it) but of any motives at all, any particular prompting of interest or volition?" It also led her to wonder whether "our ability to judge, to tell right from wrong, beautiful from ugly [is] dependent upon our faculty of thought." Put most sharply, the question posed by Eichmann's thoughtlessness is: "Do the inability to think and the disastrous failure of what we commonly call conscience coincide?"[71]

If the answer to the last question is yes (as the example of Eichmann seemed to indicate), then the ability to think becomes central to the moral life and, indeed, to politics—at least in those moments when "everybody is swept away unthinkingly by what everybody else believes in."[72] Arendt regarded such moments as "emergency situations" in which the destructive, purging effect of Socratic examination was essential for the liberation of the faculty of moral judgment. In such moments "thinking ceases to be a marginal affair in political matters" and becomes the very thing which "may prevent catastrophes, at least for myself, in the rare moments when the chips are down."[73]

This is a moving and, I think, persuasive conception of the political significance of Socratic thinking and examination. In the end, however, it is overly restrictive (for reasons I discuss in chapter 5). Suffice it to say here that the example of Eichmann points to a broader phenomenon: the superfluousness of wicked motives in the creation of many of the great political evils of the twentieth or any other century. When Arendt writes of "the nonwicked everybody who has no special motives and for this reason is capable of *infinite* evil," she puts her finger on one of the essential preconditions for political evil on a grand scale: ingrained thoughtlessness. This thoughtlessness—secreted, as it were, by the very nature of social and political life—makes most people (and not just those disposed to fanaticism) in most places and times far more likely to acquiesce in injustice or aid in the performance of evil than we care to admit. No culture—not even a liberal democratic one—is immune to it, as Thoreau reminds us.[74] We are all too likely to be carried away by the unexamined passions and resentments of group life or, like Eichmann, to let our moral life be governed by a set of "elating clichés." The implication of Socratic examination is that virtually every moral belief becomes false and an incitement to injustice the moment it becomes unquestioned or unquestionable.

Here we need to confront the sheer *strangeness* of Socrates, a strangeness that tends to be glossed over in a culture where the phrase "the examined life is not worth living" primarily serves as an "elating cliché" for the liberally educated. One aspect of this strangeness is his stated willingness to abandon any belief on the basis of the outcome of the next elenchic encounter.[75] The oddness of this stance must be fully registered. It goes far beyond a willingness to listen to other points of view or change one's opinions on the basis of overwhelming evidence to the contrary. It means holding beliefs about "the most important things" in such a way that *nothing* is allowed to become so sacred or constitutive of our being that abandoning it is unthinkable. But from a psychological perspective at least, most of us are what Michael Sandel describes as "encumbered selves" for whom certain inherited beliefs and commitments are constitutive of who we are: we cannot imagine ourselves as *ourselves* without them.[76]

For Socrates the "examined life" is (on the whole) irreconcilable with the encumbered self. Our most dearly held commitments and loyalties may be morally unsound; the only way we might have some minimal confidence that they are not is through the constant solicitation of arguments which attempt to undermine them. All protests to the contrary, very few, if any, individuals are capable of *this* degree of intellectual honesty. Indeed, the price of any faith, strong commitment, or sense of community seems to be an irreducible, underlying dogmatism: we cannot think of ourselves *otherwise*. The unexamined life may not be worth living by a human being (*Ap.* 38a), but the truth of the matter is that virtually all of us—even the most liberally educated—lead worthless lives by what is, in fact, a rigorously austere standard.[77] Our lives—human life, social life—are permeated by dogmatism of one sort or another at almost every level.

But doesn't the foregoing emphasis on negativity, disillusionment, and combating the thoughtlessness of everyday life shift the focus of Socrates' philosophical activity from *what* is believed to *how* it is believed? Doesn't it have the seemingly perverse consequence of assimilating Socrates to the existentialism of a Heidegger or a Sartre, and to the polarities of authenticity and inauthenticity, the *pour soi* and the *en soi*? Isn't there for Socrates (if not for Heidegger and Sartre) a clear *telos*, an "ultimate goal to moral development" which is substantive (the "perfection of their souls") rather than merely negative or open? And doesn't Socrates consistently judge politicians, private individuals, and even entire cities by what Kraut calls the "narrow test" of how much virtue they have or promote?[78] How else are we to make sense of Socrates' plea to his fellow citizens (29e) to give their attention to "truth and understanding and the perfection of [their] soul[s]"?

Socrates certainly does want his fellow citizens to care more for their souls than they currently do, and to make "progress toward goodness"—rather than success, wealth, and power—central to their lives. But how can they make progress if neither they nor Socrates knows what genuine goodness looks like? How can the soul be "perfected" in the absence of any real wisdom about the nature of virtue?

Here we need to acknowledge the passionate intensity of Socrates' commitment to his "mission," to the fact that he has devoted his life not to disillusionment for its own sake but in order that his fellow citizens might make moral progress. The "gadfly" rouses, persuades, and reproves them in order to prevent them from sleeping till the end of their days in a state of moral self-satisfaction (31a). What he rouses them to, however, is not a new, inspiring vision of virtue or human nobility but a sense of the injustice facilitated by their hubris, lack of wakefulness, and subservience to convention. Socrates does not present himself as the repository of philosophical wisdom about the nature of virtue, nor as virtue incarnate. Whatever moral exemplariness there is to be found in his life is a function of his having followed the imperative of avoiding injustice, regardless of cost. In the formula of the *Gorgias*, he would rather suffer wrong than do it (469c), even if this costs him his life.

As George Kateb has pointed out, Socrates' conduct is guided from start to finish by the principle of avoiding injustice.[79] His moral integrity is measured by his steadfast commitment to *this* principle and the morality of abstention which flows from it. Thus, faced with a guilty verdict from the jury and required by law to offer an alternative penalty (other than death) for himself, Socrates suggests he be punished with "free maintenance by the state" so that he might continue to offer his fellow Athenians "moral encouragement." What at first looks like a heavy-handed instance of Socratic irony in fact follows from his conviction that he never wrongs anyone intentionally (37a). He therefore cannot wrong himself by suggesting a penalty which he does not deserve (such as banishment from Athens). Socrates knowingly risks the death penalty because of his refusal to diverge even slightly from the principle of avoiding injustice. His "moral encouragement" and exhortation of his fellow citizens is designed to make them take this very principle seriously. From the Socratic point of view, moral progress—the process of perfecting one's soul—consists in the increasingly consistent and self-conscious avoidance of injustice.

This negative formulation of Socratic morality seems open to an obvious objection. How can one *know* what injustice is (and thus avoid it) without a prior knowledge of what *justice* is? Isn't any abstentionist morality ultimately parasitic, feeding upon a *positive*, fleshed-out conception of justice or the good?

In thinking about this objection (a version of which is often made by critics of liberalism with respect to *its* morality of abstention), it helps to bear in mind Socrates' own practice of citizenship during the two key moments he describes in the *Apology* (32b–e). The first incident, in 406 B.C., concerned the assembly's desire to try eight military commanders en bloc for failing to recover the dead and rescue survivors of the naval engagement off the Arginusae Islands.[80] Serving on the Council at the time (it was his tribe's turn), and acting as *epistates*, or chairman, of the presiding board of the assembly, Socrates delivered the sole dissenting vote on the proposal for a mass trial of the commanders, a proposal directly at odds with Athenian notions of due process:

> The only office which I have ever held in our city, gentlemen, was when I served on the Council. It so happened that our tribe Antiochis was presiding when you decided that the ten [*sic*] commanders who had failed to rescue the men who were lost in the naval engagement should be tried *en bloc*; which was illegal, as you all recognized later. On this occasion I was the only member of the executive who opposed your acting in any way unconstitutionally, and voted against the proposal; and although the public speakers were all ready to denounce and arrest me, and you were

25

all urging them at the top of your voices, I thought it was my duty to face it out on the side of law and justice rather than support you, through fear of prison or death, in your wrong decision. (*Ap.* 32b–c)

The second incident occurred in 404 B.C., during the short-lived regime of the Thirty Tyrants, who ordered Socrates (along with four other citizens) to bring Leon of Salamis to Athens for execution. Rather than be implicated in their atrocities, Socrates disobeyed the order of the authorities and went home—even though this course of action put his own life in jeopardy: "I again made it clear not by my words but by my actions that death did not matter to me at all . . . but that it mattered all the world to me that I should do nothing wrong or wicked" (32d). Socrates' telling of this incident strongly implies that the metic Leon, like many of the victims of the Thirty, was the innocent object of politically motivated persecution. Socrates' disobedience of authority in this instance reflects his adherence to the principle of not harming the innocent—again, a principle basic to Athenian law.

In neither instance does Socrates invoke anything like a "higher law" to justify his dissent and disobedience. Rather, in each case he attempts to hold Athens accountable to its own standards of right conduct. He refuses involvement in unjust enterprises, even though his refusal might well cost him his life. (In the instance involving Leon, he would surely have been put to death had not the regime toppled shortly afterward.) His dissent and noncompliance bespeak the seriousness with which he takes the imperative of avoiding injustice, while reflecting his awareness of how the life of active citizenship (whether in the democratic assembly or the oligarchical "commission") constantly generates injustice. Socrates' dissident practice of citizenship—one which is necessarily episodic given his general abstention from public life as such—rests on no theory of justice, nor does his abstentionist morality require one.[81] All it requires is a simple, "nonexpert" knowledge of the clearly recognizable forms of injustice.[82]

If this reading of the moral basis of Socrates' dissent and noncompliance is correct, it suggests that what Kraut calls the "narrow test" Socrates uses to evaluate politicians, private individuals, and cities— "how much virtue do they have or promote?"—should be read in similarly negative terms. It is not, in other words, a question of how closely individuals approximate virtuous excellence or the "good life" (the Aristotelian criterion), nor how closely political regimes come to realizing a worked-out scheme of distributive justice (such as we find in Plato's *Republic*). To have virtue in the Socratic sense means, first and foremost, to refuse complicity in injustice, no matter who authorizes it (popular opinion in the case of the ten commanders; political authority in the case of Leon). The avoidance of injustice, where the sense of injustice is plain and reflects widely held standards, is the heart of Socratic virtue. This, I think, is as true in the semi-Platonic *Gorgias* as it is in the more authentically Socratic *Apology*.

Interpreting Socrates' "narrow test" in this manner has, in turn, profound implications for how we read his claim in the *Gorgias* that he alone practices the "true political art." If, like Kraut, we give a decidedly positive twist to what Socrates means by virtue, then the true political art implies a kind of moral knowledge which politicians and the many clearly lack. Socrates may not be a "moral expert," yet (according to Kraut) he and his students are at least on their way to the attainment of moral expertise. His refusal to take a direct role in Athenian political life, or to encourage his students to do so, reflects his awareness that it is only with the actual attainment of moral expertise that politics becomes a means to the improvement of the *hoi polloi*. Until that time, the "true political art" consists in doing the preparatory work necessary to approach a correct definition of the virtues.[83] Philosophical inquiry, then, is the unavoidable prolegomenon to effective and radical political reform. Hence—on this interpretation at least—the withdrawal from established public life which Socrates makes so much of in the *Apology*.

If, however, we give Socrates' commitment to the avoidance of injustice the primacy of place it deserves, then the "true political art" looks quite different. It is no longer something carried on by the philosophical few who believe practice must await the advances of theory. It is, in fact, an activity which applies to everyone and is potentially open to everyone. The "false political art" is what passes for statesmanship and political leadership, namely, the ability to "flatter" the *demos* and gain popular support for particular policies. This is what Pericles did particularly well. The "true political art," conversely, consists in awakening one's fellow citizens to the ongoing need to avoid injustice, to living a life which is untainted by the "worst thing" in both its public and private dimensions. It is this art which Socrates describes when he tells the jury, in no uncertain terms, that he will not, under any circumstances, desist from his philosophical activity:

> I shall never stop practicing philosophy and exhorting you and elucidating the truth for everyone that I meet. I shall go on saying, in my usual way, My very good friend, you are an Athenian and belong to a city which is the greatest and most famous in the world for its wisdom and strength. Are you not ashamed that you give your attention to acquiring as much money as possible, and similarly with reputation and honor and give no attention to truth and understanding and the perfection of your soul? And if any of you disputes this and professes to care about these things, I shall not at once let him go or leave him. No, I shall question him and examine him and test him; and if it appears that in spite of his profession he has made no real progress towards goodness, I shall reprove him for neglecting what is of supreme importance. . . . I shall do this to everyone I meet, young or old, foreigner or fellow citizen, but especially to you, my fellow citizens. (29d–30a)

To be sure, in the *Gorgias* Socrates insists that the "good and true" political artist is always preoccupied with one thought, namely, "how justice may be implanted in the souls of the citizens and injustice banished . . ." (*Gr.* 504e). Yet this formulation contradicts the account of Socrates' philosophical activity cited earlier only if we assume that the "true political artist" approaches the many as unshaped clay to be molded in accordance with a preexisting idea of justice or the good. This is, of course, *Plato's* conception in book 6 of the *Republic*, where he makes his Socratic mouthpiece speak of "stamping on the plastic matter of human nature" the patterns of order and harmony the philosopher glimpses in the eternal realm (*Rep.* 500c–e).

Socrates' approach in the *Apology* could hardly be more different. He is not a political artist of character. He seeks to implant justice, that is, banish injustice by exhorting and examining *everyone* he meets, "young or old, foreigner or fellow citizen." In waking them up, in inducing them to perplexity about "the most important things," Socrates does not apply to the ignorant and recalcitrant many an expert knowledge available only to the few; rather, he attempts to open the philosophical vocation to everyone.[84] This is not to say he harbors the unrealistic expectation that the majority will become philosophers. It *is* to say, however, that he thinks neither age nor civic status is a bar to the kind of self-examination he has in mind.[85] What matters is not class, status, education, gender, or even freedom but the capacity to think. This capacity hinges on the ability to distance oneself, however episodically, from the routines of everyday life, the "routines" of active citizenship and political oratory included. In Socrates' view, the capacity to estrange oneself and reflect does not depend on any special rational faculties which only certain groups possess or have developed, as both Plato and Aristotle maintain. If it did, he would hardly treat all and sundry as fit candidates for exhortation and examination.

The political significance of Socrates' philosophical activity here comes into focus. Once the full import of his profession of ignorance and his commitment to avoid injustice are acknowledged, we are no longer limited to the alternatives of a full-scale withdrawal from politics, on the one hand, or an all too direct relation between philosophy and political reform, on the other.[86] What the *Apology* reveals is Socrates' intensive effort to cultivate an ethical sense in his fellow citizens which is partly distinct from the political life they share, which transcends custom and majority opinion without being reliant upon the transcendent.[87] His repeated claim is that care for one's soul—in the form of self-examination and avoidance of injustice—should take priority over care for the world and the duties of citizenship. This does not entail a monastic abandonment of the public realm: Socrates obviously cared greatly for his city and fellow citizens. Rather, it means limiting the distinctive energies of the public realm through a moral form of reflection, one which is (necessarily) cultivated and practiced elsewhere.

Viewed in this manner, the relation between "private" and "public," morality and politics, is far more indirect than what is implied by the "moral expert" argument, or by the Platonic/Aristotelian argument that any state worthy of the name is a school for virtue whose purpose is to inculcate a positive conception of the good.[88] It is precisely this indirectness which enables Socrates to respect the moral capacities of his interlocutors (in a way Plato, for example, does not) and to have a moral effect which is not predicated on either coercion or the introduction of a new dogma (as all direct versions of "statecraft as soul-craft" invariably are).[89] Socratic morality, unlike Plato's or Aristotle's, is surprisingly free of moralizing.

29

   This puts us in a better position to understand the significance of Socrates' withdrawal from the public realm. This withdrawal is not merely a strategy for self-preservation (although it is that as well). More centrally, it is about creating a space in which citizens can think what they are doing in the broad sense. This activity is impossible in the assembly or, for that matter, in any deliberative political body in which decisions on policy have to be taken.[90] In this regard, it is wrong, I think, to see in Socratic dialogue an alternative paradigm for deliberative democracy, as some have suggested. Socrates' philosophical activity takes place at a remove from the public realm, not because he is trying to "reconstitute public life in moral terms outside the formal channels of the 'state,' " but because he is trying to distance thinking and moral reflection from the all too obvious constraints of political action and judgment.[91]

   The point of this distancing—of this self-conscious breaking apart of the "harmony of thought and action"—is not to create a chasm between the way of life of the philosopher and that of the citizen (a chasm Callicles assumes in his long and hostile speech in the *Gorgias*). It is, rather, to open the possibility of a philosophical form of citizenship, one based on the self-division and (moderate) alienation from everyday civic life which accompanies all thinking. This is what the *Apology's* account of Socrates' philosophical activity makes available: not a renewed integration of thought and action but the necessarily tense relation between the two as viewed from the standpoint of morality. Moral progress and political self-limitation are *potential* products of this tension, one which introduces a greater hesitancy in action.

   By creating and maintaining this tension, Socrates is able not only to remind his fellow citizens of their best ideals but to offer a radical critique of their public-political world, a critique which traces, albeit implicitly, a "transvaluation of values." Thus, while it may be "tragic" that philosophy ultimately "disconnects" itself from politics in the history of Western thought, there is nothing tragic about the self-distancing performed by Socrates.[92] The estrangement of thought from politics, from the incessant demands of active citizenship, makes both moral individualism and dissident citizenship possible. The "good man" and the "good citizen" are not divided from each other by this estrangement but rather related in a new way. To see more fully why this is so, we need to turn from the *Apology* to the critique of Periclean democracy contained in the *Gorgias*.

The *Gorgias*

The *Gorgias* is one of the more peculiar Platonic dialogues which have been regarded, by scholarly consensus, as representative of *Socrates'* thought. For an ostensibly Socratic dialogue, it is animated by some strongly held Platonic (or proto-Platonic) commitments, ones which fit uneasily with Socrates' positions on a number of issues. Thus, while Socrates famously rejected retaliation, viewing it as always and everywhere unjust (*Crito*, 49d–e), the *Gorgias* presents him as a fierce advocate of the moral duty to discipline and punish, outstripping even Kant in this regard. Similarly, the Socrates who professes ignorance in the *Apology* is replaced, in the *Gorgias*, by a Socrates who seems utterly enamored of the supposed analogy between moral/political knowledge and the kind of knowledge exercised by an expert in such crafts as medicine or animal training. When, in the *Gorgias*, Socrates claims to be one of the few people, if not the only person, to practice "the true political art," he apparently lays claim to the kind of expert wisdom he disavows in the *Apology*. He even goes so far as to invoke a cosmic order as paradigmatic for the right ordering of the soul (*Gr.*, 507a–b) as well as a myth of the afterlife (523a–527e; cf. *Ap.* 29b). Finally, the last third of the dialogue (roughly from 502e on) is drenched in the rhetoric of moral perfectionism, insisting on the need to inculcate virtue by force if necessary (517c).

These tensions make it tempting to confine one's argument to the *Apology* in order to retain a dissident Socrates, or to expend a good deal of philosophical ingenuity in rendering the two dialogues consistent (albeit at the expense of the "disobedient" Socrates).[93] It seems to me, however, that the *Gorgias* actually deepens our understanding of the political dimension of Socrates' philosophical activity without demanding that we prematurely Platonize that activity. What is called for is a delicate sifting operation, one which uses Socrates' profession of ignorance as a kind of filter for interpreting what the *Gorgias* has to say about his political stance. Read through this filter, many of the more Platonic statements in the dialogue take on a different cast, enabling us to grasp more fully the unique quality of Socratic citizenship.

To state my own position briefly and more than a little dogmatically, I believe that: the critique of public life and Periclean democracy found in the *Gorgias* is Socrates' own; the attempt to revalue the "private" over the "public," or the individual over the communal, is what drives this critique; the Socratic doctrine claiming it is better to suffer than to do wrong—the main bone of contention between Socrates and his interlocutors, Polus and Callicles—ultimately entails a "transvaluation of values," one consequence of which is a fundamental rearticulation of the relation between "public" and "private"; and, finally, that the dialogue offers us a choice between two epistemological stances—that of a secular (rational) conscience, on the one hand, and that of moral expertise, on the other. I view the former stance as more authentically Socratic and as having profound implications for how we read Socrates' claim to practice "the true political art."

The *Gorgias* is, of course, a dialogue about the so-called art of rhetoric or oratory, an "art" taught by the rhetorician Gorgias to young Athenians with political ambitions. But Socrates' critique of rhetoric as a form of "flattery"—as, in fact, no art (*techne*) at all—is here broadened to include the values and assumptions governing Athenian public life as the dialogue moves from the encounter with Gorgias to the argument with his follower, Polus, culminating in the epic clash of values that takes place in Socrates' exchange with the politician Callicles. Like the *Apology*, the *Gorgias* delivers a critique of democratic politics which is fierce enough to seem downright antipolitical. But, again like the *Apology*, Socrates presents his philosophical activity as a kind of political activity—indeed, as "the true political art." Both dialogues depict a self-conscious distancing from "official" public life, a distancing which underwrites the curious claim that the most important part of citizenship is *not* found in participation in the deliberation of the courts and the assembly but in the kind of "private" activity Socrates makes his lifework.

The first surprise of the *Gorgias* is that its central argument is devoted *not* to proving that the philosophical life is the best life, nor that *arete* (virtue) or perfection of the soul is to be found in a set of explicitly unpolitical characteristics. Rather, it is devoted to showing that *injustice is the worst wrong*, the "greatest of evils" (469b; 477e). After having questioned Gorgias on the exact nature of his somewhat dubious calling, Socrates takes on his follower Polus's assertion that rhetoric is the most valuable of skills since it is the key to political power in the city, to the kind of power that enables an individual to *act as he pleases*, like a tyrant (466c). The rhetorically able individual is, Polus contends, among the most powerful and hence happiest in the city. From this point onward in the dialogue, Socrates' dialectical skills are devoted to showing that: (a) such "power" is not genuine power at all because it is almost always exercised in accordance with a false conception of what is good for the agent, one which produces painful consequences and which is, in fact, a form of helplessness rather than power; (b) happiness and evil are incompatible because evil is painful to the agent; and (c) doing wrong is more shameful—hence more painful and evil for the agent—than suffering wrong, and that injustice can therefore never be a route to real happiness.

The eudaemonistic psychological presuppositions of this argument aside, its most striking feature is its rigorously negative form. Socrates does not attempt to refute Polus by offering him a more edifying or noble conception of happiness. Rather, he stakes everything on getting Polus to agree that doing injustice is the most shameful evil, the worst wrong for the agent. Once this *summum malum* is established, it is relatively easy for Socrates to overturn Polus's contention and prove that the happiest man is not the tyrant or the powerful politician but the man who abstains from injustice and who thus avoids doing evil or harm to himself. The happiest man is not the embodiment of virtue but the one who "has no evil in his soul" because he has avoided injustice (478e). The Socratic doctrine that it "is better to suffer than to do wrong" (469b–c) renders the negativity of this formulation precisely. "Suffering wrong" is not made into virtue or a route to virtue (as it sometimes is in Christianity). It, too, is to be avoided, but never at the cost of engaging in the worst wrong. (We are one step away here from the Socratic doctrine of nonretaliation.)

The argument with Polus deflates the dominant Athenian conception of happiness and power, one which is all the more troubling because it was held by democrats. When Callicles enters the fray, spouting a proto-Nietzschean doctrine of "natural justice" in which the stronger or better are deserving of a greater share, he does so not as an oligarch or aristocrat but as a would-be democratic politician. When he states that it may indeed be conventionally "more shameful" to do rather than suffer injustice, but that "in my view nature herself makes it plain that it is right for the better to have the advantage over the worse, the more able over the less . . . the stronger over the weaker" (483d), he is not merely reiterating the Athenians' point at Melos.[94] He is articulating the credo of democratic imperialism—indeed of all imperialism—while displaying the corruption of character that inevitably flows from domination. His contempt for "the weaker folk, the majority" and the laws they create to tame stronger natures illustrates how the ethos of *pleonexia*—of taking more than one's share—turns inward as well as outward, infecting relations among citizens as well as those among states. Indeed, as Polus's earlier appeal to "what everybody thinks" makes clear, the antidemocratic craving for power infects not just politicians like Callicles but the citizen body as a whole, which has been seduced by the glamour of tyranny and absolute power.[95] An imperial democracy cannot stay a democracy for long since the basis of democratic justice—equal shares for all—demands a self-restraint directly at odds with the energies and ambitions of imperialism.

Here we come to the second surprise of a dialogue which, at least on the surface, anticipates so much of Plato's mature, explicitly antidemocratic position. In the exchange with Callicles it is *Socrates* who defends the democratic conception of justice and the "majority's" sense of what is more shameful. In so doing, he drives to the breaking point the contradiction between Callicles' credo of imperialism and the basic moral experience of democracy. It was this contradiction which had been so masterfully obscured by Pericles' Funeral Oration, in which the freedom and individuality of democratic culture are seamlessly interwoven with the imperial claim to cultural uniqueness and greatness. In the figure of Callicles we see the dissolution of the monumental Periclean synthesis. Socratic *elenchus* suggests that this dissolution is inevitable, given the tension between the ethos of empire and that of democracy. The Periclean ideal of a great empire that is democratic and self-moderating is revealed as an impossible fiction, one built upon a fundamental moral contradiction. The *Gorgias* represents the relentless picking apart of that contradiction and the statesman (Pericles) who tried to conceal it.

It is Socrates' claim to have proven, in the argument with Polus, that "to do wrong and evade punishment for wrongdoing is the worst of all evils" (482b), which prompts Callicles to deliver his famous diatribe against philosophy. He rejects this conclusion, which he regards as self-evidently absurd, as the product of a "trick" argumentative strategy deployed by Socrates, whom he charges with shifting from the natural to the conventional sense of justice (and back again), the better to throw his opponents off balance. But he also sees this conclusion as symptomatic of the perversity of the philosophical way of life. Socrates' refusal to acknowledge the obvious, namely, that suffering wrong is worthy only of a slave, coupled with his assertion that public life and power are corrupting lead Callicles to juxtapose the "unmanly" philosophical life with the life of active citizenship (484d–486d). According to Callicles, the immoderate pursuit of philosophy into adult life leads to an increasing ignorance of public affairs and an incompetence in public (political) argument. Philosophy may be an important component in the *paideia* of a youth, but it turns the adult into a good-for-nothing, one who shuns "the city center and marketplace, in which the poet said that men win distinction"; one who lives his life "sunk in a corner and whispering with three or four boys," incapable of "any utterance which is free and lofty and brilliant" (485d). By spending his life in this way, Socrates neglects "what [he] ought most to care for," namely, the public world and his reputation in it.

The stark contrast which Callicles sets up between the life of the citizen and the life of the philosopher reminds us of Pericles' words in the Funeral Oration: "We do not say that a man who takes no interest in politics is a man who minds his own business; we say that he has no business here at all." In the Athenian democracy, the philosopher's withdrawal from public affairs makes him immediately suspect, a possible corrupting influence on civic virtue. Unlike his fellow Athenians, Callicles argues, Socrates' "love of the things of the mind" *has* made him soft, impotent, and effeminate, to the point where any rascal could have him tried and imprisoned on trumped-up charges, confident that the "childlike" Socrates could only "reel to and fro and gape openmouthed, without a word to say" in his defense (486b). Calling on Socrates to give up "these dainty devices" for the "fairer music of affairs," Callicles warns him that he risks being "disenfranchised in his own city."

That Callicles' portrait of a dangerously unpolitical philosopher is not entirely off the mark is borne out by Socrates' repeated protestations of his relative ignorance of the forms of political speech and procedure in his own city.[96] However, we should not assume that Socrates accepts, let alone validates, the polarity Callicles constructs. To be sure, the *Gorgias* articulates a set of oppositions—between rhetoric and dialectic, philosophy and politics, citizenship and one's soul—which seems to imply a series of either/or choices. Moreover, the vehemence of Socrates' critique of rhetoric and public life creates the impression that only withdrawal from the public realm—or its radical reform—will do. The latter course might involve the application of "moral expertise," or it might attempt to "reconstitute public life outside the formal channels of the state," setting up dialogue or dialectic as a new paradigm for political discourse.[97] The problem with these alternatives—withdrawal, the appeal to expert knowledge, restructuring political discourse—is that they run counter to Socrates' claim that his *philosophical* activity is the "true political art," and that he has *always already* been engaged in politics, an engagement which presumes neither the possession of expert knowledge nor the "reconstitution" of the public realm. He has practiced the "true political art" by being a philosophical citizen.

How is this possible? The apparent paradox is lessened if we note that the craft analogy—so central to the argument of the *Gorgias*—is deployed negatively: it targets rhetoricians like Gorgias and politicians like Callicles who claim to *know* what virtue or happiness is. The knowledge they claim is, in fact, merely the "routine" of flattering the *demos*, the articulation of popular desire and prejudice. Measured by the standard of the kind of knowledge characteristic of an art or craft—that is, by the one they themselves invoke—their "wisdom" is found miserably wanting.

But even if the craft analogy is primarily used in a destructive or critical manner, doesn't Socrates' practice of the "true political art" amount to a claim of craftlike knowledge, at least when it comes to making citizens "the best that they can be"? If it did, it would not only run counter to the profession of ignorance in the *Apology* but would also make Socrates a victim of the very criterion he uses to condemn Pericles, Themistocles, Cimon, and Miltiades. For if Socrates' claim is that the most revered Athenian statesmen lacked genuine political wisdom because they failed to improve the citizenry (and, in fact, rendered them worse), then he is hoist by his own petard (cf. *Ap.* 33b). How, after all, can he condemn Pericles et al. for the fact that their fellow citizens turned on them when he himself will be tried and condemned by a large jury of his fellow citizens, who should have been improved by his practice of "the true political art"? By this standard, Socrates is an abysmally poor "trainer" of men since the animals whose ethical care he has undertaken turn on him (*Gr.* 516b). Like Pericles, he has left "the only true office of the good citizen" unfulfilled.[98]

Clearly, we need a less literal understanding of Socrates' "narrow test" of moral improvement as well as his notion of the "true political art." Such an understanding emerges when we tease out the implications of his characterization of rhetoric and political oratory as modes of "flattery." The problem with rhetoric is not that, or not simply that, it tells the *demos* only what they want to hear: Pericles' third speech in the *History* is hardly ingratiating. Indeed, political oratory *can* be harshly critical, holding up to its listeners an unflattering portrait of themselves even in times of crisis. But if rhetorical criticism is not to fall on deaf ears, it must appeal to the best selves of its audience. It must take the form of a reminder of the ideals of the city itself, ones which call forth a spirit of sacrifice. Pericles is able forcefully to confront his fellow citizens with their own lack of constancy, their own infidelity to their ideals. What he *cannot* do is subject these ideals (or the popular understanding of them) to anything like prolonged critical scrutiny. The office of the democratic leader, after all, is to persuade and to act. Hence, he must work with what is already there: the passions, goals, and values of his community. Public address allows him to select, direct, and interpret these, but it effectively forbids any fundamental questioning. Oratory is flattery because persuasion, not genuine criticism, is its goal. The demagogic political leader can, perhaps, guide us through this medium, but he cannot be truly said to *improve*.

But can the *philosopher* achieve what the politician's calling seems to prohibit? Certainly not in the sense of "doing battle with the Athenians" by entering the public realm as a citizen among citizens (521a). To directly criticize popular but unjust policies in this arena is, as Socrates reminds us in the *Apology*, not an option: "Do you suppose that I should have lived as long as I have if I had moved in the sphere of public life and, conducting myself in that sphere like an honorable man, had always upheld the cause of right, and conscientiously set this end above all others? Not by a very long way, gentlemen." (32e–33a).

Gregory Vlastos claims that this excuse for withdrawing from the public realm is self-serving. He objects to the *Phaedo*'s characterization of Socrates as "the wisest and most just of men," arguing that Socrates could have been decidedly more just had he publicly and vocally opposed Athenian policy in the assembly.[99] In cases like the Mytilenian debate, Socrates apparently fails to live up to his most basic civic and moral obligations by *not* speaking out against the grossest of political evils, namely, a proposed genocide. But the fact that Diodotus succeeds in overturning a state-ordered massacre by appealing to what is in Athens' *interest* as an imperial power suggests that moral condemnation of *popularly* decided policies is likely to be ineffective and—in the context of a direct democracy at war—possibly suicidal. In such conditions (and here we need to remember that Socrates' philosophical activity occupied a period virtually coextensive with the Peloponnesian War and its tumultuous aftermath) the kind of improvement Socrates calls for in the *Gorgias* would hardly result from publicly delivered condemnations of particular policies.

Nor could such "improvement" occur by making this treacherous public realm—the fractious arena of persuasion—more dialogical. While the theatrical character of the public realm earns it a great deal of scorn in the *Gorgias*, Socrates is careful not to imply that dialogue and dialectic could somehow take the place of oratorical public address. The public realm is what it is, and it is misguided to suggest that the mode of persuasion characteristic of philosophical discourse could ever be substituted for that of rhetoric and oratory. As Socrates repeatedly emphasizes in the dialogue, *his* brand of persuasion is not and cannot be directed at a large audience; it achieves its effects one-on-one: "I know how to secure one man's vote, but with the many I will not even enter into discussion" (474b). This is not because "the many" are so intrinsically base or stupid that they cannot rise to the level of philosophy. Rather, it is because the idea of a "dialogue" with or cross-examination of a large audience is an absurdity.

Socrates' forceful contrast of dialectic with rhetoric in the *Gorgias* reminds us that the latter is at home in the public realm while the former is not. Indeed, if Arendt is correct in suggesting that Socrates *enacts* the process of thinking in the marketplace, the lesson seems to be that *thinking* needs both a space and a form of discourse of its own.[100] To put the point somewhat baldly, thinking does not take place in the public realm—and it certainly does not take place on the public stage. Hence Socrates' withdrawal from it and his creation of a new, mobile space for his philosophical/political activity. The paradox of the "true political art" is that it is not a creature of the public sphere, nor does it try to be.

The fact that Socrates' "true political art" stands at an explicit (and carefully preserved) remove from the world of the assembly and its political leadership indicates that the kind of "moral improvement" he aims at is not something that can easily be measured, let alone provide the basis for the "narrow test" he proposes in the *Gorgias*. The virtue Socrates attempts to awaken is not something that can be inculcated by political means or through the standard channels of moral education.[101] It consists, first and foremost, in getting his fellow citizens to think what they are doing. The life of active, engaged citizenship—celebrated by both Pericles and Callicles, as well as by the civic republican tradition—militates against this possibility. Thinking what we are doing necessarily slows us down, if only because it demands that we stop acting in order to think. It moderates what Arendt (in *On Revolution*) calls the "love of public freedom" and "joy in action."

Socrates' radical suggestion to the Athenians and to all "lovers of action" is that political deliberation and judgment are no substitutes for thought or moral reflection, and that thought itself provides no solid results that can serve as the basis of further action. If his fellow citizens become at least episodically philosophical, Socrates can be said to have "improved" them by slowing them down, by loosening the grip the Periclean idea of greatness (or the Calliclean idea of power) has on their imaginations. His "true political art" can thus be understood as the attempt to de-aestheticize the public realm—not, however, by *moralizing* this realm but rather by making care for the city something distinct from and secondary to the (thoughtful) care for one's soul.[102] Only when their moral sense has been sobered by an appreciation of the worst wrong can citizens begin to free themselves from the communal intoxication of the Periclean vision and from the Calliclean corruptions which flow from it.

The nature of the "transvaluation of values" performed by the *Gorgias* should now be clear. If Socratic *elenchus* proceeds immanently, taking "commonsense" definitions of moral terms and showing how they entail contradictions with the network of moral beliefs held by the individual under examination, we cannot say the same of Socratic ethics.[103] In his role as dissenting citizen, Socrates is careful to appeal to the Athenians' established sense of proper conduct. In his role as philosophical critic and "gadfly," however, he goes well beyond the *sensus communis*. It is therefore misleading to say that Socrates calls his fellow Athenians "back to the best ideals of [their] past as criticized by philosophy."[104] The sheer intensity with which Socrates demands the avoidance of injustice puts him in diametric opposition not only to the power-worshiping of Polus and Callicles but also to the ideals of civic greatness and self-sacrifice articulated in the Funeral Oration. Callicles gets it right: if what Socrates says is true, then "surely the life of us mortals must be turned upside down and apparently we are everywhere doing the opposite of what we should" (481c). Where, in Euben's words, "being great becomes being good, courage becomes the willingness to suffer injustice rather than commit it, and the purpose of life is not to conquer Syracuse, avenge one's friends, build an empire, or leave monuments behind but to conquer tyrannical impulses [and] harm no one," we have not a purified or refined table of values but a substantively different one.[105] Socratic negativism dissolves the Periclean ideal, using the imperative of avoiding injustice to reveal the moral hollowness of aesthetic monumentalism. It points to a new moral world, one where the principle of conduct derives not from the collective desire to demonstrate greatness or cultural superiority but from the individual's desire to preserve his or her moral integrity, to not be a party to injustice.[106]

For the first time in the history of the West, the *Apology* and the *Gorgias* articulate the standpoint of a rational conscience, one whose "no" is distinct from the internalization of any creedal imperatives. Throughout both dialogues, Socrates is at pains to distinguish the kind of persuasion created by moral argument and reflection from that produced in the assembly and law courts. The latter kind is not purely irrational (however much the contrast of rhetoric and dialectic may imply this), but it necessarily takes account of (and fluctuates with) the moods and prejudices of the public. The *integrity* of the political leader or actor is subject to strict bounds because he cannot allow the desire for self-consistency to repeatedly contradict the desires, hopes, and fears of the people. Socratic integrity, on the other hand, is found precisely in the placement of the standard of self-consistency above all others. *Self*-contradiction—the betrayal of defining moral commitments—is the animating fear. Thus, Socrates answers Callicles' initial objection that he has turned "the life of us mortals" upside down by pointing out how this formulation installs common sense and public opinion as the only possible standards (481c–482b). What matters for Socrates, however, is not whether he contradicts the *demos* but whether he contradicts *himself*—his own reason and his own principles: "I think it better, my good friend, that my lyre should be discordant and out of tune, and any chorus I might train, and that the majority of mankind should disagree with and oppose me, rather than that I, *being one*, should be out of tune and contradict myself" (482c).[107]

The standard appealed to here—in explicit opposition to what "the many" think or what custom and convention dictate—is not an anticipation of natural law or of "the voice of God in man" (what conscience becomes for European Christendom), nor is it the kind of specialized knowledge which comes from a *techne*. It is, rather, *self*-agreement, the principle of noncontradiction as it applies to the fundamental moral commitment of avoiding injustice. With the articulation of *this* principle, Socrates creates the possibility of a secular form of conscience. The fact that conscience always says no, that (as Shakespeare puts it in *Richard III*) "it fills a man full of obstacles," does not in itself tell us anything about the source of the prohibitions. They could be merely the internalization of religion, custom, or law. When, in the *Apology*, Socrates appeals to his "inner voice" (*daimonion*) and to his own practice of ruthless self-examination, he is appealing to the thinking individual's capacity to generate such prohibitions—the core of any morality of abstention—not out of deference to such authorities but out of a nonexpert understanding of injustice. With Socrates, conscience (and morality) no longer depend upon the "leading strings" provided by such authorities.

Invoking the principle of noncontradiction as the test of individual moral integrity, Socrates' reply to Callicles attests to the thinking individual's relative moral independence, to the right to think and judge for oneself. Socrates demonstrates how it is possible to *conscientiously oppose* political authority, social norms, and creedal restraints with the invocation of no authority higher than the thinking, morally consistent individual. From this point forward, moral individualism—the kind expressed by Montaigne, skeptic and moralist, when he questions whether the advent of Christianity has lessened the amount of injustice in the world, or by Thoreau when he writes that "the only obligation I have a right to assume, is to do at any time what I think right"—becomes a concrete existential possibility.

Dissident Citizenship: The *Crito*, Conscience, and Civil Disobedience

This last formulation elicits the following objections: first, that Socrates was no upholder of a subjectivist doctrine of conscience; and, second, that he was no enemy of law or legitimate political authority. Indeed, he was neither—but, then, neither was John Locke, the most famous theorist of the right to revolt. The case of Socrates, however, is complicated by his apparent rejection of *any* disobedience to political authority whatever, his de facto disobedience and noncompliance notwithstanding. In the *Apology* he says that he *knows* that "to do wrong and to disobey my superior, whether God or man, is wicked and dishonorable" (29b). In the *Crito* he goes even further, stating that the escape from prison and imminent execution proposed by his friend Crito would not only be wrong but, as an act of disobedience to lawfully constituted procedures, destructive of the state as such. Impersonating the Laws of Athens, Socrates asks himself (and Crito, his would-be accomplice in "wronging the state") the following questions:

> Do you expect to have such license against your country and its laws that if we try to put you to death in the belief that it is right to do so, you on your part will try your hardest to destroy your country and us its laws in return? And will you, the true devotee of goodness, claim that you are justified in doing so? Are you so wise as to have forgotten that compared to your mother and father and all the rest of your ancestors your country is something far more precious, more venerable, more sacred, and held in greater honor both among gods and among all reasonable men? Do you not realize that you are even more bound to respect and placate the anger of your country than your father's anger? That if you cannot persuade your country you must do whatever it orders, and patiently submit to any punishment that it imposes, whether it be flogging or imprisonment? And if it leads you out to war, to be wounded or killed, you must comply, and it is right for you to do so. . . . Both in war and in the law courts and everywhere else you must do whatever your city and your country command, or else persuade them in accordance with justice. (*Cr.* 51a–c)

This is not exactly a doctrine of "my country right or wrong" since Socrates emphasizes the fallibility of both citizens and the laws themselves, insisting on the right of any citizen to persuade his fellow citizens that they have made a mistake or are acting unjustly. Nevertheless, if the attempt at persuasion fails, the unconditional duty of the accused seems to be docile and passive submission to the authority bent on his or her destruction. Anyone influenced by the Anglo-American tradition of rights-based individualism is thus bound to feel a bit queasy when reading this passage. Even Hobbes, the archdefender of political authority and the state, scarcely demanded that its victims "patiently submit" to its overwhelming force.[108] In the *Crito* Socrates seems to offer a theory of political obligation which perhaps allows protest but which *never* countenances disobedience to law.

This raises a number of questions, some of them familiar, others less so. First, how do we square the dissident spirit of the *Apology* with the authoritarian flavor of the *Crito*? Can the two dialogues be rendered consistent without collapsing one into the other? Moreover, there is the problem of whether the *Crito* can be rendered consistent with itself, since its apparent doctrine of unconditional obedience to even unjust law flagrantly contradicts the Socratic principle that we must never do wrong or commit an injustice (*Cr.* 49a). If the *Crito* indeed fetishizes obedience to law and subservience to the state, mustn't we look elsewhere for a model of conscientious, dissident citizenship? Doesn't Sophocles' *Antigone* offer a less ambiguous model of, and superior justification for, civil disobedience than anything we find in the Socratic dialogues?

The question of how much, if at all, Socrates advocates dissent and disobedience raises broader issues as well. Even if he can be said to justify disobedience under some conditions, can his motivations properly be called *political* in any sense? Can the Socratic effort to avoid injustice, to "never willingly do wrong," provide a model for citizenship, or does it express an ethical purism or moral absolutism at odds with the very idea of political action and civic involvement? Here we broach what Michael Walzer has dubbed the problem of "dirty hands" in politics, that is, the apparent impossibility of fulfilling the demands of the political vocation without occasionally engaging in action which, by almost any standard, is immoral or unjust.[109] If Machiavelli and Max Weber argue for a manly acceptance of this unavoidable burden of political "sin," Socrates apparently argues for a rejection of even the merest taint of injustice—for "clean" (albeit unpolitical) hands. Viewed from this angle, his call for "care for the soul" seems fundamentally at odds with the kind of worldliness which characterizes the political actor.

In the *Apology*, after he has refuted the charges against him and given an account of his much misunderstood philosophical activity, Socrates poses a famous rhetorical question. Suppose, he says to the jurors, you pay no attention to the charge of corruption brought by Anytus and offer to acquit me on one condition, namely, that I give up my philosophical activity, which looks so suspicious to you. What then? His answer leaves no room for doubt: "I should reply, Gentlemen, I am your very grateful and devoted servant, but I owe a greater obedience to God than to you, and so long as I draw breath and have my faculties, I shall never stop practicing philosophy and exhorting you and elucidating the truth for everyone that I meet" (29c–d). In case his fellow citizens don't get the message, he later adds: "You know I am not going to alter my conduct, not even if I have to die a hundred deaths" (30c).

Here we seem to have an unmistakable attitude of defiance, one which puts obligation to his philosophical/political mission far above any command or law against philosophizing the *demos* might issue. The tonal clash between this pronouncement and the argument of the Laws in the *Crito* could not, it seems, be greater. Yet recent interpreters have tended to downplay or even deny the gap between the two dialogues. Brickhouse and Smith, for example, argue that there is no "*Apology/Crito* problem" since Socrates' two principles—never do wrong and never disobey civil authority—can, in fact, be rendered perfectly consistent.[110] The defiant trial statement, they point out, refers to a hypothetical situation in which Socrates is offered a conditional acquittal, something the jury was not legally empowered to do. Hence, continuing to philosophize would constitute no disobedience to a "valid command of an authentic legal authority." In similar fashion, one could question the legitimacy of the newly installed political authority that sought to execute Leon, arguing that Socrates' noncompliance with the command of the Thirty was hardly disobedience to a justly enacted law. As to the larger question of what would happen should properly constituted laws command Socrates to do something patently unjust, Brickhouse and Smith reply that Socrates could fully comply without endangering his own vow to never knowingly commit injustice. Strictly speaking, the moral responsibility for the resulting injustice rests not with him who carries out the orders but with him who issues the commands. "Unjust laws may be passed; but in obeying them, the citizen does not act unjustly."[111]

The problem with this strategy for eliminating the tension between the *Apology* and the *Crito* is that it succeeds only by turning Socrates into the most passive of citizens, one whose intense aversion to injustice always gives way before the more intense demand for obedience to law. In cases where morality and legality conflict, he or any other citizen does what the unjust law commands, secure in the knowledge that they were only following orders, and thus in no way responsible for the wrongs the state has commissioned.[112] Like the child obeying his parent or the slave obeying his master, the citizen who acts unjustly when ordered to do so by legitimate authority is, by virtue of his subservient position, blameless.

This reconciliation of the *Apology* with the *Crito* exacts a high price. Not only does it demand a Socrates who rejects the very idea of justified disobedience to law; it also attributes to him a conception of political membership which relieves the citizen of any burden of moral reflection when it comes to political obligation and civic duty. *Qua* individuals we may have a duty to examine ourselves and avoid injustice, yet *qua* citizens we are not responsible actors. We are therefore free to excuse ourselves from the consequences that flow from our compliance. This is, perhaps, not exactly a doctrine of blind obedience (citizens are, after all, free to dissent, to "persuade or obey"), but it is authoritarian enough to remind us of the case of the "thoughtless" Adolf Eichmann, who not only conflated moral and legal obligation but insisted throughout his trial that what he had done was no crime since the Führer's orders had the status of law in the Third Reich.[113] Thus, Brickhouse and Smith create a "consistent" but implausible Socrates, one whose insistence on the examined life is strictly bounded by the public/private distinction. This "gadfly" may try to awaken private individuals to ethical demands, but as citizens he lets them sleep to the end of their days. Here we have a separation between the "good man" and the "good citizen" far more radical than anything imagined by Aristotle in book 3 of the *Politics*.

Richard Kraut takes the opposite tack. Rather than bend the *Apology* to make it consistent with a virtual authoritarianism, he takes the more plausible route of arguing the *Crito's* doctrine of political obligation is not nearly as rigid as it has been made out to be. For Kraut the *Apology* establishes unequivocally that Socrates believes in justified disobedience to law (his noncompliance with the order of the Thirty and his defiance of any proposed ban on philosophy expressing an unbending resolve never to do wrong).[114] The task then becomes how to read the speech of the Laws in the *Crito* so that it "open[s] the door to justified disobedience."[115] He does this by eliciting a proto-Lockean doctrine of consent from the *Crito*, one which binds the individual citizen to maintaining his "just agreements," and by presenting an interpretation of the "persuade or obey" clause which not only permits disobedience but makes it a veritable duty for the citizen who believes he or she is confronted by an unjust law.

According to Kraut, Socrates' refuses Crito's offer of escape because to do so would be to overturn the voluntary agreement he has made with the Laws of Athens, an agreement he has upheld over the course of a lifetime, an agreement which was not coerced and which did not commit him to *performing* any injustice (such an agreement would obviously have conflicted with the principle of never doing wrong). What it *did* commit him to was acceptance of the verdicts of the law courts, even though these might result in his *suffering* an injustice by being wrongly condemned. The refusal to accept unfavorable verdicts, to live up to his part of the agreement, would, if generalized, result in the destruction of the legal system and thus the state. Hence, Socrates refuses to commit an injustice or sin against the state by breaking his just agreement. He pays the price demanded by the jurors' verdict at his trial—not out of any blind obedience to authority but out of a recognition of the force of obligations imposed by agreements freely entered into, which are both fair and conditional. On Kraut's reading, Socrates recognizes that such vulnerability to legal verdicts is the unavoidable price of membership in a political order governed by the rule of law. This recognition, however, does not suspend for a moment the overarching criterion of avoiding injustice, a criterion which *demands* disobedience whenever a law or order is unjust, just as it demands fulfillment of obligations when they are the result of free and fair agreements.

But how can this criterion of never doing wrong be squared with the Laws' demand that Socrates "persuade or obey"? This clause, foreshadowed in the passage cited earlier, occurs in the second part of the Laws' speech: "We maintain that anyone who disobeys is guilty of doing wrong, on three separate counts: first because we are his parents, and secondly because we are his guardians, and thirdly because, after promising obedience, he is neither obeying us nor persuading us to change our decision if we are at fault in any way. And although all our orders are in the form of proposals, not of savage commands, and we give him the choice of either persuading us or doing what we say, he is actually doing neither" (51e–52a).

The usual interpretation of this clause is given by George Grote, the Victorian historian of Greek philosophy, who argued, sensibly enough, that what the Laws confront Socrates with is an either/or choice of obedience (in accordance with his "just agreements") *or* taking advantage of his citizenly prerogative in the assembly to convince his fellow Athenians that the law or decree they propose is unjust. Such a choice leaves no room for disobedience since Socrates' duty, like that of every other Athenian citizen, is to state the reasons why the proposed law is a bad one and, if he fails to persuade, to obey the legislation or command of the assembly.[116]

Against this interpretation, Kraut argues that the "or" in the Laws' "persuade or obey" actually conceals a "loophole" which permits disobedience to the law.[117] This opening actually occurs in the statement of the "persuade or obey" doctrine contained in the first cited passage (51a–c). There the Laws state that "both in war and in the law courts and everywhere else you must do whatever your city and your country command, *or else persuade them in accordance with justice*" (51c, my emphasis). The citizen has a duty not simply to obey but, evidently, to cleave to the requirements of justice. Thus, if Socrates escapes he commits a wrong because "he is neither obeying us nor persuading us to change our decision if we are at fault in any way" (51e). *If* the law courts are an equally tenable place for this persuasion, then the onus on the individual citizen confronted with an unjust law or decree is not simply to persuade and (failing that) to obey but to *disobey* the unjust law or decree and to *give an account* of the reasons for that disobedience in the appropriate public setting. Even if the effort to persuade fails, the act of disobedience is allowed by the Laws since the duty they impose is not to obey fallible laws but to alert the community to legally framed injustice.[118] In Kraut's words, "If someone has disobeyed a law then he must, when summoned, appear before the court to persuade his fellow citizens that disobedience was justified. . . . Persuasion is required of the disobedient citizen because he owes the parent-city with which he has made an agreement some explanation for his behavior."[119]

This reading is attractive because it places the Socratic demands for consistency and giving an account at its center. The Laws turn out to be eminently Socratic in their estimation of what is truly important, namely, the giving of reasons. But ultimately the argument that the *Crito* enables, indeed, encourages disobedience (so long as reasons are given) is unpersuasive. The rhetoric of the dialogue, and the prominence of the Laws-as-parents metaphor in this rhetoric, presents a legal order (the state) to which the citizen is eternally in debt since it *gave him his very life in the first place* (50d).[120]

47

The Laws raised him and educated him as parents do; and, as with parents and children, there is no equality of rights between the state and its citizens (51a). Indeed, compared to one's parents, one's country is "something far more precious, more venerable, more sacred, and held in greater honor among gods and all reasonable men" (51b). According to the *Crito*, then, one's life is not one's own but rather a conditional gift of the state; one must treat the state with even more honor and deference than one reserves for one's parents; and one must constantly bear in mind the fact that one is "not allowed to answer back" to the state any more than to a parent (50e).

It is therefore implausible to argue that the Laws are as solicitous of correction and as fixated on (or placated by) reasons as Kraut makes them out to be. What the speech of the Laws sets out is the unquestionable authority of the state over its citizens, an authority which the Laws clearly present as shaken by *all* acts of disobedience, not merely those which neglect to give reasons. Throughout, the state is presented "as if it were a hounded and vulnerable individual."[121] The fact that Kraut's ingenious interpretation makes the *Crito* consistent with the *Apology* does not mean that it *must* prevail over interpretations of the dialogues which recognize and preserve the tension between them.[122] Rather, it alerts us to the hazards of assuming that the Socrates Plato presents in the *Crito* is as authentic a presentation of Socrates' voice as that which we find in the *Apology*. Even within the "Socratic" Platonic dialogues, we are bound to find gradations in relative faithfulness to Socrates' thought.[123]

Does this mean that we should ignore the *Crito* when we attempt to specify the nature of Socratic politics and Socratic citizenship? Hardly, for the *Crito* provides essential evidence with regard to the nature of Socrates' ties to the Athenian democracy and his evaluation of it as a form of political association.

Toward the end of their speech, the Laws of Athens proclaim:

Socrates, we have substantial evidence that you are satisfied with us and with the state. You would not have been so exceptionally reluctant to cross the borders of your country if you had not been exceptionally attached to it. You have never left the city to attend a festival or for any other purpose, except on some military expedition. You have never traveled abroad as other people do, and you have never felt the impulse to acquaint yourself with another country or constitution. You have been content with us and with our city. You have definitely chosen us, and undertaken to observe us in all your activities as a citizen. (52b–c)

A little further on they add:

> You had seventy years in which you could have left the country, if you
> were not satisfied with us or felt arrangements were unfair. You did not
> choose Sparta or Crete—your favorite models of good government—or
> any other Greek or foreign state. You could not have absented yourself
> from the city less if you had been lame or decrepit in some other way. It
> is quite obvious that you stand by yourself above all other Athenians in
> your affection for this city and for us its laws. (52e–53a)

What these passages reveal is not a "love it or leave it" doctrine
of political loyalty but an insight into the nature of Socrates' attachment to Athens. Socrates *prefers* Athens not because he was born
there (with the Laws as his parents) but because of Athens' democratic constitution and the freedom it made possible.[124] He may regard other cities, such as the oligarchies of Sparta or Crete, as more
law-abiding and disciplined, but his refusal to leave Athens for even
brief periods reveals an appreciation of the moral distinctiveness of
a democratic constitution—a constitution which, as Pericles noted,
not only made citizens free and equal but provided a freedom of
expression and tolerance unmatched in the Greek world.

Only in Athens could Socrates have practiced philosophical citizenship in the manner he did for as long as he did. Only in Athens
did there exist the freedom and equality which allowed him to pursue the kind of moral improvement he had in mind, one which de-
pended upon individual effort, reflection, and judgment, not upon
the coercive instrumentalities of moral habituation, inculcation, and
punishment. If one insists, on the basis of the passages cited earlier,
on calling Socrates a "patriot," then it is necessary to qualify that
description as a form of *constitutional* patriotism. But even then we
risk losing sight of the true nature of his attachment. Pericles was
right: Athens' constitution makes democratic individualism possible
for the first time. Socrates fully appreciates this fact and is grateful
for it. It makes his mission—teasing out the moral implications of
this nascent individualism, getting Athenian citizens to care for their
souls and think for themselves—possible. However, his appreciation
of the Laws of Athens and the possibilities they create does not prevent him from being a fierce critic of Athenian political practice and
many of the values that guide it.

Socrates' preference for the laws of Athens, then, does not express
a loyalty to a *group* or a people. Unlike Pericles, he does not harp
on the uniqueness of the Athenians *as a people*, and he certainly does

not view them as superior in all respects to their neighbors. Moreover, unlike Plato, he points to democratic freedom as a precondition for his philosophical activity and for the moral improvement of individuals.[125] To escape from Athens, as Crito urges for him to do, would only land him in places like Thebes or Megera, which would prohibit the practice of his "true political art," or among the "indiscipline and laxity" of Thessaly, where his stories would be appreciated but his cross-examinations would not (53c–54a). Only Athens, with its democratic constitution, provides the freedom and nascent individualism necessary for Socrates' indirect (and noncoercive) art to exist. He could simply not pursue his mission elsewhere.

Assuming this is a plausible rendering of the *Crito*'s significance for understanding Socrates' brand of citizenship and the nature and extent of his civic loyalty, we still face the problem posed by the "persuade or obey" formula. If one is dubious, as I am, about this formula's accommodation of civil disobedience, then one has to admit that the Socratic legacy is ambiguous with respect to the central question of the citizen's moral relation to law. Here an advocate of dissident citizenship might well turn to Antigone as a model clearly preferable to Socrates, whose radical questioning never produces any radical *action*. If moral integrity is a matter of *meaning it*, then Antigone's active choice of death in defiance of Creon's ban on burial for her brother Polyneices leaves no room for doubt as to *what* her moral commitments are and how they stand vis-à-vis the laws of the state. Whereas Socrates offers us negativity, thought divorced from action, and a seemingly passive acquiescence in his own death, Antigone embodies a clear hierarchy of values, a positive sense of justice, and the courage to *act* on her commitments. What her sister, Ismene, calls her "extravagant action" (l. 78) in the name of familial and religious duty thrusts her into the bright light of the public realm. Her "most glorious acts" (l. 749) win her a reputation for unexcelled justice and piety and reveal the immoral basis of Creon's political authoritarianism.[126] In short, Antigone provides "lovers of action" with a moralized version of the Periclean ideal, one shorn of the vestiges of docility or quietism that mar the philosophical alternative. She, more than Socrates, seems to exemplify the heroism that true moral integrity demands.

The problem with this view is that it ignores the grounds of Antigone's disobedience to law. If, as Martha Nussbaum has argued, Creon's understanding of the moral-practical world is a radically simplified one in which all values and duties are made to conform to the "single supreme good" of civic loyalty, we cannot truthfully say that Antigone's understanding is any more nuanced or, indeed, any less rigidly held.[127] The tragedy presents us with the confrontation between a dogmatic conception of loyalty to the state as the basis for all good and an equally adamant insistence that traditional religious and family duties trump all other values. Antigone answers Creon's question—"Did you dare to disobey that law?"—in a way which brooks no argument: "Yes, it was not Zeus that made the proclamation; nor did Justice, which lives with those below, enact such laws as that, for mankind. I did not believe your proclamation had such power to enable one who will someday die to override God's ordinances, unwritten and secure. They are not of today and yesterday; they live forever; none knows when they first were. These are the laws whose penalties I would not incur from the gods, through fear of any man's temper" (494–503).

In these words of self-assured piety we find a moral temper diametrically opposed to the Socratic insistence on questioning and examination. For Antigone there is no room for doubt nor any reason to give an account. The traditional understanding of religious law and duty commands obedience because it is immemorial. Just as Creon fails to take account of nonpolitical values in the framing and enforcement of his decree, so Antigone fails to consider any values beyond her supreme duty to the familial dead.[128] To be sure, she is an *actor* in a way which Socrates is not. But her action is premised upon faith, upon a commitment which is unquestionable, and upon a conviction that she *knows* what Zeus has decreed and whose side he is on in the conflict. Her invocation of the "higher law" is no doubt genuine and not merely the deployment of a tried-and-true rhetorical technique (as Aristotle presents it in his *Rhetoric* [1375b]). But it *is* rhetorical in the sense that it gives no reasons and appeals to a traditional piety which her fellow Thebans sympathize with. (Hence the popular support for her which Haemon, Creon's son and her husband to be, describes to his impatient father.)

Unlike Socrates, then, Antigone is no heretic. If her "extravagant action" has the effect of winning her "great renown" (894), it is not because she represents individual moral judgment or conscience against the claims of the state. Her resistance to Creon, while justifiable, is deeply conservative in character. Her voice is that of ingrained custom made militant by its confrontation with political hubris. We should not be seduced by the "manliness" of her action compared to what Callicles describes as the "unmanly" pursuit of philosophy practiced by Socrates off the public stage.[129] Thus, while the "persuade or obey" doctrine of the *Crito* should give us pause before we declare Socrates the patron saint of civil disobedience, we ought not draw the premature conclusion that Antigone provides us with a better model of conscientious citizenship. Antigone does not speak with the voice of conscience, let alone a rational, secular conscience, at all.

A more serious objection to the Socratic position is made by Arendt in her essay "Civil Disobedience." Simply put, she feels Socrates cannot serve as a model of citizenship, philosophical or otherwise, precisely because his care for his soul undermines the citizen's care for the (public) world. Socratic conscience is, at bottom, a form of *self*-interest.[130] The inner dialogue of thought which *is* this conscience tells him what *not* to do. Its standard, however, is whether a proposed action allows him to remain friends with himself, with his inner partner in thought. Moral integrity, seen as a form of self-agreement, focuses all responsibility inward. Hence the formula of the *Gorgias*: "Better . . . that my lyre should be discordant and out of tune, and any chorus that I might train, and that the majority of mankind should disagree and oppose me, rather than that I, who am but one man, should be out of tune with and contradict myself" (482c). For Arendt this represents a clear turning away from the claims of action, politics, and citizenship. The *world* no longer matters to the conscientious individual; the self and its integrity does.

Arendt's charge reminds us of Hegel's critique of the "beautiful soul" in his *Phenomenology of Spirit*. There Hegel had mercilessly exposed the moral inadequacy of a form of consciousness which "lives in dread of besmirching the splendor of its inner being by action and an existence." In order to preserve its purity of heart, it "flees from contact with the actual world, and persists in self-willed impotence to renounce its self, which is reduced to the extreme of ultimate abstraction."[131] If, as Hegel claimed in the *Aesthetics*, Antigone's moral stance is "one-sided," failing to integrate the civic sphere with that of family and religion, at least it *takes a side* and engages itself determinately in the world. The standpoint of a purified conscience, on the other hand, rejects worldly involvement because it produces an inevitable moral taint. It therefore rejects responsibility for anything outside itself. It is this rejection of all *worldly* responsibility which Arendt has in mind when she labels the conscientious individualism of Socrates (and Thoreau) an unpolitical form of self-interest.

Does Socrates' abstentionist moral absolutism—his insistence on the avoidance of injustice—render him unfit for citizenship and open him to this broader moral censure, as Arendt's Hegel-inspired analysis implies? It certainly would if, as Arendt claims, he rejected responsibility for the world in order to pursue his responsibility to himself. But the either/or of world or self fails to take account of the indirect relationship Socrates is trying to establish between care for the self and care for the world. One best pursues one's responsibility to the world, to the claims of citizenship, by cultivating a certain distance between the self and the passions and energies of the *demos*. Only then does moral reflection provide a deeper sense of injustice, one which transcends the customary and everyday and does not vacillate according to the moods of the public. While Arendt is certainly correct to emphasize that the public-political realm is the realm of opinion, she is wrong in thinking that Socratic conscience implies a thorough withdrawal into a worldless intercourse with oneself, or that it claims political relevance by pretending to a privileged moral-epistemic status parallel to Plato's ranking of philosophical truth over "mere" opinion.[132]

Arendt's polemic against the "unpolitical" nature of conscience again reveals the difficulty of recognizing an "art of politics" which attempts neither to detach the private (the ethical self) from the public nor to substitute conscience or logic for political discourse. It is a question of how to open the public realm to the claims of conscience and reason, not how to force it to conform to the ethical imperatives of the thinking self. Socrates' "self-interest" is a peculiarly self-abnegating one: he never allowed himself to live an "ordinary private life," so intent was he on cultivating a desire to avoid injustice in his interlocutors (*Ap.* 36c). His "private" life was lived in public, and while he thought the "true champion of justice" must "leave politics alone" (32a), he never ceased practicing the "true political art," namely, the relentless examination and purging of opinions. In this (indirect) way, the reflective morality of the conscientious individual makes its impact—or at least tries to do so—on civic engagement and civic virtue.

It is this very indirectness, born of the distancing of thought from action, which makes the Socratic art of politics less vulnerable to

Arendt's charge than it might at first appear. For what irks Arendt most about the "politics" of conscience is the abstractness of its moral claim, its lack of concern for the concrete political consequences which follow from its unbending imperatives. Thus, she cites Thoreau's demand, in "On the Duty of Civil Disobedience," that the American people "must cease to hold slaves, and to make war on Mexico, though it cost them their existence as a people."[133] Such rigid adherence to principle at any cost is, in Arendt's eyes, the epitome of political irresponsibility, a wrongheaded literalization of the old adage "Fiat justicia et pereat mundus" (Let justice be done though the world may perish).

The contrast between Socrates and Thoreau on this point is instructive. For although Arendt (following the common view) identifies them as twin exemplars of conscientious moral absolutism, it is Thoreau, not Socrates, who transforms nay-saying and (limited) withdrawal into a call to action—indeed, to revolution: "I cannot for an instant recognize that political organization as *my* government which is the *slave's* government also. . . . When a sixth of the population of a nation which has undertaken to be the refuge of liberty are slaves, and a whole country [Mexico] is unjustly overrun and conquered by a foreign army, and subjected to military law, I think that it is not too soon to rebel and revolutionize. What makes this duty the more urgent is the fact that the country so overrun is not our own, but ours is the invading army."[134]

In Thoreau's conception, action from principle is precisely that: *action*. It is not mere disobedience or noncompliance (although it may start there). It is the thing which sets the moral scales right, "cost what it may." Thus, Thoreau writes, "action from principle,—the perception and performance of right,—*changes* things and relations; it is *essentially* revolutionary, and does not consist wholly with any thing which was."[135] His praiseworthy desire to eradicate the greatest of evils—slavery—leads him not only to assail the government which protects this institution and suggest a "peaceable revolution" in the form of a refusal to pay taxes; it also leads him to contemplate violence as, perhaps, the necessary means: "But even suppose blood should flow. Is there not a sort of blood shed when the conscience is wounded?"[136]

Thoreau's essay extends and, in many respects, deepens the Socratic idea of conscientious individualism, yet it also goes beyond that idea insofar as it is an unabashed call to action and—in the last instance—to arms. As an example of absolute morality applied to politics, it straddles the distinction between an activist absolute morality (such as we find among revolutionaries and Christian activists) and an abstentionist absolute morality.[137] As a result, its connection to the disillusioning political art of Socrates is tenuous at best. For Thoreau conscience is not simply the nay-saying voice that results from the thinking dialogue with oneself, or the product of the perplexity produced by the dialogue with others. It is the moral faculty which perceives right, and which provides a firm—indeed, unquestionable—basis for action. Thoreau's conscientious "no" to complicity with an unjust state leads to an impassioned "yes" to demonstrative, perhaps even violent, action. When we recall that the American Revolution was fought over unjust taxes, we may well find ourselves in sympathy with Thoreau's call to overthrow the far greater evil of slavery.

This would seem, at first blush, to make Thoreau *more* political than Socrates. However, if Arendt's worry centers on the worldly consequences of establishing an unpolitical, essentially individual passion (the desire for moral purity, for principle untainted by prudence and worldly compromise) above all others, then it is clear that Socrates poses less of a threat to the political realm. By this I do not mean that he is less aggressive in his moral passion (and hence less dangerous) than Thoreau or those inspired by him but rather that Socratic conscientiousness does not exclude a concern for consequences (which Max Weber famously identified as the hallmark of the responsible political actor).[138] Socrates' desire to preserve his moral integrity extends only so far as the consequences to *himself*. He would rather suffer death than do wrong. It does not lead him, as it does Thoreau, to demand the attempted abolition of an evil, regardless of its worldly consequences (in this case, the dissolution of the Union). It does not, in other words, make the quest for inner moral purity into the dominant principle of positive political action, which is Arendt's main fear.[139]

But doesn't this leave us once again with Socrates the "beautiful soul"? Not if we take into account the indirect nature of Socrates' "true political art" and the relentlessness with which he pursues it. While the desire of an individual to conscientiously avoid injustice is not the same as the desire of a group of individuals who, in the name of conscience, set out to eradicate a concrete evil through positive action, such a desire can still have radical political effects.

The more people are alive to the false virtue that underwrites political evil, the more they will be willing to say no to that evil. This is clearly the tendency Thoreau wished to encourage, despite the stridency (and occasional dogmatism) of his formulation. But for this to happen, individual citizens must first be open to the possibility that the idea of virtue *is* false. A genuine politics of conscience is thus to be found only among those citizens who have become at least partly philosophical; who know that they do not have an "expert" knowledge of virtue but who are awake to the reality of injustice; who are, as a result, far less inclined to accept state-sponsored violence as a manifestation of virtue, or complicity with it as evidence of civic virtue.

The *Via Negativa* and Citizenship

It is often remarked that mere nay-saying is not enough, that the skeptical temper can hardly provide the positive sense of morality necessary to move citizens toward a more just society. People, we are repeatedly told, need something to believe in. A life devoted to disillusionment and nay-saying may be possible for the philosophical few, but it can only have corrupting effects for the many since it deprives them of the stable sense of virtue necessary to stave off cynicism and immorality. The problem seems especially acute in the realm of politics, where a robust sense of membership apparently hinges upon something akin to a civil religion, namely, a faith in the virtues and purposes which animate the life of the collective. This need not take the literal and extreme form we find in Rousseau, who advocates not only civil religion but a regime of strict censorship in order to keep moral corruption at bay.[140] It can take the far more benign form of constitutional totemism, such as we find in the United States. Irrespective of the form, it appears that citizens are in need of something like a shared political faith or, at the very least, a strong sense of common values if they are to rise above the anomie and indifference which characterizes so much of contemporary political life.[141]

This kind of analysis rests on a desire for a more active citizenry, a more moral polity, or both. It expresses the yearning of many who want politics and virtue to come together in a renewed vision of civic virtue, a vision which restores luster and moral aspiration to the idea of citizenship. In the eyes of such critics, the liberal polity has reduced citizenship to a set of rights and entitlements, and thereby encouraged a narrowly egoistic ethos which makes citizens more like consumers (or litigants) than members of a self-governing polity. Such a polity has lost touch with what the critics claim is a fundamental truth, namely, that political associations are not simply vehicles for mutual protection and benefit but embodiments of moral ideals—which must be preserved and actively inculcated through political involvement and political/moral education lest they disappear.[142]

My reading of Socrates' philosophical practice and dissident citizenship runs counter to these widely perceived needs. From the standpoint of the moral individualism which Socrates can be said (with only slight exaggeration) to have invented, it is *not* the case that the crisis of citizenship is a kind of crisis of faith. People have not become anomic individuals because there is less to believe in, less to tie them positively together as members of a community. On the contrary, the moral individualist thinks that social life and public opinion are constantly generating shared beliefs, passions, and rarely examined convictions. Consequently, much of social life, even in the most "secular" liberal polity, has the character of a feverish dream since it is driven by misguided certainties about wherein virtue consists and who is and who is not virtuous.[143] We always find ourselves immersed in unquestioned belief and assaulted by the will to believe, all the while remaining oblivious to the moral effects of this state of affairs.

The problem, then, is not that secularization (what Weber called "the disenchantment of the world") has rendered the world meaningless, or that we stand in need of some form of re-enchantment. This is what Arendt and others inspired by the civic republican tradition seem to have thought, and why she turned to a Periclean conception of political action as a privileged form of meaning-creation. It is also what a number of recent commentators—communitarian, conservative, and neoconservative—seem to think, and what lies behind their appeal to a "thick" conception of the good to counterbalance what they see as the egoistic individualism encouraged by liberal "rights talk" and the market.[144] "Ethical substance"— what Hegel called *Sittlichkeit*—seems to have drained off, leaving the moral life of our community bereft of the kind of unifying common purpose which Aristotle identified as crucial to political life.[145]

Such analyses are tempting, if only because our public life seems to be a sad shadow of what it once was and could be again. But it is wrong, I think, to read the Socrates Plato presents in the early dialogues as feeding this yearning for a commonly shared set of virtues or conception of the best life. What the Socrates of the *Apology* presents us with is not the quest for either a meaningful common good or a "noble" form of life but rather the constant reminder that *all* such conceptions can be incitements to injustice, and that a minimally moral life consists in the relentless resistance to such incitements. From a Socratic point of view, disillusionment does not lead to the *telos* of nihilism (as Nietzsche thought) or to mere selfishness, since disillusionment is, in fact, a constant struggle against endlessly proliferating (or resurrected) illusions. It therefore requires ceaseless renewal and provocation: the gadfly's work is never done.

When it comes to moral matters, however, the last thing we are inclined to do is to question or examine, let alone dissolve, the verities of our existence. We would much prefer to affirm and assert, to feel confirmed by a "community sense" *we* share, to have *our* values triumph over those of an imagined "other." Socratic moral individualism (and the nay-saying form of citizenship it implies) robs us not only of complacency but of the highs that result from "acting together" or (worse) asserting national will. It may help us to avoid the worst in political life, but avoiding the worst often seems a poor substitute for achieving or approximating the best. This is why both Periclean democracy and the idea of a Socrates who *knows* what virtue is have exercised such a profound hold over the Western imagination and continue to inspire critics of liberal democracy, who find it banal, insufficiently energetic, or hopelessly relativistic.

It is true that Socrates spoke endlessly about *arete*, but, as I have argued, he never set out a positive alternative to the Periclean ideal of excellence or greatness. Instead, he underscored the proximity of the apparent best to the worst, a proximity laid bare by his insistence that, whatever else we do, our deepest obligation consists in the avoidance of injustice. His morality is abstentionist as its core, but this does not make it any less rigorous or demanding. Thus, Socrates teaches us to be skeptical of the "best" while helping us recognize that avoiding the worst—as individuals and as citizens—is itself a moral achievement of the highest order. The Socratic *via negativa* may not give us the "something to believe in" that so many crave, but it still gives us something to aspire to: a disillusioned and hence more authentically moral brand of citizenship.

John Stuart Mill

PUBLIC OPINION, MORAL TRUTH,

AND CITIZENSHIP

THE REMAINING CHAPTERS of this book will address the work of thinkers who struggled with the question of philosophical citizenship in an age of democratization and "mass" politics. These thinkers—John Stuart Mill, Friedrich Nietzsche, Max Weber, Hannah Arendt, and Leo Strauss—all took strong stands on the relevance of Socratic moral individualism to modern politics. Some sought to demonstrate the added importance of the Socratic stance, while others attempted to reveal its irrelevance to (or covert harmony with) a leveling, bureaucratic age. With the qualified exception of Mill, they all questioned the viability of a philosophical form of citizenship under the conditions of the nation-state and an increasingly universal suffrage. For Nietzsche the realization of genuine individuality demanded not only a withdrawal from the corruptions and stupidity of mass politics but an escape from "Socratism" (understood as a rationalizing, universalizing moralism suited to the "herd"). For Weber modern politics could provide an arena for individual freedom and action, but only for leaders. In a "disenchanted" world, neither the life of the philosopher nor the citizen retained integrity. Both Arendt and Strauss violently contest Weber's verdict—the former on behalf of the citizen, the latter on behalf of the philosopher—but neither holds out much hope for the Socratic idea of philosophical, dissident citizenship.

It is only in Mill—who wrote during the fitful, partial, and intensely contested democratization of England that took place in the middle of the nineteenth century—that we find a real commitment to the Socratic ideal in anything like its original fullness. But even Mill was prone to restrict the range of Socratic negativity and individualism when it came to politics, sensing, as he did, that his age required, above all, a more efficient diffusion of intelligence throughout society. His fear of public opinion (and of the majority tyranny it enabled) led him to focus more on the problem of "opinion leading" and civic education for the gradually enfranchised masses than on the deployment of dissolvent rationality by independent-minded individuals. This side of Mill is most evident in his early essays and in his *Considerations on Representative Government* (1861). Yet this Platonic or Aristotelian side of Mill is balanced by his fierce commitment to moral individualism and independent thought, which he viewed not only as necessary ingredients to social progress but as virtual ends in themselves.[1] This commitment finds its classic expression in *On Liberty* (1859), a book much commented upon but one which (its familiarity notwithstanding) retains its capacity to surprise and even to shock.

As Alan Ryan has rightly remarked, Mill wrote *On Liberty* as a way of repeating to a Victorian audience the Socratic lesson that "the unexamined life is not worth living."[2] *On Liberty* does not merely reiterate a well-worn lesson for a contemporary audience. It reveals just how demanding the Socratic imperative is, and how violently at odds the examined life is with much of middle-class manners and mores. For Mill, as for Socrates, the scandal of humanity is that we continually mistake local custom and convention for moral truth. The even greater scandal is that those fragments of truth provided by our culture or reflection are rapidly transformed into untruth—usually by being taken for the whole truth, or by being held in a rote, undemanding way. Mill's central example of this dialectic of falsification is the *partial* moral truths of Christian teaching, truths which, in his view, have been transformed into utter falsehoods by being taken for a comprehensive formulation of morality itself.[3] Like Socrates, Mill wants to alert us to the dogmatism of everyday life, to the fact that most of us are intellectually and morally asleep most of the time. The "examined life," whether in Socrates' formulation or Mill's liberal variant, is a ceaseless struggle against the received truths of one's own society. This struggle is morally imperative lest one find oneself lazily in accord with a *doxa* which not merely acquiesces in atrocity but is incapable of even recognizing atrocity when it is committed by those like ourselves (our leaders or our neighbors).

This is not to say that Mill, any more than Socrates, wanted to reject all customary or conventional belief. He was a subtle enough critic of philosophical radicals like Jeremy Bentham and his father, James Mill, to realize that no materialist "science" of human nature could utterly eliminate the inherited irrationalities of the past and provide a new foundation for morals and politics.[4] Moreover, he had learned from the Romantics—and particularly from Coleridge— that many established institutions and practices contained a wisdom and a value that their ideologically conservative defenders could hardly guess at or appreciate.[5] Yet he remained a resolute opponent of the power which custom and convention exercised over the mind and moral sensibility of man.

It is characteristic of Mill that he did not offer an easy, moderate synthesis of Enlightenment-inspired rationalism and tradition-friendly Romanticism. Rather, he used each to point out the partiality of the other and—more to the point—he used both to undermine regnant opinion. The conflictual model of intellectual progress he recommends in *On Liberty* is, first and foremost, a way of ensuring a level of mental energy higher than is found in most societies most of the time. And it is mental energy—clearly manifest in the individual's capacity for independent thought and judgment—which fights not only cultural stagnation but moral indolence. While *On Liberty* and *Considerations on Representative Government* are in tension at various points, they are united in their effort to promote intellectual energy as the great counterforce to the gravitational pull of custom and majority opinion. Thus, Mill's arguments for the greatest possible freedom of thought, discussion, and expression in *On Liberty* find their political counterpart in his arguments for an active, politically engaged citizenry in *Representative Government*. What is at stake in both works is how to break out of the narrow confines of received ideas, of intellectual and moral passivity.

Mill's devotion to pluralism flows from his conviction that the greatest moral threat we face is our own laziness and dogmatism, our own certainty that the dominant table of values gets morality right and provides the requisite justifications for actions which may, in fact, be the height of immorality. His desire to keep diversity of opinion alive in the face of an increasingly rigid consensus on moral matters led him to champion the figure of the religious and philosophical dissident (or "heretic"). As Mill famously argued in chapter 2 of *On Liberty*, such a figure (an obvious generalization of the Socratic "gadfly") renders society an invaluable service by revealing received opinion to be false, or by pressing it to derive a more lively impression of the truth of opinions which have become rote.[6] But the more common service rendered by the upholder of dissident opinion is that he or she reveals the one-sidedness of received opinion. This can be overcome only by the capacity to see the matter from another angle and to appreciate the new fragment of truth provided by *this* perspective. The dissident or gadfly, in other words, reminds us that the truth in morality and human affairs is likely to be many-sided, complex rather than formulaic. He or she slows us down in our desire to act or to judge in accordance with local prejudice (for example, the socially dominant interpretation of Christian morality).

It will be objected—and, in the case of Mill, has been objected *ad nauseam*—that such a stance puts us on a slippery slope that ends in relativism. To this one need only note what Mill makes abundantly clear throughout his work, namely, that the desire to see the truth in its many-sidedness and complexity is still a desire for truth, and that the desire to avoid reflexive judgment is by no means a desire to avoid judgment as such.[7] Mill sought not to relativize moral questions but to avoid their premature closure. This he tried to do by outlining a socialized form of Socratic dialectic. The greatest possible freedom of thought and discussion would, so to speak, "institutionalize" the work of the Socratic gadfly, creating an atmosphere in which *doxa* would perhaps be less likely to congeal into self-righteous immorality (the permanent threat posed by *all* social life). Of course, the freedom of thought and discussion championed by Mill in *On Liberty* is no guarantee against the commission of social or political evil, any more than Socratic dialectic was. The most one can ask from either is the creation of an atmosphere in which the habits of action flowing from social conformity are at least somewhat inhibited; in which the sleepwalkers, while not necessarily awakened from their moral slumber, are (to some degree) made aware of the contingency of their own most cherished and unquestioned beliefs.[8]

Mill was well aware that, in the coming age of democratic mass politics, the voice of the dissident or "philosopher citizen" would, at best, have episodic efficacy. What was needed was not merely the opportunity for dissident voices but a way of politically institutionalizing minority opinions. This need was all the more pressing given Mill's Tocqueville-inspired fears of the potential tyranny of the majority. Thus, the largely cultural analysis of the dynamics of public opinion and morals in *On Liberty* is supplemented by the schemes for proportional representation and multiple voting which occupy such a central place in *Representative Government*. As I shall argue, the practicality of these schemes is a far less important question than Mill's motive in supporting them. For while Mill saw that an individual "heretic" on the order of a Socrates, Jesus, or Luther could have an enormous cultural and historical effect, he also foresaw (with the aid of Tocqueville) that the new realities of politics demanded the institutionalization—indeed, the amplification—of dissident or minority voices. Even constitutional safeguards did not provide sufficient inhibition to majority will, to say nothing of the impoverishment of political judgment which flowed from a system geared toward the exclusive empowerment of majority opinion.

In what follows I trace Mill's argument as he shifts his Socratic concerns from the arena of cultural critique (*On Liberty*) to the theory of political institutions (*Representative Government*). My argument is that Mill was only partly successful in making this transition, and that the greatest cost was a dilution of his commitment to moral individualism and the program of disillusionment which he endorses in *On Liberty*. Perhaps this was unavoidable, but that does not make it any less lamentable.

I begin by tracing the emergence of the question of public opinion in Mill's early essays, particularly his reviews of the English translations of the two volumes of Tocqueville's *Democracy in America*. I then turn to the reformulation of the Socratic program which Mill offers in *On Liberty*, paying special attention to the sociocultural role he assigns to the "heretical" individual, as well as his protoperspectivism and its relation to his notion of moral progress. Finally, I turn to his attempt, in *Representative Government*, to politically amplify dissident voices, and to his conviction that a specialized "art of government"—a political *techne*—was needed to provide an efficient diffusion of intelligence and guidance of opinion in a representative democracy. The question is not simply whether, given modern conditions, this move from philosophical citizenship to "enlightened" management was inevitable but rather, whether it constituted a betrayal of the Socratic legacy Mill strained to uphold.

Public Opinion in Mill's Early Writings

Despite the enormous differences between the Athens of Socrates' time and the England of Mill's, there is one obvious similarity: both were undergoing tremendous intellectual, moral, political, and social changes. The fifth-century enlightenment, combined with Athenian political reforms and its rise and fall as an imperial power, created a remarkably fluid context, one in which traditional authorities and ways of doing things lost much of their power. The Platonic dialogues provide endless testimony to this decline in authority and to Plato's attempt to provide a new rationalist foundation for the old (corrupted) virtues.[9] Socrates' response, as I have argued, was quite different. As the *Apology* and *Crito* show, he gloried in the openness the Athens of this period afforded, preferring death to the alternative of living anywhere else. While Karl Popper's delineation of Socrates and Plato as the champions, respectively, of "open" and "closed" societies is perhaps overdrawn, it does capture an essential difference in their responses to an age of transition, an age in which the old verities were no longer persuasive.[10]

Mill, like others of his generation, was conscious of living through such an age. His first published essay, "The Spirit of the Age" (1831), dwells on the Saint Simonian distinction between "natural" and "transitional" ages, the former being characterized by authority, consensus, and the faith of the uninstructed masses in the instructed elite, the latter marked by the absence of these traits. For the young Mill there was no question as to which category his own age belonged, nor was there any question that the generalized evaporation of authority was a cause for anxiety. The old institutions and doctrines may deserve their discredit, but the common man's loss of faith in guidance provided by elites was an unmitigated disaster: "The multitude are without a guide; and society is exposed to all the errors and dangers which are to be expected when persons who have never studied any branch of knowledge comprehensively and as a whole attempt to judge for themselves upon particular parts of it."[11] From the failure of a particular set of elites the average man has drawn the faulty conclusion that it is *always* better to think for oneself and to trust one's independent judgment. The fallacy of the age is similar to that of a caravan of travelers, who "had long been journeying in an unknown country under a blind guide." "With what earnestness," Mill continues, "would the wiser among them exhort the remainder to use their own eyes, and with what disfavor would any one be listened to who should insist upon the difficulty of finding their way, and the necessity of procuring a guide after all. He would be told with warmth, that they had hitherto missed their way solely from the fatal weakness of allowing themselves to be guided, and that they never should reach their journey's end until each man dared to think and see for himself."[12]

In such a situation every "dabbler" assumes the prerogative of judgment, and every mode of judgment which transcends first appearances by drawing on knowledge and experience is deemed "false refinement." This, says Mill, is the situation of his age, and the most pressing question is how to get out of it, how to move from a "transitional age [where] there are no established doctrines [and] the world of opinions is a mere chaos [to a] natural age [where] worldly power, and moral influence, are habitually and undisputedly exercised by the fittest persons whom the existing state of society affords."[13] For this to happen, nothing short of a "moral and social revolution" is required. Only then will worldly power and moral influence be back in the hands of the "most competent" and society resume its "onward progress."

While the young Mill had nothing but contempt for traditional Tory elites, and was therefore not a conservative in the usual sense, his position in "The Spirit of the Age" is clearly paternalistic and elitist. And while his mature thought is far more in the spirit of Socrates and the Kant of "What Is Enlightenment?" (the Kant who celebrates independent judgment), it must be said that he always retained a trace of his earlier position, mixing a residual elitism with a milder, more indirect form of paternalism. It is, after all, in *On Liberty* itself that he observes that "the initiation of all wise or noble things comes and must come from individuals; generally at first from some one individual. The honor and glory of the average man is that he is capable of following that initiative. . . ."[14] And in *Representative Government* we read: "It is what men think that determines how they act; and though the persuasions and convictions of the average man are in a much greater degree determined by their personal position than by reason, no little power is exercised over them by the persuasions and convictions of those whose personal position is different, and by the united authority of the instructed."[15]

Despite the persistence of this strain in his work, the unmodulated authoritarianism of "The Spirit of the Age" (predicated on the young Mill's certainty that the examined life was beyond the average man) did not last long. Mill's encounter with Tocqueville's *Democracy in America* forced him to rethink what the average man was capable of, bereft of the guiding spirit of radical reformers (like Bentham) or the underappreciated wisdom of ancient institutions (as drawn out for the English by Coleridge). This is not to say that Tocqueville led Mill to see in the United States a republic of philosophical citizens—far from it. Yet *Democracy in America* did make him realize that the "age of transition" was, in fact, an age of democratization, and that there was no going back. The old style of authority—essentially hierarchical and based on a broad consensus as to who the fittest to lead were—was gone for good. The longer Europeans focused on the trauma of the French Revolution and its aftermath, the blinder they were to the fact that the "transitional age" had been under way for centuries, and that it had culminated in the birth of a new moral-political order: the world of American democracy.[16] The time of nostalgia for "natural" authority was past.

Mill's review of the first volume of *Democracy in America* appeared in the *London and Westminster Review* in 1835. In it he fully accepts Tocqueville's thesis that democracy is the fate of the civilized world, and that the only real question is whether this democracy will be well or ill-regulated, intelligent and restrained or immoderate and demotic.[17] In France, according to Tocqueville, democracy had been abandoned "to its untutored instincts, and it has grown up like those outcasts who receive their education in the public streets. . . ."[18] The analysis of the strengths and weaknesses of American democracy Tocqueville offers in his "new political science [for] a world become new" is intended to alert the European educated classes to their tutorial duty and to underscore the most important lessons to be drawn from the American experiment. Only those armed with these lessons can hope to exercise some control over the "irresistible current" of democracy and equality, channeling it away from majority tyranny or administrative despotism.

As his emphasis on Tocqueville's self-proclaimed desire to "educate" democracy suggests, the young Mill was initially drawn to the more conservative themes of *Democracy in America*. As in "The Spirit of the Age," we find a pronounced distrust of uninstructed and inexperienced popular judgment, which Mill regards as the force most likely to produce the new brand of despotism in both Europe and America. In an Aristotelian vein, Mill notes that "the best government, (need it be said?) must be the government of the wisest, and these must always be few."[19] Mill says this as an "enlightened partisan" of democracy, one who fears, with Tocqueville, the consequences of substituting "delegation for representation"—that is, what happens when "the crude and necessarily superficial judgment of the people themselves" is substituted for "the judgment of those whom the people, having confidence in their honesty, have selected as the wisest *guardians* whose services they could command."[20] The proper or (to use Mill's word) *rational* conception of democracy is not one in which the people are literally self-governing but one in which they are free to choose representatives, preferably from the "instructed classes," whose knowledge and experience outstrips the woefully inadequate "common sense [of] the multitude."[21] For, as Mill observes:

> When the governing body . . . is so numerous, that the large majority of it do not and cannot make the practice of government the main occupation of their lives, it is utterly impossible that there should be wisdom, foresight, and caution in the governing body itself. These qualities must be found, if found at all, not in the body, but in those whom the body trust. If the people in America, or the higher classes in England or France, make a practice of themselves dictating and prescribing the measures of government, it is impossible that those countries should be otherwise than ill-administered.[22]

Whether in a democracy or an aristocracy, the art of government is a combination of specialized knowledge (*techne*) and experienced judgment (*phronesis*). The primary virtue of citizens in either regime is "the willingness to place themselves under the guidance of the wisest among them."[23] The young Mill continues to adhere to Plato and Aristotle, rather than Socrates, in thinking that there is relatively little question as to who actually practices the "true political art," or in what it consists.

More interesting is Mill's reading of the "tyranny of the majority." Tocqueville, he correctly observes, fears the moral power a democratic majority exercises over opinion more than he does the physical power it wields over individuals and minorities. This power, according to Tocqueville, reaches into the domain of thought itself, producing a kind of "courtier-spirit" which affects almost everyone. Thus, "as long as the majority is in doubt, there is discussion; but as soon as it has irrevocably decided, all hold their peace; and friends and enemies seem equally to yoke themselves to its car."[24] If a dissident thinker or writer transgresses the "formidable circle" the majority has traced "around the province of thought," he faces a peculiar martyrdom: not an auto-da-fé or public trial and condemnation, to be sure, but a series of "everyday persecutions" and an "infinity of chagrins." "To him," Tocqueville writes, "the career of politics is closed; he has offended the sole power which could admit him into it."[25] The majority, living in "perpetual adoration of itself," is mortally offended by the slightest reproach and insists that everything about it, "from the turn of its phraseology to its most solid virtues," must be endlessly imitated and applauded. Compared to this tyranny of taste and opinion, the court of Louis XIV was a veritable utopia of free speech. As Tocqueville dispassionately but damningly writes, "I am acquainted with no country in which there reigns, in general, less independence of mind, and real freedom of discussion, than in America."[26]

It is no exaggeration to say that Tocqueville's characterization of the peculiar corruption born of public opinion had the greatest possible effect on Mill's thinking about politics and culture. It made him profoundly (and rightly) skeptical of the Enlightenment idea that public opinion, freed from the coercion of state power, was an intrinsically critical (and rational) force.[27] Under the conditions of mass democracy, the coercive, monolithic, and irrational force of public opinion could only increase, creating a tyranny of *doxa* far greater than anything Plato could have imagined. Indeed, as Tocqueville observed, faith in public opinion becomes "a species of religion, and the majority its prophet."[28] The solution, Mill thought at the time, was a more efficient "diffusion of intelligence" and the preservation of a "leisured class." By this he meant a body of individuals sufficiently removed from the pressures of the market and subsistence to maintain both independence of mind and a largeness of view. "In the existence of a leisured class," Mill writes, "we see the great and salutary corrective of all the inconveniences to which democracy is liable."[29]

Mill's reliance upon the "instructed" or leisured classes to provide a bulwark against the untutored majority undergoes a subtle but noticeable shift in his 1840 review of the second volume of *Democracy in America*. Indeed, he draws attention to this shift in his autobiography, noting that the modification of his "practical political creed" can be seen in the contrast between his review of Tocqueville's first volume and his essay on the second.[30]

What is the nature of this change? We can begin by saying that if Mill's central concern in his 1835 review was the tendency of a democratic people to substitute delegation for representation—that is, to reduce their representative to the status of mere registers of their collective will—his primary concern in 1840 is how to ensure that these same people will not become the passive clients of an increasingly centralized (and powerful) state apparatus. This is what happened in France after the Revolution. The people were admitted into the public realm, but aside from voting there were no institutions through which they could actively and positively cultivate their newly won political freedom. As Mill, paraphrasing Tocqueville, puts it,

> A political act, to be done only once in a few years, and for which nothing in the daily habits of the citizen has prepared him, leaves his intellect and moral dispositions very much as it found them; and the citizens not being encouraged to take upon themselves collectively that portion of the business of society which had been performed by the privileged classes, the central government easily drew to itself not only the whole local administration, but much of what, in countries like ours, is performed by associations of individuals. Whether the government was revolutionary or counter-revolutionary made no difference; under the one and the other, every thing was done *for* the people, and nothing *by* the people.[31]

The result, in France, was a "superficial love of freedom" combined with "the practical habit of slavery." In Mill's view, the great virtue of Tocqueville is to point out how local management of public affairs—the actual practice of self-government—served as a political education for the American people, one which saved them not only from a docility *à la française* but also from the political indifference characteristic of most "commercial" peoples. For if a centralized and overly energetic state is one of the great modern threats to freedom and public spirit, a narrow interpretation of self-interest born of the market is the other. In a passage which sounds like a working out of many of the problems and insights developed by Aristotle in book 3 of *The Politics*, Mill writes:

> The private money-getting occupation of almost every one, is more or less a mechanical routine; it brings but few of his faculties into action, while its exclusive pursuit tends to fasten his attention and interest exclusively upon himself, and upon his family as an appendage of himself;— making him indifferent to the public, to the more generous objects and the nobler interests, and, in his inordinate regard for his personal comforts, selfish and cowardly. Balance these tendencies by contrary ones; give him something to do for the public, whether as a vestryman, a jury-

man, or an elector; and in that degree, his ideas are taken out of this narrow circle. . . . The spirit of a commercial people will be, we are persuaded, essentially mean and slavish wherever public spirit is not cultivated by an extensive participation of the people in the business of government in detail; nor will the desideratum of a general diffusion of intelligence among either the middle or lower classes, be realized, but by a corresponding dissemination of public functions, and a voice in public affairs.[32]

It must be acknowledged that, like Aristotle, Mill thought that the best constitution would exclude the "mechanical" or working classes from citizenship, at least for the time being. The idea of working-class suffrage in the England of the 1840s was too radical for him; it failed to acknowledge the need for basic competencies which Mill thought an overworked (and often illiterate) working-class population had yet to gain. But Mill clearly departs from Aristotle in holding that an expanded middle class—their "banausic" attitudes and occupations notwithstanding—should be educated to citizenship through "participation in giving judgment and in holding office."[33] Only in this way, he thought, could a modern political association escape the seeming inevitability of the majority becoming "the slaves of habit and routine." The American republic had avoided the twin dangers of mental torpor and narrow self-interest by requiring the "perpetual exercise of the faculties of every man among the people," an effect it achieved through "the universal practice of submitting all public questions to his [the common man's] judgment."[34]

Mill's focus in his review of Tocqueville's second volume is quite different from that of his 1835 essay, which is marked by an emphasis upon the deficits of popular judgment and the ill effects wrought by the decline in authority. It is tempting to read this shift as an outgrowth of his agitation on behalf of the cause of reform in England. This reading, however, is too simplistic, for it fails to register the full weight of the change which has taken place. Beyond expressing a modification in his "practical political creed," the 1840 essay reflects a fundamental shift in his thinking about politics in general. For the first time in Mill's writing, the theme of political education—of education *to* citizenship—is detached from a structural reliance upon the principle of authority. Political education is no longer an "education in virtue" in which the chief virtue of the people is a willingness to defer to the "wisest among them" (the classical model that still haunts Mill's earliest writings). Rather, it is seen as a form of self-education, one enabled by the creation of opportunities for public judgment and the assumption of civic responsibility.[35]

This is not to say that Mill came to believe that *any* people, regardless of their general state of development, could become self-governing and self-limiting citizens by practicing local self-government. The idea of a minimal level of political maturity—subject to the vagaries of history, cultural development, and class position—retained a permanent and important place in his thought. But what clearly changes in the 1840 essay is his estimate of the effect that deference to authority has on the general level of intellectual energy and moral alertness. It is the slackening or diminishment of moral and intellectual energy which is the real danger, and deference to authority only feeds this tendency. In 1835 he was concerned with the excesses committed in the name of "private judgment"; in 1840 he is preoccupied by the need to expand opportunities for public judgment by ordinary citizens. As he would later confess in *On Liberty*, Tocqueville helped him to recognize that the moral and intellectual faculties are like muscles, which develop only with exercise.

But if Tocqueville showed how the Americans avoided one avenue to docility and submissiveness, he also revealed how public opinion could—and, in fact, did—become a new and more powerful form of authority in a world bereft of traditional forms. As was noted earlier, the famous thesis of the first volume of *Democracy in America*—that there reigns in America an unrivaled unanimity of opinion—captured Mill's attention in his 1835 review. He returns to this theme in 1840, more vehement about the danger but less certain (and less convincing) about how to avoid it:

> It is impossible, as our author truly remarks, that mankind in general should form all their opinions for themselves: an authority from which they mostly derive them may be rejected in theory, but it always exists in fact. That law above them, which older societies have found in the traditions of antiquity, or in the dogmas of priests or philosophers, the Americans find in the opinions of one another. All being nearly equal in circumstances, and all nearly alike in intelligence and knowledge, the only authority which commands an involuntary deference is that of numbers. . . . The idea that the things which the multitude believe are still disputable, is no longer kept alive by dissentient voices; the right of pri-

vate judgment, by being extended to the incompetent, ceases to be exercised even by the competent; and speculation becomes possible only within the limits traced, not as of old by the infallibility of Aristotle, but by that of "our free and enlightened citizens," or "our free and enlightened age."[36]

Where the "competent" have also been corrupted by the worship of numbers, and where the voice of the majority has become, as Machiavelli predicted, the voice of God, no amount of either leisure or instruction will have much effect upon the compact mass of public opinion. Of course, as Mill notes, an excess of either leisure or instruction is not to be expected in a society in which the commercial spirit reigns unchallenged. It is this spirit—the outgrowth of modernization rather than democratization—which has squandered the potential of more widely spread education and a democratic public sphere. There may be more books, but they have become commodities like everything else, quickly consumed and even more quickly forgotten.[37] More "superficial information" and half-formed thoughts fill up the marketplace, but these do not stimulate any genuine thoughtfulness, which, as Socrates taught, is the only true expression of intellectual energy and moral alertness.

Mill's response to "the dogmatism of common sense" and the unquestionable hegemony of the commercial spirit was to gesture, once again, to those social classes (agricultural, leisured, and learned) who were traditionally somewhat removed from this spirit, and to appeal to "the wiser and better-hearted politicians and public teachers [to] look upon it as their most pressing duty, to protect and strengthen whatever, in the heart of man or in his outward life, can form a salutary check to the exclusive tendencies of that spirit. . . ."[38] Fully appreciating the dangers Tocqueville uncovered but realizing that they have even deeper roots in modern society than Tocqueville supposed, Mill is reduced to envisioning benign effects flowing from England's hierarchical class structure. This differentiation, at least, promises a minimal diversity of opinion.[39]

Faced by the "growing insignificance of individuals in comparison with the mass," Mill thus grasps at whatever social articulation he can find. The paradoxical result is that the fate of the individual is subsumed by the fate of classes (Mill's distaste for the theory of class representation, which he called "the master fallacy," notwithstanding). The ascendency of the commercial middle class may be inevitable, but this, according to Mill, does not mean that the "most powerful" need be "all powerful." Similarly, the fate of modern democratic society may be inseparable from the enthronement of public opinion as the ultimate authority, but this does not mean that this opinion need be virtually unanimous. As long as there exists "social support for opinions and sentiments different from those of the mass," the Tocquevillian democratic night in which all cats are gray can be avoided.

"Heretical" Opinion, Freedom of Discussion, and Perspectivism in *On Liberty*

This revision of Tocqueville's sociology ultimately failed to convince its own author. The problem of public opinion and individuality in modern, at least partly democratic, society could not be resolved by the appeal to disparate class interests as the seedbed of more enlightened or diverse opinion. In criticizing Tocqueville, Mill had uncovered a cultural or "civilizational" dynamic behind the pathologies of mass democracy which could hardly be stayed by England's greater degree of sociological heterogeneity. If these pathologies were truly embedded in the process of modernization itself, then they assumed a power and inevitability which no set of historical-cultural contingencies could really circumvent. The escape from majority tyranny which Mill points to at the end of his 1840 review turns out to be no escape at all. The combined dynamic of commercial society and mass democracy produce an ever greater homogenization of public opinion on the most basic moral and political questions, whatever the contending interests at play in the society at large.

At its root—namely, the dogmatism of "common sense"—this is the same problem Socrates faced in fifth-century B.C. Athens.[40] What has changed, obviously, is the scale and combination of elements which conspire to reduce moral and political opinion to dogmatic one-dimensionality. Needless to say, neither Socrates' Athens nor Mill's England (nor Tocqueville's America, for that matter) were embodiments of anything approaching a literal unanimity. But if the imperial democracy failed to effectively question its reigning table of values, it at least harbored a culture of dissent and criticism of which Socrates is the most sublime example.[41] He made dissent philosophical, which is to say that he invented a form of moral criticism which rose above ideology and partisan politics, not, of course, to the level of a timeless, placeless absolute, but to a new conception of what humane values demand on the part of the individual.

Mill's problem was essentially that of Socrates, namely, how to undermine an increasingly monolithic public opinion and the natural dogmatism of "common sense." This meant more than strengthening the possibility of correction and modification; it meant clearing a space for radical moral reevaluation. By 1850 Mill had lost faith in the idea that a particular class, or the antagonism of classes (as Machiavelli thought), could provide the impetus for moral progress and the preservation of freedom. *All* classes—not just the untutored working class and the indolent aristocracy—appeared to him to be in a "low intellectual and moral state." This salutary skepticism about the contribution social classes could make to the avoidance of moral and intellectual stagnation is particularly apparent in Mill's revised attitude toward the English middle class. It is this increasingly powerful class which he characterizes in *On Liberty* as the primary enforcer of moral and intellectual slavishness.

On Liberty signals not only a turn away from conservative sociology but a revision of Mill's attitude toward the value of "negative philosophy." In his 1838 essay on Bentham, Mill had described his father's intellectual master as "the great *subversive*, or . . . *critical*, thinker of his age and country," only to add that these qualities alone would rank him among "the lowest order of the potentates of the mind—the negative, or destructive philosophers. . . ."[42] At the time Mill associated philosophical skepticism with the French *philosophes* and with Hume, "the prince of the *dilettanti*, from whose writings one will hardly learn that there is such a thing as truth, far less that it is attainable. . . ."[43] A philosopher whose primary effect was negative, consisting solely in the dissolution of mistaken opinions, could hardly be ranked among those who had positively advanced the cause of truth.

This dismissive attitude toward skeptical reason went hand in hand with the young Mill's conviction that, their vulgar psychology aside, Bentham and his father really had outlined a science of morality in the form of utilitarianism. While the mature Mill would modify their utilitarianism to the point where it was almost unrecognizable, he never discarded it (or its foundationalist pretensions). Yet he did come to see that the dogmatism inherent in public opinion and "common sense" was far more tenacious and deeply rooted than either he or his father's generation had assumed. As a result, the business of "clearing the ground a little" (to use Locke's famous phrase) could no longer be viewed as a minor service performed by Voltairian wits, while the real work of philosophy awaited the builders of systems. As *On Liberty* makes evident, "clearing the ground a little" for thought had become an endless, perpetual battle against the deadening hand of custom, conformity, and the gravitational pull of mass opinion. While Mill shied away from an explicit formulation, the argument and conception of *On Liberty* reveal a much revised attitude toward "negative" philosophy and what I have been calling dissolvent rationality. These now become Mill's primary weapons in the struggle to preserve space for moral, intellectual, and aesthetic individualism.

On Liberty is not merely Mill's attempt to remind his contemporaries of the value of the "examined life"; it is, more important, his attempt to translate the chief virtues of Socratic dialectic into a form appropriate to modern society. We know from his *Autobiography* that Mill lionized Socrates from an early age, and that he later labored over his own English translations of various Platonic dialogues, including the *Apology* and the *Gorgias*, making copious notes.[44] We should not be surprised, then, that the spirit of Socrates looms large in *On Liberty*, or that Socrates himself makes an appearance as one of the great heretical moralists condemned by a people exercising its "common sense." (Mill's other example is Jesus.)[45] Like Plato, Mill tries to work out the philosophical and political implications of the trial and condemnation of Socrates. Unlike Plato, he does not conclude that the philosophical life can be saved only by placing it above the life of the citizen; rather, he tries to imagine a society in which the practice of philosophical citizenship would not automatically lead to martyrdom.

The primary work of "translation" occurs in chapter 2 of *On Liberty*. Before proceeding, however, I should note the context Mill provides in his introductory chapter. Everyone knows that Mill wrote *On Liberty* in order to assert "one very simple principle," namely, "that the sole end for which mankind are warranted, individually or collectively, in interfering with the liberty of action of any of their number, is self-protection. That the only purpose for which power can be rightfully exercised over any member of a civilized community, against his will, is to prevent harm to others. His own good, either physical or moral, is not sufficient warrant."[46] It is perhaps not surprising that much of the scholarly discussion of *On Liberty* has been devoted to working out the application of this principle and its related distinctions (such as the one between self- and other-regarding actions) to controversial issues in our social and legal life, such as pornography and hate speech. Indeed, Mill himself devoted two of his five chapters to the question of where, precisely, society should draw the boundaries, and how the "principle of liberty" should be applied as a guide to regulation in concrete settings. Yet this legalistic focus obscures the fact that *On Liberty* is, above all, a work of moral and cultural criticism. This is made plain in Mill's introductory chapter, which sets the tone for the next two chapters, "Of Liberty of Thought and Discussion" and "Of Individuality."

Mill's grand theme is, of course, the struggle between liberty and authority, a struggle he historicizes in his introduction. In broad strokes Mill traces the historical process by which predatory but necessary rulers were brought to heel through the introduction of rights and the imposition of constitutional checks, a process which reached its culmination in the replacement of independent rulers by political powers periodically chosen by the people themselves. The rise of popular government created the illusion that tyranny was a thing of the past, that the limits previously fixed on political power were anachronistic when the will being constrained was the people's own. Experience, however, taught that the "self-government" brought into being by popular regimes was not "the government of each by himself, but of each by all the rest," and that "the will of the people" actually meant the will "of the most numerous or most active *part* of the people; the majority, or those who succeed in making themselves accepted as the majority."[47] It is now generally accepted, Mill notes, that the tyranny of the majority is "among the evils against which society requires to be on its guard."[48]

With the annunciation of this Tocquevillian theme as his theoretical and practical point of departure, Mill goes on to note that the expression of an oppressive majority will through governmental action is but one manifestation of the tyranny of the majority. The "vulgar" still fear this abuse of state power. Thinking persons, however, have

> perceived that when society itself is the tyrant—society collectively over the separate individuals who compose it—its means of tyrannizing are not restricted to the acts which it may do by the hands of its political

functionaries. Society can and does exercise its own mandates; and if it issues wrong mandates instead of right, or any mandates at all in things which it ought not to meddle, it practices a social tyranny more formidable than many kinds of political oppression, since, though not usually upheld by such extreme penalties, it leaves fewer means of escape, penetrating much more deeply into the details of life, *and enslaving the soul itself*. Protection, therefore, against the tyranny of the magistrate is not enough: there needs protection also against the tyranny of the prevailing opinion and feeling; against the tendency of society to impose, by other means than civil penalties, its own ideas and practices as roles of conduct on those who dissent from them; to fetter the development, and, if possible, prevent the formation, of any individuality not in harmony with its ways, and compel all characters to fashion themselves upon the model of its own.[49]

While reiterating Tocqueville's warning about "moral slavery," Mill here goes well beyond him in articulating the modalities and targets of such social tyranny. The great, undeniable tendency of human society in virtually all times and places is to impose its specific table of virtues upon all members, to brook no dissent, and to demonize all modes of self-fashioning which depart from the norms of the community (which present themselves as morality as such). The most important subject—morality—is invariably the one treated by human societies with the greatest narrowness and dogmatism, "so natural to mankind is intolerance in whatever they really care about."[50]

These themes inextricably link the liberal moralist Mill to the antiliberal, "immoralist" Nietzsche (for reasons I discuss later). Suffice it to note here that Mill's introduction, like the first essay in Nietzsche's *Genealogy of Morals*, leaves little question as to the historically contingent character of the development of moral values, or the strength of the human tendency to ignore their historicity and insist that the "likings and dislikings of society" are the stuff of morality itself.[51] Mill differs from Nietzsche in that he does not draw Nietzsche's fallacious conclusion, namely, that the historicity of moral values entails that there can be no such thing as morality but only *moralities*, which are culturally and historically bounded.[52]

What Tocqueville and history have shown, then, is that this great human tendency is intensified, rather than diminished, by the advent of popular government and democratic culture. All the more reason, then, to assert the "one very simple principle," which applies to all cultures that have gained a minimal level of moral maturity,[53] but especially to those in which democratization has empowered the forces of intolerance. As Mill writes, "The disposition of mankind, whether as rulers or as fellow-citizens, to impose their own opinions and inclinations as a rule of conduct on others, is so energetically supported by some of the best and by some of the worst feelings incident to human nature, that it is hardly ever kept under restraint by anything but want of power; and as the power is not declining, but growing, unless a strong barrier of moral conviction can be raised against the mischief, we must expect, in the present circumstances of the world, to see it increase."[54]

It is these two factors—the permanent tendency of mankind to pervert morality into immorality by means of moralizing intolerance and group feeling, on the one hand, and the empowerment of majority opinion resulting from modern democratization, on the other— that lead Mill to propose not only his principle of liberty as a means of protection but the Socratic reconceptualization of the public realm we find in chapter 2 of *On Liberty*.

The outline of Mill's argument for freedom of thought and discussion, and the protection of dissident opinion it requires, is simple and straightforward. Society or its authorities have no right to stifle dissident opinion, since to do so presumes infallibility. The result of such all too human hubris is to rob society of the opportunity of exchanging a false (received) opinion for a true (albeit unconventional) one. In the case where the dissident opinion is false, society is still robbed of the opportunity of obtaining, through conflict and contrast, a livelier impression of the truth of its received view. But more likely than either of these possibilities, Mill notes, is that the dissident view contains part of the truth, and that the received view would be enriched by incorporation of its perspective and its truth.[55]

Reduced to its bare logical bones, Mill's argument is likely to produce a yawn in readers who are able to take a fair degree of freedom of speech for granted, or who pride themselves on "listening to both sides of an argument" (however minimal the effect this exercise has on their final judgment). But the familiarity—indeed, banality—of Mill's logical possibilities ought not to blind us to the radical implications of his argument, nor to the surprising twists and turns that constitute what is by far the longest chapter in *On Liberty* (roughly twice the length of the others). It is no exaggeration to state that the greater part of the theoretical and moral energy that Mill invests in *On Liberty* is to be found here and in "Of Individuality," the chapter which follows.

Consider Mill's first point, namely, that the suppression of any opinion assumes the infallibility of the suppressors and commits the peculiar evil of "robbing the human race" of an opinion that might well be true. Stated thus baldly, this argument would earn easy assent from all those who are fortunate enough to live in the historical afterglow of Enlightenment principles (mainly citizens of liberal democracies). But such assent misses Mill's main point, which is that it is not only popes or churches who assume infallibility and suppress discussion.[56] Average individuals are unlikely to think themselves invariably right, largely because they have learned their own fallibility from experience. It is this very sense of fallibility at the "micro" level, Mill argues, which leads us to place our trust in the authoritative judgments of our community or culture. We compensate for the fallibility of our individual judgments by appealing to what Mill calls "the infallibility of 'the world' in general." Mill elaborates:

> And the world, to each individual, means the part of it with which he comes in contact; his party, his sect, his church, his class or society; the man may be called, by comparison, almost liberal and large-minded to whom it means anything so comprehensive as his own country or his own age. Nor is his faith in this collective authority at all shaken by his being aware that other ages, countries, sects, churches, classes, and parties have thought, and even now think, the exact reverse. He devolves upon his own world the responsibility of being in the right against the dissentient worlds of other people; and it never troubles him that mere accident has decided which of these numerous worlds is the object of his reliance, and that the same causes which make him a Churchman in London, would have made him a Buddhist or a Confucian in Pekin. Yet it is as evident in itself . . . that ages are no more infallible than individuals.[57]

To acknowledge the truth of this statement is to admit that dogmatism is woven into the very fabric of our moral being. The things we care most about—the things many of us would even kill or die for—are, to a large degree, a function of parochial prejudices which, taken together, constitute the "common sense" of our class, culture, or age. Of course, few today would defend "prejudice," but neither would they acknowledge that their fundamental moral assumptions have, for the most part, been passively inherited and dogmatically adhered to (however sophisticated the work of post hoc rationalization). As moral beings, we are inevitably "encumbered selves," creatures of habit rather than reason. Mill's point is that we don't merely accept this condition but we *will* it with our hearts and souls. Our acceptance of what is "unquestionable" for our class, culture, or age provides us with the orientation and support we yearn for in an otherwise contingent (and disturbingly pluralistic) world. Our judgment as individuals may be uncertain, but as subscribers to the collective authority embodied by the common sense of our particular "world," we provide our existence with a secure, seemingly noncontingent ground. To own up to the conditioned or accidental quality of our most fundamental judgments is to risk a kind of moral/existential vertigo or paralysis. Hence the strange combination of ferocious antipathy and smug condescension which greets all dissident opinion on fundamental moral and political matters.

The inherent tendency of human judgment to fall into rote, automatic functioning led Mill to seek a means to prevent its terminal decay. To call the "method" offered in chapter 2 of *On Liberty* "free discussion" is to banalize what is, in fact, a far more radical proposal. In Mill's view, it is not simply a question of recognizing that human judgment is fallible, and that (therefore) it is important to have open discussion as a means of filtering beliefs and correcting received opinion. As was previously noted, this is Richard Kraut's interpretation of how Socratic *elenchus* proceeds.[58] At first glance this interpretation seems even more applicable to Mill's proposal. Like Socrates, however, Mill recognizes that the human propensity to reify prejudgments runs deep, and that the achievement of even minimal moral wakefulness requires that received opinion be exposed not merely to a healthy (yet limited) skepticism but also to the peculiar dissolvent force of a culture which institutionalizes, in some manner, agonistic challenge and debate.

The model of open discussion and debate set forth in *On Liberty* is conflictual, not consensual, and its purpose is not merely to modify or "correct" established opinion but to expose that opinion to the harshest possible contrary light, so that its parochial and limited nature might be illuminated. Mill does not propose this model because he thinks "the truth will out" in an open fight in "the marketplace of ideas," or that an adversarial system necessarily produces truth as its final product. Like Socrates, he was far too skeptical of the powers of human understanding, and far too aware of the average person's capacity to be manipulated, to think any such thing. He proposes it because he thinks that the only way to soften up the ever-hardening monolith of public opinion is to subject it to constant—and radical—challenge. In a mass society one gadfly is hardly enough; the very possibility of a minimally moral society depends on the continued presence of *many* critics and the willingness to exempt no belief from their challenge.

Thus, while Mill famously describes open discussion as the chief "means" by which a fallible human understanding corrects itself, he immediately follows this characterization with a blast at those who would remove certain socially valuable beliefs from the risk of public attack.[59] The apparent social utility of any belief—even the belief in a judging God and the hereafter—gives no government or society the right to restrain those "bad men" who would "weaken these salutary beliefs." The reason for this is that all such restraint rests on a claim to certainty about the perniciousness, the "immorality and impiety," of the dissident view. Mill's choice of examples in this regard—Socrates and Jesus—leaves little doubt as to his deepest concern. The fact that these two great moral benefactors of mankind were tried and condemned for (respectively) impiety and blasphemy points not simply to the cognitive limits of received opinion but to the repeated and radical character of its moral blindness.

Mill thus joins his insistence upon the fallibility of human understanding to an even more emphatic claim about the limits of the human moral imagination and the gross immoralities these limits produce. He drives this point home by noting that the men who judged and condemned Jesus were, "to all appearances, not bad men—not worse than men commonly are, but rather the contrary; men who possessed in a full, or somewhat more than a full measure, the religious, moral and patriotic feelings of their time and people: the very kind of men who, in all times, our own included, have every chance of passing through life blameless and respected."[60] Mill extends the point to the most respectable and pious men of his own time, who, he argues, would have acted precisely as the now reviled judges of Socrates or Christ acted had they been born in a different age. The common moral sense of *any* age is as much a form of moral blindness as it is the expression of a (limited) moral vision. The blindness and the limitation hang together and, as such, are ineradicable. The only thing we can hope for is that through open discussion and the tolerance of "immoral and impious" critics, society is a little less blind in its judgments, a little less grotesque in its moralizing violence.

To some this characterization of Mill's position will sound both too radical and too despairing. Mill certainly did believe in the possibility—indeed, the fact—of moral progress. He was no Montaigne, musing on the persistent moral idiocy of mankind; nor did he think, like Nietzsche, that "there was only one Christian, and he died on the cross." Yet throughout *On Liberty* the emphasis is on the precariousness of the moral progress we have made, and on the factors—such as the dogmatism of received opinion and the built-in intolerance of any majority—which continually threaten us with retrogression. While Mill, like Socrates, had no desire to overturn *all* conventional opinion, he was quite aware of the fact that moral progress was not inherently gradualist; that the hardening of any morality into "common sense" was inseparable from its increasing distance from moral truth; and that (therefore) there was a persistent need for radicals like Socrates and Jesus to reform or reinvent moral vocabularies. To borrow from the overworked terminology of philosopher of science Thomas Kuhn: moral progress has its "revolutionary" as well as its "normal" moments. It is not simply additive (a function of the gradual elimination of fallacies) but also discontinuous—even, occasionally, "paradigm shifting."[61]

Mill's critical focus on the narrowness of human moral imagination (not to mention the inherent dogmatism of common sense) made him value the interruptions of figures like Socrates and Jesus as much or more than reformers who work within the constraints of received opinion and attempt a purely "immanent" critique.[62] The "heretical" dissident has a world-historical importance: he or she reveals not just the falsity of an opinion but of a whole network of beliefs (to say nothing of the way of life based on it). Mill makes a startling claim in this regard. While acknowledging that "we do not now inflict so much evil on those who think differently from us as it was formerly our custom to do," he asserts that his own age is more successful, not less, in stifling independent thought and "heretical" opinion. "Our merely social intolerance," he writes, "kills no one, roots out no opinions, but induces men to disguise them, or to abstain from any active effort for their diffusion. With us, heretical opinions do not perceptibly gain, or even lose, ground in each decade or generation; they never blaze out far and wide, but continue to smoulder in the narrow circles of thinking and studious persons among whom they originate without ever lighting up the general affairs of mankind with either a true or a deceptive light."[63]

It is through an atmosphere of such social intolerance (and its twin, a formal yet glacially dismissive tolerance—what Herbert Marcuse was to misleadingly describe as "repressive tolerance") that the agon is extinguished and intellectual pacification achieved. But, as Mill observes, this happens only at the cost of "the entire moral courage of the human mind."[64]

Mill's claim is radical and has more than a little in common with social critics like Nietzsche and Weber, who argued that the freedom of the modern age has been purchased at the price of the internalization of deeply conformist norms. To this it might be objected that Mill's point was perhaps valid for Victorian society but not our own; that, moreover, the last century has seen not only the emergence and diffusion of "heretical opinions" but their tremendous cost in both social stability and human life. The *bon sens* of the narrow-minded bourgeois seems an altogether marginal evil when viewed in the context of a century convulsed by "dangerous ideas."

What would Mill say to such a challenge? First, he would openly acknowledge the need to be sensitive to historical context, a point he adopted from Tocqueville's "new political science" (which was, in turn, derived from Montesquieu). Second, he would no doubt point out that the truly dangerous ideas of our or any other time have not been those which *depart* from a broad social or moral consensus but rather those which have been successful in enlisting or creating such a consensus (and the feeling of certainty it confers) as their basis for action in the world. We need to be reminded that a widely adhered to creed or ideology is, by definition, *not* a heretical idea, and that Mill used the term "heretic" to refer to figures like Socrates and Jesus, whom he viewed as challenging a "common sense" which, while not unanimous, was ingrained and morally complacent.[65] Apparently heretical ideas which rigidify received ideas through the grotesque exaggeration of certain elements (Christian fundamentalism, say) or which energize the prejudices of "common sense" for violent or self-aggrandizing enterprises (all forms of nationalism and group feeling, including fascism) are, in fact, not heretical at all. Their craziness expresses and magnifies the craziness which lurks just below the surface of any people's "common sense."(Think, for example, of the sense of racial superiority which has been the bane of European civilization since its inception.)

Mill's "heretic" is, at bottom, a critical and dissolvent force, one whose "heterodox speculations" help prevent the kind of reification that converts originally moral ideas into solid grounds for immoral actions. This is why so many passages of *On Liberty* can be read as virtually unqualified celebrations of "the heretic." This celebration is motivated not, as we might expect, by the fact that the heretic is the one who reveals the truth to a misguided public mind. On the contrary, the correction of false, conventional opinion is only one (and by no means the most important) function of the holder of dissentient ideas. Far more crucial, in Mill's view, is the contribution the dissident qua gadfly makes to the level of mental energy of a culture. Only where "heterodox speculation" is tolerated and the heretic feels free, like Socrates, to seek out an audience can mental energy manifest itself in a people. Only then does progress become possible: "Truth gains more even by the errors of one who, with due study and preparation, thinks for himself, than by the true opinions of those who only hold them because they do not suffer themselves to think. Not that it is solely, or chiefly, to form great thinkers, that freedom of thinking is required. On the contrary, it is as much and even more indispensable to enable average human beings to attain the mental stature which they are capable of."[66]

If the inherent tendency of public opinion is to congeal around a one-dimensional account of the truth, then the only time this tendency does not present an insuperable obstacle to moral progress is in those rare historical moments when "the old mental despotism has been thrown off" and "heterodox speculation" flourishes. The Reformation, the Enlightenment, the "Goethian and Fichtean period" in Germany: to these three episodes, Mill states, can be traced "every single improvement which has taken place either in the human mind or institutions. . . ."[67]

This is, of course, an exaggeration, but it points to an essential aspect of Mill's first argument for freedom of thought and discussion. Open discussion is not so much a method for arriving at truth as it is a means for dissolving misplaced certainty—the kind of certainty which adheres to the matters we care most about. The presupposition of Mill's first argument, like that of Socratic dialectic, is that we do not know what we think we know. We are eminently fallible, particularly—indeed, especially—when it comes to the most important things. Thus, the heretic Mill depicts does not wake us up (like so many sleeping beauties) with an epistemological kiss, one which moves us from the realm of dreamlike illusion to that of truth. The discontinuity characteristic of moral progress is not of this kind (something Marx failed to see). Rather, the heretic contributes to wakefulness precisely by questioning the authoritativeness of received opinion (which, by its very nature, induces a "deep slumber").[68] Similarly, the reason why Mill credits "every single improvement" in opinion or institutions to these three flowerings of "heterodox speculation" is that he wants to emphasize the mental and moral despotism that accompanies social life in most times and places. Heretical individuals—those "afflicted with the malady of thought," as Mill ironically puts it—are rare; *ages* which are characterized by independent thought are rarer still. But the only way to cultivate the potential for moral progress is to make the leap from freethinking individuals to a freethinking age. Such ages cannot be willed into existence. At best they can be fostered indirectly by means of a virtually absolute freedom of thought and discussion. Such freedom keeps the intellectual agon (with its constant disturbance of the "deep slumber of received opinion") alive.

This formulation may seem too sharp, too negative to capture what Mill actually had in mind. This impression is strengthened when we pass to the second division of Mill's argument, in which his supposition is that the received opinion is true, and his concern shifts to the manner in which this opinion is held. At first glance it seems that Mill urges free discussion not in order to *dissolve* received opinion (the case, after all, concerns received opinions which are *true*) but merely to ensure that we retain a clear and vivid apprehension of what is true in our belief. Such vivid apprehension is facilitated by being forced to fight and argue for even the best established beliefs. Thus, Mill cites "the Socratic dialectics" as a "contrivance" designed not to dissolve opinion but to force Socrates' interlocutors to know the grounds of and best arguments for their beliefs.[69] The "intelligent and living apprehension" of a truth requires an aid, a "dissentient champion," one who will not allow us to fall asleep at our posts. His episodic irritation will force us to maintain firm, knowledgeable foundations, which in turn enable us to build a more stable edifice of moral truth.

This is surely one side of Mill's argument. However, the latter is complicated by Mill's description of the very manner in which "true" opinions are held. As it turns out, the *manner* in which a belief is held is for Mill far more determinative of its truth or falsehood than one might initially think. Any person who holds an opinion without knowing its grounds, or the best arguments that can be said on behalf of opposing opinions, holds his or her·belief as a mere prejudice or superstition.[70] If Mill's first argument for freedom of thought and discussion stressed our fallibility (the fact that we do not know what we think we know), his second argument demonstrates that even when our opinions are "true," our manner of holding them effectively renders them false. The cumulative effect is not to shore up any substantial portion of received opinion but to make us less secure in our monopoly on the truth and more open to the possibility that not only dissidents but our enemies possess part of the truth.

Again, this may seem too sharply negative. The force of Mill's second argument clearly seems to be that we should take pains to learn the grounds of our opinions so that we might have warranted (as opposed to unwarranted) belief. But closer inspection reveals that Mill's standard for warranted or true belief is quite a bit tougher than expected. It is not a matter of merely knowing "both sides of the question," of being able to rattle off the stock arguments for and against a particular position. Rather, it is a matter of knowing opposing views "in their most plausible and persuasive form"; of feeling "the whole force of the difficulty which the true view of the subject has to encounter and dispose of."[71] It is no exaggeration to state that few, if any, individuals take the kind of pains or exert the kind of intellectual energy Mill demands for warranted belief. How many of us can say we know the best and most plausible arguments for and against liberalism or conservatism? Access to a few clichés about individual rights or the need for authority and order will hardly do. How many of us can claim to be thus informed about the virtues and dangers of the welfare state, global capitalism, or organized religion? On such questions even specialists tend to be ideological, one-sided defenders of a recognizable position in an overheated political debate.

Thus, even when we "know" the truth, we cannot be said to "possess" it, to really have warranted belief. And this, Mill states, is the condition of "ninety-nine in a hundred of what are called educated men . . . even those who argue fluently for their opinions. They have never thrown themselves into the mental position of those who think differently from them, and considered what such persons have to say; and consequently they do not, in any proper sense of the word, know the doctrine which they themselves profess."[72] Time has not altered this state of affairs; if anything, the "niche marketing" of opinions has sealed the educated as well as the uneducated in echo chambers inhabited primarily by those who think like themselves. Mill's demanding criterion—knowing the strongest arguments for contrary positions—is given lip service, but the fact remains that the opinions of even the best educated are held in a manner that converts most of them into falsehoods.

This puts "knowing the grounds of one's opinions" in quite a different light. Few of us can claim to have met this demand, at least as Mill conceives it. And if this is the case, then we need dissident opinion to provide something more than an argumentative workout for the intellectually lazy. The real lesson of dialectic or disputation is not (*contra* Mill's own suggestion) improved debating technique but the acknowledgment of ignorance. The nature of received opinion—even when the opinion in question is true—is that its received character makes it false. *This* is what the dissident teaches us.

Mill's point is that (all too often) received opinion attains its status at the price of its truth. Settled on by a society as true or dominant (usually after a long struggle), an opinion ceases to have genuine competitors. It is inflated into the whole or obvious truth and inculcated as such, becoming part of the common sense of the group. Now beyond discussion and contention, it takes its place as one of the unquestionable judgments that ground the culture. At this point, its content is hollowed out, its substance drained off. For once contestation ends, "not only the grounds of the opinion are forgotten in the absence of discussion, but too often the meaning of the opinion itself. The words which convey it cease to suggest ideas, or suggest only a small portion of those they were originally employed to communicate. Instead of a vivid conception and a living belief there remain only a few phrases learned by rote; or, if any part, the shell and husk only of the meaning is retained, the finer essence being lost."[73]

This process of reification and loss of substance virtually defines the manner in which an opinion becomes "received." According to Mill, it is "illustrated by the experience of almost all ethical doctrines and religious creeds."[74] Wherever "controversy flags"—wherever the agon of opinion ceases—there the meaning of an opinion or doctrine dies and its truth becomes a falsehood (or, at best, a half-truth). Only the perpetual struggle of opinion enables us to realize, however partially, some element of the truth contained in doctrines which have taken their place among "received opinions."

The stakes of Mill's argument are made clear by the example he chooses to illustrate the conversion of truth to falsehood, living doctrines into "dead beliefs." That example is the fate of the ethical teachings of Christianity. "By Christianity," Mill writes,

> I here mean what is accounted such by all churches and sects—maxims and precepts contained in the New Testament. These are considered sacred, and accepted as laws, by all professing Christians. Yet it is scarcely too much to say that not one Christian in a thousand guides or tests his individual conduct by reference to those laws. The standard to which he does refer it, is the custom of his nation, his class, or his religious profession. He has thus, on the one hand, a collection of ethical maxims, which he believes to have been vouchsafed to him by infallible rules for his government; and on the other a set of every-day judgments and practices, which go a certain length with some of those maxims, not so great a length with others, stand in direct opposition to some and are, on the whole, a compromise between the Christian creed and the interests and suggestions of worldly life. To the first of these standards he gives his homage; to the other he gives his real allegiance.[75]

It is important to see that Mill is here not accusing Christians of hypocrisy or self-serving inconsistency. What he is accusing them of is a failure to grasp the ethical import of the teachings to which they pay homage. It is because Christianity has become a "received opinion" that contemporary Christians can at once know the maxims of the New Testament (for example, that the blessed are the poor and humble) and conduct themselves without any real regard for them. The living faith has become a dead dogma, and as such has lost its power to promote our moral integrity. Again, this is the fate not merely of Christianity but of virtually all "ethical doctrines and religious creeds."

At this point, the second division of Mill's argument leads to two questions. First, does a "lively apprehension" of the truth of any opinion demand the fervor—even zealotry—of the true believer fighting for the life of his creed? Mill's contrast of early with contemporary Christians certainly seems to imply this. Second, if the truth of any opinion is lost the moment controversy flags, must false heretical opinions be propagated and preserved merely to sustain the controversy and (with it) a robust conception of the truth? Or, as Mill puts it,

Is the absence of unanimity an indispensable condition of true knowledge? Is it necessary that some part of mankind should persist in error to enable any to realize the truth? Does a belief cease to be real and vital as soon as it is generally received—and is a proposition never thoroughly understood and felt unless some doubt of it remains? As soon as mankind have unanimously accepted a truth, does the truth perish with them? The highest aim and best result of improved intelligence, it has hitherto been thought, is to unite mankind more and more in the acknowledgment of all important truths; and does the intelligence only last as long as it has not achieved its object? Do the fruits of conquest perish by the very completeness of the victory?[76]

I shall discuss the second of these two broad questions first. Thus far I have argued that the answer to the questions Mill rhetorically poses in the preceding passage is, to a surprising degree, affirmative. Mill, however, famously disputes this interpretation of his argument, stating in no uncertain terms that he affirms "no such thing": "As mankind improve, the number of doctrines which are no longer disputed or doubted will be constantly on the increase: and the well-being of mankind may almost be measured by the number and gravity of the truths which have reached the point of being uncontested. The cessation, on one question after another, of serious controversy, is one of the necessary incidents of the consolidation of opinion; a consolidation as salutary in the case of true opinions, as it is dangerous and noxious when the opinions are erroneous."[77] Mill goes on to say that the "gradual narrowing of the bounds of diversity of opinion [is] at once inevitable and indispensable."

What can he possibly mean by these pronouncements? The answer at first seems all too clear. Diversity of opinion, as well as freedom of thought and discussion, are not ends in themselves but *means* to the gradual uncovering of a complex but ultimately singular moral truth. While much of Mill's argument up to this point seemed to indicate his commitment to a robust form of pluralism—to diversity of opinion for its own sake—his real position (it seems) is defined by an additive conception of moral progress, one whose teleology is consensus on the most important issues. On this reading, the passages just cited reveal Mill's continued commitment to the Enlightenment ideal of his father and Bentham, as well as the doctrine of progress he imbibed from the Saint-Simonians and the work of Auguste Comte.[78] Thus, if *On Liberty* gives social flesh to Socratic *elenchus*, it does so in harmony with the sense of *elenchus* outlined by

89

Kraut. Absolute freedom of thought and discussion, combined with diversity of opinion and heated debate, are elements of a "method" of social discourse and inquiry, one designed to uncover the truth in moral and political as well as scientific matters.

Isaiah Berlin has given a sharp rebuke to this interpretation in his essay "John Stuart Mill and the Ends of Life." Mill's primary commitments, Berlin argues, were to liberty, variety, and justice, not truth, and his argument for freedom of discussion rests on the assumption that not only are human beings fallible but that there is "no single, universally visible truth," and that "each man, each nation, each civilization might take its own road towards its own goal, not necessarily harmonious with those of the others. . . ."[79] Mill's horror at the mounting tyranny of public opinion and the "leveling, middle class society" that went with it, coupled with his acute awareness of the progressive effacement of difference in modern life, led him to value diversity of opinion for its own sake.[80] Indeed, according to Berlin, it is Mill's conception of the individual as a self-cultivating agent capable of choosing between a variety of ends that is at "the center of his thought and feeling." It is this conception—rather than any residual commitment to utilitarianism, enlightenment, or even the sanctity of the private realm—which drives Mill's thought.

Berlin's essay has the salutary effect of reminding us of the true nature of Mill's hopes and fears; it forces us to adopt a more nuanced reading of his statements regarding "the inevitable and indispensable" narrowing of "the bounds of diversity of opinion." However, while Berlin is absolutely right to remind us of Mill's commitment to diversity not only in opinion but in "experiments in living" (a commitment which trumps his devotion to the discovery of truth), he overstates his case. Mill may value diversity of opinion more than truth, and he may be too aware of what Berlin calls the "many-sidedness of truth and of the irreducible complexity of life" to really subscribe to the Enlightenment narrative of conjoined moral and scientific progress that passages like the one cited earlier suggest.[81] Nevertheless, Mill's commitment to diversity is inextricably bound up with his commitment to liberty and moral progress, and this fact makes Berlin's assimilation of Mill to his own brand of moral pluralism (with its emphasis on the incommensurability of values) more than a little suspect.

Thus, while Mill rejected the simplistic analogy between scientific and moral truth—which led Comte to ask, "If we do not allow free thinking in chemistry or biology, why should we allow it in morals or politics?"—he also rejected the notion that the acknowledgment of plural ends relativized the idea of moral progress out of existence. For Mill there was no contradiction between increased liberty, tolerance, and diversity of opinion, on the one hand, and the increasingly universal acceptance of the fundamental moral theses of rights-based individualism, on the other. Indeed, the two went hand in hand. Fostering diversity of opinion and an openness to an indefinite number of paths to the "good life" did not mean for Mill (as it apparently does for Berlin) that we must affirm traditional religious or communal forms of life.

A Millian liberal does not question the right of such communities to exist (so long as they respect the vital claims to life and freedom from enslavement of their members), but he or she will point to the indubitable progress made when such groups accept the basic tenets of rights-based individualism (of tolerance, respect, and individual liberty) and adjust their practices accordingly. Mill did not think that diversity was undermined by the gradual containment of inflamed, intolerant, or inhumane particularisms. Berlin's brand of pluralism, conversely, is more willing to countenance the curtailment of individual rights and diversity of opinion in the name of a particular group's desire to be governed by those like themselves. Individual rights give way to the demand for group status or recognition, and variety is identified not so much with the "heterodox speculation" or "experiments in living" performed by individuals as with district cultural perspectives made manifest in particular hierarchies of value.[82]

In sum, a plausible reading of Mill must give equal weight to his desire to promote diversity *and* his belief in the actuality (if not the inevitability) of moral progress. Neither the smooth additive process of a testing and purification of opinion, culminating in a virtual consensus on moral and political matters (a kind of "end of history"), nor the cultural perspectivism of Berlin's Herderian vision do justice to these two interconnected aspects of his thought. The former is inadequate because it fails to convey Mill's appreciation of the many-sidedness of moral truth, while the latter is inadequate on both epistemological and moral grounds. To identify diversity with the "perspective" of a particular group or culture is to create a curiously inert and suffocating vision of the value of difference, one in which group values and prejudices are endowed with a false aesthetic wholeness, all at the expense of individual freedom and cultural dynamism. It is also to countenance various limited forms of authoritarianism (religious, democratic, or traditional) as valid expressions of the multiple ends of human life. This is something Mill adamantly refused to do, as the arguments of chapters 3 and 4 of *On Liberty* make clear. However, before turning to them, I need to return to the two questions raised earlier concerning the implications of Mill's second argument in chapter 2.

Must heretical opinions be tolerated merely in order to keep controversy and, with it, a "lively apprehension of the truth" alive? The answer, in fact, is no. When we combine Mill's insistence on human fallibility (on the fact that we do not know what we think we know) with his description of the peculiar reification that occurs when doctrines attain the status of "received ideas," we see just how deeply Mill appreciated the fragility of all moral progress. The possibility of retrogression is always close at hand, especially when any group or culture thinks it has access, if not to the whole truth, then at least to its greatest part. Every step forward, dogmatically rigidified, becomes a step backward. Heretical opinions are necessary not simply to revive "dead" truths but to reveal their partiality *as* truths— a point Mill emphasizes in the third and final division of his argument.

But doesn't a "lively apprehension of the truth" demand, if not continued "ignorance" on the part of a section of mankind, a certain fervor and vehemence, a certain agonistic zeal? Again, this is something that Berlin seems to think. He goes so far as to compare Mill's insistence on the need for heated controversy with Hegel's argument that war is necessary to save the human species from stagnation.[83] But this is off the mark, and not merely because Mill's battlefield is one ideally ruled by "the morality of public discussion." It is wrong because Mill did not advocate strong views (and their requisite temperament) for their own sake; nor did he think that the intellectual and moral faculties are best enhanced by active participation in the clash of debate: "It is not on the impassioned partisan, it is on the calmer and more disinterested bystander, that [the] collision of opinions works its salutary effect."[84]

The answers to these questions point to the last division of Mill's argument, in which he considers a third and final case. Rather than one doctrine being true and the other false, it is far more frequently the case that they, in fact, "share the truth between them," and that the "nonconforming opinion" is needed to "supply the remainder of the truth of which the received opinion embodies only a part."[85]

Put so sparely, this third case seems merely to round off Mill's canvassing of logical possibilities. However, the third part of Mill's argument for freedom of thought and discussion is far more than that. It is, in fact, the completion and culmination of the previous two "divisions." For it is here that Mill expands on his conception of the "many-sidedness" of truth, developing a distinctive, liberal version of perspectivism (although he never used this Nietzschean term). This conception alters the way we read the previous divisions of Mill's argument, highlighting the deficiencies of both the simple additive conception of progress toward moral truth and Berlin's insistence that different cultural value perspectives are incommensurable and irreconcilable.[86] It also points to a conception of citizenship which is more philosophical (in the Socratic sense) than Mill's advocacy of energy and participation—and his hatred of timidity, mildness, and docility—might initially lead us to expect.

Expanding on his claim that the truth is most often shared between received and heretical opinion, Mill outlines the way human understanding is always prone to take the part for the whole, to think that there are definitive, final, and freestanding answers to the basic questions of morality and politics:

> Popular opinions, on subjects not palpable to sense, are often true, but seldom or never the whole truth. They are a part of the truth; sometimes a greater, sometimes a smaller part, but exaggerated, distorted, and disjointed from the truths by which they ought to be accompanied and limited. Heretical opinions, on the other hand, are generally some of these neglected and suppressed truths, bursting the bounds which kept them down, and either seeking reconciliation with the truth contained in the common opinion, or fronting it as enemies, and setting themselves up, with similar exclusiveness, as the whole truth. The latter case is hitherto the most frequent, as, in the human mind, *one-sidedness has always been the rule, and many-sidedness the exception.* Hence, even in revolutions of opinion, one part of the truth usually sets while another rises. Even progress, which ought to superadd, for the most part only substitutes, one partial and incomplete truth for another; improvement consisting chiefly in this, that the new fragment of truth is more wanted, more adapted to the needs of the time, than that which it displaces.[87]

93

This insistence on the partiality of the truth in both received and dissident opinion, and on the constant need for new "fragments of truth," is supported by three examples. The first is cultural. Mill cites Rousseau's critique of the Enlightenment as brilliant but more riddled with error than the doctrines of his rationalist opponents. Nevertheless, Rousseau's "paradoxical" vision of the advance of science and civilization as contributing to a process of corruption and moral decline had the salutary effect of "dislocating the compact mass of one-sided [rationalist] opinion, and forcing its elements to recombine in a better form and with additional ingredients."[88] His new "fragment of truth" concerning the "demoralizing effect[s of] artificial society" and the greater value of "simplicity of life" qualifies the confidence of the Enlightenment that science and morals necessarily advance together.

Mill's second example is political, announcing a theme he will return to in the opening chapters of *Representative Government*. It concerns the truth of the "commonplace" that a healthy polity requires both a party of order and a party of reform since each articulates a part of the truth and needs to be restrained by the opposition of the other. The fact of this opposition prevents any practical monopoly on political "truth," creating a tense balance of elements which more closely approximates the reality of political life than could be achieved by the one-sided domination of either the progressive or conservative picture. "Unless opinions favorable to democracy and to aristocracy, to property and equality, to co-operation and competition, to luxury and abstinence, to sociality and individuality, to liberty and discipline, and all the other standing antagonisms of practical life, are expressed with equal freedom and . . . defended with equal talent and energy, there is no chance of both elements obtaining their due. . . ."[89] That this is more than an updating of the Aristotelian doctrines of the superiority of the "mixed regime" and the virtue of the mean is made clear by the following stunning passage, in which Mill describes the kind of truth we can approach in moral-political matters, the capacities necessary to appreciate it, and the need for an institutionalized competition to exploit and supplement the inevitable one-sidedness of most opinion:

> Truth, in the great practical questions of life, is so much a question of the reconciling and combining of opposites, that few have minds sufficiently capacious and impartial to make the adjustment with an approach to

correctness, and it has to be made by the rough process of a struggle between combatants fighting under hostile banners. On any of the great practical questions just enumerated, if either of the two opinions has a better claim than the other, not merely to be tolerated, but to be encouraged and countenanced, it is the one which happens at the particular time and place to be in the minority.[90]

The capacity for judgment, for discerning where the truth lies in "the great practical questions of life," is internally connected to what Kant called the capacity for "enlarged thought." This capacity is rare not because the ability to know and do the right thing at the right time is rare, the province of gentlemen of experience and good character (Aristotelian prudence or practical wisdom). It is rare because judgment demands a mobile perspectivism, the ability to see things from many different angles and from a distance, with a certain disinterestedness. Such a capacity is hardly the natural property of any class. (Mill's contempt for an indolent aristocracy, his hatred of middle-class conformism, and his fear of working class illiteracy and inexperience made him skeptical of Aristotle's sociology of the mental faculties.)

The fact that most individuals are not adept at the reconciling and combining of opposites, at *genuinely* looking at things from a variety of angles, means that a "rough process of struggle" is required if fair play is to be accorded "to all sides of the truth."[91] And even in this second-best case, the struggle is valuable *not* because it encourages the mobilization of partisan energy or sectarian vehemence but rather (as noted earlier) for its effect upon what Mill calls the "more disinterested bystander." This bystander—the attentive appreciator of multiple strands of the truth—potentially learns to weave a more complex pattern out of the materials presented him than can any one-sided advocate.

One-sidedness of opinion, then, is as much Mill's target as timidity, docility, or conformism. Intellectual and moral energy are not best expressed by passionate advocacy (although Mill clearly believes that this is better than apathy or the mental torpor induced by custom). They are far better expressed by the capacity to dissolve and imaginatively recombine the elements that constitute the play of moral and political debate. As with Socrates, the philosophical citizen is less an advocate or actor than a somewhat distanced judge, one who is concerned, above all, with curbing the injustices born

95

of a one-sided appreciation of the truth (the inevitable modality of partisan and majoritarian politics).[92]

It is in Mill's third example, concerning morals, that the perspectivist implications of his notion of truth as "many-sided" are most vividly displayed. Virtually all creeds, religious traditions, and ethical doctrines cannot resist presenting themselves as definitively articulating the virtues and the demands of morality. Christianity is no exception. Indeed, as Nietzsche argues, in many respects it is the paradigm of an ethical creed which presents itself as universal, complete, and superseding or excluding all others. Unlike Nietzsche, Mill does not trace this dogmatic presumption back to the teachings of Christ himself. On the contrary, Mill writes, "the sayings of Christ [are] irreconcilable with nothing that a comprehensive morality requires," adding that "everything which is excellent in ethics may be brought within them. . . ."[93] However, "it is quite consistent with this to believe that they contain, and were meant to contain, only a part of the truth; that many essential elements of the highest morality are among the things which are not provided for. . . ." Christianity is a partial truth, and it is "a great error to persist in attempting to find in the Christian doctrine that complete rule for our guidance which its author intended it to sanction and enforce, but only partially to provide." To do so is a "a grave practical evil," since this "narrow theory," unsupplemented by a variety of ancient and modern ethical ideas, fosters "a low, abject, servile type of character, which, submit itself as it may to what it deems the Supreme Will, is incapable of rising to or sympathizing in the conception of Supreme Goodness."[94]

This last sentence anticipates the critical thrust of chapter 3 of *On Liberty*, where Mill inveighs against the "Calvinist" reduction of the virtues to the duty of obedience, and (in proto-Nietzschean mode) urges a healthy dose of "Pagan self-assertion" to balance it. In the present context it is important to see how Mill's discussion relativizes Christianity not by making it *one* perspective in irreducible conflict with all others but precisely by conceiving it as a *partial* truth in grave need of supplementation by "secular sources." Mill's position is that we do not have to know (or claim to know) the nature of the whole in order to recognize a part as part. Nor do we have to think of moral truth as a kind of natural whole which particular creeds or doctrines attempt (more or less successfully) to correspond to. "Supreme Goodness" is not *the* Good, in the Platonic sense, but rather the best and fullest articulation of moral intuitions and ideas that human individuals are capable of. Such an articulation is always elusive; in principle it can never be complete, given the limits of human intelligence and the open-ended character of human experience.

Morality, then, is not reducible to the vision of one perspective or *one* set of virtues. The fact that there are and have been *moralities* does not prevent us from taking the best (and avoiding the worst) from many different ones, from looking at different codes of conduct and conceptions of human excellence in order to "reconcile and combine opposites." This is precisely what Mill does when he points out the necessity of combining a Christian ethical sense with the public-spirited virtues of Greece and Rome. *Contra* Berlin, the conflict of "ultimate" values does not prevent the liberal perspectivist from combining the seemingly uncombinable. Moral truth, like every other truth, is many-sided, always in need of "new fragments."[95]

While elusive, such a perspectivist conception of moral truth (one which rests on a "diversity of opinion") is positive in a way that Socratic, abstentionist morality is not. Indeed, it could be argued that Mill's project in *On Liberty* is less to propose his "one simple principle" than to adumbrate an alternative conception of human excellence. As we shall see, Berlin's contention that Mill wanted, above all, to put individual autonomy or choice at the head of the virtues is not entirely off the mark.[96] When we add the energetic conception of citizenship found in *Representative Government* to the picture, it is easy to view Mill as a strong spokesman for a set of distinctively "liberal virtues," as well as the champion of whatever arrangements successfully inculcate *this* particular conception of the Good Life.[97]

There can be little doubt that Mill wanted to promote intellectual and moral energy in an age dominated (or so he thought) by "industrious sheep." In this regard at least, his updating of the Socratic virtues stands as a positive conception of the kind of character a liberal society should strive to encourage and make room for. That said, however, it would be wrong to argue (as some conservative critics of Mill have) that behind his perspectivism and pluralism lurks an assumed *telos* to human life as definite as anything we find in Aristotle. Mill's perspectivism and focus on liberty imply (as he clearly saw) that there are almost as many paths to the Good Life as there are individuals; that the "Good Life" itself is as many-sided, and in need of new "experiments" and formulations, as truth itself;

that, finally, pursuing "one's own good in one's own way" is how the better part of our moral and intellectual faculties are developed at all.[98] Mill's conception of autonomy is thus an "open" as opposed to a "closed" one (such as we find in Kant). He wants to see human energy mold itself into as many novel and beautiful shapes as it possibly can, so long as it abstains from inflicting harm on the vital claims of others. (This is the abstentionist morality built into his Principle of Liberty.) And he hardly wants the state to take up a tutorial role when it comes to the formation of moral character.

To sum up, I have argued that the three divisions of Mill's argument for freedom of thought and discussion (which are so often read as a falliblist method to moral and intellectual progress) have implications which are far more negative (and skeptical) than is generally appreciated. Mill's first argument—that received opinion may be wrong and the heretic right—teaches us, as does Socrates, that we do not know what we think we know. Mill's second argument—that even if received opinion is true, heretical opinions are necessary to retain a "lively apprehension" of their truth—teaches that moral complacency leads us to falsify or drain the substance from the most valuable part of conventional opinion. In other words, even when received opinion is true, we have a way of making it false. Finally, Mill's third argument—that received and heretical opinions most typically capture only a part of the truth—teaches that moral truth is many-sided, complex, often a matter of combining opposites, and always in need of additional "fragments."

Taken together, these three arguments for free discussion deliver a strong Socratic message, albeit one cloaked in the garb of cognitive optimism. Mill's emphases on human fallibility, experience, and pluralism lead to a set of conclusions which are surprisingly skeptical. Even when we secure a part of the truth, it is the rare individual who can grasp its full meaning and set it in the context of other sides of the truth. The human propensity to dogmatism—to one-sidedness in opinion, thought, and argument concerning the things that matter most—demands that Socratic dialectic take a broader, more social form. We must somehow find a way of multiplying the number of gadflies and heretics. This is especially true in the world of democratic politics, where public opinion often rules. Despite our first impression, Mill's arguments for freedom of discussion do not present moral and intellectual progress as the process of heaping one correct conclusion on top of another but rather as a never-ending insight into the partiality of what is supposed to be the whole truth. In this way, freedom of thought and opinion help liquify overly confident understandings of moral truth, understandings that invariably spawn injustice and the suppression of freedom.[99]

INDIVIDUALITY AND CITIZENSHIP

Assuming that my characterization of Mill's argument in chapter 2 of *On Liberty* is plausible, and that Socratic *elenchus* and Millian discussion share a common (critical and negative) form and function, it might still be objected that the two philosophers are engaged in diametrically opposed endeavors. As I argued in chapter 1, Socrates deploys dialectic in order to slow his fellow Athenians down. Mill, on the other hand, wants his fellow citizens to shake off the "despotism of custom" and the mental torpor it creates. For Mill it is not a question of slowing people down but of stimulating them so that they become more active—not only mentally and in their private lives but publicly as well.

Nowhere is this apparent disparity between the Socratic and Millian projects more in evidence than in chapter 3 of *On Liberty* ("Of Individuality") and chapters 2 and 3 of *Representative Government* ("The Criterion of a Good Form of Government" and "The Ideally Best Polity," respectively). The former text is famous for its dystopian vision of a stagnant society bereft of individuality and difference, and for its call for "Pagan self-assertion" to offset the diminishment of character resulting from two thousand years of "Christian self-denial." Mill acknowledges that while it "may be better to be a John Knox than an Alcibiades," it would be better still to be a Pericles.[100] *Representative Government* expands on this theme, demanding that government cultivate the courage and originality of its people, improving them by promoting an "active and energetic character."[101] In both texts the great evil is "passivity of character," which Mill regards (in his frankly Eurocentric way) as an "Oriental" form of submissiveness.[102]

Where does this leave Mill's legacy with respect to the quest for a philosophical form of citizenship? I will argue that Mill's conception of individual self-cultivation, on the one hand, and active citizenship, on the other, introduce an ambivalent note to his otherwise fundamentally Socratic project. The modification of the Socratic project performed by these ideas is at least partially justified by the enormous differences between the contexts of fifth-century (B.C.) Athens and mid-nineteenth-century England. The Faustian energies of an Athenian direct democracy have been replaced by the industrialized regimentation of a centrally administered (and culturally conformist) constitutional monarchy, one in which the vast majority of subjects remains disenfranchised. That a champion of the central values of philosophical citizenship such as Mill should emphasize the positive dimensions of "Pagan self-assertion" and political participation is, given the circumstances, not as contradictory as it might first appear.

Yet several of Mill's formulations in these pages are strong enough to give pause. For example, the aesthetic model of self-cultivation or self-fashioning which Mill outlines in "On Individuality," leads to a very un-Socratic celebration of genius and spontaneity. It is this Romantic component of Mill's thought which leads him to assert that "the glory and honor of the average man" is found in his capacity to follow the initiatives of his less conformist, more creative betters.[103] It would clearly be wrong to take this statement out of context in order to express smug horror at Mill's "elitism." Yet even in context the statement jars, not least because it condemns most of us, if not to an "unexamined life," to a life of what might be called "reflective following."[104]

Similarly, in *Representative Government* we find Mill apparently endorsing the Aristotelian view that the function of government is to provide an education in virtue or character to its citizens. "A government," Mill writes, "is to be judged by its action upon men, and by its action upon things; by what it makes of citizens, and what it does with them; its tendency to improve or deteriorate the people themselves; and the goodness or badness of the work it performs for them, and by means of them."[105] While Mill never held anything like the view that statesmen are or ought to be "political artists of character," the combination of the Romantic rhetoric in "Of Individuality" with the formative rhetoric in *Representative Government* certainly appears to point in that direction.

What are we to make of such passages? Are they instances of self-betrayal, lapses induced by the influence of Romantics like Coleridge or classical thinkers like Aristotle? Or do they reveal the true Mill, a "liberal" less concerned with the morality of rights than with the cultivation (coerced, if necessary) of originality and character?

Is there a way of reading these statements that shows them to support rather than undermine Mill's fundamental commitments to diversity of opinion and individual freedom?

I think Mill is more consistent than is typically allowed by those who are embarrassed (or scandalized) by the rhetoric of *On Liberty*, or who think that Mill is a closet "virtue theorist" (to use Bonnie Honig's helpful phrase).[106] As I shall argue in the next section, Mill is not without his moments of self-betrayal, moments that undermine the Socratic nature of his project and his commitment to a broadly philosophical form of citizenship. However, the line of argument in chapter 3 of *On Liberty* and chapters 2 and 3 of *Representative Government* cannot be counted among such moments. What links these texts is their shared emphasis on the importance of individual energy as the sine qua non of moral progress. Where individual energy is quashed or given no outlet, the result is cultural stagnation and moral retrogression. Where citizens or subjects have no active role in the public realm, the result is a docility which promotes authoritarianism.

"Of Individuality" begins with the less than startling claim that freedom of opinion should be matched by a corresponding (but necessarily more limited) freedom of action: "Men should be free to act upon their opinions—to carry these out in their lives, without hindrance, either physical or moral, from their fellow-men, so long as it is at their own risk and peril,"[107] and so long as it doesn't injure others. However, it soon shifts to a discussion of the value of spontaneity in human life, and from there to an insistence that individuals have the right to use and interpret experience in their own way, to choose their own plan of life, and to cultivate or form themselves in an active, independent, and utterly individual way. "Among the works of man," Mill writes, "which human life is rightly employed in perfecting and beautifying, the first in importance is surely man himself."[108] Mill urges each one of us to approach his or her life as a work of art, and to think of ourselves as the artist primarily responsible for the beauty (or ugliness) of what results.[109]

The terrain of Mill's argument has shifted from morality and truth to what might be called the aesthetics of character. To make something beautiful of oneself—to "give style to one's character," as Nietzsche would say—demands an abundance of material in the form of desires and impulses to work with:

Desires and impulses are as much a part of perfect human being as beliefs and restraints: and strong impulses are only perilous when not properly balanced. . . . It is not because men's desires are strong that they act ill; it is because their consciences are weak. . . . To say that one person's desires and feelings are stronger and more various than those of another, is merely to say that he has more of the raw material of human nature, and is therefore capable, perhaps of more evil, but certainly of more good. Strong impulses are but another name for energy. Energy may be turned to bad uses; but more good may always be made of an energetic nature, than an indolent and impassive one. . . . A person whose desires and impulses are his own—are the expression of his own nature, as it has been developed and modified by his own culture—is said to have a character. One whose desires and impulses are not his own, has no character, no more than a steam-engine has a character.[110]

Mill's insistence that energy and "strong impulses" are crucial to self-cultivation refers us to Goethe and von Humboldt, as well as back to Plato and forward to Nietzsche. The roots of this conception in the history of ideas are, however, far less important than the context that provokes Mill's passionate endorsement of strong impulses and desires, an endorsement quite at odds with the usual picture of Mill as a schoolmasterish Victorian sage. The context in question is that of a mass society whose morality is dictated by the prejudices of the dominant middle class, prejudices which retain the form (if not the substance) of Calvinist asceticism and which make virtues of obedience and conformity. Drawing on the lessons of Tocqueville, Mill delivers an indictment of his society which is stunning both in its ferocity and inclusiveness:

In our times, from the highest class of society down to the lowest, every one lives as under the eye of a hostile and dreaded censorship. Not only in what concerns others, but in what concerns only themselves, the individual or the family do not ask themselves—what do I prefer? or, what would suit my character and disposition? or, what would allow the best and highest in me to have fair play, and enable it to grow and thrive? They ask themselves, what is suitable to my position? what is usually done by persons of my station and pecuniary circumstances? or (worse still) what is usually done by persons of a station and circumstances superior to mine? I do not mean that they choose what is customary in preference to what suits their own inclination. It does not occur to them to have any inclination, except for what is customary. Thus the mind is bowed to the yoke: even in what people do for pleasure, conformity is the first thing thought of; they like in crowds; they exercise choice only among things commonly done: peculiarity of taste, eccentricity of conduct, are shunned equally with crimes: until by dint of not following their own nature they have no nature to follow: their human capacities are withered and starved: they become incapable of any strong wishes or native pleasure, and are generally without either opinions or feelings of home growth, or properly their own.[111]

It is all too easy to historicize this judgment as appropriate to the Victorian grayness surrounding Mill, and of little relevance to post-sixties Anglo-American culture. But while the tonality has changed, with consumer society providing a range of styles suitable to every demographic, the individual who opts out of this marketplace—or who questions the range of choice it offers as an authentic expression of freedom—is bound to find him- or herself something of a pariah. The fact that rebellion is the favorite trope of advertisers seeking the youth market does nothing to alter the fundamental truth (and continuing relevance) of what Mill says in this passage about the basic dynamic behind society's likings and dislikings. If anything, the triumph of consumer society has made the prospect of genuine eccentricity or individuality even more tenuous.[112]

That said, the fact remains that Mill tends to exaggerate the gravitational pull of the masses, sketching a "tyranny of opinion" so monolithic that it would seemingly take an individual of both genius and extraordinary energy to tear himself (or anyone else) away from it. Sounding more like Coleridge than Tocqueville, Mill writes that mediocrity has become "the ascendent power among mankind." Real power is the property of the masses, with governments wielding it only insofar as they make themselves "the organ of the tendencies and instincts of the masses." The public opinion which Mill feared in his early writings is equated with *mass* opinion in *On Liberty*: "Those whose opinions go by the name of public opinion are not always the same sort of public: in America they are the whole white population; in England, chiefly the middle class. *But they are always a mass, that is to say, a collective mediocrity.*"[113]

This is the sociological backdrop against which Mill makes his claim that "the initiation of all wise or noble things comes and must come from individuals," and that "the honor and the glory of the average man is that he is capable of following that initiative; that he can respond internally to wise and noble things and be led to them with his eyes open."[114] While Mill explicitly repudiates "hero worship" and the idea that the "strong man" has the right to compel others into a higher, more noble form of life, the burden of his argument seems to be that only the man of genius can break through the crust of custom and convention. In this he seems to be in agreement not only with his friend Thomas Carlyle but with numerous conservative critics of mass society, from Burckhardt and Nietzsche to Heidegger and Ortega y Gasset.

Are we here one step away from Nietzsche's "philosophers of the future" or the poet-statesmen of Heidegger's *Introduction to Metaphysics*? The fact that Mill invokes neither reason nor deliberation but spontaneity and creativity would incline some to answer yes. However, as I suggested earlier, this would be to miss Mill's primary point. What is at stake in his discussion is not the overcoming of bourgeois conformity as such (in the name of something higher, nobler, or more "authentic") but rather the preservation of genuine diversity of opinion as the precondition of both perspectivism and moral progress. The problem is not that *democratization* leads to "leveling" but that *mass public opinion* tends all too frequently in one direction at a given moment, and that (as a result) it flattens or eradicates perspectives rather than multiplying or making them more distinct. The result is that it becomes increasingly difficult to practice perspectivism as an aid to independent moral and political judgment, or to derive any of the (negative and dissolvent) benefits of free discussion that Mill outlines in chapter 2 of *On Liberty*. Where men "think" in masses, in groups, they are indeed dependent upon the initiative of individuals to show them other ways of thinking and of conducting themselves.

This, then, is the context in which Mill makes his seemingly scandalous statement. When public opinion is a creature of mass culture and media, we rightly suspect the adequacy of appeals to reason, virtue, or public deliberation. The example of the heretic or dissident, of the citizen who says no, is clearly every bit as important. But beyond the heroic dissident, as Mill points out, we need as many individual centers of energy, thought, and action as possible. Otherwise human experience and opinion will fluctuate within the narrow bounds of mass culture. Only those who discover new truths and commence new practices prevent human life from becoming a "stagnant pool"; and only the "more and more pronounced individuality of those who stand on the higher eminences of thought" provides an effective "counterpoise and corrective" to the increasingly unquestioned rule of mass opinion.[115] The "more highly gifted and instructed One or Few" which Mill writes of, then, are neither philosopher-kings nor "gentlemen," neither legislators of superior virtue (Rousseau) or poetic inspiration (Shelley). They "point the way" to new ways of living and interpreting experience, of conceiving the moral life. They teach by the example of their originality, integrity, and dissent–*not* by compulsion. Without them the tendency of even the best beliefs and practices to "degenerate into the mechanical" would continue unabated.

The elitist tone of Mill's pronouncement obscures what is, in fact, a grave moral necessity. What is at stake is not primarily the preservation of the heroic or the high-minded in the midst of mass mediocrity but the preservation of human life and experience as open-ended: as multifarious in its ends, plural in its virtues, and potentially boundless in its energies. What Mill dreads is not the decline of genius or creativity per se but the moral and intellectual effects of a society deprived of innovation; a society in which individuals no longer regularly discover new truths and commence new practices; a society, in other words, which is not constantly being reminded of the partiality of its preferred forms of life and interpretation of morality. Diversity and energy are valued in themselves, but they are also valued for what they make possible (but by no means guarantee): moral progress.

The charge of elitism misses the mark, then, for four important reasons. First, because the genius (or heretic) does not compel his fellow citizens or treat them as raw material for his artistic vision; he merely "points the way." Second, because the contribution of "original" individuals does not consist in political or cultural legislation but in providing a "counterpoise and corrective" to the inherent one-dimensionality of public opinion. Third, because Mill's goal is not essentially to preserve the possibility of magnificent cultural productions but to foster as many centers of individual energy as possible. Fourth (and following from this), because he has no desire to limit freedom of thought and action to those of exceptional talents. Moral progress may be most clearly visible in the opinions and actions of a Socrates or a Jesus, but an ordinary individual living his own life in his own way (again, commensurate with the vital interests of others) is, in itself, morally valuable. It is also more likely to contribute to the diversity and progress of the species than a life spent merely imitating the dominant social character or conforming to the reigning code of conduct.[116]

But even if this is the case, Mill's argument for individuality in conduct as well as opinion seems to hinge upon his conception of progress, and (thus) upon a positive conception of morality and character. We seem a long way from the negativity of Socratic dialectic, a negativity born of relentless (and radical) questioning. Yet this distance evaporates once we see that the "commencement of new practices and experiments in living" has its effect not only in preventing a "degeneration into the mechanical" but also in revealing the partiality of forms of life and conceptions of the good life. Like Socrates, Mill is convinced that the examined life—the life of radical questioning—promotes moral ends by helping the individual detach him- or herself from the despotism of custom and the reflexive, unthinking character of group feeling and action. Like Socrates, he is convinced that moral and intellectual integrity depend upon moral and intellectual energy, as well as upon an atmosphere of freedom.[117]

Mill's argument for diversity of practices thus mirrors his argument for diversity of opinion in that its primary function is dissolvent. We *think* we know what the good or virtuous life is, as well as the code of conduct which should govern it. Freedom of opinion and practice demonstrates to us that we have taken the part for the whole and (in the process) falsified the nature of the moral life. When Mill states that "there is no reason why all human existence should be constructed on some one or some small number of patterns," he is questioning the very assumption that a phenomenon as complex as the moral life can be reduced to a single code of conduct or hierarchy of values universally applicable to all.[118] What *is* basic to the moral life is not a single ranking of the virtues but the Socratic/Millian refusal to do harm to the vital claims of others, or to allow oneself to become an instrument of such harm. What is basic to the moral life is the avoidance of injustice—especially injustice justified by the appeal to morality or the imperatives of a single, inflexible code of conduct.

This interpretation is supported by what Mill says in chapter 4 of *On Liberty*, where he not only draws the protective boundary between what is private and what is properly regulated by public authority but also decries the universal human tendency to be mortally offended by codes of conduct that are different from our own. But it runs up against additional objections when we turn to chapters 2 and 3 of *Representative Government*, which seem to promote a "liberal" version of the formative or "tutorial" state, the better to foster a particular conception of citizenship and civic virtue. How do we square this with *On Liberty's* rejection of moral or civic paternalism and Mill's plea for individuality?

In *On Liberty*, Mill notes that there was a time when political authority, hard-pressed by an excess of individuality among its subjects, asserted "a power over the whole man," the better to induce persons of "strong bodies or minds" to obey rules which "required them to control their impulses." Such a time, however, is long past. *Representative Government* gives the impression that what has replaced it is an epoch in which government, while eschewing any claim to rule "the whole man," is nevertheless the primary agency through which civic and moral energies are, or ought to be, cultivated. In a world where the public-spirited virtues have all but disappeared (thanks to Christianity's virtual effacement of the pagan virtues), Mill seems ready to deploy whatever means are necessary to promote their rebirth—even a formative state. Government, according to Mill, is (among other things) an "agency of national education," one whose purpose should be to encourage public-spiritedness, promote the virtues of "industry, integrity, justice, and prudence," and, in general, form national character.[119]

There can be little doubt about the centrality of Mill's concern with civic education in *Representative Government*. The question is: how does this education proceed, and what, precisely, is its goal? The latter can be stated simply enough. A chief criterion of a good form of government is its effectiveness in fostering an "active character" in its citizens.[120] But what does "active character" mean, and why is it to be preferred? How does civic education bring it about, and through what means? Is such political education compatible with the strong libertarian strains of *On Liberty*? Can it, moreover, be rendered harmonious with the Socratic goals of that book, and with the idea of philosophical citizenship generally?

For Mill, "active character" connotes not just energy but public-spiritedness, mental activity, courage, and originality.[121] It is to be preferred because it is the precondition of progress in human affairs. In this sphere, "things left to take care of themselves inevitably decay." A system of government is no exception to the rule. If popular in form, it demands these qualities not only in its construction but in its working and preservation. "Political machinery does not act of itself," Mill observes. A legitimate set of institutions requires not just the acquiescence of citizens but their "active participation."[122] Good government therefore principally depends upon "the qualities of the human beings" over whom it is exercised. Since there is "an incessant and ever-flowing current of human affairs towards the worse, consisting of all the follies, all the vices, all the negligences, indolences, and supinenesses of mankind," it is imperative that the active character (and, specifically, the virtue and intelligence) of the people themselves is promoted by the very form of government they have chosen or submitted themselves to.[123]

According to Mill, the primary avenue for promoting energy, virtue, and intelligence—the chief means of civic education—is political participation itself. This is a highly controversial claim, one which would seem to make Mill an ally of participatory democrats (and, to some degree, an enemy of Socrates). Indeed, much of Mill's case for a representative form of democracy rests on the myriad opportunities for political participation such a system opens up to the average person. The more people participate—the more their energies are incited by and enlisted in the political process at both the local and national levels—the more they are drawn away from the selfish pursuit of interest and "educated" to citizenship. Given a share in the public business and deliberation, the "private citizen" undergoes a transformation, widening his or her range of ideas while simultaneously developing an array of moral and intellectual faculties. According to Mill, the citizen engaged in public functions

> is called upon, while so engaged, to weigh interests not his own; to be guided, in the case of conflicting claims, by another rule than his private partialities; to apply, at every turn, principles and maxims which have for their reason of existence the common good: and he usually finds associated with him in the same work minds more familiarized than his own with these ideas and operations, whose study it will be to supply reasons to his understanding, and stimulation to his feeling for the general interest. He is made to feel himself one of the public, and whatever is for their benefit to be for his benefit.[124]

Deprived of the "school of public spirit" which participation in public business and deliberation provides, the private citizen finds all his thoughts of interest or duty utterly absorbed "in the individual and in the family"; he views his neighbor only as a rival and potential competitor. Thus, Mill observes, "even private morality suffers, while public is actually extinct."[125]

These sentiments recall Rousseau's argument in *The Social Contract*. Like Mill, Rousseau envisaged the tightest possible link between political participation and moral improvement.[126] Indeed, Rousseau's argument prefigures Mill's contention that political participation is what raises the average person from the narrow pursuit of interest to a disciplined care for the common good. For Rousseau the promise of citizenship was its capacity to transform a creature otherwise doomed to be a slave of impulse and appetite. This transformation is memorably etched in Rousseau's description of what happens when we leave the state of nature (or its socially corrupted remnant) and enter a form of polity animated by popular sovereignty. The individual who participates in the legislative activity of such a sovereign finds that "his faculties are exercised and developed, his ideas are broadened, his feelings ennobled, his entire soul is elevated to such a height that, if the abuse of this new condition did not often lower his status to beneath the level he left, he ought constantly to bless the happy moment that pulled him away from it forever and which transformed him from a stupid, limited animal into an intelligent being and a man."[127]

Obviously, *Representative Government* does not equate civic participation with legislative authority, nor can Mill be said to share Rousseau's enthusiasm for the idea that virtuous citizenship is what makes us fully human and genuinely free. Nevertheless, the similarity between their basic arguments about the moral elevation effected by participatory citizenship should take us aback. Disturbing is not simply the fact that Rousseau was an antiliberal *avant la lettre* but that his account of the general interest animating citizens is entirely hostile to diversity of opinion, faction, and individual dissent (his approving citation of Socrates in the *Discourse on the Sciences and the Arts* notwithstanding).[128] The arc he traces is one which ascends from entrapment in selfish interests to liberation through active participation in the common good and the common self (the *moi commun*). Can it be that Mill, the champion of individual liberty and diversity of opinion, is similarly fixated on consensus and a unitary interpretation of the "common good," at least when it comes to assessing the value of citizenship? Does his concern with educating

109

ordinary working-class people to citizenship trump his commitment to individuality, perspectivism, and the "many-sidedness" of truth?

It must be acknowledged that Mill, like Rousseau, expects great educative gains from active, publicly oriented and involved citizenship. This said, we should note that there is an enormous difference between the kind of citizen Rousseau wants to produce and the civic ideal of Mill. The Rousseauian citizen is educated by laws, customs, and civil religion to be a patriot, a vigilant but largely silent guardian of a univocal common good.[129] Thus, we should not be surprised that participation has a highly ritualized aspect in his account; it expresses not differences but a virtual unanimity, one made possible by an all-encompassing education in virtue and civic duty.

In contrast, Mill's focus is on cultivating and channeling energy into public pursuits, on the enlightenment and general broadening of views which sustained attention to public matters produces. His ideal is not the laconic and self-sacrificing Spartans Rousseau encountered as a boy in Plutarch but the talkative and intellectually energetic Athenians he found in his friend George Grote's history of Greece.[130] "Notwithstanding the defects of the social system and moral ideas of antiquity," Mill writes, "the practice of the dicastery and ecclesia raised the intellectual standard of the average Athenian citizen far beyond anything of which there is yet an example in any other mass of men, ancient or modern."[131] While service on juries and in "parish offices" could hardly rival the benefits deriving from the Athenians' regular attendance at public debates, it nevertheless helped to produce a "range of ideas and development of faculties" far beyond those typically available to "those who have done nothing in their lives but drive a quill, or sell goods over a counter." And, as we will see, Mill was far more appreciative than Rousseau of the deliberative dimension of popular and representative assemblies.

Mill's remarks on this score point to a crucial ambiguity in his concept of civic education, one which flows from his tendency to efface the distinction between political education and the development of critical intelligence. As Dennis Thompson has pointed out, when Mill describes the goals of participation, "he often vacillates between political education and intellectual education, evidently assuming that the development of general critical intelligence and extensive knowledge accompanies the growth of political skill and political knowledge."[132] This vacillation makes eminent sense, given Mill's commitment to democratic reform and his fear of the tyranny of public opinion. For while Rousseau measured the success of civic education in terms of how closely the sovereign assembly of the people approximated unanimity, Mill measured it in terms of how many public-spirited and energetic interpretations of the common good found their way into the political arena.

Like Rousseau, Mill eschewed the idea that the common good resulted from the "aggregation of interests"; unlike Rousseau, he recognized what Leo Strauss has called the "essentially controversial" nature of the common good.[133] The point of *Representative Government* is that we should not attempt to circumvent this controversial nature through the inculcation of patriotic norms and the avoidance of anything that smacks of "faction" (Rousseau), or by the appeal to a philosophical "umpire" who stands above the fray (Strauss). Rather, we should prefer a system which is open to an array of partial interpretations, one which recognizes democratic sovereignty and majority opinion but which also ensures that minority views are not only expressed but given real power. For only in a political system where no individual or group is doomed to passivity by the weight of majority opinion or the prestige of elites can a high level of moral and intellectual energy be maintained and "public-spiritedness" detached from a univocal conception of the common good.

This can be seen in the way Mill decries the effects of a "good despotism" of the sort advocated by Hobbes. Such a regime may respect its subjects, treating them in a nonarbitrary way, and it may indeed govern with an eye to the common good (at least as perceived by the despot). The price of avoiding political disagreement and faction, however, is the infantilization of an entire people, the narrowing of their intellectual and moral horizons. Bereft of the opportunity to act on matters of public interest, they have no incentive to develop informed views on any topic of political interest: "With the exception . . . of a few studious men who take an interest in speculation for its own sake, the intelligence and sentiment of the whole people are given up to material interests, and, when these are provided for, to the amusement and ornamentation, of private life."[134] For Mill the result of such benign paternalism must be an "Oriental" type of stagnation. Only a guaranteed entry into the agon of political life can assure "the improvement of the people themselves," one which comes from making them more self-reliant and hence more intellectually and morally active.[135] Participation in political debate

111

and contestation is necessary for the exercise of the average person's moral and intellectual "muscles."

This preference for a robust political pluralism is seen even more clearly in Mill's discussion of the proper function of popular and representative assemblies. In general, Mill accepts the thrust of Rousseau's distinction between the (popular) sovereign body and the government, applying it to popular and representative bodies. The business of the latter, he argues, is neither to administer, to act, nor even to draft legislation. These are, by nature, "skilled" activities best left to those with training and experience. However, "what can be done better by a body than by an individual is deliberation. When it is necessary to secure hearing and consideration to many conflicting opinions, a deliberative body is indispensable."[136] The primary activity of any assembly is talk, deliberation which subjects proposed laws and governmental action to many-sided debate and judgment. Mill is well aware that deliberative speech is highly regarded neither by the Western tradition of political theory (which focuses on ruling and law-giving) nor, indeed, by his contemporaries:

> Representative assemblies are often taunted by their enemies with being places of mere talk and *bavardage*. There has seldom been more misplaced derision. I know not how a representative assembly can more usefully employ itself than in talk, when the subject of talk is the great public interests of the country, and every sentence of it represents the opinion either of some important body of persons in the nation, or of an individual in whom some such body have reposed their confidence. A place where every interest and shade of opinion in the country can have its cause even passionately pleaded, in the face of the government and of all other interests and opinions, can compel them to listen, and either comply, or state clearly why they do not, is in itself, if it answered no other purpose, one of the most important political institutions that can exist anywhere, and one of the foremost benefits of free government. Such "talking" would never be looked upon with disparagement if it were not allowed to stop "doing"; which it never would, if assemblies knew and acknowledged that talking and discussion are their proper business, while *doing* as the result of discussion is the task not of a miscellaneous body, but of individual specially trained to it. . . .[137]

The place where the many-sidedness of truth finds political expression is the representative or popular assembly; the mode in which this many-sidedness is expressed is talk or deliberative speech.

Action may be the outcome of such speech, but, as Mill notes, the mere expression of different and dissenting points of view in and of itself makes such speech one of the most important activities in any polity. If such assemblies do their job properly, they question and slow down initiatives emanating from both the government and portions of the *demos*. Mill's desire to give such assemblies a Socratic twist—to make them offices of "criticism and control" rather than action—leads him to urge the separation between deliberative and administrative bodies as absolutely essential.

Finally, Mill's consistent commitment to a politics of opinion and dissent can be seen in his extended discussion of representation of minorities. Representative assemblies are essential not only for "criticism and control" of the government but to preserve antagonistic and conflicting views in the face of the dominant power in society. Echoing Machiavelli's point in the *Discourses*, Mill notes that "no community has ever long continued progressive, but while a conflict was going on between the strongest power in the community and some rival power; between the spiritual and temporal authorities; the military or territorial and the industrious classes; the king and the people; the orthodox and the religious reformers."[138] The last thing he wants is a society in which a strong sense of civic or moral virtue results in the marginalization of minority or dissenting views. While every form of government threatens to overwhelm such views, the danger posed by democracy, *On Liberty* insists, is particularly acute. For where the majority is dominant, the source of conflict built into nondemocratic forms of government (between people and ruling elite) is eliminated. Hence the "great difficulty" of democratic society is to provide "a social support, a *point d'appui*, for individual resistance to the tendencies of the ruling power; a protection, a rallying point, for opinions and interests which the ascendent public opinion views with disfavor."[139]

Mill's solution takes the form of an endorsement of Thomas Hare's scheme of plural voting, which he believed would give added moral and political weight to the most beleaguered of minorities, "the instructed few." While a staunch advocate of extending the suffrage to the working classes and women (a truly radical position at the time), Mill's anxiety about the level of competence and judgment in a mass democracy led him to propose a "universal but graduated suffrage," one in which sheer numbers would be offset by the electoral amplification of the voices of the most competent. "In human affairs," Mill writes, "every person directly interested, and not under positive tutelage, has an admitted claim to a voice, and when his exercise of it is not inconsistent with the safety of the whole, cannot be justly excluded from it. But though every one ought to have a voice—that every one should have an equal voice is a totally different proposition."[140]

Mill's endorsement of plural voting is questionable (he was to recant it himself in his *Autobiography*), but the motive behind it is clear and, generally speaking, laudable. For if the main threat to representative democracy (beyond governmental transgression of rights) is the tyranny of an increasingly uniform public opinion, then some way has to be found to offset the majority and ensure that "the interests, the opinions, the grades of intellect which are outnumbered [are] nevertheless heard."[141] The fact that Mill's proposal takes the form of an argument for the "leading" of opinion by elites ought not to blind us to his primary concern, which is the preservation of minority voices in public-political deliberation.[142]

All of these considerations help put Mill's focus on civic education and participation in a different light. The methods he recommends for inculcating public spirit and civic virtue in the average citizen (extension of the franchise, participation in local political functions as well as public debates) are not designed to articulate a univocal common interest or express anything like the General Will (which, in Rousseau's famous description, is "constant, unalterable, and pure"). But this still leaves the question as to why Mill, in *Representative Government*, places so much emphasis on the cultivation of civic virtue at the expense (evidently) of his more Socratic preoccupations.

The answer to this question can only be that for Mill citizenship is the precondition for philosophical citizenship. His fear is that the manual laborer of his day, while deserving of full political rights, nevertheless inhabits an exceedingly confined mental and moral universe, one which must be enlarged through political discussion and "collective political action."[143] The more experience the average person has of these two activities, and of a *public* ballot, the more sensitive he or she will be to the distinction between the selfish pursuit of interest and the demands of justice and the common good.[144] They will also, presumably, be more open to the kind of Socratic criticism of institutions and policies Mill points to in *On Liberty*. While the average citizen may perhaps never reach the heights of philosophical or dissident citizenship, the system of representative democracy promotes a level of civic self-cultivation and self-reliance which is far more likely to resonate with the criticism made by such a citizen. This provides a different, decidedly nonelitist spin to "the glory of the average man."

It is on the foundation of the active and independent form of civic virtue encouraged by representative democracy that Mill erects his vision of the "ideally best polity," one which manages to combine something like the public-spiritedness of Athenian democracy with the critical moral energy of a Socrates. Indeed, in Mill's eyes representative democracy, properly understood, embodied the potential for reconciliation of the democratic and Socratic spirit. Through its encouragement of independence of mind and a plurality of views on the common good, it provided an alternative to the prospect of majority tyranny—the tyranny of the dominant *doxa*—in a democratic age.

The Art of Politics in *Representative Government*

While *Representative Government* can hardly be characterized as the simple application of the principles of *On Liberty* to questions of institutional design, it is generally truer to the spirit of that book than one might initially suppose. The moral individualism of *On Liberty* is translated into a set of principles and suggestions designed to foster a high level of moral and intellectual energy in the political as well as the cultural realm. That such energy is the precondition of both public-spiritedness and morally serious criticism is, as I have tried to show, less of a paradox than it might at first appear. For example, while I am skeptical of those who would describe Socrates as primarily a "patriot," there can be no denying that he was committed to the principles of Athenian democracy, if not its policies. In *Representative Government* Mill attempts a similar synthesis, convinced that the freedom and equality of representative democracy provides the greatest stimulus for individual civic and moral development. It is not, as with Rousseau, a matter of reviving a classical conception of civic virtue. Rather, it is a matter of fostering a form of democratic citizenship that is less inclined to mistake the will of the majority for the common good, one that is at least somewhat attuned to the partial nature of the various (and conflicting) articulations of this good.[145]

This said, it is must be acknowledged that Mill placed a heavy burden on the Benthamite distinction between "sinister interests" and the "common good" and remained skeptical about the level of instrumental and moral competence the average citizen could achieve in a representative democracy.[146] Even the individual who participated in "office and judgment" (to use the Aristotelian formula) would lack the specialized education necessary to perform most political/legal functions, just as he would probably be tempted by the "sectional interests" of his class or group. The two biggest dangers confronting representative government are "general ignorance and incapacity," on the one hand, and the influence of particular (or "sinister") interests, on the other.[147]

While Mill (all too optimistically, no doubt) thought that civic education could greatly ameliorate the situation, strengthening the average citizen's commitment to the pursuit of the common good, in the short term he turned to the moral and political competence of the "instructed few" to keep political society on a progressive track. Indeed, much of *Representative Government* reads as if Mill were an unqualified proponent of a democracy run by elites, of rule by the "best and the brightest." This impression is not as mistaken as we might wish, for Mill takes "the principle of competence" seriously enough to endorse the view that there is, in fact, a *techne* of moral and political judgment. This art is not reducible to the kind of moral expertise Socrates seemingly lays claim to in the *Gorgias*. Rather, it combines moral and technical elements, as befits a mass society whose political and legal structures are both enormous and complex. In such a society, those who possess moral and instrumental competence ("the instructed few") are to lead the less competent masses—not, to be sure, by blatantly coercive means but by the force of their example and their superior reason and ability. The people, Mill hopes, will no longer defer to their social "betters" (the indolent and incompetent aristocracy) but rather to their intellectual and moral superiors.[148]

Here we encounter an unexpectedly "Platonic" dimension of Mill's thought, one which reserves an ample place for the principle of authority and relies upon a dubious political use of the metaphor of education. Given his early conviction that "the best government . . . must be the government of the wisest, and these must always be the few," it is perhaps not surprising that the mature Mill sought to balance the principle of participation by an equally strong emphasis on the principle of competence. What is surprising is the lengths Mill goes to in insisting upon the authority of specialized knowledge and the need for popular "deference to the superiority of cultivated intelligence."[149] To be sure, much of Mill's concern was generated by the specter of an unchecked and univocal majority will, one deaf to views that depart from its own. By elevating the "instructed few" into positions of power and prominence, Mill hoped to institutionalize "a social support, a *point d'appui*, for individual resistance to the tendencies of the ruling power."[150]

This is a laudable aim. The problem is that Mill's conception of the function the "educated class" fills in a representative democracy owes far too much to Plato's moral psychology and its tripartite division of the soul, a division mirrored in the hierarchical class structure of society itself (the appetitive producing or working class, protected and checked by the spirited guardian or soldier class, both deferring to the philosopher-kings, who represent the pure mind of society). While Mill hardly thought the *demos* to be an ineducable "beast" (*Republic* 493b), he obsessed about the dangers posed by its relative incompetence and lack of moral integrity (both of which would dispose it to view its selfish class interest as being in the general interest).[151] Moreover, like Plato, he believed, in the possibility of a class of disinterested intellectuals who might become selfless instruments of the common good.[152] This belief manifests itself again and again in *Representative Government*. It betrays a surprisingly uncritical view of the "educated classes," who are presented as structurally detached from "sinister interests" in a manner similar to Hegel's bureaucrats (the "universal class") or Mannheim's "free-floating intellectuals."[153] What makes this lapse so disturbing is not that Mill fails to unmask the interests of such a group (à la Marx or Weber), but that he neglects his own (Socratic) precepts and makes disinterestedness the achievement not of a skeptical intelligence fostered by *elenchus* (or its cultural equivalent) but of social position and training.[154] Like Plato he treats "mind" as if it were the distinct property of a group and, in so doing, betrays his moral individualism and his overarching commitment to a philosophical form of citizenship.

This propensity to ascribe virtues to groups rather than individuals is much in evidence in *Representative Government*, most notably in Mill's argument for plural voting (where some people are able to cast more votes than others) as a means of enhancing the influence of the "instructed few." The rationale Mill offers for his position—while everyone should have a voice, it is a far different matter for everyone to have an *equal* voice—is telling in this regard:

> When two persons who have a joint interest in any business differ in opinion, does justice require that both opinions should be held of exactly equal value? If, with equal virtue, one is superior to the other in knowledge and intelligence—or if, with equal intelligence, one excels the other in virtue—the opinion, the judgment, of the higher moral or intellectual being is worth more than that of the inferior: and if the institutions of the country virtually assert that they are of the same value, they assert a thing which is not. One of the two, as the wiser or better man, has a claim to superior weight: the difficulty is in ascertaining which of the two it is; a thing impossible as between individuals, but, *taking men in bodies and in numbers*, it can be done with a certain approach to accuracy. There would be no pretense for applying this doctrine to any case which could with reason be considered as one of individual and private right. In an affair which concerns only one of two persons, that one is entitled to follow his own opinion, however much wiser the other may be than himself. But we are speaking of things which equally concern them both; where, if the more ignorant does not yield his share of the matter to the guidance of the wiser man, the wiser man must resign it to that of the more ignorant. . . . If it be deemed unjust that either should have to give way, which injustice is greatest? that the better judgment should give way to the worse, or the worse to the better?[155]

The assumption that something which is hard to determine among individuals—namely, the possession of superior virtue or intelligence—becomes obvious when we deal with groups or classes is one abhorrent to rights-based individualism.[156] That Mill should so casually make it in order to argue that the *hoi polloi* should defer to the judgment of their intellectual or moral superiors betrays an all too common class prejudice in this, one of the preeminent moral individualists of the nineteenth century. That the people may frequently become the prisoners of some interest, prejudice, or custom goes without saying. That any elite, no matter how defined, is free of a parallel set of moral blinders is, however, a supremely un-Socratic view, one which Mill himself disparages in *On Liberty*.

Mill's endorsement of deference to authority as a balance to his principle of participation makes sense within his broader theory of political development, which sees workable political institutions as a function of the relative "maturity" of a given population. The "ruder" the population, the more authority it needs, the more it is dependent upon "leading strings" to help it to maturity and (ultimately) self-determination. A certain amount of paternalism is thus built into Mill's theory of government, even though *On Liberty* wars against both "the yoke of authority" and paternalistic instruction of the people. In *Representative Government*, Mill finds himself at one with the Western tradition of political theory in thinking that a self-instructing people is a contradiction in terms. Participation in local institutions and the reading of newspapers (the modern equivalent of the *agora*) helps, but "a school presupposes teachers as well as scholars; the utility of the instruction depends on its bringing inferior minds into contact with superior, a contact which in the ordinary course of life is exceptional, and the want of which contributes more than anything else to keep the generality of mankind on one level of contented ignorance."[157]

Here we encounter the paradox which plagues all attempts to "educate the *demos*" for self-government. From Protagoras to Rousseau, Saint-Simon to contemporary proponents of "radical democracy," the key question is not who will educate the educators but rather how will the habits of deference inculcated at the early and middle stages of development be transcended at later ones? Mill is honest enough not to construct an elaborate pantomime of self-governance such as we find in Rousseau, one in which the tutored do what they are taught but imagine they are acting independently. And he is consistent enough to insist that the civic "schooling" which grown people receive be indirect for the most part.[158] Nevertheless, the reader of *Representative Government* is struck again and again by the tension between the call for increased energy and independence of mind (on the one hand) and the insistence upon the need for a new species of authority and deference (on the other).

The most telling moment in this regard is Mill's passing judgment upon the deleterious effect that American institutions have had on national character. "The American institutions," Mill writes, "have imprinted strongly on the American mind that any one man (with a white skin) is as good as any other; and it is felt that this false creed is nearly connected with some of the more unfavorable points in

American character. It is not a small mischief that the constitution of any country should sanction this creed: for the belief in it, whether express or tacit, is almost as detrimental to moral and intellectual excellence as any effect which most forms of government can produce."[159]

The "false creed" that any man is as good as any other is, in Mill's eyes, a form of know-nothing antiauthoritarianism, one which winds up fostering an "involuntary deference" to the force of sheer numbers. Even in a democracy, Mill thinks, authority is inescapable. Better that it should be based on superior virtue and intellect than on numbers.[160]

There is another side to American antiauthoritarianism, however, one which Mill overlooks in his faithful retention of Tocqueville's analysis. This is the privilege accorded by Protestantism to "private judgment" or conscience over (and against) the demand for deference on the part of any religious, secular, or cultural authority. That this privilege is abused, that it is paradoxically often turned into yet another vehicle of conformism and the tyranny of the majority is beyond question. Yet, as Mill himself recognized in his more consistent moments, the privilege of judging for oneself lies at the heart of any minimally defensible conception of human dignity or moral and intellectual integrity. It is not for nothing that *On Liberty* rails against the deactivation of the faculty of judgment which accompanies virtually all civic and moral pedagogy.

How are we to make sense of these tensions within Mill's thought? We could contextualize in the manner Mill himself recommends, noting that the emergent working-class politics of his time threatened to unleash politically inexperienced and unschooled masses, forces which he feared would confirm the conservative case against democratization. Or we might note that the ambiguity of his stance has deep roots in his youthful appropriation of the Romantics and the lessons of Tocqueville. Neither of these points, however, really gets to the heart of the matter. How could Mill retain the Socratic, disillusioning conception of discussion and inquiry we find in *On Liberty* while adumbrating the quasi-Platonic conception of the political role of elites we find in *Representative Government*?

The answer reveals itself in Mill's reading of the Platonic dialogues and his understanding of the figure of Socrates presented therein. Like his father, Mill praised Socratic *elenchus* as a method "unsurpassed as a discipline for correcting the errors, and clearing up the confusions incident to the *intellectus sibi permissus. . . .*"[161] But he also saw no real tension between the negative quality of Socratic dialectics and the more authentically Platonic idea of politics as a specialized science or *techne*. Indeed, in his view the former provided the basis for the latter. Thus, in his 1866 review of George Grote's *Plato and Other Companions of Socrates*, Mill writes:

> It was reserved for Socrates, and for Plato, who, whether as the interpreter or continuator of Socrates, can never be severed from him, to exalt [the] negative arm of philosophy to a perfection never since surpassed, and to provide it with its greatest, most interesting, and most indispensable field of exercise, the generalities relating to life and conduct. These great men originated the thought, that, like every other part of the practice of life, morals and politics are an affair of science, to be understood only after severe study and special training; an indispensable part of which consists in acquiring the habit of considering, not merely what can be said in favor of a doctrine, but what can be said against it; of sifting opinions, and never accepting any until it has emerged victorious over every logical, still more than over every practical objection. These two principles—the necessity of a scientific basis and method for ethics and politics, and of rigorous negative, dialectics as a part of that method, are the greatest of the many lessons to be learnt from Plato. . . .[162]

This passage is remarkable for its clear-sighted recognition of the negative, disillusioning function of Socratic dialectic in its struggle with "King Nomos."[163] But it is also remarkable for its marriage of dissolvent rationality and specialized science. The former, in Mill's understanding, paves the way for the latter. The point of negative philosophy is no longer to "clear the ground a little" in order to preserve a space for moral, intellectual, and aesthetic individualism, as it was in *On Liberty*. The point, rather, is to cultivate the abilities of a select few who, after "severe study and special training," are in a position to pursue disinterested "scientific" leadership and administration.

This deduction of an "art of government" from Socratic *elenchus* is, in itself, hardly novel. Indeed, as I pointed out in chapter 1, the standard interpretation of Socrates' "true political art" in the *Gorgias* has been along similar lines. What Mill specifically does is to reinstitute, at the highest level, the Platonic distinction between *nomos* or *doxa*, on the one hand, and *techne* or *episteme*, on the other. While evidently in conflict with the translation of Socratic dialectic into the sociocultural terms of *On Liberty*, this move can, in fact, be rendered consistent with it—but only at the cost of replacing one form of authoritarianism (the tyranny of "King Nomos" or public opinion) with another (popular deference to the rule of elites). The people should become more independent-minded and intellectually energetic, but—given the built-in limits of such improvement—they should readily accede to the greater intelligence and judgment of their superiors. Mill does not want his citizens to be passive—far from it—but neither does he want them to be especially critical of those who (apparently) possess superior judgment. Mill thinks that it is only when citizens recognize such individuals as a group, and defer to them, that virtue and intelligence are able to find their proper weight in a representative democracy.

In the course of arguing for Thomas Hare's plural voting scheme, Mill declares "a democratic people would, in this way be provided with what in any other way it would almost certainly miss—leaders of a higher grade of intellect and character than itself. Modern democracy would have its occasional Pericles, and its habitual group of superior and guiding minds."[164] It is all too easy, with the benefit of hindsight, to point out the naïveté of Mill's vision of an active, engaged citizen body deferring to the judgment of the "best and the brightest." Yet the fact that we can do this—that we have been repeatedly disillusioned by horrific and shameful experience on this score—signals a deeper problem with Mill's *political* appropriation of Socrates and Plato.

This problem concerns Mill's idea that the moral judgment of the average citizen must defer to the greater instrumental and (presumed) moral judgment of the elite, and his conjoined assumption that this elite is less in thrall to the fantasies, passions, and unfounded *doxai* that constitute the bulk of popular political life. Experience has shown the idea of a science of politics or ethics to be dubious in the extreme. More important, it has demonstrated time and again that democratic elites are in thrall to their own set of fantasies, passions, and unfounded *doxai*—to their own (elite) version of "King Nomos." This is something that Socrates knew well, and it is one of the reasons why he included Pericles in his list of those Athenian political leaders who had failed to "improve" the Athenians. Mill thinks that the thoroughness of his elites' training will make them, as a group, less prey to illusion, prejudice, passion, and ambition. We know better. In morals and politics, disillusion can only be relative. The process stands in need of constant re-initiation. In *On Liberty* Mill made this point forcefully—as forcefully as it has ever been made. In *Representative Government* he appears to have either forgotten it or succumbed to the illusion that there is a social group whose education and training place them permanently beyond the reach of custom and convention, prejudice and interest.

It would be wrong to conclude from the preceding remarks that Mill favors a "democratic Platonism," one in which the representative system is so skewed that the people provide little more that a legitimation by ballot of their governing elite.[165] The principle of participation, grounded in Mill's desire to raise the average level of intellectual and moral energy in society, is too strong a presence in his political theory for this to be so. While Mill does tend to locate "mind" in the "instructed classes," it cannot be said that he restricts it to these classes. (Such a move would render actual representation of the interests of less educated classes superfluous since, as in Plato, knowledge of the "real interests" of all classes would be the cognitive property of the elite.) Throughout both *On Liberty* and *Representative Government* we find a consistent desire to expand participation in deliberation and public office, and to "broaden horizons" through the preservation of diverse perspectives. Yet I would argue that the "negative" or Socratic character of this perspectivism is far more consistently maintained in *On Liberty* than it is in *Representative Government*. Why is this the case?

We find a clue in a letter Mill wrote to Pasquale Villari in March 1858. In it Mill mentions his forthcoming "little book on liberty," which he describes as focusing on moral and intellectual liberty, something which "the nations of the Continent are as superior to England as they are inferior to it when it comes to political liberty."[166] This distinction between moral and intellectual freedom, on the one hand, and political liberty, on the other, indicates that Mill saw a gap between the cultural and political effects of the "tyranny of the majority." It was in the domain of culture that the dissolvent character of heretical and skeptical thought was most needed; in the political arena (at least in England, where government was limited and rights protected) what was needed was more trained professionalism and less rank amateurism. The "omnipresent agency of King Nomos and his numerous volunteers," so eloquently described by Mill in his review of Grote's *Plato and Other Companions of Socrates*, gives way to a more differentiated (but ultimately less rich) notion of how "common sense" impacts culture and politics.[167]

The consequences of this unexpectedly rigid distinction between politics and culture are twofold. On the one hand, it enabled Mill to formulate his vision of what a minimally Socratic culture would look like in *On Liberty*. On the other, it allowed him to give relatively free rein to his conviction that government is, above all, a "Skilled Employment," one which demands not just "special and professional study" but "a scientific mastery of the subject."[168] The focus on the *art* of politics (rather than its moral stakes and potential horrors) led Mill to endorse a narrow conception of the relevance of negative Socratic thinking to modern politics, framing it as but one element in the training of the elite.

That this conception clashes with the much broader Socratism of *On Liberty* has already been noted.[169] What needs to be emphasized here is how *that* book contains the outlines of a genuinely philosophical form of citizenship. That Mill failed to develop this aspect of citizenship in *Representative Government*, focusing instead on such Tocquevillian virtues as participation in local institutions and juries, can be explained by the need to develop citizens first and philosophical citizens later. But Mill's endorsement of the Platonic idea of politics as a "Skilled Employment" led him to neglect the development of this strand of his thought and to encourage (albeit unwittingly) the Fabian and technocratic versions of liberalism with which we are so familiar. The result is one of the great missed opportunities in the history of political thought. For if there was one theorist equipped to fully articulate a vision of Socratic citizenship for the modern age, it was John Stuart Mill.

Friedrich Nietzsche

MORALITY, INDIVIDUALISM, AND POLITICS

> *The Immoralists.* Moralists must now accept
> the fact that they are to be regarded as immoral
> because they dissect morals. . . . Men confuse
> the moralist with the moral preacher. The older
> moralists dissected too little and preached too
> much, and this it the basis for that confusion,
> and its unpleasant consequences for the moralists
> of today.
> (*Nietzsche*, The Wanderer and His Shadow)

> Socrates, simply to confess it, stands so near to
> me, that I almost always fight a battle with him.
> (*Nietzsche, unpublished note, 1875*)

ANY BOOK ON THE TOPIC of citizenship that includes a chapter on
Nietzsche must offer some explanation. Nietzsche occupies a key
point in the story I want to tell, namely, that of philosophical citizenship and its vicissitudes in the modern age. Of course, citizenship
was one of the last things Nietzsche, the "good European" and
acerbic critic of democracy and the nation-state, was concerned
with.[1] Nevertheless, Nietzsche's thought marks an essential stage in
the development of secular moral individualism after the Enlightenment. It is no exaggeration to state that he pushes the critical demands of Socratic negativity as far as they can go, even as he decries
Socratic "rationalism" and the taste for dialectics as an underlying
cause of the decadence of modern European culture.[2]

The result is a paradoxical and often infuriating mix, but one
which has had the greatest influence on how subsequent theorists
approached the themes of philosophy, citizenship, and individual
integrity in the late modern age. We simply cannot imagine Max
Weber's demystifying approach to democracy, philosophy, and the
ideal of citizenship without Nietzsche. Indeed, Weber's reformula-

125

tion of the meaning of moral and intellectual integrity in the famous "Vocation" lectures of late 1917 and early 1919 begs to be read as a "disenchanted," quasi-Nietzschean response to the Socrates of the *Apology*.[3] Hannah Arendt's recovery of the Athenian ideal of citizenship likewise stands in Nietzsche's shadow, as does Leo Strauss's Platonic defense of the philosophical life. For all these thinkers Nietzsche's provocation is fundamental, altering the terrain on which the question of philosophical citizenship is raised.

Nietzsche's importance for my topic, however, goes well beyond the question of influence. Unfortunately, his relevance is all but obscured by his fondness for hyperbole and his notorious endorsement of a "rank order" of society. These enthusiasms led him to espouse what can only be described as incredibly stupid and repellent political views, which have been labeled, with some justification, a form of "aristocratic radicalism."[4] Yet most commentators would agree that there is far more to Nietzsche than his explicit—and generally appalling—political opinions. If we look beneath the hyperbolic surface, we find much in his thought that is relevant to the themes of moral individualism and philosophical citizenship; in particular, to the question of whether such citizenship is an enduring possibility in an age of nation-states and mass politics.[5]

In Nietzsche's view, modern conditions render the Socratic balance between philosophy and citizenship untenable. Ideology has replaced opinion as the medium of an increasingly demotic public life. Thus, in *Human, All Too Human* (1878) Nietzsche observes that the imperative of swaying the masses has compelled political parties to "transmute their principles into great frescoes of stupidity and to paint them thus upon the wall."[6] Under such conditions, moral and intellectual integrity are preserved (if they are preserved at all) only if the philosopher "steps a bit out of the way," remaining silent in a public realm where "too many people . . . are speaking." In *On the Genealogy of Morals* (1887) the point is sharpened considerably: philosophers must withdraw into a "desert," away from the concerns of the public and "everything to do with 'today.' "[7] Such a withdrawal—consistently adhered to by the mature Nietzsche—radicalizes the moderate alienation cultivated by both Socrates and Mill. The resulting stance is nicely captured by a trope Nietzsche used to characterize his genealogical project, namely, that of seeing things as if from another planet.[8]

The legacy of this intensified alienation is predictably ambiguous. By increasing critical distance, Nietzsche brings into view objects—such as the forgotten and bloody history behind moral concepts and practices—which previous thinkers had largely ignored.[9] This is crucial to the fight against moral dogmatism, which typically reifies *one* (culturally and historically determinant) set of virtues into morality *as such*. But such critical estrangement also breeds misanthropy, encouraging Nietzsche to condemn a wide range of modern political forms and movements as products of a "sick animal," man (whose transfiguration Nietzsche fantasizes about when he contemplates the coming age of *grosse Politik*).[10]

Nietzsche's dramatic insistence upon philosophical alienation, combined with his complex and clearly Oedipal relationship to Socrates, makes the interpretation of his thought on political and moral matters more than a little hazardous. For the most part, the scholarly literature has succumbed to one of two temptations. On the one hand, there are those who take Nietzsche at his (generally outrageous) word, viewing him as anti-Socrates, the avatar of irrationalism and a politics of apocalyptic immoderation.[11] On the other, there are scholars influenced by the pathbreaking (but increasingly disputed) work of Walter Kaufmann, who emphasized Nietzsche's individualism and continuity with many philosophers in the Western tradition. Such commentators tend to see more than a few parallels between Nietzsche and Socrates but little that is of *political* relevance.[12] A third, more surprising, alternative has recently emerged as theorists of the postmodern persuasion have attempted to reveal a democratic Nietzsche under the aristocratic veneer.[13]

These are all more or less plausible approaches to Nietzsche's thought. What I shall attempt in this chapter is to outline a Nietzsche who is significantly but ambivalently Socratic; one who is not, in the final analysis, reducible to either an apolitical individualist or a revolutionary conservative. It is my view that Nietzsche clearly has *moral* commitments; that these commitments trump the neoaristocratic perfectionism implied by his pursuit of "noble values"; that, finally, his ethical stance is at least partly harmonious with the moral individualism of both Socrates and Mill. Thus, while Nietzsche repeatedly pointed out the deleterious cultural effects of Socratic rationalism, he deployed his own brand of critical, dissolvent rationality in order to reveal the origins of *our* moral prejudices and dogmatism, and to combat the cultural forces which war against conscience, individuality, and independent judgment. Unconcerned with citizenship per se, his investigations reveal the underlying sources of conformism, dogmatism, and docility in Western culture. His thought is thus an essential touchstone for any minimally sophisticated understanding of what the "examined life" looks like in the late modern age.

At first glance this emphasis on Nietzsche's moral commitments might seem wildly off target. Since Nietzsche aims his critique not at *a* morality but at morality in general, it would obviously be safer to describe Nietzsche as an aesthetic rather than a moral individualist.[14] To do so, however, would be to diminish the stakes of his writing. Nietzsche's critique is driven not solely by the claims of self-fashioning, but by a clear sense of the demands of intellectual and moral integrity. That he has such commitments is not, as is often maintained, an exercise in blatant self-contradiction.[15] Nor does his concern for the cultivation of individuality and energy entail a specific (aristocratic or protofascistic) politics. The fact that Nietzsche sometimes wrote as if it did—as if his critique of the dominant morality was but the prologue to a culture-and-politics-transforming "transvaluation of values"—reveals more about the severity of the standard set by Socratic negativity than it does about the "inner logic" of Nietzsche's thought.

It is, of course, undeniable that Nietzsche rejected anything like the Socratic morality of abstention (which was too passive, reactive, and "slavish" for his taste). But it is equally undeniable that he gave new impetus to the Socratic vision of moral and intellectual integrity. Intellectual honesty—the uncovering of avoidable self-deception—is the Nietzschean virtue par excellence, the virtue he demands even more than "hardness towards oneself."[16] After *The Birth of Tragedy* (with its merciless but not very convincing critique of dialectics), Nietzsche adapts Socratic *elenchus* to his own ends, reformulating it as a mobile brand of perspectivism. The conventional view has been that Nietzsche's perspectivism dissolves the very possibility of "objective" truth by emphasizing personal, cultural, or ideological "points of view." As a result, perspectivism is often cast as the antithesis of Socratic *elenchus*, which is presented as a logical tool designed to eliminate misconceptions and reveal the singular (and rationally compelling) truth.[17] This, I shall argue, is a caricature of the actual relation between Nietzsche's method and that of Socrates.

There is more at stake here than epistemology or even philosophical method. It is through the idea of perspectivism that Nietzsche tries to preserve not only the philosophical life but the form of integrity specific to it. Intellectual integrity—for Nietzsche as for Socrates—is defined by the obligation to combat dogmatism of every kind. This includes the dogmatism of philosophers like Plato and Kant, who fall short of the Socratic ideal of radical (and open-ended) questioning.[18] Perspectivism is Nietzsche's main weapon in this fight, an intellectual method he employs to save moral philosophy from the fate of merely rationalizing pregiven values.

The fact that Nietzsche, unlike Socrates, could never be counted as a "citizen among citizens" underscores the distance he felt *honest* philosophical criticism must place between itself and the culture at large (which depends upon a tissue of fictions for its moral self-image—indeed, for its very survival). We should not be surprised, then, to encounter a form of cultural critique which denies the possibility of *philosophical* citizenship. One must make a choice: one can be a philosopher *or* a citizen, but not both, since the latter role presumes that the tissue of fictions—the *doxa*, ideology, or common sense of the day—remains intact. The conclusion that philosophy and citizenship are mutually exclusive—accepted, in one form or another, by Weber, Arendt, and Strauss—is hardly novel. What makes it disconcerting is realizing that it flows from Nietzsche's radicalization of Socrates' elenchic strategy. Whether this is a *consistent* conclusion remains to be seen.

Masters and Slaves: The Genealogy of Modern Democracy

However much Mill may have feared the tyranny of public opinion, he retained his enthusiasm for popular government, properly tempered and guided. One possible reconciliation of the Socratic lessons of *On Liberty* with *Representative Government*'s emphasis on civic virtue and participation was suggested in his reviews of George Grote's two great works, the eight-volume *History of Greece* and the six-volume *Plato and Other Companions of Socrates*. In his review of the first book, Mill sang the praises not only of Pericles but of the energetic and intellectually curious Athenian *demos*. In his review of the

129

second book, he stressed the importance of Socratic negativity in philosophy's struggle with the overwhelming power of "King Nomos." What emerges from these reviews is not obvious self-contradiction but an ideal of democracy in which it is possible to have both Pericles and Socrates, an energetic *demos* and an active (and widely dispersed) philosophical temper.

The prospect of a democracy in which the majority lacked political experience prompted Mill to turn from this ideal to a representative system in which both participation and competence have their place. Hence his dual emphasis on civic education for the many and the specialized knowledge of the few. These forces, combined with the stimulus provided by near absolute freedom of thought and discussion, were (in his view) the best counterforce to the gravitational pull of public opinion. Democracy need not be the unfettered reign of King Nomos—that is, of custom, convention, popular prejudice, or public mood. However despairing the more somber passages of *On Liberty* appear, Mill's Enlightenment faith in education and progress tempered his sense of the inertness of the "compact mass" of public opinion.

This faith is totally absent in Nietzsche, and not simply because he shared philosophy's traditional contempt for the unphilosophical masses.[19] What makes Nietzsche's insistence on the *impossibility* of philosophical citizenship worth taking seriously is his tracing of the roots of *doxa* and conventional morality into the deepest recesses of our linguistic and cultural being. In this section I want to examine Nietzsche's argument on this score in order to show how it undergirds his critical view of democratic politics (discussed in the third section of this chapter).

In one of the most famous—not to say infamous—passages of *Beyond Good and Evil* (1886) Nietzsche declares:

> *Morality in Europe today is herd animal morality*—in other words, as we understand it, merely *one* type of human morality beside which, before which, and after which many other types, above all *higher* moralities, are, or ought to be, possible. But this morality resists such a "possibility," such an "ought," with all its power: it says stubbornly and inexorably, "I am morality itself, and nothing besides is morality." Indeed, with the help of a religion which indulged and flattered the most sublime herd-animal desires, we have reached the point where we find even in political and social institutions an ever more visible expression of this morality: the *democratic* movement is the heir of the Christian movement.[20]

This passage contains all the brilliance and brutal telescoping implicit in Nietzsche's critical stance of radical alienation. The struggle for democratization is lifted out of its immediate historical context and placed within a sweeping world-historical drama, which Nietzsche dubs "the slave revolt in morality." What began with the Jewish "inversion" of "noble" Roman values reaches its apogee in the French Revolution and the triumph of the "democratic" movement, in which the values of "sick" herd animals come to dominate the moral and political spheres of secular modernity.[21] In this view, the Enlightenment figures not as one the great liberators of humanity (as in Mill) but rather as a destructive force which removes the last cultural obstacles to the triumph of the "herd values" of Christian morality. These values now take the secularized form of an egalitarian morality of rights which destroys the "rank order" of society.

As violent caricatures go, this is not an entirely bad one. Indeed, many liberals would agree with the gist of Nietzsche's story (minus, of course, his terminology of "slavish" and "noble"). The democratic movement *is* the heir of the Christian movement, one which strips its moral universalism of the dross of sectarianism, otherworldliness, and superstition. But in the passage just cited, Nietzsche is not merely substituting a negative sign for what is usually presented as a narrative of progress. He is also drawing an explicit connection between Christianity's pretense to provide a code of conduct which is exhaustive and applicable to everyone and democracy's institutional structure and underlying values. The problem, in other words, is not that—or not simply that—democracy is Christianity's "heir," upholding values that have a religious or creedal origin. It is, rather, that democracy reproduces (in altered, secularized form) values that are *fundamentally* passive and conformist in nature, elevating them to the status of a universal code of conduct for society.

We have already seen a similar indictment of the spirit of Christianity in Mill. The latter, however, left the connection between Christianity and the democratic "tyranny of the majority" more or less implicit. Nietzsche, being neither a Christian nor a democrat, felt no need to practice Mill's restraint. The connection is not only made explicit but is dwelled upon. We thus encounter in Nietzsche questions which Mill's analysis glossed over. We may state these as follows: To what extent does modern democracy reproduce the narrowness of the Christian conception of the virtues? To what extent is its idea and practice of freedom held hostage by this narrow conception? As I have suggested, Nietzsche's answer to both these questions is "almost totally."

This can be seen in section 199 of *Beyond Good and Evil*. Here Nietzsche stresses how virtually *every* morality thus far has cultivated "the herd instinct of obedience" and made the need for an unconditional command ("thou shalt") the basis of the average man's conscience. Christianity builds its table of virtues on this need to obey, giving it such a universal and seductive form that even those who command in life feel they must "pose as the executors of more ancient or higher commands" lest they be overwhelmed by a bad conscience. When this table of virtues is translated into the idiom of the "democratic movement," the new morality brings forth "the herd man of Europe today," one who is "tame, easy to get along with, and useful to the herd," one whose virtues are "public spirit, benevolence, consideration, industriousness, moderation, modesty, indulgence, and pity."[22] Considered from the standpoint of "the natural history of morals," the democratic movement continues the Christian project of creating docile subjects fit, above all, for obedience. Whatever additional freedom the struggle for "liberal institutions" creates disappears as soon as these institutions are attained.[23]

Stated so compactly, Nietzsche's remarks on the connection between the Christian morality and the democratic "herd man" are merely provocative (and not very convincing). It is only when we turn to the book he wrote directly after *Beyond Good and Evil* that we get some sense of the argument behind them, and the reasons why Nietzsche felt justified in suggesting such a tight link between modern political beliefs and the "ascetic ideals" erected by early Christianity.[24]

In the second essay of the *Genealogy*, Nietzsche describes how the prehistoric "morality of mores"—the morality of custom embodied in often gruesome rituals, tortures, and punishments—eventually transformed the flighty and forgetful human animal into a moral subject, burning in a will and a memory where there had previously been little more than instinct and forgetfulness. Allowing himself an uncharacteristically teleological moment, Nietzsche writes:

> If we place ourselves at the end of this tremendous process, where the tree at last brings forth fruit, where society and the morality of custom at last reveal *what* they have simply been the means to: then we discover

that the ripest fruit is the *sovereign individual*, like only to himself, liberated again from morality of custom, autonomous and supramoral (for "autonomous" and "moral" are mutually exclusive), in short, the man who has his own independent, protracted will and the *right to make promises*—and in him a proud consciousness, quivering in every muscle, of *what* has at length been achieved and become flesh in him, a consciousness of his own power and freedom, a sensation of mankind come to completion. . . . The proud awareness of the extraordinary privilege of *responsibility*, the consciousness of this rare freedom, this power over oneself and over fate, has in his case penetrated to the profoundest depths and become instinct, the dominating instinct. What will he call this dominating instinct, supposing he feels the need to give it a name? The answer is beyond doubt: this sovereign man calls it his *conscience*.[25]

This is an extraordinary and rightly famous passage. In it Nietzsche outlines his conception of the "responsible individual"—autonomous and supramoral—as the ultimate, healthy, and altogether admirable product of what otherwise seems a cruel and repellent process stretching over thousands of years. This individual has not only mastered the instinctual aggression of Nietzsche's "noble" races (the "blond beast" of essay 1 of the *Genealogy*) but also curbs the "instinct for obedience" cultivated by the morality of mores. He is autonomous in the sense that his self-control enables him to take full responsibility for his conduct—something the Kantian definition of autonomy had promised but failed to deliver. (In *The Groundwork of the Metaphysics of Morals* and *The Critique of Practical Reason* Kant makes submission to duties derived from formal reason the sole legitimate content of "self-legislation.")[26]

It is important to see that when Nietzsche qualifies the phrase "autonomous and supramoral" by noting that "autonomy" and "morality" are (in his usage) mutually exclusive, he is not saying that the "sovereign individual" is *beyond* morality in the broad sense of the word. Rather, he is saying that this individual—the *conscientious* individual who has not merely internalized authority—is beyond custom and *what has typically passed for morality* in the recorded history of the West. Such "so-called morality" has been creed-governed, concerned first and foremost with obedience, with weakening or "taming" the individual and curbing those passions and energies which might disrupt society.[27] Even in secularized form, "so-called morality" continues this attack, erecting external authorities (such as Reason or Nature) to take the place of tradition, creed, or God.

For Nietzsche the "sovereign individual" is responsible to no such authorities, only to himself. Indeed, his pride and conscientiousness forbid him from equating morality with obedience to commands, whatever their source. From the perspective of such an agent—the mature moral subject—much of what has passed for morality will appear (quite rightly) as the source of the grossest immorality. This is especially so when we take account of the brutality and stupidity that has animated the project of "making mankind moral" over the centuries.[28] Nietzsche's fundamental point is that the consistent identification of *morality* with *obedience to authority* has stunted our moral sense, making it deeply conformist and severing it from the claims of intellectual honesty.

In all this Nietzsche is far closer to Socrates and Mill than is commonly allowed.[29] His quarrel with "so-called morality" is not that it demands self-control or involves duties toward others. (It is hard to think of a fiercer opponent of "letting oneself go" than Nietzsche.) Rather, it concerns the habitual identification of morality with authority, a reflex originally installed by the "morality of mores" and reinforced by centuries of creedal morality. The result is not only a profound deformation of the moral sense but a virtual prohibition against criticism of our understanding of fundamental moral values. As Nietzsche put it in the 1886 preface to *Daybreak*:

> Hitherto, the subject reflected on least adequately has been good and evil: it was too dangerous a subject. Conscience, reputation, Hell, sometimes even the police have permitted and continue to permit no impartiality; in the presence of morality, as in the face of any authority, one is not *allowed* to think, far less to express an opinion: here one has to—*obey*! As long as the world has existed no authority has yet been willing to let itself become the object of criticism; and to criticize morality itself, to regard morality as a problem, as problematic: what, has that not been—*is* that not—immoral?[30]

One might think that such a "positive" authority would be a prime target for philosophical criticism. In fact, Nietzsche claims that morality has very little to fear from philosophers since it possesses the "art of enchantment"—the capacity to paralyze critical thought by means of its "inspiring" qualities. Nietzsche calls morality the "Circe of the philosophers" precisely because of this intoxicating (and disarming) effect.

If the authority of the "moral interpretation" affected only philosophers, it would be a curious instance of bad faith and nothing more. The point is that the philosophers' abdication of intellectual integrity mirrors that of society at large, which remains curiously immune (not to say hostile) to questioning the dominant interpretation of the virtues. In a very Socratic, very Millian passage from *The Gay Science*, Nietzsche writes:

> I keep having the same experience and keep resisting it every time. I do not want to believe it although it is palpable: *the great majority of people lacks an intellectual conscience*. Indeed, it has often seemed to me as if anyone calling for an intellectual conscience were as lonely in the most densely populated cities as if he were in a desert. Everybody looks at you with strange eyes and goes right on handling his scales, calling this good and that evil. Nobody even blushes when you intimate that their weights are underweight; nor do people feel outraged; they merely laugh at your doubts. I mean: *the great majority of people* does not consider it contemptible to believe this or that and to live accordingly, without first having given themselves an account of the final and most certain reasons pro and con, and without even troubling themselves about such reasons afterward: the most gifted men and the noblest women still belong to this "great majority."[31]

What does this have to do with the "sovereign individual," autonomous and supramoral, of the *Genealogy*? The answer is that this individual possesses a conscience which is not merely "formal" or other-directed, a conscience which does not merely seize upon "whatever is shouted into its ears by someone who issues commands—parents, teachers, laws, class prejudices, public opinions."[32] The conscience of the sovereign individual—his "dominating instinct"—is, like Socrates' *daimon*, fully independent. It values self-agreement over agreement with others.[33] It says "no" to conduct which falls below the standard set by the individual's will and self-control. Where this conscience arises, morality ceases to be identified with external authority—or, indeed, with the internalization of externally given commands. Yet, as Nietzsche's "vivisection" of morality makes all too clear, such an individual is the rarest of finds. Instead of the "sovereign individual," the "tremendous labor of the morality of mores" actually gives birth to something botched, herd-like, and desperately in need of commands. The only thing *this* moral subject has been emancipated from is the need to ever give an account of its most fiercely held values.

What has happened? What has gone wrong in the transition from the morality of mores to a more mature moral culture, one less hostile to individual conscience and intellect? Nietzsche's answer is that we—or at least the great majority of us—have become stalled at an intermediate stage of moral development, a stage midway between the tyranny of tradition and autonomous individuality. This is the stage of guilt, bad conscience, and ascetic ideals; a stage which roughly, coincides, with "so-called morality," or morality considered as an historical, epochal phenomenon.[34] Nietzsche leaves no doubt as to how he views this stage: it is an *illness*. Those who have internalized "moral" values are, in a very real sense, *sick*, self-torturers who lack the most rudimentary psychic health. Even though Nietzsche calls this stage an illness, "just as pregnancy is an illness," the fact remains that a *healthy* version of the responsible agent is by no means the inevitable result. The "pregnancy"—two thousand years of "moral" values—may well not bear the fruit Nietzsche hopes for.[35]

Where does this "illness," this detour on the way to the sovereign individual, come from? What drives it to such unimaginable heights of moralized self-loathing (in the guise of "sin" and "sinfulness")?

Answering these questions leads Nietzsche to consider the primordial origins of organized political life. He argues that the pervasive feeling of guilt, of "bad conscience," did not come into the world by the avenue of punishments for crime or social transgressions. Nor did it have anything to do with "original sin" or the fact that human beings have drives which make them sensual, proud, cruel, or ambitious.[36] Rather, the "heaviness" that comes to blanket the earth first emerges with one of the most fundamental changes in human life: the abrupt transition from nomadic, familial, or tribal forms of social life to bounded, territorially specific political forms. "Bad conscience" arose when *the state* first appears, when "some pack of blond beasts of prey, a conqueror and master race which, organized for war and with the ability to organize, unhesitatingly lays its terrible claws upon a populace perhaps tremendously superior in numbers but still formless and nomad."[37]

But how does the appearance of the state give rise to pervasive feelings of guilt in ordinary human beings? Nietzsche's answer derives from his theory of drives, from the thesis that we are nothing other than our desires and passions, and that all higher faculties (such as reason) are but spiritualized forms of more basic drives, the economy of which is strictly regulated.[38] If the quantum of energy produced by an individual's drives is cumulative, what happens when this individual is placed in an environment where the discharge of this energy is suddenly blocked? The answer can only be that it is turned back upon the individual. Robbed of an external outlet for his or her more aggressive instincts and passions, the individual's "will to power" is turned inward. With the rise of the primordial state, the great majority of persons suddenly find themselves in precisely this position, deprived of any external outlet. Yet the drives and passions continue to make their demands.[39]

The state's prohibition against the discharge of aggressive drives and passions creates not only the feeling of heaviness or suffering but an ever deeper and more complex psychological world in which frustrated drives seek their "subterranean gratifications." The appearance of the state thus coincides with what Nietzsche calls "the internalization of man," with the development of a soul or psyche where previously there had reigned something akin to sheer animal instinct. The appearance of the state and its "hammer blows" against the animal instinct for freedom is thus the beginning of man's suffering of himself, a suffering born of the "forcible sundering from his animal past."[40]

Nietzsche, of course, does not *bemoan* this fact of primordial human history. It is, after all, the precondition of an "inner world" (the *soul*) and the growth of all culture and higher forms of individuality.[41] The key question is how human beings cope with their new condition and the suffering it causes them. This suffering is exacerbated by the fact that most human beings, while driven by pride and a yearning for distinction, are (according to Nietzsche) incapable of the energy, discipline, and sheer strength necessary to distinguish themselves. They are unable to take the raw material of their drives and inherited characteristics and transform them into something unique and beautiful.[42] In other words, they lack the energy necessary for *genuine* individuality. The majority suffer from this inability and, as a result, are resentful of anyone who can fashion a unique or distinctive life.[43]

According to Nietzsche, the suffering born of this confinement, incapacity, and resentment soon reaches an unbearable pitch. The experience of a comprehensive frustration of drives threatens to overwhelm those who suffer from it. They become so "sick" as a result of their frustration and lack of freedom that they begin to feel a "disgust with life," a revulsion which threatens their very will to live. It is at this point in his narrative of our moral prehistory that Nietzsche introduces one of his most famous "ideal types," the ascetic priest.

The ascetic priest is a figure who emerges "in almost every age," who stands for a moral ideal that says "no" to life and existence as such. His "monstrous" mode of valuation "treats life as a wrong road," locating the origin of value in an otherworldly, transcendental source.[44] Yet despite his comprehensive "no" to *this* world and *this* life, the ascetic priest (who "prospers everywhere") serves a very worldly function. He is both shepherd and physician to the "sick herd," preserving them from their enemies (the healthy) and, even more important, from themselves.[45] He does this by providing the sick with a reason for their pain and a *meaning* behind their suffering. This is accomplished by *moralizing* their feelings of discomfort, by telling the "sick" that *they themselves* are responsible for their suffering. Their discomfort is a sign of guilt and the punishment "sinful" human beings bring upon themselves for having the drives they do.[46]

The ascetic priest's explanation is, of course, a manifest lie.[47] How could we be *responsible* for our own nature, for the very drives that make us human? Nevertheless, this lie has the unexpected effect of strengthening the will to live of the "physiologically depressed." By slandering life, sensuality, aggression, the desire for distinction, and so forth, the ascetic priest manages to alter the direction of the *ressentiment* of the sick, turning it back upon themselves "for the purpose of self-discipline, self-surveillance, and self-overcoming."[48] He transforms invalids into "sinners," creating a community where there had previously been a collection of "weak, sickly, disgruntled individuals." This reinterpretation of suffering "as guilt, fear, and punishment" overcomes "the old depression, heaviness, and weariness," giving the sick a purpose, a project, and a future in the shape of creedal discipline and conformity.[49] It consolidates their shattered will to power. Thus, the contradiction of "life against life" manifest in the ascetic ideal is merely apparent. In fact, this ideal "springs from the protective instinct of a degenerating life"; it is "an artifice for the preservation of life."[50]

Nietzsche's description of the role of the ascetic priest is of great importance for understanding how otherworldly values predicated on self-denial actually serve a form of life, creating a particular kind of culture (one obsessed with obedience, equality, and conformity) in the process. It also helps us see how these values—so-called *moral* values—figure in the struggle between different forms of life and culture. For the table of values provided by the ascetic priest is not only a "medication" designed to alleviate suffering; it is also a *weapon* in the struggle against other moralities, other forms of life—the "healthy" most of all. Such individuals are the other great threat to the "herd": they threaten to dominate it, all the while inciting unbearable levels of envy and resentment.[51] Thus, the ascetic priest—the shepherd, physician, and defender of the "sick herd"— must find a way of rendering the healthy, "noble" type of man harmless. This can be done only if the healthy are somehow tricked into abandoning their own values, if they come to see their health—their very capacity to distinguish themselves—as something guilty and blameworthy.

This brings us to some of the issues addressed in the first essay of the *Genealogy*, and to the question of Nietzsche's paradoxical view of Socrates as a kind of ascetic priest.

The first essay of the *Genealogy* is Nietzsche's attempt to demonstrate that the moral categories of good and evil—which we take to be natural and universal—in fact arose historically as a reaction to the reigning aristocratic values of good and bad. Originally, Nietzsche claims, it was the nobles who possessed the "right to give names," who derived fundamental values from their characteristic way of life, patterning a table of virtues upon their own competitive, individualizing capacities and energies. Thus the value judgment "good" did not—initially at least—refer to nonegoistic actions but rather to the power, activity, and individuality of the noble. This was in contradistinction to all that was "common and plebeian." The noble took it for granted that he and those like him were "good," while the common man—the base, passive, non-noble man—was "bad."[52]

The couplet good and evil reverses these aristocratic values, transforming the "good man" of the noble valuation into the evil or malevolent man, while elevating the common man (the man incapable of competitive distinction or the life of action) to the rank of good. This reversal, Nietzsche declares, is an act of "spiritual revenge," the fruit of the intense but impotent hatred the common man feels

139

for the noble. Through it, new ideals and a new moral landscape are created, one tailored to the cultivation and preservation of the passive, ordinary man. This is the "slave revolt in morality," the dramatic and thoroughgoing inversion of the noble ideals of the Greeks and Romans.[53]

Nietzsche's infamous identification of the Jews as the initiators of the "slave revolt" should not blind us to the nuances of his (seemingly unsubtle) contrast between "noble" and "slave" moralities. The former is characterized by self-affirmation: "The noble human being honors himself as one who is powerful, also as one who has power over himself, who knows how to speak and be silent, who delights in being severe and hard with himself and respects all severity and hardness."[54] His virtues—centering on power, ability, and the active life—celebrate the distinction which individuals of great energy and discipline are able to win for themselves. For Nietzsche the noble and the active life are identical, so much so that this morality of *active* virtue fails to make any strong distinction between a doer and his deeds: one is what one does. The noble is proudly conscious of the fact that *his* virtues are available only to those like himself, to individuals who also possess great energy, power, and courage. He prizes his enemies because they enable him to demonstrate the full extent of his virtue and ability.

Slave morality, in contrast, preserves and protects those who know only toil, not action. As was noted earlier, it begins by demonizing the noble man and his defining characteristics: power, activity, sensuality, pride, and a healthy egoism. It is only after saying "no" to these aristocratic virtues that slave morality begins to create its own table of values. These values, however, are essentially inversions of noble values. As such, they are marked by the constraints of their birth. Slave morality cannot be centered on action and the active manifestation of virtue, nor can it preach individuality to those incapable (because of lack of energy, "physiological depression," or external constraint) of achieving it. Somehow the ascetic priest must make virtues out of passivity, humility, and the lack of energy or strong affect.

How is this achieved? The beginnings of an answer may be found in Nietzsche's famous parable of the lamb and the bird of prey (*GM*, essay 1, sec. 13), which displays the basic (reactive) logic behind the "slavish" inversion of the noble value "good":

140

That lambs dislike great birds of prey does not seem strange: only it gives no ground for reproaching these birds of prey for bearing off little lambs. And if the lambs say among themselves "these birds of prey are evil; and whoever is least like a bird of prey, but rather its opposite, a lamb—would he not be good?" there is no reason to find fault with this institution of an ideal, except perhaps that the birds of prey might view it a little ironically and say: "*we* don't dislike them at all, these good little lambs; we even love them: nothing is more tasty than a tender lamb."

Having (in characteristic fashion) aligned himself with the "masterly" predator, Nietzsche goes on to gloss his own parable. His point is to relativize our notions of moral agency and responsibility by questioning the grammar of action on which they rest:

To demand of strength that it should *not* express itself as strength, that it should *not* be a desire to overcome, a desire to throw down, a desire to become master, a thirst for enemies and resistances and triumphs, is just as absurd as to demand of weakness that it should express itself as strength. A quantum of force is equivalent to a quantum of drive, will, effect—more, it is nothing other that precisely this very driving, willing, effecting, and only owing to the seduction of language (and of the fundamental errors of reason that are petrified in it) which conceives and misconceives all effects as conditioned by something that causes effects, by a "subject," can it appear otherwise. For just as the popular mind separates the lightning from its flash and takes the latter for an *action*, for the operation of a subject called lightning, so popular morality also separates strength from expressions of strength, as if there were a neutral substratum behind the strong man, which was *free* to express strength or not to do so. But there is no such substratum; there is no "being" behind doing, effecting, becoming; "the doer" is merely a fiction added to the deed—the deed is everything.

The concluding pronouncement of this passage is too categorical. Given Nietzsche's general view about how our conceptual schemes shape rather than correspond to the world, calling the agent a "fiction" in the pejorative sense is not something he's really entitled to do.[55] Nevertheless, his general point is an important one. If there is no *natural* grammar of action or responsibility, and if (as Nietzsche argues) the fundamental purpose of any morality is to provide conditions favorable to a particular form of life, then the sharp distinction between doer and deed our moral epistemology takes for granted must be seen as serving a particular *type* of morality and, indeed, a particular *type* of human being. In fact, as Nietzsche suggests, the reified version of this distinction has actually been a weapon in the struggle between noble and slavish moralities.[56]

In "noble" moralities, Nietzsche maintains, one is what one does: individual identity is inseparable from the manifestation of virtues in action. In "slavish" moralities, conversely, who one is as a *moral* agent ceases to have any intrinsic connection to the active life. The morally responsible self (the "subject" or "soul") is assumed to precede all its actions or "effects." This self occupies a different (independent and superior) ontological plane, one which enables it to stand apart from the world and action in it.[57] The *inner* life—one's motivations, intentions, and psyche—becomes the primary arena and object of moral evaluation. As a result, the "slave" can be deemed moral or virtuous *without doing anything*. Indeed, the *abstention* from action—from anything that smacks of worldliness, interest, or power—is now seen as a great virtue. Impotence—the lack of power to act—ceases to be a reason for self-contempt. It becomes, instead, a sign of the slave's "freedom," his superior virtue compared to the master.[58]

Nietzsche's point in this parable is not to praise the predatory behavior of the "nobles" (although he certainly doesn't condemn it, either), but rather to indicate how our notions of agency and responsibility reflect a specific historical attempt to defame the life of action—the life of the "masters." A "slavish" hostility to action and agonistic individuality (the individuality born of great ability, energy, and *virtu*) is, Nietzsche claims, built into our very grammar of moral evaluation, one we suppose to be "natural." I should stress that for Nietzsche the travesty of this moral epistemology is not that it gets the actor's relationship to the world or his deeds *wrong* but that it underwrites a particular code of conduct, making it seem applicable to all. Everyone is to be rendered morally accountable in terms of this code, which is to say that everyone is to be rendered tame, self-surveilling, and useful to the herd. As Nietzsche argues in the *Genealogy*, the worst thing is not the existence of the "sick" but the fact that *their* morality comes to infect the "healthy"—the active, healthy, and individualistic (essay 3, sec. 14). The nobles come to internalize the "slavish" code of conduct, thereby succumbing to "the will to power of the weakest." As was suggested earlier, the "ascetic priest" plays a key role in this "corruption," mostly through his ability to seduce with a religious (ascetic) interpretation of existence. The seeming naturalness of the actor/act distinction is, however, another powerful weapon in his armory.

Surprisingly enough, Nietzsche casts Socrates in the role of such a corrupting ascetic priest, one who masterfully deploys the moral epistemology of the "slave" in order to convince the Athenians that their restless activity is blameworthy; that their deeds have brought not glory but shame. By privileging interiority and conscience, Socrates deprives the Periclean virtues of their life-sustaining atmosphere. He dissolves the protective moral horizon which had fostered Athenian energy and greatness. In "The Problem of Socrates" (from *The Twilight of the Idols*) Nietzsche describes how the "plebeian" Socrates seduces young nobles with his dialectic, causing them to turn away from the active life toward a "decadent" contemplative one. "With Socrates Greek taste undergoes a change in favor of dialectics: what is really happening when that happens? It is above all the defeat of a *nobler* taste; with dialectics, the rabble gets on top."[59]

The Socrates we encounter in *Twilight of the Idols* is an archrationalist, one who offers reason and logic as crutches to those who are no longer capable of an assured self-control or calm mastery of the passions. He is a physician to declining *aristocratic* life, and as such less a questioner than a dogmatist offering novel means for fending off imminent collapse: "Rationality was at that time divined as a *savior*; neither Socrates nor his 'invalids' were free to be rational or not, as they wished—it was *de rigueur*, it was their last expedient. . . . [O]ne was in peril, one had only *one* choice: either to perish or—be *absurdly rational*."[60] Socrates' role as an ascetic priest ministering to aristocrats who could no longer trust their own instincts makes him the great symbol of the decline of the Greeks' agonal energies.

When we contrast Nietzsche's characterization of Socrates (and Greek philosophy generally) as *decadent* with his approving citation of Thucydides as "the last manifestation of that strong, stern, hard matter-of-factness instinctive to the older Hellenes," we seem to have all the evidence we need to convict Nietzsche—not of championing evil, to be sure, but of espousing an agonistic conception of individuality, one which reserves precious little room for reflection, self-examination, and radical (philosophical) questioning.[61] Nietzsche leaves us confronting not the conflict between the citizen and the philosopher but that between the active, heroic individual and the philosopher.

If we link these aspects to Nietzsche's earlier praise of life and action-sustaining illusions in *The Birth of Tragedy* and the *Untimely Meditations*, we seem to arrive at a position diametrically opposed to that of Socrates; one in which "slowing people down" and the morality of abstention appear as symptoms of a "declining" life. One half of the rhetoric of the *Genealogy*—that of disillusion—gives way to the other—the agitated (and agitating) rhetoric of life, of *Lebensphilosophie*. This rhetoric is almost entirely unconcerned with the demands of "the intellectual conscience" since it treats illusions as a necessary dimension of practical life.

Viewed from *this* perspective, the only thing that really matters is whether a given form of life is healthy or sick, active or reactive. The fact that both healthy and sick forms require protective illusions—that they both foist simplifying fictions upon the world and the self in order to better cope with the threat of chaos and disintegration—is no objection. Rather, it underlines the necessity of "untruth" as a condition of life.[62] Thus, the "noble" Greeks upheld a vision in which self and action were inseparable, while the decadent Greeks fell under the spell of the moral epistemology of the slave.[63] In each case a particular form of life—one vital, the other declining—is preserved by a moral vocabulary which worked *for* it, just as the "sick herd" is preserved by the moral vocabulary of Christianity, which does its best to take the self out of the world.

Is this insistence upon the necessity of illusion the chief legacy of Nietzsche's genealogical investigations? Is the "sovereign individual" a chimera, a stage of moral development that is never reached, except perhaps in the fantastic form of the *Übermensch*? Instead of deepening the Socratic connection between intellectual and moral integrity, does Nietzsche, in fact, *combat* it by urging disillusion for "free thinkers" like himself but otherwise insisting upon the necessity of a closed horizon for both the "healthy" *and* the "sick"?[64]

The answers to these questions take us to the heart of Nietzsche's conception of modern democracy, which he views as the antiindividualist culture par excellence. Rather than advancing the project of autonomy, in Nietzsche's view liberal democracy retards it, giving institutional form to the "bad conscience" and *ressentiment* of the "herd." It secretes an ethos, a morality, a culture which brooks no opposition. Nietzsche's alternative to democratic institutions and the "tyranny of public opinion" *does* preserve a space for both philosophy and moral integrity, but only (apparently) at the expense of citizenship. Insofar as he is able to conceive a political role for a "philosophy of the future," it seems far from a Socratic, disillusioning one. It is, rather, disturbingly reminiscent of Plato for reasons I will shortly discuss.

DEMOCRACY, ARISTOCRATISM, AND INDIVIDUALISM

Beyond Good and Evil is the text in which Nietzsche clearly seems to endorse an antiegalitarian, antidemocratic politics, the better to promote what he calls "the enhancement of man." At the beginning of part 9 ("What Is Noble"), he expresses his evident faith in the superiority of aristocratic values, as well as his (apparent) conviction that the preservation of inequality is the key to genuine human progress:

> Every enhancement of the type "man" has so far been the work of an aristocratic society—and it will be so again and again—a society that believes in the long ladder of an order of rank and differences in value between man and man, and that needs slavery in some sense or other. Without that *pathos of distance* which grows out of the ingrained difference between strata—when the ruling caste constantly looks afar and looks down upon subjects and instruments and just as constantly practices obedience and command, keeping down and keeping at a distance— that other, more mysterious pathos could not have grown up either— the craving for an ever new widening of distances within the soul itself, the development of ever higher, rarer, more remote, further-stretching comprehensive states—in brief, simply the enhancement of the type "man," the continual "self-overcoming of man," to use a moral formula in a supra-moral sense.[65]

Admittedly there are ambiguities in this passage ("slavery in some sense or other"), but its general tendency is clear enough. When Nietzsche goes on, in the next section, to define a "healthy" aristocracy as one which does not see itself as a mere part of the social whole but rather as its "meaning and highest justification"—one which accepts, "with good conscience," the sacrifice of "untold

145

human beings who, *for its sake*, must be reduced and lowered to incomplete human beings, to slaves, to instruments"—we seem to be in the presence of a view which is (morally speaking) at least as distasteful as Aristotle's defense of "natural" slavery in book 1 of the *Politics*. In the opinion of both philosophers, the performance of virtuous activities presupposes a leisured elite and the presence of human "tools" to take care of more banal activities. A higher, non-utilitarian sensibility can flourish only where the tasks of labor and subsistence are performed by others.[66]

From this perspective, the rise of a democratic order signals the debasement of all values. The culture of democratic egalitarianism—in which no human life is worth more, in moral terms, than another—reduces the entire realm of value to its lowest common denominator (the average person, who is completely ignorant of "rarer, more remote, further-stretching states"). The equality of persons demands the fungibility of values. Moreover, it promotes a set of virtues tailored to the timidity, lack of vitality, and general conformity of the "herd animal." Hence Nietzsche's claim that "to us, the democratic movement is not only a form of decay of political organization but a form of the decay, namely, the diminution of man, of making him mediocre and lowering his value."[67]

Left at this, Nietzsche seems to offer us a simple formula. Aristocracy leads (or can lead) to the enhancement of man, democracy to his diminution—to "the dwarf animal of equal rights and equal claims." But Nietzsche also acknowledges an irrefutable fact, namely, the triumph of the "slave revolt in morality" in the form of modern democracy. Aristocratic values have been overthrown.[68] Thus, in a famous passage from *Beyond Good and Evil* Nietzsche pins his hopes on the "philosophers of the future." As "commanders and legislators," *they* will create the values which will overturn the "nonsense" of the "greatest number." Armed with this revaluation, they will mercilessly stamp neoaristocratic values on the plastic mass of a decadent Europe (which will have been softened up by "a new warlike age" and the "fight for the dominion of the earth").[69]

This is one widely circulated reading of *Beyond Good and Evil*. However, if we tie Nietzsche's criticisms of democratic culture to the basic argument of the *Genealogy*, we see that things aren't so simple. Additional complications arise when we take account of Nietzsche's earlier comments on democracy in *Human, All Too Human* (1878) and *The Wanderer and His Shadow* (1880).

As I noted in the second section of this chapter, Nietzsche's primary objection to "slave morality" is that it presents *one* code of conduct and *one* table of values as binding for all. At the heart of the "slave revolt" is the most radical possible denial of moral pluralism, that is, of the idea that different codes of conduct might apply to different spheres of life or different types of individuals or cultures.[70] Now, "moral pluralism" can mean many things, from the simple recognition that values often conflict and that codes of conduct are multiple to more robust assertions of cultural relativism. Nietzsche's championing of the active virtues of the Greeks, Romans, and the Renaissance reveals him to be no relativist, while his insistence that there can be "other, higher moralities" shows him to be a moral pluralist in the broad sense (as is anyone who disputes the idea of a single, positive code of conduct which is identical with morality itself). In Nietzsche's view, the denial of moral pluralism provides the strategic cornerstone for slave morality's victory over "noble" values. Presenting itself as fact rather than interpretation, slave morality pulls the rug out from under all other competing tables of values, creating a strong internal link between intolerance and the very concept of morality.[71]

Nietzsche's tracing (in the *Genealogy*) of the stratagems by which slave morality achieves its victory provides the background to his claim (in *Beyond Good and Evil*, sec. 202) that the European morality of his day has turned a blind eye to other "higher" moralities, insisting that "I am morality itself, and nothing besides is morality." What it is absolutely essential to note is that the ancient and contemporary forms of "slave morality" which Nietzsche attacks are *positive* or "thick" codes of conduct, derived from a distinct table of virtues. Thus, in the early (Christian) phase of the "slave revolt," meekness, obedience, pity, and all things nonegoistic are "lied" into virtues, while in the later (democratic) phase, a parallel set of values (including public spirit, benevolence, consideration, industriousness, moderation) is presented as obligatory for all.[72] In other words, what Nietzsche objects to is not the idea that any given society has a dominant morality. (He could hardly do that, given his broadly anthropological conception of the function moralities play in different cultures.) Rather, it is those instances in which the dominant form totally monopolizes cultural and psychic space, making society and the individuals who constitute it slaves to a single (dogmatic) conception of virtue.

This suggests that, appearances to the contrary, Nietzsche actually makes a distinction between politics and culture, as well as between political institutions and the type of individuals who depend on them. The contrary assumption—that politics and culture so overlap that they are ultimately indistinguishable, and that individual citizens are emanations of the laws and institutions in which they are brought up—might, for purposes of shorthand, be called the Platonic conception. Nietzsche *seems* to adopt it when he states that "the democratic movement is not only a form of the decay of political organization but a form of the decay . . . of man," and also when he refers to democratic political and social institutions as "the ever more visible expression of this [herd animal] morality."[73] But consider the following passage from *The Wanderer and His Shadow*:

> The democratization of Europe is irresistible. . . . Nonetheless, it is possible that posterity will one day laugh at this anxiety of ours and regard the democratic work of succession of generations somewhat as we regard the building of stone dams and protective walls—as an activity that necessarily gets a lot of dust on clothes and faces and no doubt also unavoidably makes the workers a little purblind and stupid; but who would wish such a work undone on that account! The democratization of Europe is, it seems, a link in the chain of those tremendous *prophylactic measures* which are the conception of modern times and through which we separate ourselves from the Middle Ages. Only now is the age of cyclopean building! We finally secure the foundations, so that the whole future can safely build upon them! We make it henceforth impossible for the fruitful fields of culture again to be destroyed overnight by wild and senseless torrents! We erect stone dams and protective walls against barbarians, against pestilences, against *physical and spiritual enslavement*![74]

This is not merely a Tocquevillian presentiment of the inevitability of democracy; it is, in fact, an appreciation of the cultural possibilities opened by modern (constitutional) democracy's distinctions between legality and morality, and between the public and private realms. These distinctions, and their institutional articulation, are the "prophylactic measures" by which the moderns separate themselves from the "physical and spiritual enslavement" characteristic of the Middle (and other, more "organic") Ages. Like Marx in his *Contribution to the Critique of Hegel's "Philosophy of Right,"* Nietzsche equates modern democracy with the secularization and relative autonomy of the political sphere, that is, with the liberation of the spheres of culture and private life from the tyranny of moral legislators (such as the Church or the Prussian "Christian Nation").[75] It is, in other words, not merely that one cannot go back ("no one is free to be a crab.").[76] More than that, one would have to be mad to want to.

This modernist appreciation of the spaces and possibilities opened up by liberal democratic institutions should make us wary of any quick assimilation of Nietzsche to what I have called the Platonic conception (in which statecraft is, above all, soul-craft, and the role of philosophers is to legislate virtue). It should also put us on our guard when we read statements from *Beyond Good and Evil* such as "the *democratic* movement is the heir to the Christian movement" (sec. 202). We know (from *Beyond Good and Evil*, the *Genealogy*, and *The Anti-Christ*) that Nietzsche regarded Christianity as a dogmatic, universalizing, and intolerant creed. Similarly, we know that he regarded *ressentiment* as the primary passion animating the movement for democratic equality, one that manifested itself in a rage against all standards of rank, whether political or cultural. But we also know that Nietzsche regarded institutions and practices as relatively autonomous entities, as *forms* which are given a specific meaning through their investment by a particular "will to power."[77] This suggests that there is an important (albeit largely implicit) distinction in Nietzsche between liberal democratic *institutions* and the *spirit* or will that drives them at any given moment.[78]

Keeping this distinction in mind, I propose a more nuanced interpretation of Nietzsche's critique of the "democratic movement" in *Beyond Good and Evil*. Democratic social and political institutions may well become "an ever more visible expression [of] herd animal morality," but that does not mean that their original or most important function was to promote the morality of enforced sameness. On the contrary, it is utterly consistent with Nietzsche's understanding to say, on the one hand, that the democratization of Europe was an absolutely essential step in separating out spheres of value which had been conflated by feudal Christianity and, on the other, that popular democratic political *movements* have often been animated by motives more ambiguous than their professed concern for social justice.

The struggle to give institutional form to the modern ideas of limited government and an abstentionist morality of rights—a struggle which opens up vast new realms of individual and cultural freedom—can, in fact, be overtaken by a passionate majority determined to impose or inflict *its* positive morality upon the society as a whole. If we read *Beyond Good and Evil* through *this* lens, we find a critique of democratic/demotic culture animated by concerns quite similar to Mill's. Like the latter, what Nietzsche fears most is the dogmatism of the majority, a dogmatism with deep cultural and psychological roots. Empowered by democratic forms of political organization, this dogmatism poses the greatest threat to individual and cultural liberty, as well as to different *types* of human beings—especially the "sovereign individual."

Nietzsche's rhetoric, of course, is far more agitated than Mill's. In Nietzsche the cultural pessimism of the earlier generation gives way to the apocalyptic tone which will characterize much of twentieth-century continental philosophy. Nevertheless, support for the idea that Nietzsche's critique rests on the modernist distinctions between culture and politics, morality and legality, a "positive" code of conduct and a more minimal one can be found in a number of places. In *Human, All Too Human* Nietzsche notes that mass politics is here to stay, and that it is pointless to try to change it: "Since this has already occurred, we must adapt ourselves to the new conditions, as we adapt when an earthquake has displaced the old boundaries and contours of the land. . . ." He goes on to observe:

> If all politics is now a question of making life tolerable for the greatest number, then this greatest number might also be allowed to determine what they understand a tolerable life to be; if they believe that the intellect is capable of discovering the appropriate means for attaining this goal, what good would it do to doubt it? They now *want* for once to forge their happiness and unhappiness themselves; and if this feeling of self-determination, this pride in five or six ideas that their heads contain and bring to light, does in fact make their lives so pleasant for them that they will gladly endure the fatal consequences of their narrow-mindedness: there is little to object to here, provided their narrow-mindedness does not go so far as to demand that *everything* should become politics in this sense, or that *everyone* should live and work according to this standard.

Demotic narrow-mindedness is not to be fought by philosophical "commanders and legislators" who impose a new, aristocratic table of values on the herdlike many. Rather, the triumph of this *mentalité* in the public realm means that the pursuit of individuality must take place *elsewhere*, in a cultural space which has not yet been "politicized" in this manner.

But, it will be objected, this is the "middle" Nietzsche speaking, the Nietzsche who did not yet see himself as a "destiny" for Europe.[79] *That* Nietzsche—the Nietzsche of *Beyond Good and Evil, Zarathustra*, and *Twilight of the Idols*—does not counsel withdrawal but a "revaluation of all values," a *cultural* revolution which must (necessarily) make use of political means if the "diminution of man" is to be reversed.[80] The "philosophers of the future" do not withdraw from the public realm. Rather, they bash it into shape, using political means of the most brutal sort in order to achieve what Jacob Burckhardt called "the state as artwork."

Certainly, the young Nietzsche was drawn to such a conception of the state, as the 1872 essay fragment on "The Greek State" bears out.[81] And the rhetoric of the mature Nietzsche often appears unambiguous. In sections 37–39 of *Twilight of the Idols* he goes out of his way to associate liberalism and democracy with cultural decline, and to praise the Roman Empire and the Russia of his day as powers sufficient to create durable institutions (unlike modern democracy or the German Reich).[82] Add to this Nietzsche's tendency to view the state as an apparatus for "breeding" a certain type of human being, and we seem to have all the evidence we need to convict him of cleaving to the Platonic conception of politics.

But before we come to this conclusion, we would do well to ponder the section of *Twilight of the Idols* entitled "The 'Improvers' of Mankind." Here Nietzsche attacks all projects—religious, political, cultural—designed to "make men moral." Whether the attempt is motivated by the desire to *tame* the human animal (as in Christianity) or to *breed* "a definite race and species" (as in Indian morality and the "law of Manu"), immoral means—often of the most gruesome sort—must be utilized. If one wills the end, one must will the means: *that* is the bottom line of the "morality of taming" *and* the "morality of breeding." Hence, from a *genuinely* moral point of view these two types of project are "entirely worthy of one another: we may set down as our chief proposition that to *make* morality one must have the unconditional will to the contrary. . . . Expressed in a formula one might say: *every* means hitherto employed with the intention of making mankind moral has been thoroughly *immoral*."[83] In *The Anti-Christ* (sec. 3) Nietzsche suggests that the Christian morality of taming is also an instance of the morality of breeding, while in *Beyond Good and Evil* he suggests that we regard the aristocratic commonwealths of the ancient Greek polis or Venice as "arrangements" ("voluntary or involuntary") for breeding certain types of individuals.

What is going on here? Why do we have seemingly contradictory messages about "the morality of breeding" in texts from roughly the same period of Nietzsche's life? If nothing else, there certainly seems to be an instability in Nietzsche's rhetoric. On the one hand, he expresses moral revulsion at the violent and soul-destroying means that have been used by different cultures in order to "make men moral." (Indeed, the *Genealogy* can be read as one long, anguished cry concerning the cruelty man performs on himself.) But, on the other, he seems to regard such "breeding" in almost value-neutral terms, as the tacit but obvious purpose of *all* religious and political forms. In the latter mode he apparently endorses whatever arrangements produce human beings endowed with the kind of active (pagan or Renaissance) virtues he so admires. This has led many to view Nietzsche as a champion of the state, his famous denunciation of it as the "coldest of all cold monsters" notwithstanding.[84]

I would suggest that here, as elsewhere, we are running up against Nietzsche's employment of a dual perspective, one which bears a curious similarity to that used by Kant in *The Groundwork of the Metaphysics of Morals*. Kant had argued that so long as we are conscious and consistent in our usage, there is no *logical* self-contradiction involved in regarding humans as, on the one hand, conditioned beings caught up in the "mechanism of nature" and, on the other, as rational agents capable of spontaneous action and moral self-legislation. Of course, Nietzsche will have nothing to do with the two-world metaphysics Kant uses to ground his two perspectives. (Kant's metaphysics comes in for sustained abuse from Nietzsche.) Nevertheless, Nietzsche does borrow from Kant the idea that, under one aspect, human phenomena can be consistently naturalized and, under another, can be regarded critically in terms of their moral significance ("moral" being used here in a non-Kantian but nevertheless strongly evaluative sense). Thus, the *Genealogy of Morals* constantly shifts back and forth between the presentation of physical and psychic cruelty as necessary to the self-formation of man (his "de-animalization," as it were), and a perspective which expresses the utmost horror at the intensification and prolongation of such self-cruelty.[85]

When we add to this the fact that Nietzsche (in his "naturalizing" mode) regards even Christianity as a "breeding" project, it becomes even harder to attribute to him a desire for politically enforced eugenics experiments. "Breeding" has become an all-inclusive metaphor, one which refers not to politically directed projects (such as we find in book 5 of Plato's *Republic*) but to *the kind of individuals* "produced" by any political/moral/cultural regime. It is clear that Nietzsche prefers the kind of agonistic individuals "produced" by the Greek polis, Rome, and Renaissance Italy to the "tame herd animal" produced by Christianity and modern European culture.[86]

In this preference he is not that far from Mill (who urged "pagan self-assertion" as a balance to Christian self-denial), although they differ on the degree to which different *kinds* of virtues can—and ought to be—embodied in the same agent. Similarly, Nietzsche is not that far from Mill in regarding some forms of despotism as appropriate to certain (early) stages of the self-formation of man.[87] Like Mill, he regards the moral taste of a particular culture as crucial to the kind of individuals (active or herdlike) it will likely produce. But nowhere does he propose using *political* means to enforce a *philosophically determined* breeding program. When, in section 3 of *The Anti-Christ* Nietzsche writes that "the problem I raise here is not what ought to succeed mankind in the sequence of species . . . but what type of human being one ought to *breed*, ought to *will*, as more valuable," he is concerned with the *reigning cultural ideals of the individual*, not who gets to have sex with whom (as in Plato). That the rhetoric of "willed" types of individuals *does not* imply the tyrannical destruction of human freedom can be seen from the fact that Nietzsche regards Christianity itself as such a *willed achievement* of a particular kind of individual. Such a will animates a particular culture and its practices; it does not entail eugenics experiments run by priests or philosophers.

If it is wrong to accuse Nietzsche of propounding an updated version of Plato's philosopher-kings—wrong because he wants nothing to do with the enforcement of the same code of conduct on *everyone*; wrong because he attacks religion and the state for undertaking precisely this "formative" project, with its attendant immoral means; wrong, finally, because his conception of "breeding" a type of individual is vague and figurative, not something planned and coercively carried out—then why does he insist (in *Beyond Good and Evil*) upon calling the "philosophers of the future" (sec. 201) commanders and legislators? Why does he speak of creating a "new ruling caste" (sec. 258) for Europe?

The answer to this question takes us back to that of Nietzsche's "sovereign individual" and the reasons why the long, hard road described in the *Genealogy* turned out to be, in large part, a dead end. The problem for Nietzsche is not how to woo the masses away from Christianity, nor how to replace liberal-democratic institutions with aristocratic ones. The masses may well need their faith; to take it away from them would only lead them to embrace worse forms of tyranny.[88] Similarly, the fault lies not in liberal-democratic *institutions* but in *us*: we have lost the vitality out of which these institutions grew.[89] Indeed, as Nietzsche remarks, "as long as they are still being fought for, these same [liberal] institutions produce quite different effects; they then in fact promote freedom mightily."[90] Once the struggle ends, the incitement to active, individualizing virtues ceases. Then the ideals of the "tame animal" come to the fore, and the culture as a whole genuflects before the lowest common denominator.

Like Mill, what Nietzsche suffers from is a kind of *claustrophobia*, a condition brought on by the usurpation of cultural space by *one* dominant ideal.[91] In such a situation—where the "healthy" are in danger of being infected by the "sick," where the liberty created by liberal-democratic institutions is subsumed by a single positive code of conduct—the greatest need is for those who can create "new" or alternative values which expand our sense of the possibilities of human existence as well as the richness of the moral life. This, more than anything else, is what Nietzsche demands from his "philosophers of the future," his new "ruling caste." That their primary responsibility is to expand cultural space and ideals rather than to "rule over" pliant masses can be seen from Nietzsche's citation of the spirits who "rule" in his own day. These include Mill, Spencer, and Darwin—mediocre Englishmen all, according to Nietzsche, but "who would doubt that it is useful that *such* spirits should rule at times?"[92] In Nietzsche's vocabulary, "ruling," like "breeding," cannot be taken at face value. It signifies a cultural influence whose importance cannot be underestimated but which hardly hinges upon the possession of political power.

The task of the "philosophers of the future," then, is to break the stranglehold on European culture of the dominant (dogmatic) values. They are called philosophers "of the future" *not* because they are a cadre of violent political artists summoned into being by the prophet Nietzsche but rather because their concern is *with* the future, with attacking the "ideal of today" and keeping cultural possibilities open.[93] We can, in hindsight, count Nietzsche among their number, exercising (posthumously) something akin to the "rule" he ascribed to Mill, Spencer, and Darwin. If a "new ruling caste" is required in Europe, it is a *philosophical* caste, one capable of breaking with the mendacity of previous philosophy's rationalization of popular morality and custom; one with the critical independence necessary to think the moral life anew, beyond the bounds of creedal conformity. What is required, in short, is not philosopher-kings (or philosopher-Führers) but thinkers whose *intellectual conscience* impels them to denounce the illusions of the past, the illusion of a single, positive code of conduct for all individuals—*the* "right way to live," *the* good, "best" or moral life as given by reason or revelation—most of all.

But doesn't even this limited goal require a break with the past more radical than anything dreamt of by the Enlightenment? Doesn't Nietzsche's call for a "revaluation of values" demand a break with all custom and convention, giving the philosopher the godlike task of a *creatio ex nihilo*?

Nietzsche often talks this way, most notably in *Twilight of the Idols*, *The Gay Science*, and the posthumously published notes that comprise *The Will to Power*. The famous declaration that "God is dead" refers not to the end of religious faith but to the structural collapse of the cultural and moral edifice of the West, one that had been grounded on a table of values "created" (and guaranteed) by the Christian God. With this collapse, an entire way of conceiving the realm of value comes to an end.[94] Nietzsche did not view this event simply as the "end of metaphysics" (the destruction of the distinction between the sensory and the suprasensory, existence and essence, etc.). Rather, he saw it as portending a cultural shift of gigantic, and potentially cataclysmic, proportions.[95]

Nietzsche seems to have thought that the partial (and semihypocritical) secularization wrought by the Enlightenment would be nothing compared to this coming cultural collapse, out of whose wreckage "new values" would have to arise. But with this prognostication he seems to have fallen prey to precisely the foundationalist logic he is so famous for attacking. He assumes that if the fundament goes, it must take everything with it. Nowhere is this (false) assumption more evident than in the contempt he directs at the "freethinking" George Elliot and her ilk in *Twilight of the Idols*:

They have got rid of the Christian God, and now feel obliged to cling all the more firmly to Christian morality: that is *English* consistency. . . . In England, in response to every little emancipation from theology one has to reassert one's position in a fear-inspiring manner as a moral fanatic. That is the *penance* one pays there. With us it is different. When one gives up Christian belief one thereby deprives oneself of the *right* to Christian morality. For the latter is absolutely *not* self-evident: one must make this point clear again and again, in spite of English shallowpates. Christianity is a system, a consistently thought out and *complete* view of things. If one breaks out of the fundamental idea, the belief in God, one thereby breaks the whole thing to pieces: one has nothing of any consequence left in one's hands.[96]

Here we confront Nietzsche's grand, self-dramatizing mistake—that of a minister's son. The desire to see Christianity as a "system" whose highest values devalue themselves (thanks to the "will to truth" it deployed in its battle with paganism) blinds Nietzsche to his own insights concerning the structure of disillusion and the nature of moral self-formation. Viewed from a distance, the "death of God" is simply another way of talking about the transformation that occurs when the West moves from a society that integrated values and spheres of life in accordance with certain publicly recognized (religious) "ultimate" values to a society in which different spheres of life gain a relative independence and autonomy. The result of this "de-centering" may be a loss of easy, unreflective answers to why we do what we do (or value what we value), but it does not destroy the moral *materials* made available by the previous form of life. Christianity lives on—not simply as the unreflective faith of many but as a tradition of moral discourse that can be secularized, appropriated, and supplemented in much the way Mill envisaged. In fact, the "death of God" makes Christian values available for morality—one is tempted to say for the first time.

Of course, this general point about the appropriation and transformation of moral teachings was something that Nietzsche (when he wasn't dwelling on "epochal transformations" or the problem of "nihilism") was perfectly well aware of. Indeed, he was himself the master practitioner of the "creative appropriation" of pagan and Renaissance virtues, prying them out of their original context and giving them a modernist, individualist spin (all interpretations of Nietzsche that present him as bloody-minded hinge—fatally, in my view—on the assumption that he desires a literal resurrection of the warlike virtues of Rome or the Renaissance). The great opportunity presented by "the death of God" is that it makes it possible for each individual to approach his or her moral self-formation in a manner similar to the process of self-fashioning Nietzsche describes in *The Gay Science*:

> *One thing is needful.*—To "give style" to one's character—a great and rare art! It is practiced by those who survey all the strengths and weaknesses of their nature and then fit them in to an artistic plan until every one of them appears as art and reason and even weaknesses delight the eye. Here a large mass of second nature has been added; there a piece of original nature has been removed—both times through long practice and daily work at it. Here the ugly that could not be removed is concealed; there it has be reinterpreted and made sublime. Much that is vague and resisted shaping has been saved and exploited for distant views; it is meant to beckon toward the far and immeasurable. In the end, when the work is finished, it becomes evident how the constraint of a single taste governed and formed everything large and small. Whether this taste was good or bad is less important that one might suppose, if only if it was a single taste![97]

I want to suggest that this image of self-fashioning has important consequences for how we understand Nietzsche's idea of autonomy, his emphasis on the "creation of values," and his notion of "the sovereign individual." Whether considered as an aesthetic or moral subject, the individual does not create him or herself out of thin air, out of a tremendous (and necessarily self-deluding) "no" to all that has gone before. Rather, the process always involves working on materials both inherited and appropriated, blending and sculpting these into something distinct, new, and individual. One can no more be a moral *individual* than a distinctive character if one's morality is simply the sum of received materials which have not been worked over, transformed, and integrated. The achievement of autonomy thus becomes a project which is fulfilled only through the continuous working over of the moral "materials" at hand. One must make these materials one's own; one must *actively* appropriate them. One must, finally, *give birth to oneself as a moral subject*. In the end, this Nietzschean process of giving birth to oneself as a moral subject is remarkably similar to what Socrates means by the "examined life."

This can be seen by turning to another passage of *The Gay Science* (sec. 335), where Nietzsche describes the lack of self-knowledge most of us betray when we engage in "moral" (or "conscientious") judgment. I here quote the opening paragraphs of this lengthy but extremely important section:

> How many people know how to observe something? Of the few who do, how many observe themselves? "Everybody is farthest away—from himself"; all who try the reins know this to their chagrin, and the maxim "know thyself!" addressed to human beings by a god, is almost malicious. That the case of self-observation is indeed as desperate as that is attested best of all by the manner in which *almost everybody* talks about the essence of moral actions—this quick, eager, convinced, and garrulous manner with its expression, its smile, and its obliging ardor! One seems to have the wish to say to you: "But my dear friend, precisely this is my speciality. You have directed your question to the one person who is entitled to answer you. As it happens, there is nothing about which I am as wise as about this. To come to the point: when a human being judges '*this is right*' and then infers '*therefore it must be done*,' and then proceeds to *do* what he has thus recognized as right and designated as necessary—then the essence of his action is *moral*."
>
> But my friend, you are speaking of three actions instead of one. When you judge "this is right," that is an action, too. Might it not be possible one could judge in a moral and in an immoral manner? *Why* do you consider this, precisely this, right?
>
> "Because this is what my conscience tells me; and the voice of conscience is never immoral, for it alone determines what is to be moral."
>
> But why do you *listen* to the voice of your conscience? And what gives you the right to consider such a judgment true and infallible? For this *faith*—is there no conscience for that? Have you never heard of an intellectual conscience? A conscience behind your "conscience"? Your judgment "this is right" has a pre-history in your instinct, likes, dislikes, experiences, and lack of experiences. "*How* did it originate there?" you must ask, and then also: "What is it that impels me to listen to it?" You can listen to its commands like a good soldier who hears his officer's command. Or like a woman who loves the man who commands. Or like a flatterer and coward who is afraid of the commander. Or like a dunderhead who obeys because no objection occurs to him. In short, there are a hundred ways in which you can listen to your conscience. But that you take this or that judgment for the voice of conscience—in other words,

that you feel something to be right—may be due to the fact that you have never thought much about yourself and simply have accepted blindly that what you had been *told* ever since your childhood was right; or it may be due to the fact that what you call your duty has up to this point brought you sustenance and honors—and you consider it "right" because it appears to you as your own "condition of existence...."

In this passage Nietzsche is primarily concerned with drawing out the dogmatism of everyday moral judgment, especially its "conscientious" form. Specifically, he is concerned with the distinction between what, in *Beyond Good and Evil*, he calls a merely "formal" conscience and the more authentic (more genuinely Socratic) conscience of the "sovereign individual."[98] For Nietzsche, as for Socrates (but not Rousseau), moral integrity cannot be detached from intellectual integrity. Conscience without "intellectual conscience" is not autonomy, but (to use the Kantian term) heteronomy, the internalization of what is prescribed by custom, family, religion, or society. For most people the "inner voice" is nothing more than a socially given command which has been internalized, although (as the passage just cited indicates) obedience to this voice can have a number of different tonalities. The fact that conscience is merely formal in most people—that it commands "thou shalt unconditionally do something, unconditionally not do something" in a manner which leaves little room for thought or judgment—should not surprise us, according to Nietzsche, since "nothing has been exercised and cultivated better and longer among men so far than obedience." This need to obey—bred into the human animal by the morality of mores and custom—effectively prevents conscience from becoming an independent moral faculty in most people.[99]

When Nietzsche concludes this section by insisting: "Let us therefore *limit* ourselves to the purification of our opinions and valuations and to the *creation of our own new tables of what is good*, and let us stop brooding about the 'moral value of our actions'!" what does he mean? I would suggest that what is involved in the Nietzschean "creation" of values is not artistic posits of the will (as Aladair MacIntyre has argued)[100] but a far more involved process of "making one's own"—a process of the creative and critical appropriation of values. The emphasis in Nietzsche's ethical thought, as in Socrates,' is that the individual cannot be a mere receptacle for a given code of conduct, whether this code is transmitted by society, tradition, or

creed. To merely take in—as opposed to taking up and transforming—a set of values more or less guarantees one's eventual
complicity with evil. No virtue, whether derived from Socrates or
the Renaissance, becomes part of a *moral* life unless it has been
worked over intellectually and existentially by its appropriator. Otherwise it will be "mere moral tinsel," a fig leaf for immorality (which,
unfortunately, is what most "tables of virtues" wind up being).

If to "create" values is to make them one's own through a process
initiated (and sustained) by the *intellectual* conscience, then we see
that Nietzsche stands much closer to Socrates and Mill than is usually acknowledged. The "instinct of obedience" in matters of moral
judgment must be replaced by the critical activity of making one's
own, and *this* process is not mimetic but creative. "Creating one's
own values" refers to the process through which the morally sensitive (and intellectually active) individual appropriates and interprets
values, evolving his or her own code of (independent) conduct.[101]
Such "creation" is not the usurpation of a Mosaic prerogative;
rather, it should be seen as the goal of moral maturation, as the
movement from an "other-directed" moral sense to a self-directed
one. What distinguishes Nietzsche from Mill (or Kant) is his awareness of just how deeply such "other-directedness" penetrates our
being: autonomy is always the exception, and the focus of a ongoing
struggle (the process of "self-overcoming").

This, I think, is what Nietzsche means by the "sovereign individual" and, to some degree, the "value-creating" philosopher. The
problem, of course, is that Nietzsche confuses the issue when he
polemically juxtaposes pagan or Renaissance virtues to the "reactive" values of slave morality. The process of critical appropriation
here gives way to the struggle between values, to an aggressive and
polarizing form of moral pluralism. This gives Nietzsche's critics
the opportunity of charging (with some plausibility) that his attack
on dogmatic codes of conduct is grounded on a dogma of its own,
namely, that of "noble" (albeit nonuniversal) values.

Here we must face the fact that Nietzsche's project has its "reactive" side. This is seen in his unwillingness to contemplate (as did
Mill) the possibility that one "type" or table of values could actually
complement another, their basic tension notwithstanding. It can
also be seen in Nietzsche's celebration of the sheer energy or vitality
of figures like Alcibiades, Cesare Borgia, and Napoleon (in contrast
to the "timidity" of the "herd animal"). If these individuals can be

characterized as "creative," it is only because they arrogate unto themselves a space of action beyond accepted moral standards, asserting their right to exception through the sheer greatness or audacity of their deeds. But such exemplars of life "beyond good and evil" take us a long way from Mill's "heretic," and an even longer way from the Socratic idea of conscience. They highlight the apparently Faustian dimension of Nietzsche's "creative" individual.

But *should* we take Alcibiades, Borgia, and Napoleon to be paradigmatic instances of "the sovereign individual"? The latter, Nietzsche reminds us in the *Genealogy*, is characterized by his independence and his *conscience*, by his "right to make promises" and bind himself to the future through a long chain of will (essay 2, sec. 2). The sovereign individual is not simply one who possesses great energy or *virtu* but an individual who has internalized a will to self-consistency. Only this kind of person can be counted on to keep his word no matter what. Such consistency or integrity is a far cry from what we find in Alcibiades, Borgia, and Napoleon. They may have each possessed great ability, but they all lacked conscience in this sense.

Even if Alcibiades, Borgia, and Napoleon are not good examples of the "sovereign individual," might not Nietzsche's admiration of them still reveal something essential about his conception of the "philosophers of the future"? After all, Nietzsche characterizes the latter as "commanders and legislators [who] first determine the Whither and For What of man."

Here it is helpful to turn to the text once again. In section 212 of *Beyond Good and Evil* (the locus classicus of the charge that Nietzsche's "philosopher" is indeed a "Caesar of the spirit") Nietzsche writes:

> More and more it seems to me that the philosopher, being *of necessity* a man of tomorrow and the day after tomorrow, has always found himself, and *had* to find himself, in contradiction to his today: his enemy was ever the ideal of today. So far all these extraordinary furtherers of man whom one calls philosophers, though they themselves have rarely felt like friends of wisdom but rather like disagreeable fools and dangerous question marks, have found their task, their hard, unwanted, but inescapable task, in being the bad conscience of their time.
>
> By applying the knife vivisectionally to the chest of the very *virtues of their time*, they betrayed what was their own secret: to know of a *new* greatness of man, or a new untrodden way to his enhancement. Every

161

time they exposed how much hypocrisy, comfortableness, letting oneself go and letting oneself drop, how many lies lay hidden under the best honored type of their contemporary morality, how much virtue was *outlived*. Every time they said: "We must get there, that way, where *you* today are least at home."

It is difficult to imagine a more Socratic formulation of the role of philosophy than the one given in this passage. Genuine philosophers are "the bad conscience of their time [and] the enemy of the ideal of today." Their essential task consists in exposing the moral and intellectual laziness that supports the elating clichés of the present. Their ethos is "critical discipline and every habit that is conducive to cleanliness and severity in matters of spirit," the closest possible marriage of intellectual honesty and moral integrity in the face of the "tartuffery" of everyday moral judgment.[102] Should we need more proof of the kind of individual Nietzsche has in mind, he goes on to instance Socrates as precisely such a philosopher, one who enlisted irony as a signpost pointing toward "greatness of soul" in a decadent (morally and intellectually lazy) age.

This characterization of the task of the philosopher seems directly at odds with the "legislative" or prescriptive role Nietzsche seems to argue for in *Beyond Good and Evil*: "*Genuine philosophers, however, are commanders and legislators:* they say *thus* it *shall* be! .... Their knowing is *creating*, their creating is a legislation, their will to truth is—*will to power*" (sec. 211). Here we seem to have a typically Nietzschean dialectic of negation and affirmation: the "vivisection" performed on the "ideal of today" is coupled with the demand for, or promise of, a new set of (radical) normative prescriptions.

A dialectic of this sort is certainly at work in Nietzsche's thought (see the last section of this chapter). But we should note that Nietzsche's rhetoric in this and other passages of *Beyond Good and Evil* is again more than a little ambiguous. It is not simply that we can read "commanding and legislating" as referring to a different (nonpolitical) form of cultural innovation and influence. It has to do with the fact that when Nietzsche states his positive ideal of "greatness," it turns out to have little to do with fantasies of power and everything to do with maintaining independence and intellectual honesty in a mendacious and conformist world:

> Facing a world of "modern ideas" that would banish everybody into a corner and "speciality," a philosopher—if today there could be philosophers—would be compelled to find the greatness of man, the concept of

"greatness," precisely in his range and multiplicity, in his wholeness in manifoldness. He would even determine value and rank in accordance with how much and how many things one could bear and take upon himself, how *far* one could extend his responsibility. . . . [T]oday the concept of greatness entails being noble, wanting to be by oneself, being able to be different, standing alone and having to live independently. And the philosopher will betray something of his own ideal when he posits: "He shall be greatest who can be loneliest, the most concealed, the most deviant, the human being beyond good and evil, the master of his virtues, he that is overrich in will. Precisely this shall be called *greatness*: being capable of being as manifold as whole, as ample as full." And to ask it once more: today—is greatness *possible*?[103]

The great individual is no demon of *virtu* like Alcibiades, Borgia, or Napoleon. Rather, he is an individual like Socrates—like Nietzsche—who is capable of "being alone, being different" as well as creating "wholeness" out of a multitude of strong drives, affects, and characteristics. Not for nothing does Nietzsche describe Socrates in *The Wanderer and His Shadow* as the great exemplar of "moral rational" individualism. Socrates is the source of "the most divergent philosophic ways of life"; his characteristic feature was that he "shared in all temperaments." It is this "wholeness in manifoldness" (*Ganzheit im Vielen*) which constitutes *great* individuality for Nietzsche.[104] Utilizing an openness to perspectives and affective states, such individuality breaks through the endless mimesis of social life and transcends the limits set by "the social construction of the self." As *genuine* philosophers, Socrates and Nietzsche are more than the enemies of the ideal of their respective times and places. They are paradigms of the independent, nondogmatic life. Hence Nietzsche can state, with only slight exaggeration, that "it is my fate that I have to be the first *decent* human being."[105] Only he and Socrates can legitimately claim to stand outside the "mendaciousness of millennia."

Perspectivism, Self-Fashioning, and Independent Judgment

Of course, none of this implies that Nietzsche's "genuine philosopher" looks at things *sub specie aeternitatis*. The idea of such a "view from nowhere" defined the kind of philosophical dogmatism

Nietzsche devoted himself to combating. The notion of a pure knowledge, untainted by either interest or will, demanded a similarly ideal object realm. According to Nietzsche, both ideas are ultimately Platonic in origin. The "dogmatist's error"—the presupposition of a Truth beyond time and chance, a Truth available only to an eye that had stripped itself of all the contingencies of perspective—derives from Plato's "invention of the pure spirit and the good as such."[106] This invention "meant standing truth on her head and denying *perspective*, the basic condition of all life"—indeed, of all knowledge. But how is it that the aristocratic Plato came to invent the Ideal, this most comprehensive denial of life? "Did the wicked Socrates corrupt him after all? Could Socrates have been the corrupter of youth after all? And did he deserve his hemlock?"[107]

These questions from the preface to *Beyond Good and Evil* invert the story I have been telling, in which Nietzsche positions himself as the true—and perhaps only—heir to Socratic radical questioning and negativity. Thus, while it certainly is plausible to view Socrates as a "genuine philosopher" in Nietzsche's sense, it is clear the later Nietzsche prefers to cast him in a different role: not, it is true, as the *inventor* of philosophical dogmatism but rather as its plebeian inciter. There seems to be no escaping the picture of Socrates as an ascetic priest who corrupts the Athenian aristocracy with his dialectics. In the later work, the Mill-like tone of *The Wanderer and His Shadow* (where Socrates is presented as the great hero of moral individualism) is replaced by the most mocking of attacks.

It is no coincidence that this particular swipe at Socrates comes in the middle of an attack on the presuppositions of philosophical dogmatism. In *Beyond Good and Evil* Nietzsche opposes his idea of perspectival knowledge not just to the notion of a singular, unchanging Truth but (by implication) to the very "method" of dialectics which defines the Socratic approach to philosophizing. Any doubt is apparently removed by Nietzsche's characterization of dialectics as an "expedient" deployed by Socrates to "devitalize" his opponents' intellect, forcing them to bow down before the tyranny of logical consistency.[108] If we are to trust the mature Nietzsche, perspectivism and Socratic *elenchus* are diametrically opposed. The former recognizes that all views are interpretations, while that latter seems to promise that the *true* view is the logically consistent one.

I think this contrast is more apparent than real. It tells us more about Nietzsche's narrative self-fashioning—and his Oedipal struggle with Socrates—than it does about the nature of his philosophical project. Nevertheless, the issue is important for the light it sheds on the question of just who can do without the idea of a singular moral truth, discoverable by reason or revealed by faith. Such people, according to Nietzsche, have overcome the "dogmatist's [Plato's] error" not in order to return to the deep slumber promised by custom and convention (the fate, apparently, of most of Europe) but rather to pursue what Nietzsche calls the "task of wakefulness itself."[109] This, of course, is also the task of the Socratic gadfly. Socrates, however, saw it as an important *political* one, aimed at preventing his fellow citizens from sleeping till the end of their days.[110] For Nietzsche wakefulness (and the ethos of disillusion it implies) is necessarily the task of the few, whom he dubs "free spirits."

In this section, I want to explore Nietzsche's reasons for insisting upon this limitation. Why is perspectivism an existential-cognitive attitude open only to the few? Are these few (the "free spirits") free of illusions or do they simply recognize their own entrapment in illusion, unlike the dogmatic many? And why are the many "naturally" dogmatic? What—besides the gravitational pull of custom, convention, and received opinion—keeps them from pursuing wakefulness or responding to those who do? The answers to these questions provide important clues to Nietzsche's view of the prospects for independent judgment in a "disenchanted" age. For reasons which I've already partly discussed, Nietzsche was far more pessimistic than Mill on this point. His pessimism infected virtually every major European thinker who came after him, and it continues to color the way we respond to the idea of "philosophical citizenship."

In the introductory section of this chapter I said that the standard opposition between perspectivism and *elenchus*—an opposition Nietzsche seems to endorse—caricatures the actual relation between these two methods of thought. It is a caricature because it relies on a simplistic (and mistaken) interpretation of both terms. *Elenchus* is the diametric opposite of perspectivism only if we assume two things: first, that Socrates' method practices a strictly circumscribed negativity, one which clears away confusions but whose *telos* is a positive (and ultimately singular) moral truth; and, second, that perspectivism is the doctrine that there is no such thing as truth, only interpretation, and that therefore any particular view is as good as any another, epistemologically speaking. If Nietzsche's view is that no perspective can claim epistemic privilege over all the others, then (it is assumed) a more or less total cognitive relativism follows. I have indicated my doubts about the first set of assumptions (concerning *elenchus*) in chapter 1. Here I want to say a word or two about the mistakenness of the second set.

The standard view makes sense only if we assume that Nietzsche, like the "dogmatists" he combats, held that there is a "real world" whose structure or features *genuine* knowledge was supposed to represent accurately. The difference between Nietzsche's position and that of "dogmatic" philosophers would then be that the latter think some such relation of representation is possible, while Nietzsche does not. The "world"—reality in itself—remains forever beyond our grasp, and our representations of it cannot even claim an "objectivity" based on the structure of our cognitive faculties (thanks to the variability of culture and language).

Such a view, a radicalization of Kant's position in his *Critique of Pure Reason*, seems to have been held by Nietzsche in his early years.[111] But (as Clark, Nehamas, and others have pointed out,[112]) Nietzsche came to reject the distinction between reality and appearance (or the "thing-in-itself" and the order of representation) upon which such cognitive pessimism is based. Once this distinction is rejected, the notion that a view is a "mere" interpretation goes with it, since not even the abstract possibility of correspondence to "reality in itself" remains. "Reality in itself"—uninterpreted, unperceived, prior to judgment and language—turns out to be the last "Konigsbergian" remnant of the "ideal world" posited by Plato, a word fetish that continues to exert a certain seductive (if nevertheless diminished) charm.[113] This does not mean that the world is revealed to be a fiction but rather that the world we talk about, manipulate, know, and feel alienated from is nothing apart from its appearances and interpretations. Humanly speaking, these constitute reality.[114]

Once the idea of a "real world" lurking behind appearances is rejected as a metaphysical holdover, the idea that a given cognitive perspective (Christianity, say, or modern science) is a "mere" interpretation must also be set aside. A perspective may radically simplify the world (and in that sense falsify it), but we become aware of such falsification only thanks to the availability of other perspectives. Every cognitive perspective is, qua perspective, limited: the appearances it selects, accentuates, or leaves out is determined by the set of interests and the form of life it serves. "Perspectives" in Nietzsche's sense are not like glasses we put on and take off at will. They arise as a result of the needs of different forms of life, and cannot be casually discarded nor easily synthesized.[115] The assumption that there is, or ought to be, a synoptic view that seamlessly combines different perspectives is also a metaphysical holdover, a Hegelian version of the "view from nowhere."

But doesn't this radical unmooring of perspective from the "real" world (and the correspondence theory of truth which it underwrites) result in a fundamental relativism? If we cannot judge a particular perspective in terms of a reality independent of it, nor in terms of a more adequate synoptic perspective, how can we judge it at all? The problem is made more pressing by the fact that Nietzsche clearly believes that some perspectives are better than others. And, while he famously claims that "untruth" is a condition of life, he also claims that certain perspectives and values are "errors, nothing but errors."

Clearly, there is a tangle here. How is it possible to pursue an ethos of disillusion when there is not only no truth independent of perspective but also no perspective that is free of illusion or error?

It is this kind of question that Nietzsche seeks to dispose of when he says paradoxical things like "truth is an error necessary for life" or suggests that there is ultimately no *essential* opposition between "true" and "false," only "degrees of apparentness ... lighter and darker shadows and shades of appearance."[116] From Nietzsche's point of view, the fact that a perspective falsifies reality by simplifying it is no objection, since such simplification is an essential condition of all knowledge, of all "seeing."[117] The primary thing that enables him to label a perspective as "error, nothing but error" is its pretense to stand above all interpretation, to offer an unvarnished view of the world. Like Socrates and Mill, Nietzsche starts from the ubiquitous phenomenon of the reification of a belief or opinion into a privileged (and thus unquestionable) truth. The greater the reification, the more unavoidable "untruth" converts itself into avoidable (discoverable or refutable) error. Where Nietzsche departs from Socrates and Mill is in his insistence that *all* truths—even the most necessary or seemingly self-evident ones—are the result of a similar process of reification. Seen in this way, perspectivism—the view that all truths (even those of physics; see *Beyond Good and Evil*, sec. 14) are part of the world-constituting order of interpretation—

figures not as the abdication of the will to truth or disillusion but as its logical outcome. It does this by dissolving all claims to providing a complete or final truth, one beyond time and chance, revision or repudiation.

Does this mean that Nietzsche's perspectivism picks up where Mill's notion of the partiality of truth leaves off? In one sense yes, but in another, more important, sense no. Mill had argued that any particular view or theory converts itself into falsehood the moment it presents itself as being the last word. Because the truth of any subject (morality, say) is complex and many-sided, we will need many different views, vocabularies, and examples of codes of conduct in order to have something approaching an adequate grasp of it. Cleaving to a single moral vocabulary or code (whether it be Christianity or pagan *virtu*) will produce a one-dimensional sense of the moral life, as well as a stunted conception of human nature and possibility. Hence the central importance to Mill of an open, additive conception of moral truth. Without this, the idea of moral progress becomes either unfeasible or banal (the idea that mere passage of time is identical with the moral maturation of the species).

Nietzsche, of course, had no use for the idea of progress, let alone moral progress. The ascendance of the "herd animal"—of man made small and unheroic—seemed to him to provide the most weighty contrary evidence to the idea that the species was getting "better" as the centuries passed.[118] But this does not get to the heart of the matter, for Mill also bemoaned the "taming" of man. Nietzsche's real radicalism is found not in his low estimation of the moral energy and worth of his contemporaries but rather in his rejection of the idea that anything like a synthetic view was, in fact, possible. This strand of Nietzsche's thought extends at least as far back as the *Untimely Meditations*, in particular his attack on historicism in "On the Utility and Liability of History for Life" (1874). There Nietzsche inveighed against the flaccid eclecticism of his contemporaries, their lack of a defined and limited horizon which might provide both perspective and rank.[119] However, it is more deeply (and interestingly) worked out in *The Gay Science*, where Nietzsche writes:

> *Our new "infinite."*—How far the perspective character of existence extends or indeed whether existence has any other character than this; whether existence without interpretation, without "sense," does not become "nonsense"; whether, on the other hand, all existence is not essen-

tially actively engaged in *interpretation*—that cannot be decided by even the most industrious and most scrupulously conscientious analysis and self-examination of the intellect; for in the course of this analysis the human intellect cannot avoid seeing itself in its own perspectives, and *only* in these. We cannot look around our own corner: it is a hopeless curiosity that wants to know what other kinds of intellects and perspectives there *might* be; for example, whether some being might be able to experience time backward, or alternately forward and backward. . . . But I think that today we are at least far from the ridiculous immodesty that would be involved in decreeing from our corner that perspectives are permitted only from this corner. Rather, the world has become "infinite" for us all over again, inasmuch as we cannot reject the possibility that *it may include infinite interpretations*. Once more we are seized by a great shudder; but who would feel inclined immediately to deify again after the old manner this monster of an unknown world?[120]

In this passage Nietzsche is engaged in an anti-Kantian thought experiment, one which suggests that our cognitive capacities cannot take their own measure; nor can they rule out other (non-Kantian, non-Newtonian, non-European) possible ways of constructing the world. We "cannot see around our own corner" means that the perspectival character of understanding is at once irreducible and inescapable. A world which is constituted from many different perspectives turns out to be a world which is interpretation "all the way down." It also turns out to be a world whose multifariousness exceeds the bounds implicit in the Millian idea of the partiality of any given truth, as well as in the cognate notion of a "many-sided" truth. Nietzsche's "new infinite" reveals the parochial nature of even Mill's conception of truth, which tacitly assumes that partial truths can be added together because the perspectives represented by them are ultimately commensurable.

Nietzsche, it should be pointed out, does not insist on any *necessary* incommensurability between perspectives. His pluralism is fluid, not objective. Indeed, as we shall see, he argues for the superiority of the agent who is able to "employ a *variety* of perspectives and affective interpretations in the service of knowledge."[121] Nevertheless, the force of the preceding passage is to reveal a residue of rationalist teleology built into Mill's sense of human fallibility. There is, for Mill, a *telos* to human moral and cognitive development, one we are slowly but clearly approaching. For Nietzsche, conversely, a world constituted by interpretation means a world finally freed from any teleology whatsoever. This is the liberation promised by perspectivism and the "new infinite," a liberation from metaphysical comfort so radical that it threatens to induce a kind of existential vertigo.[122]

In such a world what purpose can an ethos of disillusion serve? Why does Nietzsche cling as ferociously as he does to the virtue of intellectual honesty (the "intellectual conscience") if the process of disillusionment brings us no closer to truth? Why should we not (as Nietzsche likes to say) prefer error or illusion to the negative, disillusioning, or even terrible truth?

These questions raise the issue not only of what counts as disillusion in Nietzsche but of the relation between an ethos of disillusion and what Kant called "maturity" (*Mündigkeit*).[123] Nietzsche clearly believes that those who take the perspective of perspectivism are more "mature"—more capable of independent judgment and less in need of comforting fictions—than the many "constrained spirits" (as he calls them in *Human, All Too Human*). The "free spirit" is the embodiment of intellectual honesty, the sworn enemy of moral dogmatism and hypocrisy. Such an individual, according to Nietzsche, has experienced the "great liberation" which comes when all that has previously been loved, valued, and submitted to suddenly appears as both arbitrary and alien.[124]

This shattering of the sense of "being at home"—the source of both moral complacency *and* what usually passes for moral idealism—is the first step toward becoming a sovereign individual, someone who is master of his virtues rather than *mastered* by them. Alienation from one's self and community give rise to a solitude which provides a kind of convalescence from predetermined goals and valuations (the baggage of the "encumbered" self).[125] Such alienation is the fundamental precondition for grasping "the perspectival element in every valuation." It creates the distance necessary not only for questioning custom and convention but for entertaining the idea of a "new infinite" born of perspective seeing and perspective knowing.

The *value* of such an alienated existence is not found (*pace* Mill) in any direct utility to society at large. As Nietzsche never tires of emphasizing, the will to truth—to intellectual honesty at all costs—is, in essence, *dangerous* to the settled judgments and conventions that provide culture with its very foundation. The "free spirit" exploits the vistas opened by perspectivism in order to become a virtuoso of dissolvent rationality, one who ignores the limits tacitly respected by both the Socratic philosopher and the Millian discoverer of new truths. This could lead to the charge of grave irresponsibility were it not for the fact that the "free spirit" seeks solitude, not engagement with the public or political power.

Nietzsche is adamant on this point, but not out of any misplaced solicitude for the many (who require the crudest of illusions—and the most uncomplicated of moral certainties—to carry on). His insistence on the apartness of the "free spirit" is underscored by his contempt for what usually passes as "free thinking." In *Beyond Good and Evil* he heaps scorn on self-styled freethinkers (*Freidenker*) not because they lack courage or even decency but because they are "without solitude, without their own solitude."[126] To think requires not only the space opened up by perspectivism but the *distance* afforded by withdrawal from all things public. Nietzsche radicalizes *elenchus* in several ways, most prominently by using perspectivism to question not simply particular moral beliefs but the entire process of moral valuation (with its "faith in opposite values" and numerous other prejudices). He also radicalizes it by insisting that it be removed from the public realm (the Greek agora or Millian space of free discussion) almost entirely. For Nietzsche the only truly free thoughts are those which have not been corrupted by the prejudices and needs of the day, which have not lost their claim to honesty by having as their a priori enlistment in some cause. Hence, free spirits—the true free thinkers—must be the "sworn, jealous friends of solitude."[127] Nietzsche does not describe himself as "the last antipolitical German" for nothing.

This withdrawal from the public realm has the most traditional of philosophical antecedents, Plato's parable of the cave in *The Republic* being the most obvious. But Nietzsche's ferocious insistence that the free spirit *cannot* be a "citizen among citizens" is not made for the sake of an *ideal* but rather for the sake of intellectual integrity itself. Like any other human being, the free spirit cannot wrest him- or herself entirely free of illusion in order to occupy an Archimedean point above the world and beyond perspective. But he or she can, through the consistent "reversal" of perspective, attain a *relatively* disillusioned standpoint, one from which many unquestionable assumptions of the day at last become both visible and questionable. The loss of faith in a metaphysical (or positivistic) truth opens the way to a new form of objectivity, an objectivity born of distance and the capacity to see things "with many eyes":

Precisely because we seek knowledge, let us not be ungrateful to such resolute reversals of accustomed perspectives and valuations with which the spirit has, with apparent mischievousness and futility, raged against itself for so long: to see differently in this way for once, to *want* to see differently, is no small discipline and preparation of the intellect for its future "objectivity"—the latter understood not as "contemplation without interest" (which is a nonsensical absurdity), but as the ability *to control* one's Pro and Con and to dispose of them, so that one knows how to employ a variety of perspectives and affective interpretations in the service of knowledge. . . . the *more* eyes, different eyes, we can use to observe one thing, the more complete will our "concept" of this thing, our "objectivity," be.[128]

In its endorsement of multiple perspectives and the antidogmatic capacity "to control one's Pro and Con," this passage could easily serve as a credo of liberal, skeptical inquiry. But Nietzsche, unlike Mill and Socrates, is quite insistent that this ability is necessarily rare, as is the kind of judgment it enables. "Independence is for the very few; it is a privilege of the strong"; the rest of us will never even begin to "see around our own corners" or detach ourselves from the "nook" into which we were born.[129] Why is it so hard to "reverse perspectives," to practice the kind of distanced and independent judgment enabled by perspectivism and the "great liberation"?

One answer is that the pull of custom, convention, and received opinion is not only strong but virtually overwhelming. Nietzsche thinks human beings are the kinds of animals who generally find comfort in numbers and in sameness (the "noble" type is, by definition, the exception to the rule). In this regard he does not depart significantly from either Socratic or liberal moral psychology (despite the radically different conclusions he draws about the proper audience for disillusionment). But there is another, deeper reason for his insistence that the free spirits are among the rarest of rare species. This has to do with the insights born of perspectivism and the idea of a world which is interpretation "all the way down."

Arthur Danto has observed that from the standpoint of perspectivism, the contrast between "commonsense" and "mere" interpretation collapses. Yet even if our commonsense view of the world (and of moral values and moral agency) is, in broad terms, a "fiction," it is, as Danto points out, a useful and necessary one.[130] To paraphrase Nietzsche, it makes a certain form of life possible. However, it would be wrong to infer from this that the value of certain types of action (for example, altruistic behavior) is found in their utility, or that the moral truth of a particular culture is simply what "works" for it. As Nietzsche's investigations in the *Genealogy* and elsewhere demonstrate, all kinds of dubious propositions concerning moral psychology, moral agency, and the nature of morality itself (the faith in opposite values; the reified distinction between an actor and his acts; the idea that what is a virtue for one type of person must be a virtue for all, regardless of circumstances) are preserved in contemporary practices, often with deleterious consequences for the culture at large. Why is this the case? Why can't the errors of the past simply be abolished and mankind liberated from their enervating thrall?

The answer is that in a world with no structure other than that created by our moral and cognitive vocabularies, excising "errors" is a tremendously problematic (and potentially traumatic) endeavor. As Tracy Strong writes, for Nietzsche "language pulls together and is the world: *this* language, *this* world, *these* men."[131] The moral categories that contribute to our commonsense understanding of the world are our very flesh: they make us who *we* are.[132] If the philosopher, in his role as "cultural physician," attempts to dissolve such errors through the therapeutic use of ordinary language analysis, he will be sorely disappointed. Concepts and categories hang together, constituting not just a web of interpretation but the practices which make up our form of life. Thus, to want to abolish one set of particularly mistaken or obnoxious metaphors (such as Nietzsche detects in the Christian interpretation of the world) is not to set oneself a limited, isolated target, since language and the world are so deeply intertwined. To throw off one set of structuring metaphors would, in actuality, demand a transformation in the very form of life that unconsciously deployed them. Hence, "to escape from the prison of this world, all must be made new."[133]

This is not to say that progress never takes place because of the "prison house of language." Nor is it to say that Nietzsche conceives his task (and that of the "philosophers of the future") as performing or inciting such a radical remaking of the world. Nietzsche's position is far more sophisticated than either of these alternatives allows.

According to Nietzsche, the "success" of a morality depends, in large part, on its ability to *narrow* perspective and make fundamental assumptions and distinctions unquestionable.[134] This narrowing

and falsification—performed through and inscribed in language—
creates and preserves a form of life. Moreover, it is essential to all
"education of the spirit."[135] But what happens when that form of life
declines and becomes "decadent"? At that point certain fundamental
judgments, concepts, and categories cease to form the tightly woven
network they once did. They become available for questioning and
(potentially) for discarding. It is the free spirit who will first notice
this state of affairs, and who will press the process of dismantling—
and of cultural shift—forward:

> With the strength of his spiritual eye and insight grows distance and, as
> it were, the space around man: his world becomes more profound; ever
> new stars, ever new riddles and images become visible for him. Perhaps
> everything on which the spirit's eye has exercised its acuteness and
> thoughtfulness was nothing but an occasion for this exercise, a playful
> matter, something for children and those who are childish. Perhaps the
> day will come when the most solemn concepts which have caused the
> most fights and suffering, the concepts "God" and "sin," will seem no
> more important to us than a child's toy and a child's pain seem to an old
> man—and perhaps "the old man" will then be in need of another toy
> and another pain—still child enough, an eternal child![136]

This passage suggests how moral progress is possible, but it does
so in a way which avoids the Enlightenment assumption of a linear
or cumulative process of disillusionment, one aimed at the discovery
of a singular (rational) moral truth. The primary consequence of
perspectivism is a heightened awareness of the contingency of our
moral and cognitive vocabularies. Our most cherished beliefs—the
ones we feel to be central to any adequate conception of morality—
may, from a future perspective, look both quaint and beside the
point. Thus, secularization suggested that belief in the divinity is a
far less necessary (and far more ambiguous) basis for morality than
previously assumed. More recent history suggests the same thing
with regard to the Kantian idea of a rational grounding for morality,
one untainted by desire or interest. Indeed, one can imagine a time
in which the entire anxiety concerning a religious or philosophical
"foundation" for morality—one beyond time and chance—will be
outgrown. (Of course, reasoned justification of, and rational argument about, moral concepts and practices occupies an entirely different plane. They are hardly things we—or Nietzsche—would
want to consign to the "childhood" of humanity.)

In Nietzsche's view, one task of the free spirit is to suggest the depth of contingency on these matters without pretending to have the right answer.[137] This heightened sense of contingency underscores the wrongheadedness of assuming that free spirits (unlike the rest of us) speaks from a definitively disillusioned perspective. They may be adept at looking at things through many different eyes and even (like Nietzsche) at reversing perspectives. But if they have genuinely absorbed the lesson of the "new infinite," they will recognize that they, too, are inevitably children of their time and place, however much they are enemies of the "ideal of today." Progress can only look like progress from a given perspective, a given stage of maturity, one which we may also "outgrow." Disillusionment is always relative and (therefore) never complete. In this sense, we are indeed "eternal" children.[138]

This indicates an unexpected epistemic humility, coming as it does from a thinker whose "autobiography" includes chapters entitled "Why I Am So Wise" and "Why I Write Such Good Books." Like Socrates, Nietzsche knows that human knowledge is founded on ignorance, and that human wisdom begins with the admission of ignorance.[139] But this Socratic humility does nothing to erase the gap between the free and the "constrained" spirit, between the few and the many. And it is here that we encounter the irreducible difference between Socrates and Nietzsche. Socrates pursued the ethos of disillusion for the sake of his fellow citizens. He tried to show them that moral integrity demanded intellectual integrity. Nietzsche, by contrast, pursues an ethos of disillusion to expand the distance between himself (and his fellow free spirits) and the "ideal of today." While he doesn't detach the pursuit of intellectual honesty from moral integrity, he certainly does detach it from a larger "social" mission. Why does Nietzschean "education" depart so radically from the Socratic model on this score?

It is not that Nietzsche thinks of humanity as presently divided between two types, the "nobles" and the "slaves," who follow two radically opposed moralities. If he did, this would certainly explain his desire to remain aloof from the *hoi polloi*. But in *Beyond Good and Evil* he clearly states that today one encounters the mixture and mediation of moralities, often "within a single soul."[140] There remain "higher" and "lower" individuals, to be sure, but the "pathos of distance" between two distinct human types has been mostly eradicated.[141] Yet, surprisingly, the answer to the question of why

Nietzsche's mission is so determinedly nonpublic is, to a large extent, found in the *Genealogy*. What light, then, does this book shed on his reasons for restricting the ethos of disillusion to the narrowest of circles, and for severing philosophy from citizenship?

As its title suggests, the *Genealogy* is concerned with matters of descent. The history of moral values is of interest to us because they are usually presented as naturally, rationally, or divinely given, that is, as without a *history* in the usual sense of the word. Thus, Nietzsche traces the presumed moral value of altruistic actions back to the slave revolt in morality precisely in order to highlight this forgotten history. He takes pains to describe the form of life which this new, ascetic morality preserves and maintains, as well as the kind of agent formed by its practices, concepts, and valuations. What makes this endeavor a "history of the present" is that the primordial history of the subject lives on in its contemporary fruit. The result of millennia of self-torture is the passive "herd animal" of today, the individual who has a "formal conscience" (one programmed for obedience to custom, convention, and authority) but lacks an intellectual conscience (one capable of saying no to all three agencies).

What disturbs many readers of the *Genealogy* is Nietzsche's insistence that human beings have been bred to be the kinds of animals they are by means of mostly forgotten (or repressed) disciplinary practices, punishments, and moralized self-torture. But what is perhaps even more disturbing is his denial that there is any logic of history whereby the inheritance of these archaic practices is thrown off, discarded upon the ash heap of history. Genealogy, as both Deleuze and Strong have emphasized, is directed by Nietzsche *against* any such notion of a dialectical progress at work in history.[142] Thus, the "bad conscience" bred into the human animal in one epoch remains the psychic bedrock of the "responsible individual" in another, even when the intensity of belief in sin and guilt is a shadow of what it once was. To put the matter perhaps too colloquially: the fruit never falls far from the tree. The (modern) democratic movement is the "heir to the Christian movement" not simply because they share certain egalitarian moral ambitions but (more fundamentally) because its underlying moral-psychological structures are the same.[143]

This is why the "sovereign individual," the *ripest* fruit, is such a rare occurrence. As conceived by Nietzsche, freedom and individuality require far more than the capacity to resist the gravitational pull of custom and convention (the moral imperative of Socrates and Mill). They require the strength to *make explicit* and *individualize* those layers of the soul that remain hidden to most people, the unquestioned (and unquestionable) fundament of our existence. One can overcome what Nietzsche calls the "will to the unconditional" only by thoroughly excavating that part of the soul which incessantly demands it. Only then does it become possible to stop willing an authority to obey (the genealogical inheritance of the "slave revolt") and begin commanding oneself.[144] Only then does it become possible to transform the structure of the "formal conscience" into a conscience grounded upon intellectual honesty.[145]

This outcome cannot be achieved by any exercise in "consciousness-raising" or by a simple repudiation of the superstitions of the past. It requires (as previously quoted section 290 of *The Gay Science* intimates) a long, difficult process of work on the self. But for Nietzsche such work on the self has an ultimately moral and not merely aesthetic valence.[146] While it is true that Nietzsche, in opposition to Aristotle, does not reduce the development of character to moral terms, he hardly severs the connection between moral concerns (broadly construed) and the pursuit of self-fashioning. When, in *The Gay Science*, Nietzsche asks: "What does your conscience say?—You must become who you are," he is suggesting the most intimate of connections between moral/intellectual integrity and the achievement of genuine individuality.[147]

The injunction to " 'give style' to one's character," in other words, does not imply that the criterion of taste or stylistic consistency has been rendered independent of the imperative of intellectual honesty. Rather, the two go together, inciting us to an endless struggle against the mimetic character of social life, the "goal" being the attainment of an as yet unrealized individuality.[148] This notion of honesty to an ideal of an individuality which is *achieved* rather than revealed was already articulated in "Schopenhauer as Educator." "The human being who does not want to be a part of the masses need only cease to go easy on himself; let him follow his conscience, which cries out to him: 'Be yourself! You are none of those things that you now do, think, and desire.' "[149] Consistency of style is worth nothing if it remains mired in the mendaciousness that constitutes much of contemporary morals and politics. Yet one does not escape this mendaciousness by viewing the self as an aesthetic object; in *that* case one simply invents a new form of aesthetic ideology.[150]

It cannot be stressed strongly enough that Nietzsche has no a priori criteria to distinguish those who will fashion themselves as genuine individuals from those who will not. Birth, class, ethnicity, religious background, gender: all have nothing to do with it (despite the fact that Nietzsche is notorious for the nasty things he says about women, Christians, Jews, and Germans). It is, ultimately, a question of the energy one is capable of enlisting in the cause of intellectual and moral honesty—in the cause of separating oneself from the mendaciousness that surrounds one, which is constantly usurping one's (potential) individuality in the name of some group, creed, ideology, or "so-called" morality. Those who *do* succeed in "becoming who they are" will, of course, be few; but this has nothing to do with any notion of a natural (or "socially constructed") elite. The project—forming oneself as a genuine individual—is potentially open to everyone. As Nietzsche writes in *Human, All Too Human*: "*Talent.*—In a humanity as highly developed as the present one, everyone acquires by nature access to many talents. Everyone has *innate talent*, but only a few are born with and trained to a sufficient degree of tenacity, persistence, and energy that any one of them really becomes a talent, that is, *becomes* what he *is*, which is to say: discharges it in works and actions."[151] As in Mill, vitality or energy is the key. It by no means guarantees that individuality, much less intellectual or moral integrity, will be achieved. But, like Mill, Nietzsche thinks *none* of these characteristics can be cultivated without it. Each is, in its own way, a form of energy.

Stepping back, we can appreciate the curiousness of the picture Nietzsche has drawn for us. His genealogical investigations reveal the deep (and unedifying) roots of contemporary moral and psychological structures, while his perspectivism and aesthetic individualism offer a sharp rebuke to any kind of determinism (whether of nature or culture). As with many other aspects of Nietzsche, this is not evidence of incoherence but rather a sign of his repudiation of the metaphysical faith in "opposite values." Famous for his (supposed) psychological/biological determinism *and* for his radicalization of the Kantian idea of autonomy, his real position lies elsewhere. As he puts it in *Beyond Good and Evil*, "The 'unfree will' is mythology; in real life it is only a matter of *strong* and *weak* wills."[152] "Strong" precisely because the "herd instinct of obedience" is inherited best, and because only those with great reserves of affect and self-discipline can hope to break even partially free of it. For Nietzsche human freedom is a function of disciplined and focused individual energy, a striving to distinguish oneself not only in style but in intellectual honesty and moral responsibility, a responsibility for *all* one's actions. Everything else is unconscious mimesis.[153]

The problem, of course, is that Nietzsche takes intellectual integrity and the achievement of individuality so seriously that he insists on a withdrawal from the public realm; he lacks any concern for the "wakefulness" of his fellow citizens. Indeed, for Nietzsche it was a point of pride that he didn't *have* any fellow citizens, just kindred spirits in the past and (presumably) in the future. It was even more a point of pride that his judgments on issues moral, aesthetic, cultural, and psychological were *his* judgments, the fruit of the development of a unique set of talents, coupled with an ingenious capacity for "reversing" perspectives. This pride is manifest in his discussion of the "philosophers of the future" in *Beyond Good and Evil*:

> Are these coming philosophers new friends of "truth"? That is probable enough, for all philosophers so far have loved their truths. But they will certainly not be dogmatists. It must offend their pride, also their taste, if their truth is supposed to be a truth for everyman—which has so far been the secret wish and hidden meaning of all dogmatic aspirations. "My judgment is *my* judgment": no one else is entitled to it—that is what such a philosopher of the future may perhaps say to himself.
>
> One must shed the bad taste of wanting to agree with many. "Good" is no longer good when one's neighbor mouths it. And how should there be a "common good"! The term contradicts itself: whatever can be common always has little value. In the end it must be as it is and always has been: great things remain for the great, abysses for the profound, nuances and shudders for the refined, and, in brief, all that is rare for the rare.[154]

One can read this, as one can read so much in Nietzsche, as elitism pure and simple. However, to do so would be to miss the underlying philosophical point. As is often the case, Nietzsche is here making an argument against Kant, one which questions the Kantian idea that "the power of judgment rests on a potential agreement with others."[155] Perspectivism as Nietzsche practices it may entail something like a Kantian "enlarged mentality" (the ability to be able to "think in the place of everybody else"), but the validity of its judgments *does not* derive from its success in eliminating all "subjective" factors, nor from its capacity to generate universal agreement.[156] For

Nietzsche, on the contrary, the "objectivity" of a judgment reflects the specific character, distance, and range of affects which the judging individual brings to the process. The greater the "objectivity" of a judgment, the *less* likely it will elicit universal agreement. For Nietzsche it is almost a principle that the most universally accepted judgments will rank among the falsest.

This is not simply the attitude of an inveterate contrarian, nor of an aesthetic snob for whom a generalizable "judgment of taste" is necessarily the judgment of *bad* taste. More fundamentally, it is the position of a moral-aesthetic individualist, one who sees the Kantian test of universalizability as more an indicator of the prejudices of "common sense" than as a reliable unmasker of partial interests or idiosyncrasy. As usual, Nietzsche states his position in the most extreme terms. But before we dismiss it, we would do well to ask whether the judgments of a Socratic or Thoreauvian conscience could be reduced, without the greatest possible violence, to the kind of formal test Kant offers. "Universalizable" reasons are better than disingenuous ones, and certainly better than no reasons at all. All too often, however, they dress up what is, in fact, a widely shared prejudice or viewpoint in the garb of what Jürgen Habermas calls "communicative rationality."[157]

From a Nietzschean perspective, the test of universalizability provides, at most, a preface to judgment, one best directed at those inclined to mistake their own interests, or most outrageous prejudices, for the "common good." It serves, in other words, as a set of training wheels for those unfamiliar with the rudiments of "objective" judgment. It cannot do the work of individual judgment, nor can it compensate for an unwillingness to take a stand *against* what may seem to be "good reasons" in a particular time and place.

Although, there are certain broad similarities between Nietzsche's stance and that of Socrates or Thoreau we must be clear about the differences. For Socrates and Thoreau conscientious judgment is the highest capacity of the individual considered as an independent, moral being. Socrates suggested that the moral superiority of such judgment ultimately rested upon a commitment to intellectual integrity. Without this commitment, conscientious judgment is likely to devolve into yet another form of dogmatism.

Nietzsche makes the relation between the moral and intellectual integrity even tighter. He suggests that the will to intellectual integrity is itself a kind of morality, one which overrules (or should overrule) everyday dogmatic morality, at least for those who are capable of attaining a high degree of intellectual "cleanliness." Thus, whereas Socrates stands for the novel suggestion that genuine moral integrity demands intellectual integrity, Nietzsche stands for the more radical suggestion that the only version of moral integrity worth striving for is that secreted by the ethos of intellectual honesty. The ethos of disillusion—of the "intellectual conscience," of the free as opposed to "constrained" spirit—is morality enough, however damaging it may be to the "tartuffery" of what usually passes for morals.

DISILLUSION, AFFIRMATION, AND POLITICS

An obvious objection arises here. If the Socratic morality of abstention can be criticized as derivative of a positive conception of the good, surely the same criticism can be made concerning Nietzsche's attempt to identity intellectual conscience with a "nonformal" conscience. Moreover (the critic might add), it is simply not the case that Nietzsche was satisfied with an ethos of disillusion. His never completed "revaluation of all values" was to pick up where his negative or deconstructive work left off. In it he was to attempt nothing less than the "legislation" of a new table of values for a postnihilistic age. Far from being the champion of a Socratic brand of skepticism, Nietzsche pointed to a post-Socratic and post-Christian ethical world, one in which the claims of both reason and faith would take a backseat to the myth and value-creating powers of art, itself elevated to virtually religious status.[158]

I think such claims are overblown, but they do point to an interesting problem. Nietzsche clearly viewed skepticism as an impotent and ultimately untenable attitude and took pains to distinguish it from his own "philosophizing with a hammer."[159] In addition, he did have a positive (alternative) vision of virtue, one which he hoped would contribute to the revival of an increasingly decadent European culture.[160] Tempting thought it may be, we cannot simply bracket these Romantic/apocalyptic aspects of his thought nor deploy the public/private distinction in such a way that safely domiciles them in the sphere of individual self-creation.[161] We are thus faced with a question: What does it mean when an "ironist" like Nietzsche folds politics into culture so that the pursuit of "private self-perfection" (becoming who one is) seems to get tangled up in the broader project of renovating the public realm and in providing a new *public* source of meaning and ranking of values?

I argued earlier that there is a fairly clear (but often implicit) set of distinctions in Nietzsche between the public and the private, politics and culture, institutions and their "spirit." Such distinctions are operative when he criticizes the "improvers" of mankind for foisting a positive morality upon their unwitting victims, or when he praises the "prophylactic" quality of modern political institutions and innovations. But Nietzsche ignores these distinctions just as often as he relies upon them. His episodic conflation of culture and politics, for example, is responsible for generating the widely varying characterizations of his attitude toward politics. Thus, while it would be a gross exaggeration to claim that Nietzsche *identifies* politics with culture in his mature thought (see section 4, "What the Germans Lack," in *Twilight of the Idols*), he certainly links the prospects for increased vitality and individualism to the state of culture in general. In itself this is no great cause for alarm. Mill does the same thing, as does Tocqueville. But Nietzsche's linkage goes deeper than theirs, having to do with his diagnosis of the state of European culture as well as his conception of the role ideals and beliefs play in any given society.

One of Nietzsche's earliest and most persistent themes is that every society, every culture, ultimately rests on a protective bed of illusion. Its fundamental beliefs, practices, and table of values provide the necessary narrowness of perspective, one which enables it to orient itself in the world and act in a hostile environment. In a famous passage from "On the Utility and Liability of History for Life," Nietzsche writes:

> And this is a universal law: every living thing can become healthy, strong, and fruitful only within a defined horizon; if it is incapable of drawing a horizon around itself and too selfish, in turn, to enclose its own perspective within an alien horizon, then it will feebly waste away or hasten to its untimely end. Cheerfulness, good conscience, joyous deeds, faith in what is to come—all this depends, both in the instance of the individual as well as in that of a people, on whether there is a line that segregates what is discernible and bright from what is unilluminable and obscure. . . .[162]

Untruth is here more than a *condition* of life; it is the sine qua non of a healthy life, whether for an individual or a people. Nietzsche never really abandoned this psychological/anthropological insight, however much his own philosophical practice was guided by the opposite imperative (that of disillusion). To state it in an overly simple formula: as a philosopher Nietzsche followed the broad example of Socrates, but as an anthropologist and analyst of culture he basically agreed with Pericles. Disenchantment had to make way for re-enchantment by a civil or some other form of religion lest the culture in question find itself fatally weakened by a promiscuous openness to other perspectives. The life-sustaining narrowness of a given horizon had to be maintained if the individual or culture at its center was to thrive.

This theme provides the context for Nietzsche's critique of Socrates, from *The Birth of Tragedy* to *Twilight of the Idols*. Socratic rationality is presented as acting like a corrosive acid on the life-sustaining horizon of the Greeks, one constituted by tragedy, myth, and custom. Indeed, Nietzsche attacks Socrates not because of any supposed *dogmatism* (the charge he lodges against Plato) but precisely because Socratic rationality is *dissolvent* in the sense I discussed in chapter 1. Thanks to Plato and Christianity, the undermining effect of the Socratic "will to truth" becomes a central feature—perhaps the defining feature—of Western culture, with the consequence that we are driven to endlessly search for something which does not exist (a single, foundational, and transhuman moral truth). The fact that Christianity was initially able to successfully deploy the will to truth against animism and paganism does not prevent this will from turning on monotheism itself. Christianity is incapable of stopping the "disenchantment of the world" to which its own war on myth gave such powerful impetus.[163] Truth after truth is revealed to be just another myth, a process which culminates in the debunking of the "truth" of the Christian divinity. In this sense Christianity becomes a victim of its own morality, its own worship of the truth.[164]

Nietzsche thought that the inevitable outcome of a culture whose central value is truth was nihilism: "The highest values devalue themselves. The aim is lacking; 'why?' finds no answer."[165] After two thousand years, the center of gravity provided by the idea of the Christian God dissolves, falling prey to science and secularization.

183

But neither of these two "new" truths proves sufficiently strong or different enough to overcome the heaviness and depression which accompanies the "death of God." A near suicidal pessimism or "Buddhism" follows, with an increased need for narcotics of all kinds.

According to Nietzsche, the only thing that can stop this fatal "weakening of the will," this slide into the utmost decadence, is a new set of revivifying values—a new "sun" to replace the one which has burned out. Hence the idea of a "revaluation of all values" and of philosophers as "commanders and legislators" who provide "the Whither and For What of man." As I argued earlier these philosophers need not be politicians in the literal sense. What is crucial, however, is that their creation of values exceed the limits of the self and provide a new *public* source of meaning, a new *direction* for culture.

Does this make the "philosophers of the future" a band of ascetic priests? The answer is no: Nietzsche has no interest in ministering to the sick "herd." But he *does* have an interest in renovating culture, and this project has indefinite public/political dimensions. I say indefinite because Nietzsche thinks it can be accomplished in various ways, through various (and unpredictable) channels. The idea that it could be accomplished by a twentieth-century philosopher-king or "ruling caste," however, seems least plausible. Meaninglessness is not overcome, nor is the human being enhanced, if the few succeed in reenslaving the many by bringing back the ancien régime or contriving some bastardized modern version of it. Besides, man is not a crab: he cannot walk backward. Democratic institutions are here to stay. The question is how to invest these institutions (and the culture they inhabit) with some of the more "noble" values they have all but vanquished. In other words, the "creation of values" Nietzsche proposes enables so-called noble values to reclaim parts of culture. This reclamation is something more than the personal experimentation celebrated by Nehamas and Rorty in their influential interpretations, and something decidedly less than the totalitarian fusion of culture and politics which Strauss and his followers fear. It is, above all, maddeningly vague and ambiguous.

From the perspective I have offered, it is neither the vagueness nor ambiguity which should surprise us. It is, rather, the extent of Nietzsche's self-betrayal. How is it that the champion of perspectivism and the "new infinite," the antidogmatist par excellence, should succumb to the idea that our greatest danger comes not from the reification of illusions or partial truths as Truth but from skepticism and the dissolvent force of rationality? How is it that Nietzsche, who lays claim to being the greatest paragon of intellectual honesty since Socrates, should, in the end, urge something that certainly looks like dishonesty, if not willful self-deception?

The answer, I fear, is that Nietzsche radically overestimated the role the "will to truth" plays as a disillusioning imperative in Western culture and radically underestimated the extent to which illusions reproduce and proliferate in even the most secular of cultures. It is simply not the case that the "death of God" wipes away the horizon, or that a widely shared sense of purpose or meaning is required for a culture to be minimally healthy. Yet Nietzsche seemed to think (as contemporary conservatives and communitarians do) that our primary problem is not that we still believe too deeply but rather that we "believe in nothing very deeply at all."[166] It is for this reason that he castigated liberal skeptics and felt the need to yoke disillusion to affirmation and value "creation."

Contemptuous, like Montaigne, of man's persistent moral idiocy and teetering on the brink of misanthropy, Nietzsche winds up being surprisingly solicitous of the human need for meaning in a "disenchanted" age. This would have involved no self-betrayal if he had been as clearly oriented to the private quest for self-perfection as some have made him out to be, or if he had remained true to aphorism 156 of *Beyond Good and Evil*. There Nietzsche writes: "Madness is rare in individuals—but in groups, parties, nations, and ages it is the rule." With this thought Nietzsche articulates a fundamentally Socratic insight: it is not the "will to truth" which causes our greatest calamities but the "will to meaning." Philosophers must become citizens not in order to provide their fellow citizens with a "Whither and For What" but rather to help them to see the injustices that such a *public* demand for meaning inevitably generates.

Max Weber

CONFLICT, INTEGRITY, AND

THE ILLUSIONS OF POLITICS

THE TOWERING WORK of Max Weber stands as an almost insurmountable obstacle to anyone who claims that "philosophical citizenship" is an important, or even relevant, possibility in the late modern age. This is because Weber, in his reflections upon the status of theory and the shape of modern society, did more that any thinker to debunk the ideals of philosophy, on the one hand, and citizenship, on the other. The world he inhabited was one in which reason, humbled by both empirical science and Nietzsche's radicalization of Kant's *Critique*, could no longer claim (in good faith) to adjudicate between different ways of life, nor to offer any genuine guidance as to how to live and how to act. Least of all could it pretend to be the kind of "super science" it was for Hegel, synthesizing the findings of cognition and offering up the meaning of history in one grand, all-encompassing narrative.

"The fate of an epoch which has eaten of the tree of knowledge," Weber famously wrote, "is that it must know that we cannot learn the *meaning* of the world from the results of its analysis, be it ever so perfect; it must rather be in a position to create this meaning itself."[1] General views of life and the universe could never be the legitimate result of "increasing empirical knowledge." In this regard, science was as impotent as philosophy. Having outgrown both metaphysics and positivism, it was time to acknowledge the inescapable, namely, that the "highest ideals," the things "which move us most forcefully," are always and everywhere "formed only in the struggle with other ideals which are just as sacred to others as ours are to us."[2]

The same held for the idea of citizenship. If, in days past, it was plausible for writers and activists to invoke (in good conscience) the famous Aristotelian definition of citizenship as "participation in judgment and authority," it was no longer.[3] The growth of an increasingly rationalized world more or less squeezed the space for this kind of citizenship out of existence. In its place were the enormous bureaucratic structures of the modern, centralized nation-state, structures which demanded not virtuous citizens but armies of "trained officialdom" in order to be properly run.[4] Even in the arena of mass democratic politics, the role of the citizen was at best that of a foot soldier on the "battlefield of elections."

While Weber was a vehement critic of the bureaucratic tendency in modern life, he nevertheless thought that the professionalization and rationalization of politics was unavoidable. There could be no getting around the fact that notions such as "civic virtue" or the "education of the *demos*" had very little purchase in a political world characterized by huge party "machines" and "intellectually proletarianized" masses.[5] Deliberative rationality and civic virtue were increasingly rare—and superfluous—commodities, at least among the ordinary citizens of a parliamentary democracy. In such a system, the successful pursuit of power was based almost entirely upon the "exploitation of mass emotionality" and the political actor's ability to mobilize a personal following whose motives were self-interested and "predominantly base."[6]

The worlds of knowledge and politics delineated by Weber thus offer surprisingly little room for either philosophy or citizenship, let alone "philosophical citizenship." When we add to this mix Weber's distinctive views about the "actual relation" of ethics and politics, there seems ample warrant for labeling him, rather than Nietzsche, the true "anti-Socrates." On just about every issue, Weber's views seem in diametric opposition to those of Socrates.

First, there is Weber's repeated insistence that all politics is conflict, and that it operates "with very special means, namely, power backed up by *violence*."[7] If force and coercion are the characteristic instrumentalities of the modern state, then it appears that political action involves either the threat and possible application of force (for example, in the enforcement of law or strike-breaking) or the attempt to gain control of the state's monopoly on "legitimate violence" (the shared goal of electoral and revolutionary struggle). The political actor must therefore be prepared to accept the moral burden of "dirty hands." Indeed, in his celebrated lecture "Politics as a Vocation" Weber goes so far as to redefine the concept of political responsibility in terms of the political actor's understanding of and willingness to take on this particular burden. For Weber the responsible political actor is not one who *avoids* violent and unjust means in the pursuit of good ends but rather one who recognizes their absolute necessity in certain situations, is unafraid to use them, and owns up to the consequences of his actions. The ethical imperative that guides him is not "avoid injustice" but "do what must be done."

Second, there is Weber's firm rejection of *any* ethos that conflates the demands of the public and the private, that sees itself as offering a guide for conduct across a wide range of different "spheres of life." This is not to say that Weber thinks that politics is simply about power and therefore has no relation to ethics (this was the position of the Athenians at Melos). On the contrary, he feels that politics must be understood as a relatively autonomous sphere of life, one which has characteristic means and poses unique dilemmas and requires an ethic specific to it if it is undertaken *seriously*, that is, "as a vocation." Weber's attempt to delineate an ethic specific to politics leads him, famously, to reject the potential chiliasm of an "ethic of ultimate ends" and to view with intense skepticism any and all attempts to apply an absolute (or context-independent) morality to politics. Socratic ethics—in particular the doctrine of nonretaliation—would strike him as just such an absolute morality, the herald of a dangerous and unmanly attitude toward the world.

Third, and perhaps most contrary to Socrates, there is Weber's lack of concern with the ethical standing of the ordinary citizen, his almost exclusive focus on the problem of *leadership* and the kind of moral character it requires. "Politics as a Vocation" examines what it means to have the "calling" for politics. It is tightly focused upon the characteristics and commitments of the authentic political leader. Indeed, it is not wholly incorrect to view Weber's lecture as an updating of Machiavelli's *Prince*.[8]

This focus on "leading politicians" flows, in part, from Weber's analysis of the professionalization and rationalization of politics in the modern age. Where "power is exercised neither through parliamentary speeches nor through monarchic enunciations but [rather] through the routines of administration," the only source of meaning in politics which potentially transcends the narrow bounds of bureaucratic rationality is the "charismatic" leader.[9] Given the marginality of the citizen to the actual workings of modern power, it is not surprising that Weber turns his attention to the possibility of a "spiritual aristocracy" which might, through sheer force of will and dogged moral consistency, endow the "machine" of modern politics with a purpose beyond its own mechanical functioning and reproduction.[10] But whatever the source of this almost desperate focus on leadership, it sits uncomfortably with the Socratic attempt to create more thoughtful citizens.

These differences between Weber and Socrates are both real and deep. They do not, however, tell the whole story. For along with the obvious differences, there are some less obvious but no less real and deep continuities. These are apparent in the way Weber insists upon an utterly sober approach to the political realm, one immune to the "intoxications" of both power politics and the revolutionary pursuit of justice; in the way he deploys an "ethic of responsibility" (*Verantwortungsethik*) to stimulate conscience and slow the political actor down in his use of force or coercion; and in the way his analysis of the interpenetration of reason and domination in the modern world helps disabuse his readers of some of the more characteristic (and naïve) tropes of the Enlightenment. Indeed, from this perspective it is possible to view Weber, along with Socrates, as one of the great "disabusers" in the Western tradition of political thought. Both seek to wake us up, to make us see things clearly, and to purge us of the opinions that blind us to the ubiquity of injustice and domination in the world of politics. Both challenge the beliefs and longings that make us complacent about our virtues and self-righteous about our politics. In the end, however, Weber accepts brutality as the price of a meaningful politics in a "disenchanted" age.

This limited (and highly unexpected) convergence of Weber and Socrates comes to the fore when we compare their respective formulations of the demands of moral and intellectual integrity. With the possible exception of Nietzsche, it is difficult to name a thinker in the Western tradition who takes these two forms of integrity more seriously than Weber, for whom conduct based on willful self-deception or avoidable illusion was the greatest of sins. Hence Weber's insistence upon the need for a manly intellectual and moral maturity in a "disenchanted age." There is no more predictable response to the "disenchantment of the world"(*Entzauberung der Welt*) than the urge to re-enchant it, even among secular intellectuals. The eschatological Marxism of Weber's younger contemporaries, Ernst Bloch and Georg Lukács, is only the most obvious case in point.[11] (As we shall see in the next chapter, Leo Strauss's "tentative return" to the "classical political rationalism" of Plato and Aristotle also represents such an effort, as does Hannah Arendt's attempt to meld the best of the Periclean and Socratic heritage.)

This is not to say that Weber was himself completely free of illusions, or of the will to believe. In reading Weber, we would do well to bear in mind Karl Jaspers's observation that Weber "could appear as the complete relativist—and yet he was the most fervent believer of our time."[12] This is an overstatement, to be sure, but it underscores a central and troubling dynamic in Weber's thought. If modernity is, as Weber maintained, an age in which the forces of rationalization have definitively vanquished the old sources of meaning and mystery in human life, then the question inevitably arises as to *what* makes life meaningful in a disenchanted age. Weber had contempt for those who yearned for new prophets "in a godless and prophetless age," as well as for those who could not "bear the fate of the times like a man" and required the embrace of "the arms of the old churches."[13] But he also had contempt for those "last men" savagely depicted by Nietzsche in *Zarathustra*—the philistine, bourgeois secularists of the late modern age who cheerfully, and without sacrifice, endorsed the ideology of progress and material happiness.[14] This revulsion toward the undemanding values of his own class led Weber to take more seriously than he should have the mystic antimodernism of Tolstoy, whom he presents as having precisely formulated the problem of the supposed "meaninglessness" of modern life.[15]

This concern with the "meaninglessness" of modern life—the phenomenon Nietzsche dubbed "nihilism"—led Weber to crucially qualify his allegiance to the Socratic ethos of disenchantment and to what he called the "plain duty" of intellectual integrity. To state the matter more precisely, it led him to a somewhat idiosyncratic formulation of the nature of this duty and the kind of moral integrity it underwrites. For Weber the practice of intellectual integrity meant having the courage to relentlessly clarify "one's own ultimate standpoint."[16] This Socratic injunction, however, stops short of dissolving the grounds of any particular "ultimate" standpoint (for example, Christianity, socialism, or aestheticism).[17] Largely accepting the cultural implications of Nietzsche's thesis concerning the "death of God" (that is, of a centering metaphysical source of value), Weber thought that an avenue of escape lay in the meaning created by the struggle of the many "new gods" which had recently ascended from their graves. The clash of "ultimate standpoints"—of religious, political, scientific, and cultural values liberated from the confines of the Christian value hierarchy—would continue to provide meaning in a disenchanted world.

This is not to say that, despite all his warnings about the need for "sobriety," Weber leaves the door open to a full-scale "re-enchantment" of the political sphere. He is, however, curiously accepting of a certain form of illusion in the public sphere and curiously uninterested in deliberation as a public-political process of "clarification" and disenchantment. For Socrates and for Mill this was an—if not *the*—essential function of public argument.[18] For Weber public argument is *simply* fighting: in the arena of mass politics, deliberation necessarily gives way to demagogy and propaganda. Weber would defend his inattention to the "clarifying" function of deliberation by reminding us of the unedifying realities of modern electoral politics, just as he would defend the ethos of "passionate devotion to a cause" by reminding us of the deadening "rule of officialdom" that lurks behind all nonideological politics. This disinterest would hardly be noteworthy were it not for the supreme value Weber places upon intellectual integrity in *other*, less directly political, contexts.

In what follows, I trace the tensions within Weber's conception of moral responsibility and intellectual honesty and the roles they play in the public sphere. As in previous chapters, the Socratic formulation of these ideas provides something of a critical standard as well as an invaluable contrast. I begin by examining Weber's idea of politics as struggle, showing how this idea is articulated in a number of registers in the course of his reflections on politics and culture. I then turn to a consideration of Weber's peculiar brand of agonistic pluralism and the impact this has on the reformulation of the ideas of moral and intellectual integrity he attempts in the "Vocation" lectures. The last two sections examine these "disenchanted" formulations in some detail. *Contra* some of Weber's critics, I suggest that he retains an important link to the Socratic conception, despite obvious (and major) differences. On the surface Weber's work debunks anything like the idea of "philosophic citizenship"; on a deeper level, however, it manages to keep alive some of the most important elements of this ideal.

The Politics of Struggle: Machtstaat, Parliamentary Democracy, and Culture

In "Parliament and Government in a Reconstructed Germany" (a series of articles first published in the *Frankfurter Zeitung* in 1917), Weber declared that "politics means conflict."[19] While the type of conflict Weber had in mind (at least in this context) was not that between states, his stress on the conflictual character of politics was neither new nor atypical. From his prophecy (in his 1895 inaugural address) of the "eternal struggle" facing future generations of Germans, to his "sociological" definition of politics (in "Politics as a Vocation") as the struggle to "share power or striving to influence the distribution of power, either among states or among groups within a state," Weber consistently derided visions of politics which turned a blind eye to the reality of the will to power and the sheer depth of ideological and national differences.[20] Neither perpetual peace nor unforced social harmony were realistic *political* goals. To think that they were was to engage in willful self-deception and to ignore the positive contribution of such struggle in the preserving freedom in a world characterized by "the irresistible advance of bureaucratization."[21]

What was true in the political realm was even more the case in the domain of culture. Here, too, struggle was the primary, unavoidable reality, as different "value spheres" (art, morality, religion, politics, science, and economics) created conflicting obligations and radically divergent approaches to life. Indeed, for Weber the modern age was characterized by the "disaggregation of value spheres," a process commensurate with the secularization of Western culture initiated by the Renaissance and the Reformation. The result of this disaggregation was that the conflict between different sets of ultimate values—suppressed for a thousand years by "the grandiose moral fervor of Christian ethics"[22]—could once again come to the fore and permeate life at every level. No longer would the virtues of the citizen, the soldier, the merchant, or the politician be superficially integrated in terms of their common subservience to the ruling "ultimate values" of the Catholic church. Once the cultural hegemony of this institution came into question, a new "polytheism" was born; not, to be sure, in the realm of religious belief but in the sphere of life itself. As Weber famously put it in "Science as a Vocation":

> We live as did the ancients when their world was not yet disenchanted of its gods and demons, only we live in a different sense. As Hellenic man at times sacrificed to Aphrodite and at other times to Apollo, and, above all, as everybody sacrificed to the gods of his city, so do we still nowadays, only the bearing of man has been disenchanted and denuded of its mystical but inwardly genuine plasticity. Fate, and certainly not "science," holds sway over these gods and their struggles. One can only

understand what the godhead is for the one order or for the other, or better, what godhead is in the one or in the other order. . . . Today the routines of everyday life challenge religion. Many old gods ascend from their graves; they are disenchanted and hence take the form of impersonal forces. They strive for power over our lives and again they resume their eternal struggle with one another.[23]

Our primary responsibility as moderns is to confront this pluralism of values (and the resulting fragmentation of existence) soberly, without the false hope of discovering a new, integrative source of ultimate cultural authority. It is from the "irreconcilable conflict" of the different spheres of life with each other that the possibility of individual choice—and individual freedom—emerges. Confronted with the conflicting ethical demands of the Sermon on the Mount ("turn the other cheek") and the code of everyday "manly" conduct ("resist evil—lest you be coresponsible for an overpowering evil"), the individual "has to decide which is God for him and which is the devil. And so it goes throughout all the orders of life."[24]

Weber's emphasis on struggle between states, within states, and across cultural values traces a voluntarist metaphysic which can be appreciated fully only against the backdrop of his fears for the future. The latter are most graphically articulated when Weber, responding contemptuously to the goals of the leftist "literati" in 1917, outlines the likely outcome of a German transition to socialism:

State bureaucracy would rule *alone* if private capitalism were eliminated. The private and public bureaucracies, which now work next to, and potentially against, each other and hence check one another to a degree, would be merged into a single hierarchy. This would be similar to the situation in ancient Egypt, but it would occur in a much more rational— and hence unbreakable—form.

An inanimate machine is mind objectified. Only this provides it with the power to force men into its service and to dominate their everyday working life as completely as is actually the case in the factory. Objectified intelligence is also that animated machine, the bureaucratic organization, with its specialization of trained skills, its division of jurisdiction, its rules and hierarchical relations of authority. Together with the inanimate machine it is busy fabricating the shell of bondage which men will perhaps be forced to inhabit someday, as powerless as the fellahs of ancient Egypt. This might happen *if* a technically superior administration *were to be the ultimate and sole value* in the ordering of their affairs, and

193

that means: a rational bureaucratic administration with the corresponding welfare benefits, for bureaucracy can accomplish this much better
than any other structure of domination. . . . Who would want to deny
that such a potentiality lies in the womb of the future?[25]

The enormous dystopian potential inherent in a world in which
"technically superior administration" was the "ultimate and sole
value" impels Weber to seek out sources of resistance to the un-
bounded rationalization of society. It is a question not of reversing
the overall direction of development of occidental culture (for
Weber, a patent absurdity) but rather of limiting the domination of
officialdom in specific sectors of life. The fact that nation-states,
political parties or associations, and cultural values all demand loyalty from the individual in their various struggles against each other
opens up a potentially rich source of alternative values and sources
for meaning. The ideas of choice and struggle in the political realm
exert a tremendous attraction on Weber because they point to powers which, to some extent, can "check and effectively control" the
"tremendous influence" of bureaucracy on society at large.

This explains, in part, why the notion of struggle plays such a
prominent role in Weber's political and cultural thought. Its shaping
influence upon his ideas of moral and intellectual integrity can
hardly be exaggerated. All the more reason, then, to ask whether his
notion of struggle remains static, signifying an unvarying principle
of existence, or evolves as we move from his early to mature thought.
The answer is, a little of both—something that becomes apparent
when we compare his usage in the inaugural address to that in "Parliament and Government" and the "Vocation" lectures. It is my contention that Weber's reliance on the idea of politics as struggle expands rather than contracts as he moves from the consideration of
interstate relations to the constitutional form of postwar Germany
and, finally, to the conflict of values in a "disenchanted" world.

The 1895 address on "The Nation State and Economic Policy"
reveals the young Weber as an unabashed nationalist and imperialist.
Building on the findings of his earlier inquiry into "The Conditions
of the Agricultural Workers in the East Elbian regions of Germany,"[26] the lecture is ostensibly a consideration of the "the role
played by physical and psychological racial differences between na-
tionalities in the economic struggle for existence."[27] Weber takes as
his example the shifts in population in the agrarian lands of West

Prussia, where German peasants and day laborers are declining, while Polish peasants and laborers are becoming ever more numerous, threatening the German character of the region. The lecture, however, scarcely confines itself to the policy questions that this particular case study presents. On the contrary, Weber uses his example as an occasion to reflect publicly on the role of political economy in promoting the interests of the nation; on the kind of ideals that should guide Germany in its competition for power with other nations; and on the relative political maturity of the "rising classes" (the bourgeoisie and the workers) in Germany. The lecture is a warning about the dangers faced by the German nation, a stern rebuke to its "political" classes for their lack of leadership, and a call to arms for a new generation, one ready to face the challenges of the future.

Given the stakes of Weber's agenda, the problem with which he opens the lecture seems almost trivial. What, he asks his audience, accounts for the counterintuitive phenomenon of the more advanced ethnic group (the German peasants) coming off worse in the economic struggle for existence in the east? How is it that the West Prussian agricultural crisis (which finds the aristocratic Junker landlords struggling to maintain their hegemony in the face of increased market pressure) creates a "process of selection" which rewards the "inferior" Poles?

Weber's answer is couched in the social Darwinist rhetoric of the time, albeit to make a point which runs counter to the popular understanding of how "natural" processes of selection are bound to work. "Why is it the *Polish* peasants who are gaining ground?" Weber asks. "Is it because of their superior economic intelligence or capital resources? It is rather the opposite of both these things."[28] The superior adaptability of the Polish peasant to the proletarianization of work conditions in West Prussia lies in his ability to "*minimize* his own requirements," to make fewer "physical and ideal demands" than his German counterpart, for whom the yearning for freedom retains its power.[29] In the case of West Prussia, then, the all-powerful "process of selection" works *against* the "racially and culturally" superior (who are unable to adapt) and *for* those who are at a lower stage of material and moral development.

While Weber's use of racial and ethnic generalizations in the first part of his lecture grates on contemporary sensibilities, the lessons he draws from his case study are far more disturbing. The fact that

195

German peasants are "coming off worse in a silent and bleak struggle for everyday economic existence in competition with an inferior race" reveals the falseness of assuming that the "process of selection" invariably works in favor of the more developed or advanced. But it also points to the falseness of assuming that economic development is creating a world in which the root causes of competition between nations and ethnic groups are being gradually being done away with, heralding an international economic order of peace and prosperity. "The somber gravity of the population problem alone," Weber writes, "is enough to prevent us from being eudaemonists, from imagining that peace and happiness lie in the womb of the future, and from believing that anything other than the *hard struggle of man with man* can create any elbow-room in this earthly life."[30]

Scarcity—of food, employment, and lebensraum—is the fundamental fact underlying the existential struggle of one nation against another. That is why, according to the young Weber, the science of political economy must abandon not only "optimistic hopes of happiness" but the idea that appropriate standards or ideals for humanity can be derived from economic considerations alone. It is, Weber asserts, an "optical illusion" to think that economics can or ought to secrete such "ultimate" values: "The truth is that the ideals we introduce into the subject matter of our science are *not* peculiar to it, nor are they produced by this science itself; rather, they are the old general types of human ideals."[31] This means that the science of political economy must take its bearings from the *character* of the particular people it happens to serve—the "particular strain of humankind" whose existence it seeks to promote in the "eternal struggle."[32] Economic policy must acknowledge the fact that "the expanded economic community is simply another form of the struggle of the nations with each other, one which has not eased the struggle to defend one's own culture but made it more *difficult*, because this enlarged economic community summons material interests within the body of the nation to ally themselves with it in the fight *against* the future of the nation."[33] Political economy, in other words, must acknowledge the priority of the political.

What is at stake in this competition between nations? The answer is not simply access to markets, riches, or the "well-being" of future generations. Every nation struggles for its *existence*; a great nation, however, struggles to enhance the "quality of human beings" reared by its particular socioeconomic regime. "We do not want to breed well-being in people, but rather those characteristics which we think of as constituting the human greatness and nobility of our nature."[34] It is a mistake to think that making a nation's economic culture "as advanced as it can be" automatically ensures success in the pursuit of *this* goal since—as the example of the Polish versus German peasants bears out—strictly economic processes of selection often work in favor of the "lower" type.

With this striking recasting of political economy as an auxiliary in the struggle of nations and cultures to "stamp" the future of humanity, Weber gives a quasi-Nietzschean twist to the "dismal science." In order to be meaningful, the economic struggle must be cast in terms of the struggle for power, and the latter must be seen as a struggle of ideals. Nations can be carriers of ideals; commerce, labor, and markets cannot. Moreover, economic success ultimately depends upon political power, for it is political power (in the form of aggressively pursued empire-building) which opens markets and gains access to raw materials. But if this is the case, who will be the bearer of the nation's "sense of political purpose"? What group can be trusted to advance the "specifically political interests" of the nation?

With this question Weber turns to the last and, in many respects, most characteristic topic of his lecture: the relative political maturity (*Mündigkeit*) of the rising classes in Germany. Given that economic development has not lessened but exacerbated the struggle between nations, which class in Germany is politically mature enough to lead? Which of the "leading economic and political strata" is able to grasp the nation's "enduring economic and political power interests" and has both the ability and the discipline to "place these interests above all other considerations"?[35] The Junkers are politically adept but economically declining: they can no longer be trusted to place the nation's interest above their own (something illustrated by their openness to Polish workers). Can the bourgeoisie pick up where the Junkers left off? Can they provide Germany with the political leadership that a *Machtstaat* (power state) demands?

Weber's answer is a contemptuous "no." He depicts the bourgeoisie of the previous generation as politically immature, beset by an utter lack of political judgment and any developed instinct for power. Raised in the formidable shadow of Bismarck, the German bourgeoisie found itself deprived of any meaningful opportunity for political participation (and political education) by its "Caesarist"

leader. Moreover, the previous generation conspired in its own political infantilization, happily shrugging off political tasks and responsibilities, the better to enjoy the fruits of German unification
and the thirty years of peace Bismarck's policies made possible. Bur-
dened by this "unpolitical past," the older generation (according to
Weber) lacks all sense of the "vocation" for politics. It is split between the big or haute bourgeois, who yearn for another protector
à la Bismarck, and a broader section of petit bourgeois, who are
mired in the "political philistinism" of the lower middle classes,
cheering the acquisition of colonies and the belligerent rhetoric of
the kaiser with little or no sense of the stakes involved. Weber sees
nothing that can alter this attitude or make up for "a century of
missed political education."[36]

If the German bourgeoisie was politically immature, the German
working class hardly presented an alternative. The fact that this class
was relatively well organized and able to assert itself in the *economic*
struggle for power did not alter the fundamental *political* state of
affairs. Unlike their English or French counterparts, the German
working class was never confronted with the compulsory political
education that results from absorbing the "reverberations of a position of world power."[37] In addition, in Weber's estimation, their
leaders were even greater political philistines than the bourgeoisie,
"wretched minor political talents" who postured as if they were "the
successors of the men of the [French Revolutionary] Convention"
but who utterly lacked "the great *power* instincts of a class with a
vocation for political leadership."[38]

"What is *threatening* about our situation," Weber surmises, "is the
fact that the bourgeois classes seem to be wilting as the bearers of
the *power*-interests of the nation, while there is still no sign that
the workers are beginning to become mature enough to take their
place."[39] The "*political* qualification of the *ruling and rising* classes,"
not the "economic situation of the ruled" (which, Weber admitted,
was one of "enormous misery"), was the crucial "socio-political
problem." Hence, "the aim of our socio-political activity is not to
make everybody happy but the *social unification* of the nation, which
has been split apart by modern economic development, and to prepare it for the strenuous struggles of the future."[40] Since no class's
arm is currently strong enough to bear "the spear of leadership,"
there is "an immense task of political education to be done," some-

thing that can be accomplished only if all see that "there is no more serious duty" than "contributing to the *political* education of our nation."[41] Only the achievement of a hard political maturity—one which eschews dreams of "happiness" and the belief that "it is possible to replace political with ethical ideals"—will enable the current German nation to become "precursors of an even greater epoch."

The young Weber took great delight in the controversy stirred by his inaugural address. "The brutality of my views have caused horror," he wrote, with more than a little satisfaction.[42] His liberal nationalist contempt for "eudaemonism" is certainly unapologetic, as is his insistence on the priority of the political and his description of *Staatsraison* (reason of state) as "the ultimate criterion for economic policy."[43] But what is most striking about the inaugural address is not its enthusiastic endorsement of realpolitik but the way it deploys the notion of struggle to support a supraeconomic politics of ideals, one which demands responsible, self-denying stewards with a sense of historical mission.[44] This is why the question of maturity looms so large even in the young Weber's thought. The worst fate is to be consigned to the role of political epigoni, overshadowed by the feats of one's predecessors. His father's generation seemed strangely (and, in Weber's view, contemptibly) comfortable in this role. Weber wants his generation to be different, to appreciate its responsibilities before the nation and history. The only way to escape the fate of epigoni is to become "the precursors of an even greater epoch." Maturity in the distinctly Weberian sense of *responsibility to an ideal* is found not in the rising classes but in the rising generation—or so the young Weber would have his audience believe.[45]

Between the *Freibürger Antrittsrede* and "Politics and Government in a Reconstructed Germany" there lies the death of an overbearing father; a personal breakdown which forced Weber to give up teaching; a long period of inactivity and recuperation, followed by frenzied scholarly production; and, of course, a world war which transformed the world and Germany's place in it. We should not be surprised, then, that the view of politics held by the fifty-three-year-old Weber is significantly different from that held by the aggressive thirty-year-old liberal nationalist. Nevertheless, the thematic continuities are striking. The emphasis on the political immaturity of

Germany's "rising" classes; the focus on the need for widespread political education; and the insistence that politics is a necessary process of both *struggle* and *selection*—these elements of the young Weber's political worldview are on ample display in his later political writings. Their content, however, underwent an important shift as the reality of the war—and the mendacity and stupidity of the German ruling class—led Weber to see the role of the *Machtstaat* in the international arena as more of a burden than an opportunity for self-assertion or the promotion of ideals. Weber never renounced his nationalism, but he increasingly came to focus on politics within the state rather than between states. It was in the former arena that adequate room for maneuvering and real opportunity for reform existed. The realm of international politics, conversely, presented a far more rigid and impenetrable logic of power.[46]

This change in attitude appears in a short essay Weber published in 1916 in the journal *Die Frau*. "Between Two Laws" is a response to a Swiss Christian pacifist who had attacked the assertion of Weber's friend, the German feminist Gertrud Bäumer, that war confronts women and citizens with inevitably conflicting duties. Unsurprisingly, Weber frames his response by drawing a stark contrast between small political communities, such as Switzerland, and *Machtstaaten* like Germany. The former have renounced political power and so are free to cultivate what Weber calls "the simple, bourgeois virtues of citizenship and true democracy," which have "never yet been realized in any great *Machtstaat*."[47] Germany, on the other hand, has a "responsibility before history" to help determine "the character of culture in the future." The future of Europe will be "shared out, without a struggle, between the regulations of Russian officials on the one hand and the conventions of English-speaking 'society' on the other," unless the German people "throw [their] weight into the balance on this historical issue."[48]

The struggle that Germany is obliged to undertake, however, is not an agonistic opportunity freely grasped in order to show which nation is most deserving of the respect of future generations. It is, rather, "an accursed duty and obligation to history." In the world of *Machtstaaten*, there can no withdrawal from such responsibilities since the balance of power among states can only be preserved *actively*. Thus, Germany *had* to enter the war to aid Austria. It is easy for Swiss pacifists to think that politics should follow the moral teachings of the New Testament, for they are unburdened by such a fate and have absolutely no appreciation of the "tragical historical obligations incumbent on any nation organized as a *Machtstaat*."[49] The latter have no choice but to recognize the "laws of power" that govern their existence and act accordingly. They exist in the abysslike gap between politics and ethics, between the demands of Christian morality and worldly, historical duty.

This fatalism is echoed in a passage from Weber's famous 1917 essay "The Meaning of 'Ethical Neutrality' in Sociology and Economics." Discussing the ambiguity of the concept of "adaptation" in social science, Weber pauses to note:

> Conflict [*Kampf*] cannot be excluded from social life. One can change its means, its object, even its fundamental direction and its bearers, but it cannot be eliminated. There can be, instead of an external struggle of antagonistic persons for external objects, an inner struggle of mutually loving persons for subjective values and therewith, instead of external compulsion, an inner control (in the form of erotic or charitable devotion). Or it can take the form of a subjective conflict in the individual's own mind. It is always present and its influence is often greatest when it is least noticed, i.e., the more its course takes the form of indifferent or complacent passivity or self-deception, or when it operates as "selection." "Peace" is nothing more than a change in the form of the conflict or in the antagonists or in the objects of the conflict, or finally in the chances of selection.[50]

The ineradicable nature of conflict—between nations, social groups, individuals, and drives within individuals—demands not only the abandonment of dreams of international cooperation or social harmony but also (it would seem) any *democratic* hopes whatsoever. But Weber, unlike his student Carl Schmitt, did not draw the expected Hobbesian moral about the nature of domestic politics. Rather than assert the necessity of an all-powerful "Caesarist" leader, he became a fierce advocate of parliamentary democracy in postwar Germany. The reasons for this change of position are complex, but they point to an appreciation of how nonviolent political struggle, in the form of competition between parliamentary parties, can serve both the interests of freedom and political education in a mass democratic state. In "Parliament and Government" Weber drew a lesson similar to that offered by Machiavelli's *Prince* and the

Discourses, namely, that while conflictual interstate relations may be subject to a strict logic of power, the conflicts within a "free republic" can, in fact, be "the cause of liberty."[51]

Unlike Machiavelli's *Discourses*, however, "Parliament and Government" does not focus on the politically mediated conflict between social classes as a potential source of "good laws and institutions." Instead, it focuses on the tension between the bureaucratic reality of the modern state and the opposing demands of political judgment and leadership. If, as Weber writes, "in a modern state the actual ruler is necessarily and unavoidably the bureaucracy," and if the "irresistible advance of bureaucratization" also encompasses modern political parties, turning them into professionalized entities, where can we turn for the cultivation of specifically *political* talents? Where might strong and independent political actors be formed who can "check and effectively control the tremendous influence of this [bureaucratic] stratum"?[52] Weber's answer is simple: only within a parliament elected by universal suffrage; a parliament which wields real power and is not just a "rubber stamp" for the ministries.

This makes it sound as if Weber's sole concern is creation and selection of strong parliamentary leaders, since (in his view) politicians are the only effective "countervailing force against bureaucratic domination."[53] Indeed, this is an extremely important dimension of Weber's commitment to parliamentary politics. But it is misleading to view Weber's preference for a strong parliament as simply instrumental, a function of his somewhat desperate search for powers that would offset the stifling (and politically disastrous) rule of the officials.[54] It is better, I think, to follow Wolfgang Mommsen's suggestion and view Weber's stress upon the need for a strong parliament—one with genuine authority—as part of his broader commitment to democratization and the cultivation of freedom-preserving political struggle.[55]

It is true that Weber did not think that the average citizen had much to contribute to this struggle, or would find life dramatically transformed by greater democratization of the political system. Weber notoriously thought that democracy was simply one of several forms of domination (*Herrschaft*) characteristic of the modern world.[56] To think that democracy as a form of government would overcome the distinction between ruler and ruled was to delude oneself. The best that could be said about mass democracy was that it was a form of domination in which the leaders were freely elected.[57]

Yet this form of domination also preserved the maximum amount of freedom for the individual and contributed (at least in its parliamentary form) to the political education not only of elites but of the nation—no small achievement in the infantilized political culture of post-Bismarck Germany.

The emphasis on political education is evident throughout "Parliament and Government." As he had done twenty-two years earlier in the *Antrittsrede*, Weber constructs a close link between political education and political struggle. His sober view of the realities of modern democratic politics—in which party regulars are motivated by the pursuit of jobs and perks, and the masses by interest and *ressentiment*—led him to eschew the edifying but irrelevant classical view of politics as an "education in character" for the citizen.[58] More surprisingly, it made him dubious of the more limited Millian claim that political participation helped cultivate the capacity for "enlarged" judgment among ordinary citizens, even though he insisted (at least formally) that participation "is the precondition for developing political judgment."[59]

This deemphasis on the participatory "education of the *demos*" flows from the nature of modern electoral politics, which leaves the average citizen with a much diminished role. "Even in mass parties with very democratic constitutions," Weber writes, "the voters and most of the rank and file [party] members do not (or do not formally) participate in the drafting of the program and the selection of the candidates, for by their very nature such parties develop a salaried officialdom." The result is that "the voters exert influence only to the extent that programs and candidates are selected according to their chances of receiving electoral support."[60] For the most part, the average citizen is "completely inactive," the more or less passive target of propaganda efforts, demagoguery, and what Weber calls "the exploitation of mass emotionality."[61]

Where, then, and how does "political education" take place? Weber's twofold answer is deliberately dismissive of pretensions of egalitarian "literati" and what he condescendingly refers to as "the democracy of the street." For the average citizen, the political education provided by a strong parliamentary system consists *not* in any opportunity for direct political participation beyond voting but rather in the *public* character of parliamentary debate and inquiry. This, more than anything else, distinguishes "rule by politicians" from "rule by officials," for whom virtually every internal policy matter falls under the category of a "service secret." The relative political maturity of the English people can be accounted for by a parliament which was not simply an organ of impotent criticism (as was the Reichstag), but a real authority over the bureaucracy, one whose system of working committees not only cultivated competent political leaders but served to ensure "publicity of administration." It was the latter, in Weber's view, which was a precondition for the "political education of the leaders and led."

Even with strong parliamentary oversight and the principle of publicity, the fact remained that the daily business of governing had precious little to do with the "will of the people." Here, as elsewhere, Weber brought a notably "disenchanted" sensibility to the analysis of parliamentary democracy. As he famously remarked in a letter to his student Roberto Michels, "Concepts such as 'popular will' and genuine will of the people do not exist for me anymore. They are fictions."[62] The brute reality of the modern state is that "the actual ruler is necessarily and unavoidably the bureaucracy" which is responsible for the "routines of administration."[63] Citizens are simply "those ruled by bureaucracy," while modern parliaments are "primarily representative bodies of those ruled with bureaucratic means."[64] Escape from the *Obrigkeitsstaat* constructed by bureaucratic domination could only come from a source powerful enough to train and select political actors of such talent and will that they would be able to bend the apparatus of party and state to their own purposes: "Politicians [*not* 'the people'] must be the countervailing force against bureaucratic domination."[65]

What is this source? Where, in other words, do real "politicians" (as opposed to bureaucrats manqué) come from? They come from the political process of struggle and selection found only in a parliamentary or representative democracy. It is in the struggle for party leadership and victory on the electoral battlefield, in the competition with other political actors in the working committees of a strong parliament, that the most important form of political education, the education of leaders, occurs.

Parliament and not the ministries is the appropriate "recruiting ground" for *political* talents: "For the modern politician the proper palaestra is the parliament and the party contests before the general public; neither competition for bureaucratic advancement nor anything else will provide an adequate substitute."[66] Weber is intensely aware that the rhetorical and demagogic talents required by the po-

litical actor have long been the target of opprobrium from the up-
holders of "expert knowledge." From Plato to more recent technocratic critics of "partisan struggle," the operative distinction has
been between political rhetoric (a mere "technique of persuasion,"
according to the *Gorgias*) and the more specialized knowledge of
how to rule (the so-called royal art, or *basilike politik*). Weber leaves
little doubt as to where he stands with regard to *this* debate. Democratization and the increasing importance of demagogic speech go
hand in hand: next to a political actor's "qualities of will," the force
of his demagogic speech is "above all decisive."[67]

Weber's defense of "the much-maligned 'craft of demagoguery' "
is unapologetic—but it is also limited. While a necessary weapon on
the "battlefield of elections," it can also lead to "striking misuses."[68]
However, one must be willing to risk a Cleon if one would have a
Pericles.[69] The fact of the matter is that modern politics is, to a
great extent, a matter of "written and spoken *words*."[70] The advent
of parliamentary democracy makes speech-making the primary
means of waging "political combat" and building a mass following.
But while Weber stresses the importance that such "charismatic authority" assumes in the struggle against bureaucratic authority, he
is also careful to emphasize the training and struggle that takes place
within parliamentary bodies themselves. "Ignorant demagogy" can
only be overcome by politicians who have been schooled in the com-
mittee work of a strong (that is, politically powerful) parliament.[71]
The *last* thing Weber wants to do is encourage the irresponsible and
ignorant rhetoric of the "literati" or political dilettantes. Gladstone,
not Robespierre or Lenin, is his model of the "charismatic" parliamentary demagogue.[72]

This is why Weber insists that the struggle for power which takes
place *within* parliament is at least as important an arena for the
selection of leaders as "the battlefield of elections." In a "working"
parliament

> every conflict . . . involves not only a struggle over substantive issues,
> but also a struggle for personal power. Wherever parliament is so strong
> that, as a rule, the monarch entrusts the government to the spokesman
> of a clear-cut majority, the power struggle of the parties will be a contest
> for this highest executive position. The fight is then carried by men who
> have great political power instincts and highly developed qualities of
> political leadership, and hence the chance to take over the top positions;

for the survival of the party outside parliament, and the countless ideal, and partly very material, interests bound up with it require that capable leaders get to the top. Only under such conditions can men with political temperament and talent be motivated to subject themselves to this kind of selection through competition.[73]

This brings us to a central feature of Weber's idea of political struggle as the chief vehicle for the enhancement of freedom in the modern world. As is evident from his focus on the recruitment of leaders and his dismissal of the quasi-anarchic "democracy of the street," Weber had little interest in stimulating the political passions of the masses. These are, in his estimation, invariably tainted by *ressentiment* and the desire for booty of one sort or another.[74] Genuine *political* action, therefore, is not (as Hannah Arendt would maintain) a matter of ordinary citizens "acting together, acting in concert." Rather, the human capacity for initiation and freedom is best exemplified by the political leader who creates a disciplined following in pursuit of clear, demagogically articulated goals.

Weber's version of agonistic politics—part of his overall strategy to combat "Saint Bureaucratius" and the *Obrigkeitsstaat*—is obviously vulnerable to criticism. Most damning is the charge that his focus on leadership, demagogy, and charisma added little to the "political education" of ordinary Germans and helped—albeit unintentionally—to pave the way to fascist dictatorship.[75] It is, however, a little too easy to claim (in hindsight) that "increased democratic deliberation" is "the only solution for dangers inherent in the reliance of democracy upon leadership" since it "harnesses the contest amongst ambitious leaders to the necessity of giving good public advice."[76]

We must remember that Weber's guiding concern was, in effect, how to "jump-start" the process of political education in Germany. He thought this could best be accomplished through a process of political "struggle and selection," one which cultivated authentically political talents and contributed (though the enhancement of representative institutions) to the development of "independent thought" and judgment in the nation at large.[77] The fact that he considered the radical democratic project of extending political deliberation and decision-making to "the people" a utopian fantasy should not blind us to the underlying point of his conception of politics as a process of struggle. Weber thought that an agonistic parliamentary politics would help shape responsible political leaders and parties of a sort previously unknown in Germany. The institutionalization of such struggle would, in other words, give birth to the powers needed to "check and effectively control" the rule of officialdom, helping to preserve whatever traces of "individualist" freedom remained in the modern state.[78]

The institutional setting of Weber's agonistic politics quiets some of the fears aroused by his radical deemphasis of the deliberative (Millian or "Socratic") functions of representative government. In "Parliament and Government," his understanding of power balancing power reassuringly approximates the Montesquieuian conception that guided the American founders—his emphasis on the necessity of a strong state notwithstanding. However, when we turn from the struggle of politicians and parties to that between conflicting values—that is, to Weber's uncompromising version of value pluralism—we find that many of the old fears return. For it is in his conception of a "new polytheism" that the ethical consequences of his tragic understanding of a world riven by struggle become most apparent. And it is here that his deemphasis on deliberation as a potential vehicle not of consensus but of clarification and disillusion seems most extreme.

In general, it can be said that Weber's concept of struggle evolves from that of a quasi-Hobbesian competition between nations for survival and power (the *Antrittsrede*), to an instrumental conception of political struggle as a *means* for the selection of leaders ("Parliament and Government"), to (finally) a more "tragic" conception of the fundamental irreconcilability of different ultimate values, none of which can be read off from the structure of the world. It is in his reflections on value conflict that Weber, like Nietzsche, discovers a realm which, by its very nature, is resistant to the leveling demands of bureaucratic ("formal") rationality. Because ultimate values conflict, the expanding tyranny of instrumental reason (the "iron cage") is bound to run up against the ineradicable fact of human choice and commitment. But *this* fact seems to place the entire realm of ultimate values forever beyond the reach of any rational adjudication whatsoever. Hence the charge that Weber's moral pluralism is "decisionist" in a way that, say, Mill's is not.[79]

In my view this criticism has been overdrawn for reasons I discuss in the fourth section of this chapter. Suffice it to note here that what we find in Weber is not a subjective philosophy of value resting on a one-dimensional conception of formal reason but an "objective" form of moral pluralism which presents unique challenges of its own.[80] The fact that (as Habermas argues) the modern "value spheres" of science, morality, and art raise validity claims in distinct ways, subject to the broad forms of argumentative rationality appropriate to each, does nothing to alter the deeper, more recalcitrant truth that values can and do conflict. No theory or practice of argumentative rationality can tell us when, say, equality should triumph over liberty in matters of law or social policy, let alone how to decide between weltanschauungen. To be sure, we expect arguments and good reasons in these matters. Yet in many, if not most, cases reasonable people will continue to disagree over where the "force of the better argument" resides.[81]

Habermas is right, however, in saying that Weber tends to ontologize the distinction between facts and values.[82] This disposes him to abandon prematurely the claims of political and moral argument and to neglect the disillusioning effects such argument can potentially promote. This emerges most clearly in the "Vocation" lectures. As noted earlier, in these lectures Weber presents the separation of value spheres as the defining characteristic of modern life. But he also presents the value harmony characteristic of an earlier age as a culturally specific *illusion*, one whose grip we are still struggling to break free of. Faced with a fragmenting world of value, the temptation has been to look for a substitute for the integrating powers of faith. For modern man the most likely candidate has been science, which (in its more immodest moments) promises to root out the sources of tragic conflict and discover the grounds of social and political harmony.[83] This is why, in "Science as a Vocation," Weber targets not the pretensions of faith (which have been badly shaken if not destroyed) but those of science—*Wissenschaft*—and its teachers. In response to the yearnings of youth, the latter have allowed themselves to be set up as a new authority, one which answers the ultimate questions about the value and conduct of life.

A good part of Weber's lecture is thus given over to smashing these pretensions, to showing that the "value of science" is far less grandiose than some of its "devoted disciples" have imagined.[84] Science may once have promised to open the way to "true being," "true art," "true nature," and "true happiness," but it no longer does so. Tolstoy was right: science gives no answer to the question: "What shall we do and how shall we live?" The only remaining question, according to Weber, is "the sense in which science gives 'no' answer, and whether or not science might yet be of some use to the one who puts the question correctly."[85]

Science (the German *Wissenschaft* encompasses both the natural and cultural sciences) gives no answer in the sense that it cannot demonstrate the ultimate worth of the knowledge it produces: it must simply presuppose its value. According to Weber, physics, chemistry, and astronomy "presuppose as self-evident that it is worthwhile to know the ultimate laws of cosmic events as far as science can construe them," just as modern medicine presupposes that the maintenance of life is (almost) always desirable, and juris-prudence presupposes that certain legal rules are, in fact, binding.[86] In each case the *value* of the object of knowledge—the mechanism of natural phenomena, of the human body, or of legal rules—is and must be *assumed* by the particular science in question.

If science can give no account as to *why* the knowledge it provides is or should be existentially valuable to mankind, its intervention on behalf of various "party opinions" concerning political and moral matters is absolutely worthless. Knowledge which is incapable of demonstrating the ground of its meaning for human life is even more incapable of deciding between conflicting values or welt-anschauungen. The "art of measurement" pursued by the Platonic Socrates in the *Protagoras* is obviously nowhere to be found in the specialized sciences. The latter contain no standards for the ranking of values or ways of life, nor even for providing a convincing justifi-cation of their own activities.[87] " 'Scientific' pleading is meaningless in principle because the various value spheres of the world stand in irreconcilable conflict with one another."[88] Far from offering a substitute for faith or a value-ranking "substantive" reason (what the philosophers once called "right reason"), the specialized sciences simply provide the tools to help us realize pre-given but basically unexamined ends.

When we combine Weber's fierce insistence that *Wissenschaft* is powerless to answer the most existentially important questions with his utter contempt for the pieties of the "old churches," we seem to have all the elements necessary for a return to philosophy (under-stood as an inquiry into ultimates). But this is precisely what Weber denies himself and his audience. He was intensely skeptical of the rationalist conception of reason as something independent of both power and interest. While philosophers had traditionally viewed reason in either transcendental or teleological terms (that is, as occupying a plane of existence above and apart from interest, or as revealing the fundamental human ends toward which these interests blindly groped), Weber, like Nietzsche, saw Western rationalism as a peculiar product of cultural struggles for power.[89]

This is not to say that Weber was guilty of the vulgar Nietzschean sin of believing that the extremely this-worldly origins of Western rationalism determined its development and ultimate nature, or that he thought (as do some disciples of Foucault) that rationalism was little more than an ideological vocabulary designed to disguise power relations. One can hardly read the *Vorbemerkung* to his studies in the sociology of religion and doubt Weber's conviction that Western rationalism, however specific its course of cultural development, was a phenomenon of universal significance.[90] Rather, it is closer to the mark to say that Weber (again, like Nietzsche) thought that philosophy's pretension to provide a disinterested assessment of conflicting values flowed from an underdeveloped intellectual conscience. Such a project appeared plausible only as long as one retained the fiction of a transcendental reason beyond time and chance. The "fate of an epoch which has eaten from the tree of knowledge" is simply to know better.

It is this deep sense of the "impure" nature of reason, combined with a very concrete historical sense of how values conflict within and across cultures, that led Weber to insist so vehemently that the conflict between values was ineradicable. Reason, it turned out, was powerless to reduce different virtues and tables of values to a common denominator—the presupposition (as Plato realized) of any effective "weighing up." Once Western rationalism acknowledged its own contingent origins and unexamined presuppositions—in particular, the monistic assumption that values must be commensurable because there can be only one correct answer to the question of how man should live—the project of providing an ethical "science of measurement" must be given up.[91]

Thus denuded of its metaphysical pretensions, reason was resolved into the specific contents of the specialized sciences, on the one hand, and the formal structures of law, government, and economics, on the other. This led Weber—prematurely—to conclude that the end result of the rationalization of the world was the triumph of a purposive rationality whose essential function was not critical but instrumental. Reason—in the form of the sciences and increasingly impartial (and egalitarian) norms and rules—was a tool which both organized the world and increased power, but which was utterly dependent upon value "posits" for its direction, meaning, and justification. Sealed off from the authority of a reason capable of a comprehensive moral evaluation, the realm of "ultimate values" presented the visage of unending and unresolvable struggle. We are doomed to choose among them, without the comfort of the idea that there are universal, logically undeniable "facts of value" which human reason is uniquely equipped to uncover. As Weber wrote in a famous passage from "Science as a Vocation," "So long as life remains immanent and its interpreted in its own terms, it knows only of an unceasing struggle of these gods with one another. Or speaking directly, the ultimately possible attitudes toward life are irreconcilable, and hence their struggle can never be brought to a final conclusion. Thus, it is necessary to make a decisive choice."[92]

It is the overcharged atmosphere of such choices, as well as the "disenchantment" of a comprehensive or metaphysical notion of rationality, which dictates the limits of philosophy for Weber. Because the moral terrain we move and act in is so overcrowded and conflict-ridden, philosophy (in the traditional sense) can appear only as an exercise in bad faith, or as another weapon in an ongoing struggle. In this regard, Weber's brief characterization of Socrates' "discovery" of the concept as "a handy means by which one could put the logical screws upon somebody," forcing him to admit "either that he knew nothing or that this and nothing else was truth, the *eternal* truth" is particularly telling.[93] It betrays a kind of philosophical tone deafness, one which is oblivious to the disillusioning, clarifying mission of Socratic *elenchus*. Weber takes it for granted that Socrates is engaged in a foundationalist project. The dissolvent character of Socratic rationality—its critical, negative dimension—is nowhere to be seen.

Given that Weber looms large in our tradition as a prophet of "disenchantment," this is more than a little odd. How do we account for it? What drives Weber to reduce Socratic dialectic to the status of a logical weapon in the fight to provide a new foundation for ethical conduct?

I would suggest that Weber, like many influenced by Nietzsche (and Marx), viewed philosophy as a form of Platonism, at least insofar as it aspired to be something more than a theory of knowledge.[94] This led him to regard Socrates' philosophical activity *not* as a form of radical questioning aimed at overturning the rule of "King Nomos and his numerous volunteers" but as a naïve and mystified form of science, one which aimed at producing definitive *answers* to the questions of what virtue is and how we should lead our lives. But there is another reason as well, one which takes us to the heart of Weber's ambivalence about the entire process of occidental rationalization.

Weber's acceptance of the Nietzschean story about Western culture's internal nihilistic dynamic predisposes him to regard rationality in general as corrosive and destructive of meaning.[95] As a result, like Nietzsche he was inclined to view skepticism and aggressively dissolvent forms of rationality in a particularly grim light (even though, again like Nietzsche, he practiced a relentless form of demystification). Given the disenchantment of the world by science and bureaucratic rationality, Weber felt we should be grateful for whatever dimensions of life slow this "irresistible" advance. Hence his emphasis on the conflictual aspect of politics as a response to its inevitable professionalization and rationalization. For similar reasons he emphasized how the "death of God" breathes new life into the "warring gods," which represent the different value spheres of human life. The recrudescence of the value conflict repressed by the "grandiose moral fervor" of Christianity meant the expansion of the arena of human freedom and existential choice.

The "death of God," then, does not leave us free to "create" values or systematically revive those of a nobler past; it does, however, enhance our awareness of the complexity of the moral terrain we inhabit, revealing tensions and choices that are unavoidable. Value pluralism means the proliferation of existential choices (at least for some) even within the confines of the "iron cage" of bureaucratic rationality. More than anything else, it is the fact of value conflict which enables Weber to think that it may indeed be possible to preserve more than a few "remnants" of "individualist freedom" in the face of a cold and (in his view) bleak future.[96] Yet the sphere of values can harbor this hope only so long as the "warring gods" themselves do not fall prey to the tyranny of bureaucratic rationality, with its cult of "technically superior administration."

Weber thought that the only way to resist the "irresistible" advance of rationalization was to insist that the arena of "ultimate" values lay (in some important sense) beyond the reach of reason's disenchanting, content-destroying powers. And here we see the deeper reason for Weber's dismissive identification of Socrates' philosophical activity with Platonism. To acknowledge another, nondogmatic form of philosophizing, one whose critical force was in no way dependent upon metaphysical posturing, would have been to strengthen the very meaning-destroying "intellectualism" that Weber so detested, and precisely in the sphere that mattered most: the arena of free decision among ultimate values.

From Weber's standpoint, in the late modern age Socratic dissolvent rationality is at best superfluous and at worst a kind of Trojan horse, one which can only contribute to the destruction of the last intact realm of meaningful decision and action. This sphere is already being eaten away by a colonizing instrumental reason (*Zweckrationalität*). There is, in Weber's view, no need to accelerate this process by philosophically undermining the robust plurality of competing values, however "irrational" these might appear. Hence philosophy must be put in its place as an "illusion" of the "enchanted" past.

POLITICS, ETHICS, AND MORAL
INTEGRITY IN "POLITICS AS A VOCATION"

The fear of "meaninglessness" determines the ultimate valence of the concept of struggle in Weber's work. It also underlies his famous and somewhat tortured attempt to revive and secularize the Calvinist conception of the calling (*Beruf*) in the "Vocation" lectures.

In Weber's view, the new bureaucratic order encompassed the whole of modern life and was fabricating a docile, subservient individual to fulfill its functions. The passivity and immaturity bred by Germany's peculiar political-historical development was exacerbated by the demands of an increasingly rationalized world, which made specialization and conformity to routine the sine qua non of economic security and a firm status position. The administered world resulted in the proliferation of *Ordnungsmenschen*, that is, human subjects who yearned for the stability provided by adherence to authority. The last thing such human cogs could be expected to demonstrate was the combative attitude necessary for struggle in any form, whether between nations, parties, or values. If the meaning and freedom of human action were to be preserved in the evolving "shell of bondage," it would be by those individuals who had empowered themselves through the discipline demanded by service to a cause, that is, through a secularized version of the "calling."

The theme of how such individuals are created or "bred" came to occupy an increasingly central place in Weber's later work. We have already seen how he hoped parliamentary politics could provide a mechanism for the selection of genuine politicians. In the "Vocation" lectures the focus shifts from the question of the institutional reforms necessary to create such a mechanism to that of how the *character* of such an empowered individual is formed. This change of focus places Weber in line with such political thinkers as Plato, Aristotle, and Machiavelli. Like Plato and Aristotle, he is concerned with how to breed a "spiritual aristocracy" which will serve as the selfless instrument of concerns bigger than itself.[97] But, like Machiavelli, he is more concerned with what conduces to action, energy, and power than he is with what conduces to right. This is not to say he is Machiavellian in his approach to the sensibilities of potential leaders—far from it. Weber demands a degree of ascetic self-sacrifice and self-denial that the Machiavellian political actor would find positively Christian.

What accounts for Weber's insistent linkage of power and self-denial? Why are the disciplines which form genuine leaders and political actors necessarily *ascetic* in character? The answer has to do with Weber's quasi-metaphysical notion of struggle and with his sense of the "corruption" born of the bureaucratic *Ordnungsmensch*.

Weber's pluralism, as I have noted, is of an objective—but also objectifying—sort. There is little possibility of mediation between conflicting ends, nor any sense that the truth is many-sided and requires mobility of perspective. For Weber truth in the great questions of life is a function of struggle, *not* the ability "to control one's Pro and Con" and see a multiplicity of aspects. The empowered individual must learn how to be a self-sacrificing warrior to his "cause," an agent whose ethos of service prepares him for a form of spiritual combat.[98] It is only through struggle for a cause that the self overcomes its baser nature and dedicates its life (and its death) to an ideal.[99] Politics is *one* (easily corrupted) arena for this form of self-discipline, that of the warrior/servant. Serving a cause, the genuine politician constantly and selflessly *fights* for his ideal. He can be trained to do this only if he is habituated, over time, to the rigors of an ascetic discipline, to the *practice* of selfless devotion to a cause. Such ascetic devotion is what distinguishes the genuine politician not only from the bureaucrat but from all merely self-interested "power politicians."

The notion of being a "soldier for a cause" is (at least on the face of it) obviously and deeply anti-Socratic. The fact that Weber bases his conception of "vocation" on such quasi-military devotion raises many doubts. Indeed, as Harvey Goldman points out, Weber's agonistic brand of liberalism is often about as illiberal (not to mention antiphilosophical) as one can get, predicated as it is on the never-ending struggle of ascetic devotees of conflicting weltanschauungen.[100] When we add to this Weber's deep and never-repudiated nationalism, we seem to have the real anti-Socrates, one far more convincing than Nietzsche ever was.

Weber's enemies were bureaucratic inertia, bourgeois self-interest, and the decline in the "power instincts" of the ruling classes. He wanted to energize leaders and peoples for the great struggle between nations and cultures; he wanted to throw off, so far as possible, the deadening hand of rationalization and counter the hegemony of the economic forces unleashed by capitalism. He turned to the idea of the calling, with its religious and military overtones, to create a new political elite, one which would save politics from bureaucratic banality and economic determinism and restore meaning to the life of the nation.[101] As a result, slowing people down and making them more thoughtful were not high on his list of priorities.

This is one account of Weber's motivation. It is, in many respects, persuasive. There is, however, another set of reasons for Weber's intense interest in the idea of a "calling." In the "Vocation" lectures we do not simply confront Weber's recipe for creating "empowered" agents out of politicians and students. We also encounter his attempt to redefine the notions of moral and intellectual integrity for the late modern age. As I have argued, these are the notions upon which the ideal of Socratic citizenship is built. Weber has very little interest in reviving *this* ideal. Yet his reformulation of the ideas of moral and intellectual integrity is of permanent interest to those who do. For it is in this reformulation that we see the promise—and the perils—which the "disenchantment of the world" holds for Socratic citizenship.

"Politics as a Vocation" sets out a conception of the moral integrity proper to the *political* actor. But it also provides Weber's largely student audience with a *tour d'horizon* of the nature and constraints of a political career in an age of mass politics. Indeed, a good three quarters of the lecture is given over to a sweeping historical/sociological narrative of the rationalization, professionalization, and massification of politics in Europe and America. It is only after he has subjected his audience to unwanted instruction in the fundamental realities of modern politics that Weber turns, in the final part of his lecture, to consider the questions of what "inner enjoyments" a career in politics might afford and, far more important, what "personal conditions [are] presupposed by one who enters this avenue" of life.[102]

One could do worse than to read this part of the lecture as an extended exercise in forcing idealistic youth—inflamed by the passions of the Bavarian revolution of 1918—to view politics in its least appealing aspect, entirely stripped of the euphemisms political theory normally deploys to disguise the exercise of power. Weber's focus on the state as a "compulsory association" based on force; on *violence* as the characteristic *means* of politics; on professionalization, the rise of officialdom (on the one hand) and mass parties (on the other); and, finally, on the intellectual and moral "proletarianization" that accompanies the new, "plebiscitarian" form of democracy—all these comprise a prolonged cold shower intended to disabuse the young of their shallow and (from Weber's point of view) morally deficient idealism. For it is only the disillusioned who will be able to "measure up to the world as it really is," who will be both mature and strong enough to experience the vocation of politics in "its deepest meaning."[103]

Politics, as delineated by Weber, is a sordid, violent, competitive, and—for all but a few—debasing game, soul-destroying not only for losers but for winners. He opens his lecture by telling the assembled students that his talk "will necessarily disappoint you in a number of ways."[104] Foremost among these disappointments is the realization that no conviction or cause, no matter how pure or successful, can transform the stuff, the material, of politics into something edifying. One always comes back to the competition for power, the need for a party "machine," and the fact of the "soullessness" of any mass following.[105] Hence Weber's emphasis, throughout the lecture, on the motives, means, and interests of the typical (or "auxiliary") political actor, as well as his scattered remarks on the nature of the "followers." For the most part, the former "lives off" politics, viewing political action and party maneuvering as so many opportunities

216

for personal enrichment, the extension of influence, or the procurement of status. Similarly, the majority of party followers expects some form of "personal compensation" from the victory of its leader on the "battlefield of elections."[106] In short, there is little—very little—evidence of virtue in the realm of politics. Here, as elsewhere, the motivating force is usually personal gain or factional interest, regardless of the ideological trappings under which it presents itself.[107]

This said, I should note that Weber's lecture is hardly an "unmasking" in the Marxian or Nietzschean sense. It "disappoints" not because it reveals the true interests at work behind ideological posturing but because it presents the structural limits to political action in such a blunt way. Rarely has the space of political action appeared so constricted, the political stage more confined. Once the would-be political actor takes into account the nature and tactics of the political "machine," the role of the party "boss," and the dubious or marginal nature of the careers from which "professional politicians" are culled (law, journalism), he or she might well be excused for taking youthful idealism elsewhere. Moreover, these external constraints, while responsible for the cynicism or destruction of many a promising individual, are nothing compared to the burden imposed by the irony of political action itself—the fact that "the final result of political action often, no, even regularly, stands in completely inadequate and often even paradoxical relation to its original meaning."[108] Taken together, the obstacles and ironies of contemporary politics cast whatever freedom the political actor is able to exploit in a very dubious light. In ways almost too numerous to recount, Weber presents political struggle as debasing and all but futile.

And yet "Politics as a Vocation" famously affirms the possibility of political leadership—and thus of freedom—in an age of bureaucratized, mass politics. Such an affirmation is *possible* because Weber thinks that plebiscitary democracy is rapidly overtaking parliamentary democracy, thereby reviving the importance of the demagogue in Western politics. The affirmation is *necessary* because without what Weber calls "inwardly called" leadership, politics devolves into the nihilism of administrative despotism, the rule of the "clique" through the "machine." When Weber insists that "there is only the choice between leadership democracy with a 'machine' and leaderless democracy, namely, the rule of professional politicians *without a calling*," he is claiming that there is but one avenue by which *modern* politics can become a realm of meaningful, free action.[109] That avenue is the exercise of power by the charismatic leader who is able to combine passionate devotion to a cause with a similarly strong sense of "objective responsibility."

Weber's long, "disappointing" prologue thus juxtaposes the inevitable professionalization of politics with the increasingly marginal role of the citizen and, indeed, of mere party members. There *is* a space for responsible political action, but, according to Weber, it is to be found only at in the highest reaches of the political realm.[110] As a result, Weber's discussion of free political action moves the inquiry away from the virtue of the citizen (the focus of the republican tradition in political thought) to the *virtu* or character of the political leader. "What kind of a man," Weber asks, "must one be if he is allowed to put his hand on the wheel of history?"[111] As noted earlier, this is the question of Plato and Thucydides, Machiavelli and Nietzsche. It is *not* the question of Socrates, nor of liberalism. Weber, the ostensible liberal, revives the concern with the soul and *virtu* of the leader precisely because the souls of citizens are—and must be—corrupt and because *procedures* promote routinization and obedience rather than justice. The character of the leader is thus the one area of politics in which the notion of *moral* integrity has any purchase. It is, for Weber, the sole vehicle through which the activity of politics—of struggle and domination—can be even partially ennobled.

Weber's discussion of the "internal" conditions for pursuing politics as a vocation begins by distinguishing varieties of leaders according to this criterion. To have the "calling" for politics is to possess a specific and rare form of moral integrity, an inner consistency and steadfastness of purpose which most "leading" politicians lack. According to Weber, the latter tend to fall into two categories: "sterilely excited" intellectuals who are "intoxicated" by politics and mere "power politicians" who are intoxicated with themselves, pursuing power for its own sake.[112] What Weber calls the "two deadly sins of politics"—lack of objectivity and irresponsibility—are rooted in such human, all too human vanity and excitation. *Only* the leader who is able to combine passion with a keen sense of personal responsibility for the consequences of action has the inner strength and moral integrity to withstand the debasing realities of mass politics and international competition.

The most important element in the leading politician's internal constitution is, then, *passion*, which Weber is careful to distinguish from both "sterile excitation" and the (no doubt enjoyable) feeling of power. Passion is the core of the "inwardly called" leader's moral integrity, but only if it is passion "in the sense of *matter of factness*, of passionate devotion to a 'cause,' to the god or demon who is overlord."[113]

This is a strange formulation, and we should pause to consider it. In "Politics as a Vocation" Weber goes out of his way to anathematize the immaturity of the student idealist, the sterile excitation of the intellectual, and the egotism of the power politician. Both political idealism and the pursuit of power for its own sake are tainted by the sin of self-indulgence, by the wish to enlarge the self through righteous action or the accumulation of power. The political actor who values moral integrity can rise above these temptations only by practicing an ascetic form of self-fashioning, by adhering to a set of disciplines that will make him not the impresario but the *servant* of his cause. This is what having a *calling* means for Weber: the passionate devotion to a cause manifest in the agent's fashioning him- or herself into a *tool* of a given profession or ideal.

In *The Protestant Ethic and the Spirit of Capitalism* Weber showed how the Puritans pioneered a systematically rationalized form of life conduct, the better to demonstrate that they had been "called" to do God's work in *this* world and hence were among the few "elect."[114] In "Politics as a Vocation" Weber secularizes this form of active, ascetic self-control, insisting that only constant reference to the end or cause, the "god" or "demon" that control's one's (political) life, brings method, constancy, and integrity to the energies of the political actor.[115] Paradoxically, in the context of a routinized world, the freedom and integrity of the political actor is preserved through a kind of willed self-objectification. The truly responsible politician is able to maintain a "distance to things and men," a distance which includes, above all, self-detachment and self-distance.[116] But it is this very detachment and renunciatory discipline which, for Weber as for the Puritans, provide the means to a genuinely empowered self.

Like Plato in the *Republic*, Weber emphasizes the "firm taming of the soul" necessary for the genuine leader. And, again like Plato, he insists that this taming can be achieved only through ascetic discipline in the service of something bigger than ourselves. However, for the prophet of a disenchanted age, this "something bigger" obviously cannot be the Good. As Weber makes amply clear in his historical/sociological prologue, the world of politics is the world of the cave, which one cannot get out of. Thus, while ascetic disciplines may empower the self, making it ready to join in the struggle that *is* politics, they do not enable the "turning around" of the soul (the Platonic *periagoge*) or its ascent. Hence, for Weber the soul is tamed and character is formed through devotion to an innerworldly "cause" rather than an otherworldly "truth." For the *responsible* politician, the cause becomes the existential a priori of a consistent character, the gravitational center that prevents him from "becoming a [mere] actor."[117] The "god" or "demon" one serves provides the foundation for one's conduct in the world, the organizing ground that gives one's actions unity, meaning, and coherence.[118] As Weber puts it:

> The serving of a cause must not be absent if action is to have inner strength. Exactly what the cause, in the service of which the politician strives for power and uses power, looks like is a matter of *faith*. The politician may serve national, humanitarian, social, ethical, cultural, worldly, or religious ends. The politician may be sustained by a strong belief in "progress"—no matter in which sense—or he may coolly reject this kind of belief. He may claim to stand in the service of an "idea" or, rejecting this in principle, he may want to serve external ends of everyday life. However, *some kind of faith must always exist*. Otherwise, it is absolutely true that the curse of the creature's worthlessness overshadows even the externally strongest political success.[119]

The action of the "leading" political actor can have meaning if and only if it refers back to a cause. Success in "imposing one's will" (Weber's definition of power in *Economy and Society*) is no criterion. Indeed, in the absence of selfless devotion, such success is inevitably corrupting, no matter how virtuosic or charismatic the political actor. In this sense, Weber can be seen as reiterating the moral of Thucydides' well-known contrast of Pericles and Alcibiades. The speech and action of Pericles were guided by the star of Athens' greatness, not his own. The efforts of Alcibiades, however, served only himself. The "worthless creature" is a political actor like Alcibiades, one who lacks any "substantive purpose."[120] *Contra* Nietzsche, such an actor cannot achieve consistency, unity of style, depth of conduct or, indeed, genuine power. He cannot, in other words, achieve moral integrity. He is doomed to be a mere "actor."

Weber's strict and unvarying emphasis on selfless service to a cause is the prelude to his consideration of the "ethos of politics as a cause" and the place of political action within what he calls "the total economy of human conduct." This includes his famous attempt to specify the *actual* (as opposed to imagined) relation of ethics to politics by means of the contrast between an "ethic of ultimate ends" (*Gesinnungsethik*) and an "ethic of responsibility" (*Verantwortungsethik*). Before turning to that discussion—and the vehement critique of all forms of moral absolutism which animates it—I wish to note the radical divergence which has already occurred between the Weberian and Socratic conceptions of moral integrity, as well as their respective programs of disillusionment.

In the *Apology* Socrates defends himself against the charge of corrupting the youth by describing his constant practice of cross-examination as a service he owes to the god Apollo, whose oracle at Delphi had commissioned him, so to speak, through her answer to his friend Chaerephon's query. One can, as a result, view the whole of Socrates' philosophical/political activity as an expression of faith or piety, one framed in terms of ascetic yet manly devotion quite similar to Weber's. Socrates's response to his own rhetorical question of whether he feels any compunction at "having followed a line of action which puts [him] in danger of the death penalty" is to cite Achilles' contempt for death and the fact that consistency or integrity is *worth more* than life itself: "The truth of the matter is this, gentlemen. Where a man has taken up his stand, either because it seems best to him or in obedience to his orders, there I believe he is bound to remain and face the danger, taking no account of death or anything else before dishonor." (28d). Socrates goes on to say that it would be a "shocking inconsistency" for him to have remained at his post in battle and to abandon the post to which the god had appointed him—the *duty* to lead the philosophical life, examining himself and others (28e). Framing his "seeking and searching" as "obedience to the divine command," an occupation that has kept him "too busy to do much either in politics or my own affairs" (23c), Socrates refuses the possibility of acquittal, on the condition that he give up philosophizing, with the following words: "I owe a greater obedience to God than to you, and so long as I draw breath and have my faculties, I shall never stop practicing philosophy and exhorting you and elucidating the truth for everyone that I meet" (29d).

221

Here, in Socrates' account of the nature of his philosophical duty and his utter devotion to it, we *seem* to have a conception of moral integrity that exactly mirrors Weber's idea of a calling. Self-consistency, steadfastness to one's commitments, devotion to one's calling—all are given dramatic expression in Socrates' defense in the *Apology*. Even Socrates' "piety," which at first looks so distant from the "religiously unmusical" Weber, fits the schema of an ascetic, rationalized life conduct organized around a commitment which is ultimately grounded in faith. The life of rational examination which aims at purging others of their unreflective opinions seems to rest, finally, upon an unavoidably dogmatic commitment. It is upon this faith that Socrates appears willing to stake his life: "Here I stand, I can do no other."

Yet the image of a pious Socrates is mistaken, at least if we understand piety in the usual sense of the word.[121] For while the conception of moral integrity found in "Politics as a Vocation" is one which structurally depends upon *some* faith, Socratic moral integrity in fact does not. As I argued in chapter 1, Socrates' integrity is grounded upon his urgent desire to avoid injustice rather than to fulfill some positive obligation (to the god, to philosophy, to the idea of virtue or the Good Life). His philosophical activity is designed to make his fellow citizens aware that unquestioned beliefs about virtue, happiness, and the individual's duties as citizen are a major source of much of the moral horror generated by politics. Thus, while Socrates speaks in the *Apology* of trying to get the citizens of a city "which is the greatest and most famous in the world for its wisdom and strength" (29e) to attend to the "perfection of [their] soul[s],"[122] the better formulation is that found in the *Gorgias*: he wants them to "care for [their] souls." To care for one's soul, in Socrates' sense, is not to withdraw from the world—*he* certainly did not—but to move the moral center of existence away from the unmediated claims of both citizenship and group identity, which are the primary sources of (uncynical) political injustice. To "care for one's soul" in the Socratic sense is to be aware of the myriad moral compromises and incitements to commit injustice which the life of active, democratic citizenship—the life praised by Pericles—constantly generates.

Such "care for one's soul" is open to two related objections. First, there is Callicles' point (in the *Gorgias*) that the strict avoidance of injustice is possible only for children and unmanly philosophers who shirk their responsibility as citizens and public men and who, as a result, "know nothing of the laws of their city [and are] completely without experience of men's characters" (*Gorgias*, 484d). Second, there is the Arendtian point that such focused care for one's soul in fact constitutes a kind of selfishness or self-interest. Socratic moral absolutism, Arendt argues, is more concerned with maintaining the self's moral purity than with preserving the public world or resisting the all too present evil which threatens it.

Callicles' insistence that, from the standpoint of the political life, a consistent avoidance of injustice is both "ridiculous and unmanly" anticipates the arguments of all political "realists," including Weber. Arendt's objection is more interesting, and it points to an idea we find in Weber and in Machiavelli, namely, the idea that there is an ethic *specific to* politics, one which is far more defensible—and ultimately more moral—than Socratic abstentionist morality, at least in the world of politics.

The public and the private, Weber and Machiavelli argue, are not morally homogeneous realms. To think that they are is to submit to the rationalist or theological fallacy that there is a *single* moral principle that can be applied universally across the various spheres of life, one capable of guiding our conduct in both the public and private realms, overriding the peculiar character (and ironies) of each. It is precisely this assumption that Weber subjects to critical assault in "Politics as a Vocation." "Is it true," he asks, "that any ethic of the world could establish commandments of identical content for erotic, business, familial, and official relations? . . . Should it really matter so little for the ethical demands on politics that politics operates with very special means, namely, power backed up by *violence*?"[123]

Weber's point here is that *any* ethic that denies the pluralism of life spheres, and the modes of conduct appropriate to each, is a dangerous and morally irresponsible fantasy. Such a unitary ethic promotes a kind of self-interest (the care for one's soul or the "pure flame of one's intentions") to a hegemonic but ultimately unjustifiable position in the "total economy of human conduct." The results are devastating not only from the standpoint of the "public thing" (the *res publica*) but also from the standpoint of human freedom. One simply cannot posit a continuity between public and private virtues, political and nonpolitical codes of conduct, if one is to live up to one's responsibility as a political actor and help preserve the very framework that makes the pursuit of *private* morality and virtue possible.

Thus, while it is perhaps a little misleading to say that "Politics as a Vocation" is Weber's rewriting of *The Prince*, there is at least one sense in which this is absolutely true. Following Machiavelli, Weber questions the overly simple relationship between politics and ethnics posited by Western rationalism and "the grandiose moral fervor of Christian ethics." The rationalist/Christian tradition seems to offer only two alternatives: either ethics and politics "have nothing whatever to do with one another" or "the ethic of political conduct is identical with that of any other conduct."[124] It was, of course, the great originality of Machiavelli to perceive what we, following Isaiah Berlin, might call the "monotheistic" distortions built into this apparently exhaustive pair of alternatives, and to raise the possibility of a specifically political ethic. Such an ethic is manifest in the civic republican ethos which animates the *Discourses on The First Ten Books of Titus Livy*, in which the virtues of patriotism, public-spiritedness, and a fierce love of liberty are championed over and above the Christian virtues of universalism, meekness, and resignation to providence. As Isaiah Berlin reminds us, Machiavelli's values may not be Christian, but "they are moral values."[125] They are not merely strategic (means to the preservation of the polity) but *ultimate*.

Like Machiavelli, but in a far more self-conscious manner, Weber underscores the falseness of this apparently exclusive dichotomy concerning how ethics relates to politics. He does this by stressing the irreducible fact of multiple life spheres and the plural codes of conduct that govern them. Viewed from this pluralist standpoint, moral absolutism and unprincipled pragmatism are equally irresponsible since neither pays sufficient attention to the fact that the characteristic *means* of politics—its very medium, as it were—is "power backed up by violence." Once this fact is acknowledged and given its proper weight, the various ethical possibilities, quandaries, and paradoxes distinctive to politics emerge. In a life sphere characterized, above all, by power backed up by violence, the moral integrity of the political actor cannot consist in the avoidance of injustice but, rather, *only* in the strict avoidance of excessive violence.[126]

The notion that the *responsible* political leader practices a strict "economy of violence" is not the only link between Machiavelli and

Weber. Both are equally concerned to point out the disastrous political *and* moral consequences of taking a code of action which governs
everyday life and applying it to the political realm. Thus, in the famous discussion in chapters 15 to 18 of *The Prince*, Machiavelli demonstrates how the *private* virtues of generosity, mercy, and honesty
transmute into dangerous vices when they are carried over, without
modification or limitation, to the public realm. Princely generosity
breeds resentment, mercy is construed as vulnerability (which leads
to conspiracy and factional violence), and honesty puts the state at
risk in the prince's dealings with less scrupulous political actors.

We find a quite similar discussion in "Politics as a Vocation."
Weber questions the virtues of charity, nonviolence, and truthfulness
when rigidly adhered to in the political realm.[127] His point is not
simply that the champions of these virtues pay insufficient attention
to the *consequences* of their code of conduct (which, in the context of
national defeat and the hunt for a guilty party, were bad enough).
More important, his point is that the *moral substance* of these virtues
dissolves when they are not adhered to with the greatest possible
rigor and consistency—a rigor which makes them patently inapplicable to the governing of conduct in the political sphere.

Weber's target is the selective invocation of the "absolute ethic of
the Gospel" by pacifists, socialists, and trade unionists. This ethic,
he states, "is not a cab, which one can have stopped at one's pleasure;
it is all or nothing."[128] Thus, from the perspective of the Sermon on
the Mount, "fighting is everywhere fighting" and one's *moral* duty
is to turn the other cheek: nonretaliation. According to Weber, for
such an ethic to have dignity it must be adhered to relentlessly, without exception. One must be "saintly in everything; at least in intention, one must live like Jesus, the apostles, St. Francis and their like.
Then this ethic makes sense and expresses a kind of dignity; otherwise, it does not."[129] Only *total* consistency gives this ethic the heroic
dimension needed to elevate it above hypocrisy or self-debasement.
From the Weberian perspective, then, Socrates becomes a hero not
merely by professing the doctrine of nonretaliation (in the *Crito*) but
by drinking the hemlock, that is, by being consistent unto death.

For Weber the core of the "absolute ethic of the Gospel" is the
doctrine of nonretaliation, and it is precisely this which renders this
ethic inapplicable to the political world: "If it is said, in line with the
acosmic ethic of love, 'Resist not him that is evil with force,' for
the politician the reverse proposition holds, 'thou *shalt* resist evil by

force,' or else you are responsible for the evil winning out."[130] From Weber's standpoint, anyone engaged in political struggle—whether against capitalists, Prussian Junkers, or revolutionary socialists—is engaged in fighting, and in fighting against something perceived as *evil*.[131] Moreover, the winner in a fight always exercises his rights at the expense of his opponent, since power is a limited commodity. As a result, the absolute ethic of a Jesus or Socrates makes sense— has inner strength and meaning—*only* if it dictates a withdrawal from the agon which *is* politics. (As we have seen, Socrates would not entirely disagree with this; yet he nevertheless found a way to fulfill his civic obligations and avoid injustice.)[132] Those who choose to participate in the agon must be willing to be "soldiers for their cause." Otherwise, they will fail to achieve the degree of consistency and moral seriousness that Weber demands of the responsible politician. They will fail to live up to the "ethos of politics as a '*cause*.' "[133]

We begin to see how Weber appropriates the Socratic idea that moral integrity involves consistency and steadfastness to one's commitments. If anything, Weber is even more adamant than Socrates on this score. The compelling difference, however, flows from the pluralism he shares with Machiavelli, and the conviction that what is a virtue in one sphere is not necessarily a virtue in another. In the end, the virtues of the public man are, as Callicles insisted, simply different from those of the philosopher or saint: one fights, the other doesn't. Hence, anyone who would dare answer the "calling" of politics first has to get straight about the form moral integrity takes for the *political* actor. Otherwise devotion to a cause will be confused with the quest for purity of the self. Such confusion, Weber maintains, is one of the greatest threats to moral integrity in the public realm since it issues in a form of asceticism which is not a "calling" in the true sense of the word. Instead of empowering or promoting an activist stance toward the world, it subordinates conduct to the *disempowering* demand that moral cleanliness be maintained at all costs. Weber, echoing Machiavelli, insists that one must decide which one loves more: one's city or one's soul.[134] Unless the political actor is clear about the answer to *this* question, he or she will attain only a bastardized form of moral integrity.

This brings us to the heart of Weber's argument about what moral integrity can mean in the realm of politics. Weber's somewhat startling thesis is that the *kind of consistency* demanded by an absolutist (or private) ethic is qualitatively different from that demanded of the professional politician or leader. The latter must be keenly aware of the ironies of political action, the fact that good ends are often achieved through morally dubious means. He also needs to be sensitive to the *costs* of political action, both in terms of human suffering and injustice. Yet he must be willing to employ such means and incur such costs; otherwise he fails to live up to the responsibility imposed by his vocation. Socratic moral consistency—the avoidance of injustice as a way of ensuring "clean hands"—is simply not an option for him. Nor is the kind of "devotion to a cause" which insists that "the flame of pure intentions" must not be quenched.[135] (The latter attitude, characteristic of what Weber calls the "ethic of ultimate ends," is found in all movements—political, religious, social—which abstract from the short- and long-term consequences of their programs of action.)

The moral integrity of the political actor, then, cannot be demonstrated by the purity of his or her intentions nor by a misplaced fastidiousness concerning the means of politics. It can be demonstrated only by the "inner strength and consistency" that animates actions, which—from the standpoint of Socratic moral integrity or the "ethic of ultimate ends"—appear to be either gross lapses into injustice or unforgivable compromise. The mature politician recognizes that action in the political realm *cannot* be separated from moral guilt, given the nature of politics' characteristic means: power backed up by violence. His moral integrity consists in the willingness to bear this burden, to assume a *personal* responsibility for the *costs* of political action, its *unavoidable* dimension of injustice. Weber issues a stern warning to those who think that the goodness of their intentions, or the glory of their success, in any way absolves them of this guilt. To be a clear-sighted political actor is, necessarily, to "love one's city more than one's soul" since even the most responsible political action—the most parsimonious use of "power backed up by force"—is soul-staining. To quote Weber, "Everything that is striven for through political action operating with violent means and following an ethic of responsibility endangers the 'salvation of the soul.' "[136]

Integrity, then, involves something more than a "devotion to a cause." Such devotion may be the "guiding star" of action in a morally ambiguous world, but unless it is coupled with a heavy sense of responsibility for the consequences of action—unless, in other words, it is accompanied by a high degree of moral angst—it cannot

227

in itself produce moral integrity.[137] This is why, at the end of his lecture, Weber insists that the contrast between an "ethic of ultimate ends" and an "ethic or responsibility" is not as abyssal as it first appears:

> If now suddenly the *Weltanschauungs*-politicians crop up *en masse* and pass the watchword, "The world is stupid and base, not I," "The responsibility for the consequences does not fall upon me but upon the others whom I serve and whose stupidity or baseness I shall eradicate," then I declare frankly that I would first inquire into the degree of inner poise backing this ethic of ultimate ends. I am under the impression that in nine out of ten cases I deal with windbags who do not fully realize *what they take upon themselves* but who *intoxicate themselves* with romantic sensations. From a human point of view this is not very interesting to me, nor does it move me profoundly. However, it is immensely moving when a *mature* man—no matter whether old or young in years—is aware of a responsibility for the consequences of his conduct and *really feels such responsibility with heart and soul*. He then acts by following an ethic of responsibility and somewhere he reaches the point where he says: "Here I stand; I can do no other." That is something genuinely human and moving. And every one of us who is not spiritually dead must realize the possibility of finding himself at some time in that position. In so far as this is true, an ethic of ultimate ends and an ethic of responsibility are not absolute contrasts but rather supplements, which only in unison constitute a genuine man—a man who can have the "calling for politics."[138]

Weber's insistence that the passion which characterizes an "ethic of ultimate ends" must (somehow) be yoked to the realism, maturity, and "sense of proportion" which characterizes the "ethic of responsibility" must be given due weight lest we fall into the trap of some of his harsher critics, who argue that he promotes passion for the sake of passion and commitment for the sake of commitment.[139] Such readings are hardly without grounds, as the foregoing analysis of Weber's politics of meaning and struggle makes clear.[140] But they do ignore, or vigorously diminish, the role the "ethic of responsibility" plays in distinguishing mature "service to a cause" from mere intoxication or enthusiasm.[141] Weber's notion of the integrity suitable to the political actor may do little to cultivate detachment from struggle—indeed, just the opposite is the case—but it does not promote passion for the sake of passion. One must bear in mind that his overarching concern in "Politics as a Vocation" is to *dampen* enthusiasm, not incite it. This distinguishes him not only from the vitalism of the young Nietzsche but from many champions of an "agonistic politics" in recent political theory.[142]

What *is* absent from Weber's account is a consistent emphasis on the moral uses of disillusionment. The long, disillusioning prologue leads not to a skeptical account of leaders and causes but to the insistence that devotion to a cause is the sine qua non of moral integrity. Ultimately, *some* form of unquestionable devotion is the precondition of all meaningful (and morally responsible) politics for Weber. He adopts the language of polytheism because, like Kant, he wants to limit reason in order to make room for faith, one which has been freed from the tyranny of Christian moral universalism and the confines of religion generally. Weber's heroic political actor may be "sober" rather than "intoxicated," self-denying rather than self-aggrandizing, but he is still an active servant of his cause, one for whom the questioning of his faith (in liberalism, nationalism, socialism, etc.) is as unthinkable as it was for the Puritan laboring in his "calling." What distinguishes him from lesser political actors is not a higher degree of intellectual integrity or "conscience" but a full awareness of the "ethical paradoxes" that await anyone who acknowledges the "ethical irrationality of the world" and the fact that the end *sometimes* justifies the means. His commitment to "the cause" is what helps him bear up under this heavy burden and propelled him to take up the hazardous vocation of politics in the first place.

"Politics as a Vocation" begins by attacking the *illusions* of politics and political idealism, particularly those of revolutionary socialism and self-serving power politics. Yet its ultimate effect is to sanctify some very old illusions. Chief among these is Weber's faith that the *character* of the leader not only can ennoble a generally sordid profession but can also redeem the "diabolical means" which political power must employ. Bolstered by his single-minded devotion to his cause, the Weberian leader accepts the heavy moral burden of political power, never deluding himself that it is possible to govern innocently. It is this clear-sighted acceptance of the fact that (in Strauss's words) "political action cannot be performed without moral guilt" that sets the responsible leader apart, endowing him with a moral pathos otherwise unknown in the political realm.

The problem is that Weber's emphasis upon the moral pathos of the political actor who recognizes his own "dirty hands" can easily be misconstrued as a call to action for those who are man enough to act "in spite of all"—that is, in spite of what political action will do to their souls and to the bodies and souls of others. For Weber does not focus on the "diabolical means" and dreadful responsibility of political action in order to slow people down. His goal, rather, is to call forth a "spiritual aristocracy" that will not immediately be corrupted by the use of "bad means" in the pursuit of "good ends." The "leading politician" will not die with clean hands, but—as one who has internalized the "ethic of responsibility"—his injustices will always be less than those of his moralizing counterpart, the political idealist—or so Weber contends.

We must ask whether such an ethic is enough to balance Weber's injunction to serve a cause with passionate devotion by joining the struggle which *is* politics. Ultimately I think the answer must be "no." The essential problem is not, as Strauss and Goldman contend, that Weber encourages potential leaders to have passion but little reason, urging them to take up their standards as ignorant armies clash by night. Weber's morally praiseworthy critique of political idealism and power politics is not undermined by this, but rather by an ethic which, in the end, is all to respectful of the claims of action and Machiavellian "necessity."

Of course, Weber is no champion of sheer expediency or prudence without principle. But neither does he shy away from urging those who think they might have the "calling" for politics to "do what must be done." He insists on limiting the consequences of injustice while urging action that must, inescapably, be unjust. Indeed, the "inner strength" of action for Weber is never found in the intention of the actor, nor even in the consequences of his act, but in his *character*, his ability to withstand the corruption bred by both power and ideals. Hence the "spiritually strong"—and only they—can wield the "diabolical means" of politics without destroying themselves. Only they have the "calling" for politics.[143]

This trust in character, in the possibility of forming a new "spiritual aristocracy" through the discipline of the "calling," is the flaw at the heart of Weber's conception of political leadership and, indeed, his idea of a vocational ethic specific to politics. The problem is not that *all* political actors are "human, all too human." Rather, it is the seductive idea that character or "integrity" somehow lessen injustice, that the unjust actions of the noble or self-denying man are morally justifiable in a way that those of mere power politicians or callow idealists are not. This lie has a long and illustrious history in Western political thought, from Plato and Aristotle to Nietzsche and Weber, and even to many contemporary champions of what is sometimes referred to as "statesmanship." But a moral atrocity committed by a Pericles or a Lincoln is still a moral atrocity, regardless of the character—and the moral pathos—of the one who issues the commands. Nietzsche, at least, was honest enough to see this and to dispute the idea that "bad conscience"—the experience of the tragic weight of judgment, command, and action—somehow altered the fundamental reality.

Weber's quasi-Platonic (and supremely un-Socratic) faith in the ability of a neoaristocratic character to alter the tonality of blameworthy political action is, of course, overshadowed by his uncritical, passionate devotion to that greatest of fictions: the nation. It is also overshadowed by his earlier acceptance of imperialism as an ideology useful in bringing about a "fundamental liberalization of German society."[144] The faith in "responsible" leaders, national will, and imperialist self-assertion hang together as an "intellectual sacrifice" almost as great as any made in the name of a religious creed. Politically, at least, Weber's disenchantment, his will to disillusion, does not go nearly deep enough: it cannot begin to match the depth of Socratic negativity. Nor can his tortured political ethics begin to match the responsibility exemplified by Socrates' abstentionist morality.

INTELLECTUAL INTEGRITY AND THE ETHOS OF DISENCHANTMENT IN "SCIENCE AS A VOCATION"

Perhaps the most disappointing aspect of "Politics as a Vocation" is Weber's willingness to contemplate the "intellectual proletarianization" of average citizens. For there to be a charismatic leader of the sort Weber desires, the masses "must obey him blindly." This, Weber dryly observes, "is simply the price paid for guidance by leaders."[145] There is a truth here, but it tells us more about the category of leadership than anything else. Nothing could be more anti-Socratic—indeed, antiliberal—than this abdication of the commitment to cultivate some degree of independent judgment in the average citizen. Yet the concepts of authority and domination loom too large in Weberian social science for this commitment to be seen as anything other than a pipe dream. Hence, Weber may fear the growth of "ever new 'aristocracies' and 'authorities' " in the late modern age, but his ultimate response is to juxtapose one "good" form of authority (charismatic) to another "bad" one (bureaucratic).

It is only when we turn to the lecture he gave the year before "Politics as a Vocation" that we see an alternative, antiauthoritarian path laid out by Weber, albeit one confined to the fields of teaching and scholarship. Like its companion piece, "Science as a Vocation" addresses itself to those who would assume the mantle of what is, by its very nature, an exclusive and demanding calling: *Wissenschaft*. Like the later lecture, "Science as a Vocation" emphasizes selfless devotion to the task at hand: extending the boundaries of knowledge through increasingly specialized (and rapidly obsolescent) scholarly work. Where it differs from "Politics as a Vocation" is less in its depiction of this "calling" than in the quality of self-restraint it demands of science's "devoted disciples," who must stick to the facts and not give in to the urge to become prophets on the academic platform. Weber urges such self-restraint in the name of intellectual integrity. This may *seem* to detach scholarship and teaching from any *moral* tasks whatsoever—a reading of Weber popular among positivist social scientists and their critics (such as Strauss and Habermas). Yet the goal of "Science as a Vocation" is to show us how a "disillusioned" science can still "serve moral forces" by performing what is, in the end, a Socratic and antiauthoritarian function. The sad thing is that Weber failed to carry this message over to his consideration of politics and the moral integrity of the political actor.

Weber begins his lecture by considering the "external" aspects of the vocation of scholarship in Germany and America, where the future of the academic "calling" might be seen in outline. After a depressing but accurate depiction of the hazards attending the commencement of any academic career, he turns to the question of what it means to have the "*inward* calling for science." Weber emphatically tells his student audience that "science has entered a phase of specialization previously unknown and that this will forever remain the case." As a result, only the "strict specialist" can ever hope to achieve something "truly perfect": "A really definitive and good accomplishment is today always a specialized accomplishment."[146]

This does not mean there is anything automatic or merely technical about the advance of knowledge. On the contrary, the specialist must perform his or her increasingly narrow task with "passionate devotion" if this work is to make even a small contribution.

Weber emphasizes the sheer labor and frustration of scholarship because he wants to disabuse his audience of the idea that such work is—or ought to be—the means to express one's "inner self" or cultivate one's "personality": "In the field of science only he who is devoted solely to the work at hand has 'personality.' " One must be the servant, not the "impresario," of one's subject. Great scholars, like great artists, are devoted to their work. They serve it and nothing else.[147] *Contra* Goethe (and Nietzsche), one cannot make one's life a work of art without destroying the quality of the work itself. In the end, there is the work and only the work. Unless one can bear the extraordinary level of commitment and self-denial this entails, one "may as well stay away from science."

This opposition of methodical self-denial to romantic self-expression is the first stage in Weber's disabusing strategy. The second is a radical restriction of the purpose and authority of science in a "disenchanted" age. This Weber does by raising the question of the value or *meaning* of scientific progress. Characterizing this progress as "a fraction, the most important fraction, of the process of intellectualization which we have been undergoing for thousands of years," Weber asks whether it ultimately has "any meanings that go beyond the purely practical and technical?"[148] He puts this question in the starkest possible form by invoking Tolstoy's claim that progress had rendered death—and hence life—meaningless for contemporary, civilized man. Weber asks, What stand should one take? What makes the "vocation of science" meaningful within "the total life of humanity"? Is it simply a tool for mastering the world and ourselves?

Any attempt to assess the "value of science" must begin by acknowledging the "tremendous contrast" between what science meant for our ancestors and what it can mean *for us*. Here Weber embarks on a breathtaking summary of what science has meant for the greatest epochs in the history of the West. In broad strokes he describes the energies which historically have driven the scientific quest for truth. For Plato and the Greeks science (*episteme*) promised the ability to grasp the true being of the right, the good, and the beautiful. It seemed to open the way "for knowing and teaching how to act rightly in life and, above all, how to act as a citizen of the state."[149] For the Renaissance, and especially for artists/investigators like Leonardo da Vinci, the scientific experiment seemed to offer a path to true art, and "that meant for them the path to true *nature.*"[150] For those in the shadow of the Reformation Protestantism, scientific investigation uncovered traces of a transcendent God's purposes by revealing the hidden structure of his creation. Science seemed to show the way to God. Finally, for the Enlightenment and the nineteenth century (up to and including Weber's father's generation) science seemed to provide the way to human happiness, to progress and human flourishing.

Weber, like Nietzsche, is devastating in his criticism of each of these culturally specific illusions. Indeed, the mere recitation of these moral, metaphysical, and theological demands is enough to convince us that science can no longer bear the burden of meaning placed on it by our ancestors. The question, then, is what meaning does the vocation of science have once these "former illusions" (science as the way to true being, true nature, true God, and true happiness) have been dispelled? Weber cites Tolstoy's answer in order to sharpen the question and clarify the stakes: "Science is meaningless because it gives no answer to our question, the only question important to us: 'What shall we do and how shall we live?' "[151] Specialized science, denuded of its earlier hopes and pretensions, apparently *has* no meaning beyond the merely technical and professional.

As I noted in the second section of this chapter, Weber affirms Tolstoy's conclusion, but with a notable qualification: "That science does not give an answer to this question is indisputable. The only question that remains is the *sense in which science gives 'no' answer*, and whether or not science might yet be of some use to one who puts the question correctly."[152] This remark compels us to look at Tolstoy's formulation more closely. Despite its apparent Socratic resonance (see *Gorgias*, 500c), Tolstoy's question is framed in such a way as to equate *meaning* with *authority*. Science turns out to be meaningless not because it asks the wrong question but because it fails to supply an authoritative *answer* to the question of how we should live. For the mystical Tolstoy this fact is enough to damn science as a pretender to moral authority. For Weber, conversely, this is precisely what makes the scientific ethos—the contemporary form of the will to truth—of interest in a disenchanted age.

In what sense does science give "no" answer, and how might it still be of some use to one "who puts the question correctly?" *If* we

234

recognize that there is no such thing as science "without presuppositions," and *if* we acknowledge that each of the specialized sciences can only *assume* but never *demonstrate* the value of the kind of knowledge it provides, *then* we are forced to admit that science—while *assuming* the value of prolonging life in the case of medicine, or of binding legal rules in the case of jurisprudence—leaves the fundamental *question* unasked. This fundamental question is not "How should we live?" but rather "Why should we know what the specialized sciences teach us?" Because a particular branch of science or scholarship is based on a set of unarticulated value judgments concerning the *worth* of its subject matter (whether these be cosmic laws or aesthetic objects), it can never offer a genuinely impartial account of its contribution to "the totality of human conduct."[153] It cannot even sincerely question whether it *makes* a contribution, or whether (seen from a different perspective) its value presuppositions are mistaken or corrupting rather than true and ennobling.

Yet the constant tendency within science (broadly construed) is to assume that one's speciality does indeed have something to say (however indirect) about "fundamental" questions. The yearning for authoritative answers manifest in Tolstoy's question is, of course, a yearning felt by many students and laypeople. Scientists and scholars, Weber thinks, are all too willing to respond to this need, offering themselves up as prophets for the young and untutored. The resulting situation is similar to the one Socrates confronted with the sophists and rhetoricians in fifth-century Athens: youth demands answers to the questions of how to live and how to act, and there are plenty of "experts" around willing to provide them.

The difference, of course, is that Socrates was able to deploy a negative form of philosophy against such bogus authorities and, indeed, against positive or unmediated authority in general. Two thousand years later, philosophy itself appears discredited, a pseudo-science which pretended to render judgment from an Archimedean point above the conflicts of *this* world. Philosophy's self-disgrace (in the form of dogmatic metaphysics and foundationalism) opened the door to another, would-be authority: empirical, specialized science. Thus, in "Science as a Vocation" Weber devotes considerable moral energy to pointing out what science is and is not, and to showing what it can and cannot do if it desires to remain intellectually honest. If the teachers and practitioners of science are to maintain even the most basic intellectual integrity, they must give up the Archimedean pretenses (and realist self-deceptions) their enormous accomplishments and social prestige encourage. A rigorous, self-imposed epistemological modesty is in order. More than anything else, scientists, scholars, and teachers must resist the temptation to step into the shoes of the priest, the prophet, or the dogmatic philosopher.

This is why Weber places so much emphasis on self-restraint as the virtue par excellence of teacher/scholars. Precisely because all scientific/scholarly objectivity is a fragile, constructed attainment, one which hinges upon an array of methodological prophylactics and scholarly self-denial, Weber repeatedly stresses the need for self-restraint and the unbridgeable gap between scholarship, on the one hand, and demagogy or advocacy, on the other. To fail to see this gap and act accordingly is, in Weber's view, to set science or scholarship up as one more authoritarian force in a political culture already crippled by its relative immaturity. *This*, and not any positivist fantasy of an utterly *wertfrei* social science, is the underlying force behind pronouncements like the following:

> To take a practical political stand is one thing, and to analyze political structures and party positions is another. When speaking in a political meeting about democracy, one does not hide one's personal standpoint; indeed, to come out clearly and take a stand is one's damned duty. The words one uses in such a meeting are not means of scientific analysis but means of canvassing votes and winning over others. They are not plowshares to loosen the soil of contemplative thought; they are swords against the enemies: such words are weapons. It would be an outrage, however, to use words in this fashion in a lecture or in the lecture-room.[154]

In insisting upon the enormous difference between taking a "practical political stand" and "analyzing political structures and party positions," Weber is, in effect, redrawing the distinction Socrates makes in the *Gorgias* between rhetoric and philosophy, persuasive speech (*peithein*) and dialectic (*dialegesthai*). He redraws the distinction not in order to remove the last vestige of moral concern from the arena of *Wissenschaft* but to preserve the relation between scholarship and moral (as opposed to political) forces in a disenchanted world. For Weber, as for Kant, the most important thing is that his audience come to "have the courage to use [its] own understanding."[155] This it will never do so long as scholars are dishonest enough to set themselves up as prophets or demagogues before an

audience which cannot answer back: "To the prophet and the demagogue, it is said: 'Go your ways out into the streets and speak openly
to the world,' that is, speak where criticism is possible."[156]

But how does the severe self-restraint Weber preaches actually
"serve moral forces"? If the teacher should aspire only to "serve
the students with his knowledge" rather than incite or indoctrinate,
doesn't this leave the "ultimate values" of his audience untouched
by anything like critical scrutiny? Doesn't learning then become an
entirely instrumental affair, much like buying groceries from the
grocer? (This is the "American" conception of the learning "transac-
tion" Weber cites in his lecture.)[157]

To this objection we may answer that Weber's ethos of intellectual
integrity is severe enough to prefer such a strictly instrumental understanding to the idea that the teacher is there to sell the student
"a *Weltanschauung* or a code of conduct." But Weber's conception is
far more Socratic than this seemingly "hands off" attitude implies.
This can be seen in his insistence that the "primary task of a useful
teacher is to teach his students to recognize 'inconvenient' facts—I
mean facts that are inconvenient for their party opinions. And for
every party opinion there are facts that are extremely inconvenient,
for my own opinion no less than others."[158] Science/scholarship may
not be able to adjudicate among competing ideologies, but it can
certainly affect the manner in which such views are held. It can help
inoculate people against the idea that any creed or set of beliefs is
all-knowing or without inconsistencies. By forcing his audience to
own up to such "inconvenient facts," the Weberian scholar confronts students with the irreducible *abstractness* of all party/creedal
positions. Insofar as it punctures the dogmatic bubble of all such
views, this seemingly modest scholarly exercise constitutes a "moral
achievement."

It is noteworthy that Weber's central discussion of value pluralism
and the "warring gods" follows on the heels of this broadly Socratic
point. Teachers and scholars have gotten into the habit of using their
disciplines to "plead" for various causes. Yet, as Weber observes,
" 'Scientific' pleading is meaningless in principle because the various
value spheres of the world stand in irreconcilable conflict with each
other."[159] We can read "Science as a Vocation" as Weber's attempt
to remind his peers of this particular "inconvenient fact" about the
late modern age. Because science, no more than philosophy, occupies an Archimedean point, it must withdraw from direct participa-

tion in the battle of the "warring gods" if it is to remain true to itself. What would it mean, Weber asks, to decide "scientifically" on the relative value of French versus German culture? Or to "refute scientifically" the Sermon on the Mount? Its impotence in such areas is manifest for all those who maintain a minimal level of intellectual integrity. With regard to such questions, "the individual has to decide which is God for him and which is the devil."[160] No "authority" can honestly preempt the space of individual judgment.

These two strands of Weber's argument enable us to see just how wide of the mark the oft-lodged charge of "decisionism" ultimately is. For what Weber wants to combat with his insistence on "inconvenient facts" and the impossibility of "scientific pleading" is the idea that there exists some substitute for the "grandiose rationalism of Christian ethics," one which can adjudicate or serve as an umpire for the most intractable political and moral conflicts. His opponent in "Science as a Vocation" is not reasonable argument per se but the *false authority* of the unquestioned creed or teacher.

This aspect comes out most clearly in Weber's enumeration of the contributions science/scholarship can make to "practical life" in the broad sense. First, it contributes to calculation and control of "external objects" and "human activities." Second, it contributes tools and methods of thought. Third—beyond these strictly pragmatic considerations—science can help students gain "clarity." By "clarity" Weber means as full an awareness as possible about the means necessary to pursue, and the consequences likely to result from, a particular moral or political stance. According to Weber, science/scholarship must force its addressees to face the following dilemma: "*If* you take such and such a stand, then, according to scientific experience, you have to use such and such a *means* in order to carry out your conviction practically. Now, these means are perhaps such that you believe you must reject them. Then you simply must choose between the end and the inevitable means. Does the end "justify" the means? Or does it not? The teacher can confront you with the necessity of this choice. He cannot do more, so long as he wishes to remain a teacher and not to become a demagogue."[161]

At first glance this may seem a remarkably emasculated conception of scholarship's contribution to "practical life," one that leaves little space for the Socratic question: "What kind of life should one live?" (*Gr.* 500c). But is it really? Weber does not elaborate unduly on what seems to follow from such an effort, nor from what he calls the "primary task" of the teacher, namely, to force his students to recognize "inconvenient facts." Yet, taken together, such efforts "serve moral forces" in a most Socratic way. By confronting the student with the question of means and consequences, along with various "inconvenient facts," the intellectually honest scholar plays a disabusing role. The "inconvenient facts" put into question the presumed adequacy of a particular creed or ideology, while the insistence on the issue of means and consequences serves to dissolve the abstractions on which it is built. In short, the job of the "intellectually honest" teacher is neither to preach nor impose what Reason—or his particular science or politics—evidently demands. Instead, like Socrates, he *purges*.

Of course, such purging is not pursued as aggressively by Weber's "teacher" as it is in the Socratic dialogues, nor does Weber place this task front and center in his lecture. Yet the practice of "clarification," of drawing out the inconsistencies, tensions, and costs of a particular moral-political stance is, in fact, a Socratic one, with a quintessentially Socratic goal: forcing the student to give an account of his or her position and conduct. The "clarification" pursued by science consists in showing how

> in terms of its meaning, such and such a practical stand can be derived with inner consistency, and hence integrity, from this or that ultimate *weltanschauliche* position. Perhaps it can only be derived from one such fundamental position, or maybe from several, but it cannot be derived from these or those other positions. Figuratively speaking, you serve this god and you offend the other god when you decide to adhere to this position. And if you remain faithful to yourself, you will necessarily come to certain final conclusions that subjectively make sense. . . . [I]f we are competent in our pursuit (which must be presupposed here), we can force the individual, or at least we can help him, to give himself an *account of the ultimate meaning of his own conduct*. This appears to me as not so trifling a thing to do, even for one's own personal life. Again, I am tempted to say of a teacher who succeeds in this: he stands in the service of "moral" forces; he fulfills the duty of bringing about self-clarification and a sense of responsibility.[162]

"Moral forces" are served by forcing the intellectually and morally lazy to recognize the tensions, costs, and inconsistencies of their positions; they are served by revealing the tragic nature of many, if not all, moral-political choices. If "Politics as a Vocation" stressed the moral burden of the political actor's unavoidable recourse to "morally dubious means," then "Science as a Vocation" stresses the illusory nature of any apparently cost-free synthesis or harmony of values. One cannot be a champion of social equality without sinning against individual liberty, just as one cannot be a champion of unfettered liberty without sinning against democratic equality.[163] And so it goes throughout the tension-ridden landscape of moral-political life, where conflicting values make intense and by no means easily ranked claims on our loyalties.

"Giving an account" of the ultimate meaning of one's conduct, then, means the acknowledgment of such tensions and the moral loss involved in adhering to a particular position. The more thorough and honest this acknowledgment, the greater the possibility that students or laymen will have to reconsider their commitment to their "ultimate *weltanschauliche* position." It may be that they are willing to make the value sacrifice that political commitment implies, or they may come to the painful realization that they owe equal allegiance to two or more "warring gods." If so, their integrity will be measured not by any linear consistency but by their ability live, act, and think within the resulting tension.

But here an obvious objection arises. Even if one grants the moral importance of this kind of "clarification," doesn't Weber's restriction of science have the ultimate effect of affirming an agonistic relationship to a world of conflicting values? And doesn't this mean that science helps the student to become a "soldier for his cause," working less to purge opinions than to bring consistency and discipline to what are often vague and inchoate commitments? This is Harvey Goldman's reading of "Science as a Vocation." According to him, Weber's overarching concern is not to disabuse or demand an account but to demonstrate that the real calling of science consists in teaching "the reality of the *war* of the gods and the need to enlist in combat."[164]

Such a reading is evidently confirmed by Weber toward the end of his lecture. Summarizing his main points about the limits of scientific authority, Weber returns to Tolstoy's question, giving what is, at first glance, an alarming answer:

Science today is a "vocation" organized in special disciplines in the service of self-clarification and knowledge of interrelated facts. It is not the gift of grace of seers and prophets dispensing sacred values and revelations, nor does it partake of the contemplation of sages and philosophers about the meaning of the universe. This, to be sure, is the inescapable condition of our historical situation. We cannot evade it so long as we remain true to ourselves. And if Tolstoy's question recurs to you: as science does not, who is to answer the question: "What shall we do, and, how shall we arrange our lives?" or, in the words used here tonight: "Which of the warring gods should we serve? Or should we serve perhaps an entirely different god, and who is he?" then one can say that only a prophet or a savior can give the answers.[165]

We seem to be but one step away from Heidegger's despairing observation that "only a god can save us" and the damning conclusion that Weber is a theologian manqué. Weber seems driven to limit reason in order to make room for faith and (thus) meaning. This harmonizes all too well with the emphasis on the saving power of charismatic leadership in "Politics as a Vocation."

But immediately following this passage, Weber informs his audience that "the prophet for whom so many of our younger generation yearn simply does not exist." We are destined to live in "a godless and prophetless time."[166] I take this to mean that neither religion, nor science, nor political ideologies can give the kind of authentic answer to Tolstoy's question that so many yearn for. Indeed, in an epoch characterized, above all, by the "disenchantment of the world," the very attempt to create such a *public* source of meaning to fill the void can only result in monstrosities similar to those created by an ill-conceived "monumentalism" in art.[167] Here, as in so many other places in his work, the antiprophetic Weber proved to be prophetic, as the kitsch aestheticism of fascism and National Socialism bore out.

In "Science as a Vocation," what Weber calls "the plain duty of intellectual integrity" trumps all other values. The resulting ethos is neither one of strict value neutrality nor disinterested scholarship. Rather, it is the ethos of disenchantment, of a dissolvent rationality whose ultimate effect is to undermine all creeds, traditions, and ideologies. As Weber emphasizes in his lecture, the very development of science (this "specifically irreligious power") embodied this dialectic over the course of two thousand years. Weber's attempt to make German students realize that the prophet they yearn for is not to be found in the academy nor, in fact, anywhere else is a self-conscious continuation of the process of disenchantment. *No one* possesses the kind of knowledge that German youth craves, the knowledge which answers the question of which god or demon they should serve. This, I would suggest, is the negative wisdom born of the ethos of disenchantment. It is also the wisdom of Socrates. As a scholar—that is, an upholder of the "plain duty of intellectual integrity"—Weber's ethos *is* the Socratic ethos, for disenchantment and negativity go hand in hand.[168]

Of course, by insisting on the difference between teachers and leaders and between scientific work and political speech, Weber leaves open the possibility of each choosing his or her own god or demon blindly. He seems, at points, to suggest that authentic leaders or even prophets might lurk elsewhere, outside university lecture halls. But despite such moments, the preponderant sense of "Science as a Vocation" is that such creatures no longer exist except in the most bastardized form. No amount of posturing can hide the fact that "rationalization and intellectualization" have permanently altered the landscape of belief and its relation to *public* values. And even though "many old gods ascend from their graves," taking the form of impersonal forces ruling our lives, the fact that they are disenchanted means that they can no longer be the sources of an unreflective, ego-diminishing faith.

One must choose one's god or demon, then, in full view of either's lack of divinity. If, in the "Vocation" lectures, Weber often sounds as if he's willing to pay almost any price for the enhancement of meaning and freedom, his intellectual integrity suggests that the need for redemption—for faith, for *public* meaning—is our most dangerous need, a sign of immaturity, dishonesty, or both.

Weber concludes "Science as a Vocation" by citing the Edomite watchman's song (from the Old Testament book of Isaiah) as a warning to "the many who today tarry for new prophets and saviors." The passage reads: "He calleth to me out of Seir, Watchman, what of the night? The watchman said, The morning cometh, and also the night: if ye will enquire, enquire ye: return come." Weber tells his audience, "The people to whom this was said has enquired and tarried for more that two millennia, and we are shaken when we realize its fate. From this we want to draw the lesson that nothing is gained by yearning and tarrying alone, and we shall act differently."[169] The task of the intellectually sober is to "set to work and meet the demands of the day, in human relations as well as in our vocation." For Weber anything less is self-deluding and self-destructive.

CITIZENSHIP, LEADERSHIP, AND THE ILLUSIONS OF POLITICS

Weber's word's were directed at a specific audience at a specific (and traumatic) historical moment, in which the pretensions of German nationalism had come crashing down. It was a moment in which the need for a new prophecy, a new public source of meaning and value-ranking, was all but overwhelming. To this understandable yearning Weber delivers a stern and uncompromising "no." But if "Science as a Vocation" attempts to disabuse German youth of the need for prophets and nostalgia for a time when "the ultimate and most sublime values" blazed brightly in the public sphere, "Politics as a Vocation" holds out the prospect of a limited re-enchantment of the world. The disdainful contrast of the intellectually honest teacher with the demagogue on the academic platform gives way to the affirmation of the "responsible" demagogue on the "battlefield of elections." The latter is a noble soul who, like Nietzsche's ascetic priest, risks depravity by leading a (necessarily debased) mass following. It is his "passionate devotion to a cause" which, Weber believes, will save him from the ignominious fate of becoming a mere "flatterer" of the *demos*—the fate to which Socrates consigned the leading politicians of Athenian democracy at its height, Pericles included.

It is on this issue—and on the role of struggle in engendering meaning and freedom—that we encounter the limits of a "Socratic" reading of Weber's lectures. *Contra* Strauss, this limit has little to do with the difference between a philosopher who believes in the possibility of a positive moral knowledge which might serve as the basis of *true* statesmanship and a social scientist who denies the very category of "facts of value." Rather, the real locus of the difference is between a strategy of disenchantment which stops short of the category of leadership itself (Weber) and one which includes this category among its primary targets (Socrates). Of course, the *Gorgias* can be read as proof of Socrates' commitment to the oligarchical idea of a "royal art." It is better read, as I suggested in chapter 1, as a critique of the pathologies of plebiscitary democracy and "Caesarist" leaders, a critique made by a committed yet ironic constitutional democrat (the Socrates of the *Crito*, who prefers the *laws* of Athens to all others).

If we combine the commitment to a democratic constitution upheld by Socrates in the *Crito* with the abstentionist morality we find in the *Gorgias* and *Apology*, we have a position harmonious with the moral core of liberalism. But, like Thoreau, Socrates knew that a democratic constitution is no bar to the commission of injustice; that the natural tendency of democracy is to become a state like any other, promoting acquiescence among its citizens and injustice abroad, if not also at home. A democratic constitution cannot be left to run by itself, nor can it afford the complacency of those who think that they inhabit the "best regime." To be minimally moral, democracy requires more than a few morally independent citizens, whose ultimate allegiance is not to their city or nation but to "care for their souls"—to the avoidance of injustice rather than the affirmation of a positive (that is, local or parochial) morality. The blistering critique of Periclean democracy in the *Gorgias* reminds us that Athens at its most heroic was also morally blind when it came to the most important things. Socrates' self-appointed mission is to remind his fellow citizens of these things, of how prone *every* polity is to the performance of injustice and the commissioning of atrocity.

Measured by this standard, Weber's legacy in the "Vocation" lectures falls short. While light-years away from the bellicosity of the *Antrittsrede*, "Politics as a Vocation" reflects Weber's merely instrumental commitment to democracy and limited government, one contingent upon the room for demagogic leadership this system creates. Weber's Platonic self-deception in "Politics as a Vocation" is that mass politics can be "ennobled," given depth and moral dignity through the heroic character (and moral pathos) or its leaders rather than through the wakefulness of its citizens. Weber's spiritual aristocracy descends, like Plato's philosopher, into the cave of mass politics, the cave of envy and *ressentiment*, risking its own nobility for the sake of its calling.[170]

The Socratic insight is that no leader—neither Pericles, nor Lincoln, nor Churchill—is a "moral expert," the possessor of a *phronesis* that elevates prudence to new and heroic moral heights. Democratic leaders are, if anything, often more craven than their followers. Hence, the impetus for morality in politics, for avoiding injustice, can only come from "below," from more or less average citizens who are part of the "psychically proletarianized masses" which Weber, like Plato and Nietzsche before him, writes off as creatures of envy and *ressentiment*. As Mill pointed out, this impetus will arise only when some of these citizens have been pestered into moral wakefulness by a "gadfly" rather that stirred to dream more deeply by a political prophet (a "charismatic leader") who labors in and for his faith.

At his best—in "Science as a Vocation" and in the critique of the ethic of absolute ends in "Politics as a Vocation"—Weber recognizes the pious cruelty which attends all unexamined belief. At his worst, he, like Machiavelli, justifies calculated cruelty by the political leader as the lesser evil. Insult is added to injury when he tries to dignify the claims of Machiavellian necessity with an idealistic appeal to "passionate devotion to a cause" and the moral anguish of the political actor. Here clarity is replaced by self-deception, disenchantment by willful illusion, sobriety by a particularly dangerous form of intoxication, namely, that of the angst-filled leading politician who soldiers on for his cause.

As the first part of this chapter documents, the unsober side of Weber flows from his almost metaphysical belief in the energy- and meaning-creative powers of social and political struggle. This belief retains a strong hold on the theoretical imagination, as the writings of twentieth-century agonists from Carl Schmitt to Chantal Mouffe bear out. The fact that contemporary agonists are apt to champion the *demos* over elites or rival nations makes little difference. In the end, the myth of the revivifying power of "the cause" returns, and with it the unwitting cruelty that no amount of vocational responsibility can transform or eradicate. What is forgotten by all is the Millian lesson that the true beneficiary of the agonistic struggle of values, opinions, and "causes" is the individual who stands somewhat apart from the struggle itself and so learns the partiality—and relative injustice—of all sides.

Hannah Arendt and Leo Strauss

CITIZENSHIP VERSUS PHILOSOPHY

WEBER'S DEPICTION OF A responsible politician who is a hero "in the sober sense of the word" reflects his quest for sources of purpose, energy, and meaning in an increasingly routinized world. Unlike Nietzsche he did not labor under the illusion that we (or at least some of us) could become Greeks again. However, like Nietzsche he saw asceticism and the will to truth as the twin bases of capitalist, scientific culture—one in which the rationalization of everyday life left the individual precious little room for maneuver. The way out for Weber was not Nietzsche's resuscitation of pagan or Renaissance *virtu* but the discipline of the "calling," which would create an elite of empowered yet responsible political leaders. Fighting enormous obstacles, these individuals would direct the energies of mass politics toward genuinely national goals. By such means, modern politics could be partially ennobled, becoming a source of meaning rather than debilitation.

For many readers Weber's self-denying leaders will seem but a faint echo of Plato's philosopher-kings, who likewise formed an aristocracy of character, one educated to selflessly serve the common good. The echo is faint because Weber eschewed any appeal to philosophic wisdom, thinking it dishonest to cloak the exercise of power in the garb of transcendental truth. Weber's "leading politician" may be an ascetic, but he is a *this-worldly* ascetic. His passionate devotion to a cause is amplified by his capacity for manly self-denial, for *service* to an ideal in the real world of politics. This service cannot be animated by the reckless enthusiasm (or moral purism) which characterizes all ethics of "ultimate ends." Rather, it must be performed in accordance with a severe code of *personal* responsibility for consequences. This means eschewing all forms of eschatology and self-intoxication and the disciplined taking up of the "long and slow boring of hard boards."

Weber's vision of modern politics is chastened and stoic, particularly when compared to the emancipatory hopes of revolutionary socialism and nineteenth-century liberalism's faith in progress. Nevertheless, it is a vision in which political action emerges as *potentially* meaningful and noble—albeit only for a few. Philosophy and citizenship have been banished from the scene, the former for its insupportable pretensions to universal wisdom (a "view from nowhere"), the latter for its reliance upon virtues which are simply not sustainable in the world of mass politics. Having dispelled these "illusions"—of philosophical wisdom and republican citizenship—Weber focuses on responsible leadership as the one ray of hope in the otherwise bleak political landscape of modernity. Everything else—from "inalienable rights" to "the will of the people"—is viewed as willful self-deception, the kind of avoidable illusion Weber's ethos of disenchantment sternly prohibits. Thus, while Weber recognizes limited government as essential to the preservation of ever-smaller spaces of freedom, he insists that it lacks any metaphysical or even strong normative grounding.

In turning to Hannah Arendt and Leo Strauss, one is struck by how much their political theories respond to the limited possibilities sketched by Weber. To state the matter in preliminary, oversimplified terms: both Arendt and Strauss struggle against Weber's constricted vision of modern politics and his realist view of political power—Arendt in the name of the citizenly ideal (the *bios politikos*), Strauss in the name of philosophy and the philosophical life. Against Weber's "disenchanted" vision, these two products of the agitated intellectual climate of Weimar Germany argue for a recovery of what are, broadly speaking, traditional ideals.[1] They offer vivid portraits of the life of the citizen and the life of the philosopher, the better to remind us of forgotten or repressed possibilities which may help us escape from the political, moral, and philosophical cul-de-sac outlined by Weber.

Their opposition to Weber notwithstanding, Arendt and Strauss hardly share a common conception of politics, philosophy, or the relation between the two. Whereas from the standpoint of contemporary liberal theory they may look very much alike (a reverence for the Greeks coupled with a dim view of most modern politics), seen in their own terms they are virtual antipodes. In *The Human Condition* (1958) Arendt emerged as the foremost modern proponent of a Greek-inspired participatory politics, an ideal she modified but never abandoned in *On Revolution* (1963). In both works she presented the public realm as the privileged site of human freedom, a tangible freedom manifest in the political speech, debate, and action of diverse equals.[2]

Strauss, on the other hand, turned to the classical political rationalism of Plato and Aristotle in order to combat the relativism he saw fostered by Weberian social science and the philosophical historicism of Nietzsche and Heidegger. But his return to the standard of "what is right by nature" was also aimed at the idols of the cave, that is, at the egalitarian prejudices of a democratic age. Thus, while Arendt aligns herself with the politics of opinion born in democratic Athens, Strauss aligns himself with the Greek philosophical critics of popular rule. To caricature their positions (but only slightly): Arendt takes up the part of Callicles (minus, of course, the latter's admiration of the unjust, superior man), while Strauss assumes that of the *Platonic* Socrates. One defends the life of the citizen as most worthy, while the other sees the quest for understanding as the true source of human dignity.

Having framed the opposition between Arendt and Strauss in these simplified terms, we must take a step back. The careful reader of either theorist will recognize a latent tendency to question this stark opposition between citizenship and philosophy. Their respective commitments notwithstanding, Arendt and Strauss both flirt with the idea of the "philosopher-citizen." It is not surprising that they draw closest to this idea in the course of meditations on Socrates.

In this chapter I explore the "Socratic" dimension of Arendt and Strauss, showing how it complicates our sense of what these two thinkers stand for. I begin by drawing out the idea of the "philosopher-citizen" as it emerges in Arendt's and Strauss's depictions of Socrates. I then show how (and why) they back away from the complexity which the idea of a "political" Socrates introduces into their work. Their retreat is telling. It indicates a certain blindness and a certain failure of nerve, one which is all the more peculiar given Arendt's and Strauss's desire to challenge the *doxa* of our day.

In terms of the story I have been telling in this study, Arendt's and Strauss's retreat to the verities of civic republicanism, on the one hand, and philosophical elitism, on the other, reflects a broader failure of the contemporary theoretical imagination. This is the failure to articulate a genuinely critical conception of citizenship, one based not on the morally dubious foundations of shared values or absolute truths but rather upon skepticism, intellectual honesty, and the will to avoid injustice.[3] That this failure comes on the heels of Mill's misplaced faith in the contributions of a specialized "art of politics," Nietzsche's betrayal of his own individualism, and Weber's tragic despair makes it all the more poignant and—from our perspective at least—regrettable.

ARENDT: PHILOSOPHY AND POLITICS

It is a banality to observe that Arendt's conception of authentic politics was modeled on the example provided by the Greek polis, and democratic Athens in particular. In Homer and Thucydides and in Sophocles and Aristotle she found the materials she needed to remind modern readers of a time when appearing in public and participating in political affairs were the things which made life worth living. For Arendt, what the Greeks had seen with unparalleled clarity—and what we have forgotten—is how the capacity for speech and action with others distinguishes a genuinely *human* life from both animals and barbarians.[4] Yet these capacities remain unrealized so long as human beings do not share a space of public freedom distinct from the rhythms of labor and the necessities of the household realm. For the Greeks, a life spent within the darkness of the household—the life of a woman, child, or slave—was not a fully human life since it never knew the freedom manifest in sharing words and deeds with others, in the "bright light" of the public realm.[5]

The most startling idea contained in *The Human Condition* is precisely that a "life without speech and without action . . . is literally dead to the world; it has ceased to be a human life because it is no longer lived amongst men."[6] In making this claim, Arendt is not anticipating the ideas of contemporary communitarians, who stress the importance of shared values and the need for a less egoistic and more associative culture. Rather, she is insisting on the Greek idea that human freedom is actualized only in an artificially constructed realm of political equality, where an individual can speak and be recognized by his fellow citizens.[7] On this understanding, full humanity is restricted to those who were members of a political community, that is, to *citizens* with political rights. To be deprived of political membership meant that one was deprived of the joys of action and appearing in public. But it also meant that one was deprived of recognition as a free and equal being who had a unique perspective on the shared public world. It meant, in short, that one was deprived of full human reality.

Even if we acknowledge that there are conditions under which citizenship might well be *the* essential vehicle of freedom and equality, Arendt's claim that citizenship provides an outlet for our distinctively human capacities will strike most contemporary readers as outlandish. Like Aristotle, she seems to be laboring under the illusion that there is and must be a natural hierarchy of more or less "good" lives, a hierarchy which runs from the relative worthlessness of a life devoted to production and consumption (at the bottom), to the eminently more worthwhile activities of philosophy or politics (at the top).[8] Such hierarchies among *bioi*, or ways of life, clash with liberal pluralism and egalitarianism insofar as they posit (a priori, as it were) the idea that the life of a cobbler possesses less value and dignity than that of a philosopher or political actor.

In Arendt's defense it can be said that she appeals to the traditional hierarchy not in the name of "nature" but rather to fight what she sees as the dominant trend of modernity. From the emergence of a market economy down to our own global capitalist age, modern thinkers have been united in their praise of technology and the productivity of labor, as well as their disparagement of such "unproductive" activities as philosophy and politics.[9] In the hierarchy of human activities she presents in *The Human Condition*, Arendt focuses on how the modern age *inverted* the traditional ordering of the active life, placing labor at the top (by virtue of its productivity) and action—the sharing of words and deeds—at the bottom. What is at stake, in other words, is less an elitist (and antipluralist) insistence on the "best life for man" than a systematic revaluation of the (increasingly degraded) public realm and the activities properly at home in it. For it is only when we become aware of the presuppositions underlying our own, largely implicit, hierarchy of human activities that we become open to the idea of other possible orderings. And it is only upon realizing that political action is more than a burden or distraction that we question the idea that the public realm is a mere support mechanism for production and the market.

It is the human capacities for revelatory speech and initiatory action that Arendt is most intent on saving from their contemporary

oblivion. She turns to the public realm of the polis because it provides a vivid picture of these capacities in full bloom. Her great attraction to Athenian democracy results from the fact that it realized,
to an unprecedented extent, a politics of speech and persuasion—of
agonistic debate, deliberation, and exchange of opinion among
equal citizens. Like Mill in his review of Grote's *History of Greece*,
she emphasizes the sheer energy, intelligence, and talkativeness of
the Athenian *demos* as it engaged in political debate and decision in
the assembly. Thus, the public realm of the polis did not merely
provide a refuge from natural necessity and the repetitive tasks of
the household. It also provided an arena in which each citizen could
try to "prove himself the best of all" by expressing his political intelligence and judgment in public words and deeds. Such agonistic citizenship—a peculiar and never equaled mix of public-spiritedness
and individual competitiveness—was the real hallmark of Athenian
democracy. It is this mixture which Pericles celebrates in his Funeral
Oration and which Arendt pays tribute to throughout *The Human
Condition*.

According to Arendt, a politics of talk and exchange of opinion
does far more than develop the latent moral and intellectual faculties
of ordinary citizens (its primary function, in Mill's view). It also
makes genuine *individuality* possible. For it is only by appearing on
a public stage, in front of an audience of our peers, that we assume
a tangible public self and a recognizable identity. It is one thing to
presume one's uniqueness (as we moderns are wont to do), quite another to demonstrate it in a worldly and disciplined way. This is
achieved through the opinions and consistent perspective an individual communicates to his fellow citizens "in the bright light of the
public sphere."

In taking this position, Arendt challenges the preconceptions of
both liberal and romantic individualism. Self-fashioning is not a
matter of cultivating one's eccentricity or expressing one's inner
psychological depths. Rather, it is a highly theatrical exercise which
takes place in public, before an audience of one's peers. It is this
audience—one's fellow citizens—who render judgment on the
words and deeds of the political actor, thereby contributing in an
essential way to the actualization of his unique (public) identity.[10] If
this judgment is not to be viewed ironically, the negation of the
political actor's efforts and strivings, the public persona he assumes

must display consistency and firmness of purpose. The political actor must work very hard to ensure that his words and deeds clearly manifest the principles (such as honor, glory, or love of equality) which inspire them.[11]

The public-political self, then, is a performing self, and the performing self is, according to Arendt, the *real* self—at least when the performance takes place in a shared space of appearances and is not a calculated act of deception (à la Shakespeare's Richard III). Only in the public "space of appearances" does the self succeed in transcending the inchoate world of passions, drives, and physical needs. It is for this reason that Arendt claims that political action—acting and speaking in the public realm—*discloses* the agent, revealing his "unique distinctness" in a manner unparalleled by any other human activity.[12]

This is a remarkable claim to make for political action and, indeed, for the life of the citizen. But Arendt does not stop there. In addition to disclosing the unique identity of the agent, political action—the sharing of words and deeds—also discloses the *world* shared by a particular group of citizens. It is by talking about matters of public concern that the "world"—the otherwise taken for granted backdrop of our everyday practices—is "lit up" and endowed with meaning.[13] This illumination through discourse occurs only where the citizens are genuinely plural and diverse; only, that is, where there exists a multiplicity of perspectives upon the common world. Freely adapting Nietzsche's perspectivism for her own purposes, Arendt frames the very reality of the public world not in terms of a single "objective" truth but rather in terms of a multitude of perspectives. In a remarkable passage from *The Human Condition* she writes:

> The reality of the public realm relies on the simultaneous presence of innumerable perspectives and aspects in which the common world presents itself and for which no common measurement or denominator can ever be devised. For though the common world is the common meeting ground of all, those who are present have different locations in it, and the location of one can no more coincide with the location of another than the location of two objects. Being seen and being heard by others derive their significance from the fact that everybody sees and hears from a different position. This is the meaning of public life, compared to which even the richest and most satisfying family life can offer only the

prolongation or multiplication of one's own position with its attending aspects and perspectives. . . . Only where things can be seen by many in a variety of aspects without changing their identity, so that those gathered around them know they see sameness in utter diversity, can worldly reality truly and reliably appear.[14]

Without political speech and action—without the public manifestation of human plurality expressed in the medium of opinion and persuasive speech—the world is "dimmed down" to the monochromatic shades of the household.

Like Mill, Nietzsche, and Weber before her, Arendt fears the "unnatural conformism of mass society"—but for decidedly different reasons. It is not (or not only) the advent of a docile *Ordnungsmensch* that she dreads but the "destruction of the common world." When the life of the citizen is replaced by an increasingly isolated, atomized "mass man," the preconditions for a common world and for genuine human plurality disappear. In place of unique public selves and multiple, mutually illuminating perspectives, we find a mass of human beings "imprisoned in the subjectivity of their own singular experience, which does not cease to be singular if the same experience is multiplied innumerable times." The end of the common world has come "when it is seen only under one aspect and is permitted to present itself in only one perspective."[15]

This formulation might tempt us to say that Arendt borrows a liberal sociology (born of Tocqueville and Mill) in order to make a familiar civic republican point, namely, that the life of active citizenship is the best life, and that we moderns are on the brink of losing this possibility forever thanks to the advent of mass society and the reign of an undifferentiated public opinion. Yet this is too glib since it ignores the deeper ontological and aesthetic commitments animating Arendt's political thought. Active citizenship is important, but not because it makes or keeps men virtuous (as Aristotle, Machiavelli, and Rousseau thought). It is important because it preserves a realm of freedom for beings who would otherwise be overwhelmed by the dictates of nature and the rhythms of production and consumption. But the preservation of such a realm of freedom is only the beginning. A robust public realm, in which words illuminate rather than conceal (as in the case of ideology, propaganda, or advertising), is literally another (fuller) reality for human beings. It is a reality where speech and action, as well as the memory of the words and deeds of previous generations, generate unlimited meaning and interpretation. It is a reality where great words and deeds light up the world, making it a thing of beauty.

In her focus on the reality-enhancing power of great words and deeds, Arendt comes close—perilously close—to Pericles' stance in the Funeral Oration. Like Pericles (and like Nietzsche in certain moments), she tends to view authentic politics as a form of culture.[16] We shouldn't be surprised, then, that she cites Pericles' words (as rendered by Thucydides) whenever she wants to emphasize the links between public-spiritedness, the sharing of words and deeds, and the maintenance of a humane culture or civilization.

These links are most apparent in her essay "The Crisis in Culture," where she contrasts the worldly, lasting quality of Greek and Roman culture to the ephemerality of culture in our society (in which it becomes one more article to be consumed). In order for the public realm to be something more than a protective fence for subsistence and reproduction, a certain *mentalité* must be present: citizens must approach the *res publica* (literally "public thing") with the kind of solicitude ordinarily reserved for artworks. Such solicitude—which Arendt generally refers to as "care for the world"—is driven by an appreciation of the way a relatively permanent public sphere preserves an artificial space for freedom and for meaning, enabling human existence to transcend the repetitive cycles of the life process. Arendt finds this solicitude perfectly captured by Pericles' articulation of the Athenian ethos, which she renders as follows: "We love beauty within the limits of political judgment, and we philosophize without the barbarian vice of effeminacy."[17]

For Arendt, this is the credo of a public-spirited aestheticism, one consistent with Pericles' observation that in Athens "each individual is interested not only in his own affairs but in the affairs of the state as well. . . . [We] do not say that a man who takes no interest in politics is a man who minds his own business; we say that he has no business here at all."[18] That such public-spiritedness is internally linked to an appreciation of the sheer beauty that the public realm (as an arena for "great words and deeds") makes possible is driven home by Pericles' final appeal to his fellow citizens: he would have them look upon Athens and "fall in love" with her beauty. Such love and appreciation for the state as artwork will fortify them for the ultimate sacrifice. In this appeal, patriotism and a masculine aestheticism effortlessly combine.[19]

For Pericles the greatness of the city is inseparable from its beauty. The true test of citizenship, therefore, is how much one cares for the beauty—the glory, the appearance or "shining forth"— of the city, and how much one adds luster to it by one's own words, deeds, and sacrifices. Arendt's endorsement of this Periclean stance is evident from numerous passages in *The Human Condition*, perhaps most strikingly in her insistence that greatness—not success or failure, justice or injustice—is *the* standard by which authentic political action should be judged. As with Pericles, her attitude toward public life seems to elevate aesthetic above moral criteria. Our trepidation is only increased when Arendt explains that action "can be judged only by the criterion of greatness because it is in its nature to break through the commonly accepted and reach into the extraordinary."[20]

This emphasis on the heroic or theatrical character of action has led some of Arendt's critics to underscore the tension between what they see as the agonistic and deliberative dimensions of her political theory, and to recommend that we abandon the "expressive" model of action underlying the former in favor of the "communicative" model implied by the latter.[21] There is more than a grain of truth in this critique, but it misses an essential point. For Arendt virtually all genuine political action is speech between civic equals, and she rigorously distinguishes action thus understood from violence, coercion, strength, and force.[22] The Homeric rhetoric of *The Human Condition* aside, exemplary political action for her does not consist in the singular heroic feats of an Achilles, nor even in the exceptional practical wisdom of a Pericles. Rather, it is to be found in the debate and deliberation of diverse equals. This formulation applies as much to her "Greek" theory of action in *The Human Condition* as it does to her consideration of the modern revolutionary tradition in *On Revolution*. The main difference between the two is (as we shall see) more a matter of emphasis than substance.

Bearing this in mind, we see that there is no *conceptual* confusion involved when Arendt cites the speeches reported by Thucydides and the debates attending the drafting and ratification of the American Constitution as instances of exemplary political speech. Nor is there a *necessary* tension between her focus on the deliberative dimension of political action and her theatrical (or aestheticizing) conception of the public realm. As the passage from *The Human Condition* cited earlier demonstrates, Arendt ingeniously adapts Nietzsche's perspectivism to the needs of the public realm, using it to show how human plurality supports the reality of a common public world. Deliberation and the exchange of opinion are much more than a means to an end; they do not simply serve the purpose of generating a "rational will" or consensus. Far more important for Arendt is the way these activities preserve human plurality and amplify public reality, drawing out the many-sidedness of public-political questions and revealing an open-ended, potentially infinite, richness. Arendt's insistence on the potential beauty of the public realm—the "space of appearances"—is, in fact, part of her systematic effort to redeem the faculty of opinion from its entrenched philosophical devaluation.[23] These two sides of her thought—the theatrical and the deliberative, appearance and opinion—are not opposed but rather flow together.[24]

Yet even if Arendt's focus in *The Human Condition* is upon debate and deliberation and not just "great deeds," problems remain. First, an agonistic politics of debate and contestation does relatively little to foster either thoughtfulness or conscience (Mill's idealized depiction of the Athenian assembly as an institution of public learning notwithstanding).[25] The aim of such a politics is not slowing people down but rather speeding them up—enlisting their energies in a continuous process of debate, struggle, and decision. The Faustian dynamism of the Athenian democracy stands as a clear warning in this regard. Its populist and competitive energies—stimulated by debate in the assembly—left little time for reflection on the ends of political action, for questioning the pursuit of greatness and glory from a moral point of view. Democracy and empire became inextricably linked.[26] Second, the cultivation of agonal energy threatens to splinter a community from within since it encourages competitive individualism in the *political* sphere. Again, the history of Athenian democracy offers ample testimony concerning *this* tendency, as evidenced by the extraordinary ambition of Alcibiades and the considerable envy of his enemies.[27]

Arendt was not unaware of these problems. Indeed, it is possible to read *On Revolution* as an attempt to obviate the excesses of an agonistic individualism. In contrast to her focus in *The Human Condition* on "individualizing" action, *On Revolution* explores more "associational" forms, including (but not limited to) the mutual promises and agreements ordinary citizens make when constituting a new form of government or creating a new political society. Arendt's chief examples in *On Revolution*—the Mayflower Compact; the debates of the American Founding Fathers; the political self-organization of soldiers' and workers' councils in the Paris Commune, the Russian revolutions of 1905 and 1917; and the German revolution of 1918–19—reveal how even the most initiatory and spontaneous political action is, in fact, always a matter of people "acting together, acting in concert." Moreover, her emphasis on the American revolutionary pursuit of *public* happiness and freedom creates a strong link between the founding and the civic republican tradition's idea of responsible citizenship. In this model, care for the public world is manifest not in the pursuit of greatness or glory but in attentiveness to the "speech-making and the decision-taking, the oratory and the business, the thinking and persuading" required by public affairs.[28]

This shift to more associational forms of political action in *On Revolution* makes its tempting to argue that Arendt abandoned her strong "Greek" conception of action for a more citizen-friendly republican model. But even if this is the case—even if *On Revolution* effectively severs the link between public-spiritedness and "aesthetic monumentalism"—the essential problem remains. Simply put: does a more "solidaristic" or associational model of political action (such as we find in *On Revolution*) expand or constrict the space for philosophical citizenship?

Even the most charitable reading of *On Revolution* must, I think, acknowledge that Arendt's turn to the less exotic idiom of civic republicanism does little to enhance the prospects for such citizenship. Indeed, the clear force of Arendt's insistence in *On Revolution* that freedom, if it means anything at all, means the capacity to be a "participator in government" renders the (moderately alienated) philosophical critic an *irresponsible* citizen. When "participation in government" is posited as *the* standard to determine who is and is not a *responsible* citizen, Callicles' judgment of Socrates stands.[29] This holds as much for a conception of political action which centers on "acting together, acting in concert" as it does for an agonistic politics of self-display.[30]

Impatience with the moderate alienation characteristic of philosophical citizenship underlies Arendt's discussion of the eighteenth-century idea of "public happiness." Taking issue with the standard liberal interpretation of the American founding as (essentially) the creation of limited government, Arendt emphasizes how the Consti-

257

tution's creation of a new system of power provided a new "house for freedom" and enabled the pursuit of *public* happiness—the happiness that comes from being a "participator in government."[31] It was the desire for a share in public power, not the wish to be protected from it, which drove the American founders to take the steps they did, and to create a new form of government in which power balanced power. For them the "right to be seen in action," coupled with the "joys of discourse, of legislation, of transacting business, of persuading and being persuaded," came first, taking priority over the guarantee of individual rights.[32]

This clear sense of the priority of *public* freedom was soon lost. The founders' original emphasis on *political* freedom and a share in public power (the contents of the Constitution) gave way almost immediately to an emphasis on *civil* liberty (the Bill of Rights).[33] The freedom *for* politics gave way to the freedom *from* it, and the suggestive ambiguity implied by Jefferson's elision in the Declaration of Independence ("life, liberty, and the pursuit of happiness") was ultimately removed by the consumption-centered idea of happiness imported by generations of impoverished European immigrants.[34]

Much of *On Revolution* is devoted to tracing this dramatic falling away from the twin ideals of public freedom and participatory citizenship. Like most narratives born of the civic republican tradition, this is a story of creeping *corruption*, one which focuses attention on the "loss of the revolutionary spirit" and the rising tide of privatism, materialism, and conformism. Taken together, these developments transformed the ingenious new system of political power created by the Constitution into a mere instrumentality of the economic or social realm, replacing self-government with what is, for all intents and purposes, a de facto oligarchy.[35]

However tempting it might be to agree with the broad outlines of this story, the fact remains that Arendt presents us with an overly stark choice: *either* a renewed commitment to active citizenship and the power of joint political action or the fateful solidification of our status as jobholders and mere clients of the state. In her view, our culture has become so utterly privatized that the resurrection of citizenship and a "taste for public freedom" figures as *the* critical project par excellence. Insofar as philosophical citizenship tends to be skeptical of appeals to civic virtue (no matter how novel their form), it obviously offers little to Arendt's attempt to recover the "lost treasure" of the modern revolutionary tradition. One could go so far as to say that, from the perspective of *On Revolution*, "alienated" citizenship (no matter what the mode) is precisely the problem. What is needed is civic engagement, solidarity, "acting together."

This message has made Arendt an attractive thinker to communitarians, participatory (or "radical") democrats, and proponents of "new social movements" (feminism, gay rights, ecology, etc.), all of whom find her emphasis upon the activist and solidaristic dimensions of citizenship congenial. Arendt, however, was too independent and idiosyncratic a thinker to be satisfied with an "associationist" updating of the civic republican tradition. Indeed, while her primary project was to restore dignity to politics, political action, and the life of the citizen in the eyes of her contemporaries, her secondary project was to underscore the importance of independent judgment in the public realm. She took up the latter project in various essays dating from the sixties, as well as in the posthumously published *Lectures on Kant's Political Philosophy* and the first volume of *The Life of the Mind*. It received a remarkable preview, however, in an essay Arendt wrote (but did not publish) four years prior to the appearance of *The Human Condition*.[36]

"Philosophy and Politics" contains some of Arendt's most suggestive thoughts about the nature and possibility of philosophical citizenship. In brilliant and surprising fashion, she focuses on the character of Socrates' philosophical-political activity, starkly contrasting it with the authoritarian (and antipolitical) activity philosophy would become under Plato. The fact that in this essay she is a little *too* successful in reconciling philosophy and citizenship is perhaps less important than what her attempt signals, namely, a certain unease about a political realm in which only "immanent" criticism is allowed, one in which philosophy has no place.

Arendt begins "Philosophy and Politics" with a sweeping and (for some) shocking statement: "The gulf between philosophy and politics opened historically with the trial and condemnation of Socrates, which in the history of political thought plays the same role of a turning point that the trial and condemnation of Jesus plays in the history of religion."[37] According to Arendt, the death of Socrates caused Plato to despair of polis life and to doubt the validity of *persuasion* as a form of speech. Socrates had tried to persuade his fellow citizens that he was innocent of corrupting the youth of Athens—all to no avail. He had tried to address the many as he addressed his interlocutors in the marketplace, but his dialectic came across as an unorthodox (and impoverished) form of rhetoric. His truth was reduced to but one more opinion among many.

The Athenians' condemnation of the wisest and most just man among them led Plato to pose strong and inflexible oppositions between rhetoric and dialectic, and between opinion and truth. According to Arendt, the lesson Plato drew from Socrates' trial was that neither philosophy nor justice would be safe until the democratic privileging of rhetoric and opinion was overturned, to be replaced by the authority of philosophical speech and an absolute truth. Far from being distracted "good for nothings," philosophers were the last, best hope of a polity grown hopelessly corrupt. For only philosophers had access to a truth beyond *doxa*, to an idea of the good which was not context-dependent.[38] Only they could create a polity safe for philosophy, a community in which the thinker's concern with the eternal would no longer render him an object of contempt for the more civic-minded masses.

Arendt's picture of Plato's proposed solution—a "tyranny of truth" designed to remedy the deficiencies of the opinion-centered politics which sent Socrates to his grave—is, perhaps, painted in overly broad strokes. But if she exaggerates the opposition between truth and opinion, dialectic and rhetoric, and philosophy and politics in the Platonic conception, it is for good reason. She wants to highlight the difference between Plato's idea of philosophy (born out of the trauma of Socrates' trial and death) and the philosophical *activity* of Socrates. For if Plato upheld the prerogatives of philosophy *against* the politics of opinion, in Arendt's view Socrates attempted to show his fellow citizens how philosophy could help reform this very politics, making it better by making it more truthful.

But what does it mean to say, as Arendt does, that for Socrates truth was not the opposite of opinion, and that dialectic (*dialegesthai*) was not the opposite of rhetoric and persuasion (*peithein*)? Thanks to the sheer conceptual power of Plato's *Gorgias* and his *Republic*, we have come to take these oppositions for granted—so much so that the suggestion that things might be otherwise seems paradoxical. Tutored by both Plato and Christianity, we assume that there is *one* truth and many (mostly false) opinions. Yet according to Arendt,

Socrates viewed things differently. He did not regard *doxa* as false-hood but rather as "the formulation in speech of what *dokei moi*, what appears to me":

> The assumption [which Socrates shared with his fellow Athenians] was that the world opens up differently to every man, according to his posi-tion in it; and that the "sameness" of the world, its commonness (*koinon*, as the Greeks would say, common to all) or "objectivity" (as we would say from the subjective standpoint of modern philosophy) resides in the fact that the same world opens up to everyone and that despite all differ-ences between men and their positions in the world—and consequently their *doxai*—"both you and I are human."[39]

This "world," of course, is the public realm of the polis, the "realm of appearance," which is constituted by a multiplicity of per-spectives. Thus, the *truth* of a given *doxa* in no way depends upon its ability to approximate a "view from nowhere." Rather, it depends upon how well the individual establishes his own position, his *doxa*, vis-à-vis those of his fellow citizens. This requires not just the "shar-ing of words and deeds" on a public stage but a concentrated effort at the full articulation of one's perspective and the perspectives—the *doxai*—of others. Such effort is likely to occur only when the competitive agon has been suspended and citizens are free to talk something through without the usual intense pressure of public business. Only "friendly" discussion—which aims at neither victory nor decision—allows the individual citizen to grasp his fellow citi-zen's *doxa* and (thus) his "position in the common world." Moreover, it enables the individual to become fully aware of his *own* opinion and its specific truth.[40]

Like Mill, Arendt thinks that the effort at such articulation is rarely made. Even in talkative, democratic Athens, it had to be pro-voked and teased out by a "gadfly." This was Socrates' chosen role: waking his fellow citizens up, inciting them to make the effort in-volved in the full articulation of *their* perspective, *their* truth. Ac-cording to Arendt, Socrates tried, by means of *elenchus*, to refine the individual citizen's "opening to the world"—its specificity, internal coherence, and relation to the standpoints of others. Thus, his goal was not the destruction or transcendence of *doxa* but its *improvement* one viewpoint at a time. In Arendt's striking formulation:

Socrates wanted to make the city more truthful by delivering each of the citizens of their truths. The method of doing this is *dialegesthai*, talking something through, but this dialectic brings forth truth *not* by destroying *doxa* or opinion, but on the contrary reveals *doxa* in its own truthfulness. The role of the philosopher, then, is not to rule the city but to be its "gadfly," not to tell philosophical truths but to make citizens more truthful. The difference with Plato is decisive: Socrates did not want to educate the citizens so much as he wanted to improve their *doxai*, which constituted the political life *in which he too took part*.[41]

But even if Socrates is a philosopher-citizen rather than an aspiring philosopher-king, the question remains: How could *this* goal be achieved given the agonistic politics of democratic Athens? Where individual citizens constantly vie with one another to show who is "the best of all," there seems little opportunity for "talking things through" in the manner Arendt describes. But this (according to her) is precisely Socrates' motivation. He saw the destructiveness—both to the polis and to truth—which the "intense and uninterrupted contest of all against all" produced. Hence, his conversations in the agora had as their object not simply the deliverance of specific truths but the broader purpose of making "friends out of Athens' citizenry."[42] The Socrates of "Philosophy and Politics" supplements the agonistic debate of the assembly with the "dialogue between friends" in the agora and elsewhere. Here, in an indirectly political space, the claims of dialectic and the topic under consideration trump those of contest and competition. (Arendt denies Nietzsche's contention that dialectic is simply a new form of agon.) The cultivation of *this* kind of talk served to focus the attention of citizens on what they shared, on the fact that their individual and political differences were mediated by something held in common. Thus understood, dialectic, unlike rhetoric, allows civic friendship (Aristotle's *philia*) to emerge and, with it, the sense of community sorely needed by a fiercely competitive political realm.

Arendt's depiction of a Socrates who promotes community by means of the "dialogue between friends" is decidedly different from the moral individualist I outlined in chapter 1. Similarly, her interpretation of Socratic questioning as "help[ing] others give birth to what they themselves thought anyhow" closes the gap between truth and opinion—but at the cost of robbing *elenchus* of much of its critical power. Her "maieutic" Socrates—one who is essentially a "midwife" to the thoughts of others—may well strike us as a kind of philosopher-therapist since his purpose is to draw out the specific truth of individual perspectives while establishing a conversational bond of friendship between diverse members of the group.

The Socratic project, however, cannot be reduced to moderating the agonal spirit by means of dialogue and civic friendship. That this is something Arendt clearly recognized is underscored by the remarkable discussion of the relationship between solitude, thinking, conscience, and citizenship which comprises the core of "Philosophy and Politics." Before we accuse her of imagining a Socrates who is a mere facilitator of Periclean politics, one who smoothes away its Hobbesian excesses, we must take account of this discussion, which has no counterpart in her entire oeuvre.

Commenting on Socrates' insistence (in the *Gorgias*) that "it is better to be in disagreement with the whole world than, being one, to be in disagreement with myself," Arendt notes that the possibility of self-contradiction hinges on the fact that each of us is a "two-in-one" when we are engaged in thought. The Socratic formula teaches that moral integrity is based on self-agreement or self-consistency, that is, on making sure that a fundamental harmony is maintained in the inner dialogue between me and myself. Arendt glosses this by explaining that the greater one's experience of the inner dialogue of thought (not to be confused with the mere stream of consciousness), the more likely it is that self-contradiction will be experienced as something painful, as something which conflicts with our self-conception and thus stimulates the voice of conscience.[43]

According to Arendt, however, the Socratic formula also teaches a deeper and more paradoxical lesson. Thoughtful solitude, our being alone with ourselves, is what provides us with our basic and, in many ways, most important understanding of human plurality, ethical relationship and, indeed, friendship itself. The relationship each individual establishes with his or her partner in thought serves as the basis for the kind of relationships he or she establishes with others. In Arendt's formulation, "only someone who has had the experience of talking with himself is capable of being a friend, of acquiring another self."[44] What Socrates teaches is that the only civic friendship worth having is based upon the ability of specific individuals to live together with themselves in thought. *Philia*, then, is not a function of community (although it may help to create it); rather, it is rooted in our capacity for thoughtful solitude.[45] Thinking—being together with oneself—prepares us both ethically and ontologically for the plurality of the world; it also provides the basis for a conscience which is not simply the internalization of creedal norms. Solitude, which "before and after Socrates was thought to be the prerogative and professional *habitus* of the philosopher only," turns out to be "the necessary condition for the good functioning of the *polis*, a better guarantee than rules of behavior enforced by laws and fear of punishment."[46]

Arendt's characterization of the Socratic project in "Philosophy and Politics" thus centers on the creation of a *conscientious*, reflective citizenry. Socrates' goal, in other words, was not to tone down competitive individualism simply by fostering a sense of dialogical community but rather to cultivate a *thoughtful* brand of individualism, one born of the capacity for solitude. This reflective individualism would, in turn, provide the basis for a civic friendship which is tonally different from that promoted by contemporary communitarians and virtue theorists. Arendt's radical suggestion in "Philosophy and Politics" is that, according to Socrates, the experience of thought is the true basis of conscience, and that this—and nothing else—is the ground of *authentic* citizenship.

We are here a long way from Aristotle. But we are also far from the position that Arendt, in her published work, usually takes. Her characteristic stance is Periclean or civic republican; it is to question solitude and all forms of individualism—romantic, egoistic, or philosophical—which might draw our attention away from the public realm and undercut the life of the citizen. Thus, it comes as no surprise when, in her 1970 essay "Civil Disobedience," Arendt attacks the Socratic idea of conscience as a form of "self-interest," one more concerned with maintaining the individual's purity of soul than with living up to worldly commitments and responsibilities.[47] Reverting to the civic republican voice familiar from *On Revolution*, she condemns both Socrates and Thoreau for leading latter-day civil disobedients astray, making them think that their protests are not political in nature but essentially ethical or religious. Reading these pages, we are reminded why "Philosophy and Politics" is such an exceptional moment in Arendt's thought. Nowhere else is she willing to entertain the claims of moral individualism so seriously and to view them not as the enemy but the friend of a humane politics. Nowhere else does she present Socrates not simply as a great *thinker* but as a great *citizen*. Finally, nowhere else does she present the possibility of a genuine, if episodic, reconciliation between philosophy and politics.

The unique place of "Philosophy and Politics" in Arendt's oeuvre is further underscored by her 1971 essay "Thinking and Moral Considerations." This essay, which develops many of the same themes as "Philosophy and Politics," contains important—and telling—shifts in emphasis. Once again the focus is on the relationship between thinking, morality, and politics, and once again the central figure is Socrates. Yet the Socrates of "Thinking and Moral Considerations" no longer fills the role sketched out in "Philosophy and Politics." He remains a "citizen among citizens," but his moral-political effect is indirect, limited, and (as described by Arendt) more than a little ambiguous.

Arendt begins the essay by telling us that the idea that thinking might "condition" men against evildoing was aroused by her observation of the shallow and thoughtless Adolf Eichmann at his trial in Jerusalem. The doer of monstrous deeds turned out to be no demon but a creature largely defined by the "language rules" of whatever context he happened to find himself in (whether it be a Nazi bureaucracy or a trial for crimes against humanity). His capacity to adapt to the rules required by the situation—to accept that "what he had once considered his duty was now called a crime"—indicated the absence of any independent perspective on actions and events, even when their consequences were horrific. "This total absence of thinking," Arendt writes, "attracted my interest."

> Is evil-doing, not just the sins of omission but the sins of commission, possible in the absence of not merely "base motives" (as the law calls it) but of any motives at all, any particular prompting of interest or volition? Is wickedness, however we may define it, this being "determined to be a villain," *not* a necessary condition for evildoing? Is our ability to judge, to tell right from wrong, beautiful from ugly, dependent upon our faculty of thought? Do the inability to think and a disastrous failure of what we commonly call conscience coincide? The question that imposed itself was: Could the activity of thinking as such, the habit of examining and reflecting on whatever comes to pass . . . could this activity be of such a nature that it "conditions" men against evil-doing?[48]

These questions concerning "the inner connection between the ability or inability to think and the problem of evil" led Arendt to reconsider—some sixteen years after "Philosophy and Politics"—the moral and political significance of Socrates' philosophical activity.

Of course, the idea that thinking somehow "conditions" men against evildoing is one of the most cherished verities of the Western philosophical tradition. Generally speaking, however, this tradition has limited the moral efficacy of thinking to the philosophical few, or to reason's capacity to provide a supposedly indubitable foundation for a code of conduct. Yet if thinking is to have the kind of preventive (and morally salutary) effect Arendt desires, it must be an activity open to everyone, not just a philosophical elite. Moreover, it must be shorn of its pretensions to provide knowledge or a directly usable practical wisdom. Such pretensions are built on the conflation of thinking and knowing and reinstate the Platonic assumption that thought and practical reasoning are a kind of "expert knowledge."

It is for these reasons that Arendt turns not to any of the "professional" thinkers of the tradition but rather to Socrates—"a man who counted himself neither among the many nor among the few . . . ; who did not aspire to being a ruler of cities or claim to know how to improve and take care of the citizens' souls; who did not believe that men could be wise and did not envy the gods their divine wisdom in case they should possess it; and who therefore had never even tried his hand at formulating a doctrine that could be taught and learned."[49] This Socrates—neither a teacher nor a "wise man"— can serve Arendt as a model thinker/citizen since he does nothing and claims nothing beyond what "every citizen should do and has a right to claim."[50] While Arendt does not specify *what* every citizen "should do" and has a "right to claim," it is safe to say that she believes that thinking and judging for oneself are the right and responsibility of every citizen.

The moment we turn to Arendt's description of Socrates' philosophical activity, however, the "model" status she confers upon him becomes problematic. After all, this particular Athenian does something quite peculiar and exceptional in his encounters with his fellow citizens. While he certainly doesn't teach them virtue, neither can it be said that he teaches them how to think. Rather, he *arouses* them from their mental and moral slumber; *purges* them of their unexamined prejudgments, and *paralyzes* them with his own perplexity concerning matters that are usually taken for granted. He is—to cite the famous similes from the *Apology, Sophist*, and the *Meno*—a gadfly, a midwife, and an "electric ray" or stinging fish.[51]

We have encountered these similes before. In "Thinking and Moral Considerations" Arendt emphasizes how each figure captures a moment or aspect of Socrates' effect on people. But what makes her discussion in this essay especially noteworthy is how she presents his overall effect. Gone is her emphasis on Socrates as a cultivator of talk among those who possess different "openings to the world." In "Thinking and Moral Considerations" the gadfly Socrates still "arouses" his fellow citizens, but *not* to the effort of full articulation. Wakefulness is now simply identified with thought, with "examining matters." Socrates still helps deliver others of their thoughts. He does this, however, by fulfilling the traditional Greek midwife's function "of deciding whether the child [the particular thought or opinion] was fit to live or, to use Socratic language, was a mere 'windegg,' of which the bearer must be cleansed."[52] Arendt's description of how Socrates fulfills this task (cited in chapter 1 of this study) is worth quoting again, if only to measure the distance between the Socrates of "Thinking and Moral Considerations" and the seemingly more benign Socrates of "Philosophy and Politics":

> Looking at the Socratic dialogues, there is nobody among Socrates' interlocutors who ever brought forth a thought that was no windegg. He [Socrates] rather did what Plato, certainly thinking of Socrates, said of the sophists: he *purged* people of their "opinions," that is, of those unexamined prejudgments which prevent thinking by suggesting that we know where we not only don't know but cannot know, helping them, as Plato remarks, to get rid of what was bad in them, their opinions, without however making them good, giving them truth.[53]

Even allowing for the fact that her use of "opinion" here departs from her usual meaning (a rational faculty rather than a mere prejudice or prejudgment)[54] this is an extraordinary reversal for Arendt. Of course, she does not renege on her endorsement of a (democratic) politics of opinion as opposed to an (authoritarian) politics of absolute truth. Nevertheless, she utterly recasts Socrates' role within the debate and deliberation that constitutes the Greek/Arendtian politics of talk. Socrates no longer builds opinions up by eliciting their specific truth; rather, he uses *elenchus* to reveal their inadequacy. He deploys cross-examination in order to *dissolve* what had seemed solid to his interlocutors, offering nothing—not even a "subjective" truth—to take its place.

This surprising turn to the "negative" Socrates is highlighted by Arendt's gloss of the third simile: Socrates as a kind of "stinging fish," one who *paralyzes* his interlocutors by questioning, creating perplexity in the place of certainty. As Arendt notes, the idea that Socrates' effect is like that of an "electric ray" seems to run counter to the idea that he is a gadfly who arouses. But the contradiction is only apparent, since the "paralysis" of thought is quite different from the "slumber" of unexamined opinion. While the latter is utterly consonant with an active life (and, indeed, may even be its prerequisite), the former calls a halt to action so that the individual's energy can be redirected to intensified mental activity. One must stop what one is doing in order to think, and it is this "stop and think" which Socrates is so masterful at inducing. Thus, whereas from the outside the experience of thinking appears as the cessation of all activity, from the inside it is experienced as a "wind" or "storm" of thought, as "the highest state of being alive."[55]

The "paralysis of thought" has another quality as well. Once aroused, the "winds of thought" undo what words—concepts, sentences, definitions, doctrines—have "frozen into thought." Moreover, this same thinking activity restlessly does away with its previous manifestations. Like Penelope at her loom, it continually undoes its own work and begins again.[56] In other words, thinking itself is negative or dissolvent in nature: it takes the concepts or meanings reified in language and "unfreezes" them, leaving perplexities where there were once certainties and agreed-upon meanings. Hence, as Arendt notes, thinking "inevitably has a destructive, undermining effect on all established criteria, values, measurements for good and evil, in short, on those customs and rules of conduct we treat of in morals and ethics."[57]

Viewed from this angle, the Socratic questioning Arendt describes in "Thinking and Moral Considerations" does not merely slow people down. It has the further ambiguous effect of questioning the foundations of practical and moral conduct. Where the perplexities of thought are held in check by a commitment to avoid injustice at whatever cost, this "dangerous and resultless enterprise" will not issue in any "immoralist" conclusions. However, as Arendt points out, men who, like Alcibiades and Critias, were "aroused" by the gadfly took the "nonresults" of Socratic examination and converted them into negative results. "If we cannot define what piety is," they reasoned, "let us be impious"—a conclusion directly at odds with Socrates' intent but perfectly logical nevertheless.[58]

"Thinking," Arendt writes, "is equally dangerous to all creeds and, by itself, does not bring forth any new creed."[59] This, it appears, is both its strength and its weakness. It is a strength in that it undermines dogmatism and suspends the more or less automatic application of general rules to the conduct of everyday life. It is a weakness insofar as few are able, as Socrates is, to leave open, without answer, the questions raised by thinking. Ultimately virtue *is* defined or "new values" are produced by reversing the old. This, in Arendt's view, is what Nietzsche did when he "reversed" Plato, or what Marx did when he turned Hegel "upside down."[60] Such "negative results" of thinking are fated to be used "as sleepily, with the same unthinking routine, as the old values; the moment they are applied to the realm of human affairs, it is as though they had never gone through the thinking process."[61] Thoughtlessness has a way of becoming the "result" of thought, if only because so much philosophical thinking is guided by the ambition of rendering further thinking unnecessary. If only some ground—whether in Nature, History, the Will to Power or the abyss of Being—can be discovered, perhaps the perplexity (and the paralysis) induced by thinking will disappear. Or so, at least, philosophical revolutionaries like Marx and Nietzsche hoped.

The thoughtlessness inherent in such "revolutionary" reversals has its nonphilosophical counterpart in the conventionalism of most people in most times and places. Like Socrates (and like Mill and Nietzsche), Arendt thinks that our natural tendency is to hold fast to prescribed rules of conduct. This tendency preserves us from disorientation and nihilism, but it also makes us morally and intellectually vulnerable in the manner described by Mill in *On Liberty*. The *form* of ready-to-hand rules or catechisms takes precedence over a "lively apprehension" of their moral content. The result—in times of crisis or upheaval—is that many people will accept the reversal of their previously cherished values so long as this reversal is presented in the form of a new code of conduct. Indeed, as Arendt concludes,

The faster men hold to the old code, the more eager will they be to assimilate themselves to the new one: the ease with which such reversals can take place under certain circumstances suggests indeed that every-

269

body is asleep when they occur. This century has offered us some experience in such matters. How easy was it for the totalitarian rulers to reverse
the basic commandments of Western morality—"Thou shalt not kill" in
the case of Hitler's Germany, "Thou shalt not bear false testimony
against thy neighbor" in the case of Stalin's Russia.[62]

Eichmann serves as an exemplar of those who fetishize form over
content in this manner, reducing morality to the structure of rules
or law as such. Thus, while thinking may be dangerous when it
comes to moral-political matters, nonthinking—garden-variety
thoughtlessness, the dogmatism of everyday life—is clearly more so.

At this point in her argument Arendt seems to have backed herself
into a corner. She wants to maintain that thinking has salutary moral
effects, but she is too honest to pretend that the claims of thinking
coincide with the claims of everyday morality or conduct. Thinking
reduces these claims to one perplexity among others. It tempts those
without Socrates' self-control to draw negative conclusions, to dismiss common decency as either unnatural or arbitrary.[63] Yet common
decency itself seems to reside on the shakiest of grounds, ready to be
abandoned with little regret or comprehension in times of crisis. The
dilemma is only deepened when we recall that "pure" thinking—
the kind which does *not* arrive at set conclusions, the kind Socrates
practiced—does not offer usable practical wisdom: it does not tell us
how to act or judge. In short, almost everything Arendt has to say
about thinking in "Thinking and Moral Considerations" seems to
point to its political and moral irrelevance, if not its actual harm.

And yet, according to Arendt, the Socratic project—and thinking
itself—does have moral efficacy, albeit of a limited kind. How so?
How does a destructive and unproductive activity, one which com-
mences ever anew, dispose its practitioners to avoid injustice and
complicity with evil? Isn't it closer to the truth to say that it simply
encourages withdrawal from the world and the kind of civic *irresponsibility* which Arendt decried throughout her career as a political
thinker and a public intellectual?

Arendt's response to this conundrum returns her to the terrain
of "Philosophy and Politics." As in the earlier essay, her claim in
"Thinking and Moral Considerations" is that thinking—the dialogue between me and myself—creates an inescapable inner voice,
a partner in thought who is heard whenever we are alone with ourselves. This voice—our conscience—says "no" to actions which con-

tradict the sense of self created by thoughtful "intercourse with one-self." Conscience is not, Arendt insists, the "voice of God in man," the *lumen naturale*, or anything like Kant's practical reason.[64] It is, rather, a voice which is invariably heard by those experienced in thought, who have become "friends" with their thinking partner. Those who, whether through constant distraction or the avoidance of solitude, are relatively unfamiliar with the dialogue of thought will feel little discomfort when they contradict themselves in word or deed. At best their "conscience" will consist in the internalization of creedal norms.

Arendt's conscience—a *secular* conscience born of thinking itself, a form of conscience discovered by Socrates—may sound like the sole prerogative of thinkers and philosophers, but she insists this is not the case. "Thinking in its non-cognitive, non-specialized sense as a natural need of human life, the actualization of the difference given in consciousness [our "inner" plurality], is not a prerogative of the few but an ever-present faculty of everybody. . . ."[65] Conscience arises out of the two-in-one of consciousness, which finds its most fully articulated form in the dialogue of thought, of me with myself. The "voice of conscience" expresses the inner disharmony created when I subvert the understandings and agreements I have made with myself. All this—indeed, the basic formula of secular conscience— Arendt thinks is implied by Socrates' statement in the *Gorgias*: "It would be better for me that my lyre or a chorus I directed should be out of tune and loud with discord, and that multitudes of men should disagree with me rather than that I, *being one*, should be out of harmony with myself and contradict *me*" (482c).

There is, however, a striking difference in the way Arendt deploys this statement in "Thinking and Moral Considerations" and the way she used it in "Philosophy and Politics." In the earlier essay Socrates' statement is invoked as evidence of our inner plurality, which is then linked to the outer plurality of the world.[66] Thought and conscience help us to know and live with ourselves. More important (from a political point of view), they prepare us for friendship with our fel-low citizens. Thoughtful solitude is here presented as the basis of an authentic being-with-others.[67] In "Thinking and Moral Consid-erations," however, civic friendship—and the whole painstakingly established connection between our inner and outer plurality— drops out of the picture. When Arendt invokes the Socratic formula for moral integrity in the later essay, it is bereft of all specifically *political* connotations. It simply stands as an *ethical* imperative for the conscientious individual (who may well be a noncitizen or have no particular involvement in the political life of his or her society). It connects to the world of politics only by virtue of the close link it establishes between thought and conscience, between our restless, "destructive" inner dialogue (which dissolves all certainties) and the capacity to say "no" to oneself and the world.

But even this link is indirect and situational. Conscience may be, as Arendt terms it, a "side effect" of thinking, but thinking itself "remains a marginal affair for society at large *except in emergencies*."[68] What she has in mind are extreme situations—like the rise of Nazism in Germany or Stalinism in Russia—where "mere anarchy is loosed upon the world" and "everybody is swept away unthinkingly by what everybody else does and believes in. . . ."[69] Then and only then does the negative, purging element of thinking come into its own, becoming "political by implication" as it sets about destroying "values, doctrines, theories, and even convictions."

Such purging, in Arendt's view, is not something the thinker practices on others in "emergency" situations but rather the precondition for creating one's own thinking space in the midst of collective fantasy and denial; the precondition, in other words, of creating a space for moral and political *judgment*. Through its purgative effect, thinking *liberates* the faculty of judgment. The latter, according to Arendt, is the faculty of judging particulars (events, actions, etc.) "without subsuming them under those general rules which can be taught and learned until they grow into habits that can be replaced by other habits and rules."[70] Thinking and judging are distinct but inextricably linked. As Arendt suggests in the concluding paragraph of "Thinking and Moral Considerations,"

> The faculty of judging particulars . . . the ability to say, "This is wrong," "This is beautiful," etc., is not the same as the faculty of thinking. Thinking deals with invisibles, with representations of things that are absent; judging always concerns particulars and things close at hand. But the two are interrelated in a way similar to the way consciousness and conscience are interconnected. If thinking, the two-in-one of the soundless dialogue, actualizes the difference within our identity as given in consciousness and thereby results in conscience as its by-product, then judging, the by-product of the liberating effect of thinking, realizes thinking, making it manifest in the world of appearances, where I am never alone and always much too busy to think. The manifestation of the wind of

thought is no knowledge; it is the ability to tell right from wrong, beautiful from ugly. And this indeed may prevent catastrophes, at least for myself, in the rare moments when the chips are down.[71]

For the most part, then, thinking remains a solitary affair, "manifesting" itself politically only when reigning "common sense" has become monstrous and monolithic. Perhaps "politically" is too strong a word in this context since Arendt insists that the capacity of thinking to prevent "catastrophes" is limited to its ability to preserve the *individual* from complicity with state-sponsored evil—one which the majority simply fails to recognize.

As Arendt claims in "Thinking and Moral Considerations," the purgative quality of Socratic *elenchus* is an inherent quality of thinking itself. But what thinking enables is not a new, disillusioning form of citizenship, one dedicated to revealing the immorality woven into virtually all forms of patriotism or moral "common sense." Rather, it creates an individual practiced in the art of gaining distance on the *doxai* of the day; an individual who prefers the harmony of his inner dialogue to the highs (and the self-loss) offered by the enthusiasms of political participation or the distractions of social life.

The lesson of "Thinking and Moral Considerations," then, is not that philosophical *citizenship* is possible or even desirable but that solitary thinking can save *any* individual from complicity with evil so long as that individual is sufficiently attentive to his or her thinking partner and willing to withdraw in order to maintain good relations with it. In "emergency situations" this conscientious refusal to participate, to be drawn in, is, to be sure, a *kind* of dissent. While it may not be as theatrical as Socrates,' it is nevertheless *indirectly* political: "When everybody is swept away unthinkingly by what everybody else does and believes in, those who think are drawn out of hiding because their refusal to join in is conspicuous and thereby *becomes a kind of action*."[72] Yet this political quality is, so to speak, accidental. It occurs only where the idea and practice of citizenship are so hopelessly compromised that *anti*citizenship—the refusal to acknowledge the claims of the public—somehow becomes more authentically political than the practice of citizenship. To repeat, Arendt thinks such situations are rare.

What are we to make of this Socratic tangent, this zigzag on the question of philosophical citizenship, in Arendt's thought? Her attempt to reconcile philosophy and politics in the 1954 essay is

273

prompted by a rare anxiety over the moral and political effects of agonistic individualism. This anxiety—no trace of which is to be found in *The Human Condition*—led her to turn to Socrates as a kind of philosopher-mediator of the public sphere, one who attempted to rechannel agonal energies into the effort to fully articulate one's *doxa*. Had she been less bent (in her later work) on presenting philosophy as the inveterate enemy of the realm of opinion, she might have acknowledged how the perspectival public world she describes depends not just on a *plurality* of diverse citizens but on the efforts of a gadfly who draws out the specific truth of individual *doxa*. In *The Human Condition* Arendt, like Pericles and like Mill in his review of Grote, implies that this effort at articulation is fully supplied by the citizens themselves; in "Philosophy and Politics" she reveals her doubts that such a robust perspectivism is adequately generated by the public realm itself. While she chose not to emphasize (or even record) these doubts in her published work, their trace remains. Consider, for example, the well-known passage on the nature of *political* thinking from her 1965 essay "Truth and Politics":

> Political thought is representative. I form an opinion by considering a given issue from different viewpoints, by making present to my mind the standpoints of those who are absent; that is, I represent them. This process of representation does not blindly adopt the actual views of those who stand somewhere else, and hence look upon the world from a different perspective; this is a question neither of empathy, as though I tried to be or to feel like somebody else, nor of counting noses and joining a majority but of being and thinking in my own identity where actually I am not. The more people's standpoints I have present in my mind while I am pondering a given issue, and the better I can imagine how I would feel and think if I were in their place, the stronger will be my capacity for representative thinking and the more valid my final conclusions, my opinion.[73]

This is Arendt's version of Nietzsche's observation (in the *Genealogy*) that "the *more* eyes, different eyes, we can use to observe one thing, the more complete will our 'concept' of this thing, our 'objectivity,' be."[74] But for such perspectivism to become the *method* of thought, as Arendt suggests in the preceding passage, there must be a prolonged and concentrated effort at representing the standpoints of others (an effort quite distinct from the empathic idea of understanding so popular today). The suggestion of "Philosophy and Politics" is that philosophy serves politics by cultivating the habits of mind necessary for "representative thinking." Dialectic, unlike rhetoric, encourages the imaginative mobility (and willingness to bracket one's own prejudgments) which genuine *political* thinking demands.

Yet for this to be the case—for the philosopher to contribute to the growth of representative thought among ordinary citizens—certain preconditions must be met. Representative thought cannot take place if the dominance of an ideology, or the homogenization of public opinion, effectively flattens the range of perspectives, making all see from more or less the same standpoint. In the first case—which Arendt dealt with in *The Origins of Totalitarianism*—the public sphere goes dark as one perspective acquires a monopoly on public speech and "truth." In the second case—addressed at length in *The Human Condition*—the public sphere remains "illumined," but the light it casts has grown decidedly false. There are, Arendt acknowledges, places and times where Heidegger's "perverse sounding statement [that] the light of the public obscures everything" goes to the very heart of the matter.[75] She appeared to think that the West was entering such a period with the rise of "laboring society" and the enforced privatization of much of daily life.[76] Even where public life is robust, as it was in democratic Athens, "representative thinking" is hardly a matter of course. The Athenians needed Socrates—needed philosophy—to cultivate the mental habits necessary for a genuinely doxastic politics.

But where does this leave *us*? If the Socrates of "Philosophy and Politics" underscores the deficits of an agonistic politics, while the Socrates presented in "Thinking and Moral Considerations" demonstrates the moral effects of thinking in "emergency situations," it is difficult to see how either figure is directly relevant to *our* situation. It is only when we stress, with the Mill of *On Liberty*, that it is the nature of social life to secrete unquestioned (and seemingly unquestionable) regimes of opinion that we have a way of connecting Arendt's Socrates to the problems of the present. Once we take this Millian step, we see that the analysis of Socratic thinking contained in "Thinking and Moral Considerations" applies to a far wider range of circumstances than Arendt is willing to allow. The dissolvent, purgative effect of Socratic thinking creates a space for independent judgment within the field of received ideas and thoughtlessly regurgitated ideological fragments (the greater part of political speech and journalism). It also fosters the kind of intellectual mobility required by "representative thinking," albeit not for the purpose of achieving consensus with others. The most important effect of this mobility is not the elimination of everything private and idiosyncratic (the aspect emphasized by those commentators who wish to draw a parallel between representative thinking and Kant's conception of moral judgement) but the creation of the distance necessary for independent judgment.[77] "Representative thinking" does not contain the outline of a "decision procedure" for either ethics or politics. What is does contain is the outline of a method of thought for those who wish to judge for themselves.[78]

Yet despite her great admiration for figures like Socrates, Arendt tends to downplay the gravitational pull of custom, convention, and received opinion in her political theory. Why is this the case? Why is she not alive to the dangers of public opinion in all but the most extreme of situations?

The answer has to do with her desire to preserve the realm of opinion from the coercive force of an absolute Truth, whether of philosophical or religious provenance. Arendt thought—rightly, in my view—that the greater part of Western philosophical and religious thought about politics was bent on eliminating (or at least radically curtailing) the diversity of opinion which human plurality creates.[79] But her vehement anti-Platonism led her to exaggerate the vulnerability of the realm of opinion to *external* threats and to ignore those which arise from within. The dogmatic temper is hardly confined to philosophy or religion, however spectacularly it may manifest itself in these pursuits. The realm of opinion itself (left to its own devices, as it were) is as great a threat to the many-sidedness of truth, thanks to the human propensity for dogmatism and mimetic thought and behavior. Hence the need for an endlessly dissolvent, critical enterprise of the Socratic sort, the end of which is not procurement of truth but resistance to the narrowness of perspective (and moral inertia) encouraged by socially dominant views of what is right and what is wrong.

This is an aspect of the Socratic project which Mill recognized most clearly. But while Arendt occasionally comes close to Millian formulations (the passage on representative thought is a good example), her overall tendency is to be far more solicitous of "common sense" than a thinker of her critical capacity ought to be. She wants to preserve the "community sense" of reality since she sees this as the ultimate ground of any robust politics and civic responsibility. This is not to say that, ultimately, Arendt privileged one perspective above all others, and that her emphasis on human plurality and diversity of opinion is only superficial or a sham. On the contrary, "common sense" for her is both the precondition and result of a plurality of opinion, its origin and goal. It is that sense of a shared world which enables diverse perspectives to recognize each other as perspectives on the same thing.

Looked at from a position external to her political theory, however, Arendt's musings on the importance of common sense—the *sensus communis*—serve a theoretical function parallel to the young Nietzsche's emphasis on the need for an unquestionable horizon to orient and preserve a "healthy" culture or form of life.[80] As she puts in it her *Lectures on Kant's Political Philosophy*, "One judges always as a member of a community, guided by one's community sense, one's *sensus communis*."[81] "Common sense" appears here as the nonfoundational ground of moral and political judgment, the faculty which enables a perspective to be a perspective, an opinion to be more than a prejudice, and a judgment to be potentially "universal," that is, shared by the judge's fellow citizens, who have been persuaded by his words and reasons.

Arendt's drawing a horizon around the perspectival exchange of opinion—her insistence on the necessary priority of a preexisting moral world—makes the same methodological-epistemological point we find in much "hermeneutic" social science and philosophy. The activity of judgment has an irreducible and inevitable interpretive dimension, one which feeds on shared meanings and practices. However, as with the young Nietzsche and contemporary communitarians, Arendt gives this plausible point a strong normative spin. In its broadest terms, she is convinced that a healthy politics must remain firmly attached to *this* community, *this* culture, *this* "world." Hence her Socrates, unlike Mill's, is no heretic, nor can he possibly be construed as the creator of a new moral world. He is, rather, a "citizen among citizens," one who helps others to fully articulate their *doxa* and (if the situation absolutely demands it) to "stop and think." He draws out the richness of a plurality which is already inscribed in a particular moral-political world, but he does little to *relativize* that world or put its most fundamental assumptions into question. In this respect Arendt—again like the young Nietzsche—fears the dissolvent effects of the "will to truth" on the world of opinion and political action. Hence the "model thinker" (Socrates) must be recuperated as a citizen, first and foremost, lest his questioning lead to unpolitical or "nihilistic" results.

In the end Arendt is far more devoted to preserving what Michael Ignatieff has called "the myth of citizenship" than she is to promoting moral and intellectual integrity (the Socratic project).[82] This is not to say she is against these virtues, or that she is an unwitting promoter of moral and intellectual dishonesty or self-deception. Rather, her fears regarding the continued viability of an authentically *public* reality led her to strictly circumscribe the role of the "philosopher-citizen," despite her profound insights into the nature and roots of modern political evil (that is, evil as *policy*). Striving to preserve an authentic realm of opinion from the assaults of the philosophical tradition, on the one hand, and the enormous pressures of modernity, on the other, she limited the political relevance of the "purgative" Socrates to "emergency situations" where "all are carried away." If there was, in fact, an episodic reconciliation of thought and action, philosophy and citizenship, it was to be found not in the open-ended questioning of the dissident philosopher but in the all too friendly *elenchus* of a thinker who sought to promote community and the "birthing" of the opinions of individual citizens.

STRAUSS: PLATO, SOCRATES—OR ARISTOTLE?

Arendt's straying, by way of Socrates, into the problem of philosophical citizenship is fascinating and unexpected. It is, however, a *detour* from her primary theoretical task, which is to rescue political action and citizenship from their philosophical (and cultural) devaluation. For the most part, Arendt's mature theoretical work stresses the *conflict* between philosophy and politics, the *vita contemplativa* and the *vita activa*. In "Philosophy and Politics" she raises the question of whether the origins of this conflict were historical and contingent—the result of Socrates' condemnation and death—or somehow rooted in the nature of the activities themselves. While she hardly underestimates the impact of Socrates' trial and death, she tends to the latter view. The life of action, the *bios politikos*, is one lived in public, in the world of appearances, among one's fellow citizens. It is a life devoted to civic responsibilities, to political action and judgment. The life devoted to thought or contemplation, conversely, entails both a withdrawal from the world and a cessation of activity. Only then can the inner dialogue of thought fully come into its own; only then can the sheer wonder at existence—the pathos that gives rise to philosophy—be experienced.[83]

In turning to Strauss, one is initially struck by his general agreement with Arendt as to the *causes* of the conflict between philosophy and politics. For Strauss philosophical thinking requires a withdrawal from the world of appearances; it is essentially the contemplative attempt to grasp the nature of the whole.[84] Such activity stands in the sharpest possible opposition to the active pursuit of glory or greatness in the political realm (the Periclean conception), one which never leaves the conventional world of the polity behind, which never concerns itself with the "invisibles" which are the proper object of the philosopher's "what is?" questions. For Strauss the tension between *physis* and *nomos* (nature and law or convention) in ancient Greek thought mirrors the fundamental opposition between what Arendt calls the citizen's desire for worldly immortality (achieved through words and deeds) and the philosopher's experience of the eternal, which "can occur only outside the realm of human affairs and outside the plurality of men."[85]

But if Arendt's analysis in *The Human Condition* stressed the way the philosopher's concern with the eternal is "inherently contradictory and in conflict with the striving for immortality, the life of the citizen," Strauss stipulates a kind of continuity between the world of "the cave" and the philosopher's pursuit of wisdom. In his view the philosophical project is not one of dissolving or negating *doxa* but (to use the Platonic metaphor from book 7 of the *Republic*) of *ascending* from *doxa* to what is "natural" and not merely conventional. As Strauss puts it, "even Socrates is compelled to go the way from law to nature, to ascend from law [*nomos*] to nature."[86] Socratic dialectic is nothing other than the means by which the ascent from "common sense" is achieved.[87]

However, it is one thing to say that Socrates necessarily *begins* with "common sense" (as Strauss does) and quite another to say that his mission is maieutically to tease out the truth of a particular *doxa*. Arendt's formulation in "Philosophy and Politics" stands squarely opposed to Strauss's conception of the aim of classical political philosophy and political philosophy as such. The point for Strauss is to move beyond the realm of plurality and conflicting opinion, to ascend dialectically to a comprehensive standpoint far removed from the "it appears to me" of the situated citizen. Describing the character of Socratic philosophy and dialectics in *Natural Right and History*, Strauss writes:

> Philosophy consists, therefore, in the ascent from opinions to knowledge or to the truth, in an ascent that may be said to be guided by opinions. It is this ascent which Socrates had primarily in mind when he called philosophy "dialectics." Dialectics is the art of conversation or of friendly dispute. The friendly dispute which leads towards the truth is made possible or necessary by the fact that opinions about what things are, or what some very important groups of things are, contradict one another. Recognizing the contradiction, one is forced to go beyond opinions toward the consistent view of the nature of the thing [justice, piety, wisdom, virtue] concerned. That consistent view makes visible the relative truth of the contradictory opinions; the consistent view proves to be the comprehensive or total view. The opinions are thus seen to be fragments of the truth, soiled fragments of the pure truth.[88]

On this account, the *doxai* have not exactly been "destroyed," but it is clear that the fact of their plurality restricts their value to raw material for the philosopher. For Strauss the aim of Socrates is to ascend from the many (*doxai*) to the one (truth), while remaining conscious of the limits of human knowledge. Nothing could be further from Arendt's Socrates, who, as a "citizen among citizens," has as his goal the *improvement* of *doxa* one opinion at a time.

Strauss's formulation of the Socratic project is echoed in his description of the nature and goal of political philosophy in "What Is Political Philosophy?" (1954–55). The opening of this essay finds Strauss at his most Platonic: the conception of political philosophy he offers is structured almost entirely upon the distinction between knowledge (*episteme*) and opinion. Philosophy is defined as the "quest for universal wisdom, for knowledge of the whole." *Political* philosophy—a discipline Strauss argues was founded by Socrates—is a "branch" of philosophy proper. Thus, in a well-know passage, Strauss writes:

> Political philosophy will then be the attempt to replace opinion about the nature of political things by knowledge of the nature of political things. Political things are by their nature subject to approval and disapproval, to choice and rejection, to praise and blame. It is of their essence not to be neutral but to raise a claim to men's obedience, allegiance,

decision or judgment. One does not understand them as what they are, as political things, if one does not take seriously their explicit or implicit claim to be judged in terms of goodness or badness, of justice or injustice, i.e., if one does not measure them by some standard of goodness and justice. *To judge soundly one must know the true standards*. If political philosophy wishes to do justice to its subject matter, it must strive for genuine knowledge of these standards. Political philosophy is the attempt to truly know the nature of political things and the right, or good, political order.[89]

Political philosophy, then, is the "conscious, coherent, and relentless effort to replace opinions about political fundamentals by knowledge regarding them."[90] This definition of political philosophy assimilates the Socratic position to Plato's, and it is (evidently) motivated by the demand that there be *some* way of rationally adjudicating the fundamental questions and controversies of political life (What is the best regime? Who shall rule?). The political philosopher, as the classics conceived him, was no therapist to citizens but rather "the teacher of legislators." Even more important for Strauss, the political philosopher is the one whose knowledge of political things places him in a privileged position of judgment: "The umpire par excellence is the political philosopher. He tries to settle those political controversies that are of both paramount and permanent importance."[91] The political philosopher is suited to this task because only he—as opposed to the politician, "political thinker," or intellectual—is neither partisan nor constrained by the "here and now."[92] His inquiry into the "what is?" questions directs him toward knowledge of the good life and the good society. It enables him to address what Strauss calls the "essentially controversial" meaning of the common good in a comprehensive rather than partial or partisan fashion.[93]

Strauss's conception of political philosophy obviously takes its bearings from Nietzsche's analysis of European nihilism in *The Will to Power*. Like Nietzsche, Strauss emphasizes how the West has become "uncertain of its purpose" and mired in relativism.[94] But his notion of political philosophy is also—and more directly—a response to Weber's value pluralism and the historicism of Heidegger's fundamental ontology. Weber's denial that reason can find solutions to value conflicts by uncovering a natural hierarchy of values occasions Strauss's most polemical and intemperate prose.[95] The sometimes misleading rhetoric of *Natural Right and History* aside, Strauss does not dogmatically assert that reason *can* indeed solve such conflicts.[96] His primary intent is to question the "dogma" that—given the plurality of values, goods, and "ultimate commitments"—reason is unable to aid us in ranking or choosing among the "warring gods" of politics, philosophy, or art (or, for that matter, nationalism, socialism, or liberalism). Similarly, his critique of historicism—particularly the "radical historicism" of Heidegger—is motivated by what he sees as its rejection of the question of the good society and its insistence that all answers to this question are historically conditioned. (Indeed, the question itself is seen as the result of one particular fateful dispensation.)[97] Thus, Strauss sees Weber's contempt for the idea of an overarching, adjudicative reason as matched by Heidegger's contempt for such "permanencies" as the distinction between the noble and the base. It was this contempt, Strauss suggests, which led directly to Heidegger's affiliation with National Socialism in 1933.[98]

It is in *this* context that we must understand Strauss's "necessary and tentative or experimental" return to the possibility opened by classical political philosophy.[99] "Social science positivism" (Weber) and historicism (Heidegger) both deny that an ascent can be made, that there is any way out of the "cave" of opinion or historical "world views."[100] Viewed as symptoms of the creeping nihilism analyzed by Nietzsche, they both stand for the proposition that "man cannot understand himself in light of the whole, in the light of his origin or his end."[101] The "end of philosophy" recently trumpeted by Richard Rorty and Jacques Derrida was for Strauss already fully perceived (and fully expressed) by Weber and Heidegger. Strauss's response is apparently to uphold philosophy's traditional ambition to view things *sub specie aeternitatis*, to rise from convention to nature and thus to gain a comprehensive grasp of the whole. (Hence the rhetoric of *Natural Right and History*, in which what is "right by nature" is presented as the sole object of the philosophical quest.) I should stress that this response flows not from any simple nostalgia for the ancients, nor from a misplaced faith that they possess the answers to contemporary political problems.[102] Rather, it must be seen as a conscious rebellion against the (historicist/relativist) spirit of the times.

Strauss's suggestion that we combat the nihilism of the present by resurrecting what seems (for all intents and purposes) to be a metaphysical conception of reason clashes violently with what I have been calling the "ethos of disenchantment." Evidently his response to the "dogma" of historicism is dogmatically to assert that the "natural order" sought by Plato and Aristotle exists, and that we (armed with their texts and authority) can rediscover it. Beyond time and chance lurks the firm yet elusive foundation of what is right by nature. This, and only this, can help to make us confident of our purpose once again. For Strauss only philosophical reason—in the form of the rationalism of the Greeks—can save us from the destructive effects of a "will to truth" that relentlessly corrodes substantive rationality.[103]

The contrast with Arendt, both in terms of diagnosis and prescription, is clear. For Arendt the modern "crisis in authority" wrought by secularization has wide-ranging consequences, not least of which is a fundamental questioning of the traditional Western assumption that political legitimacy is—or could be—a function of some transcendental source, whether natural or divine.[104] Thanks to the dissolvent logic of the "will to truth," the field of metaphysical rationality finally closed in upon itself, to the point where the distinction between essence and existence no longer signified. Glossing Nietzsche's famous aphorisms about the "death of God" in her introduction to *The Life of the Mind*, Arendt writes that for us "What has come to an end is the basic distinction between the sensory and the supersensory, together with the notion, at least as old as Parmenides, that whatever is not given to the senses—God or Being or the First Principles and Causes (*archai*) or the Ideas—is more real, more truthful, more meaningful that what appears, that it is not just *beyond* sense perception but *above* the world of the senses. What is "dead" is not only the localization of such 'eternal truths' but also the distinction itself."[105]

Arendt goes on to describe the *opportunity* presented by the demise of metaphysics and philosophy (as traditionally understood): "It would permit us to look on the past with new eyes, unburdened and unguided by any traditions. . . ."[106] This sense of opportunity echoes her appreciation—some twenty years earlier in a 1954 lecture to the American Political Science Association—of Heidegger's contribution to the study of politics. Praising his concept of historicity (*Geschichtlichkeit*) because it led Heidegger to reject the Platonic/Hegelian assumption that *theoria* occupies a standpoint from which the whole can be grasped, Arendt notes the revolutionary implications of this concept for philosophy and (ultimately) the study of politics. For with this notion "the philosopher left behind him the claim to being 'wise' and knowing eternal standards for the perishable affairs of the City of man," a claim that had force so long as the philosopher, unlike the citizen, was understood to dwell "in the proximity of the Absolute."[107]

Indeed, with Heidegger philosophy can rightly claim to have "left the arrogance of all Absolutes behind." The realm of human affairs no longer appears as an object fit for philosophical comprehension and domination, as it had for the tradition from Plato to Marx. According to Arendt, Heidegger's "rejection of the claim to wisdom" in principle opens the way to "a reexamination of the whole realm of politics in light of the elementary human experiences *within this realm itself,* and demands implicitly concepts and judgments which have their roots in altogether different kinds of human experience."[108]

Of course, from Strauss's standpoint Heideggerian historicity hardly facilitates a return to basic political problems and phenomena; rather, it is responsible for creating (in Strauss's striking image) a kind of "artificial pit" beneath the cave of human affairs. Like other, less radical forms, Heidegger's historicism casts the "natural horizon of human thought" into oblivion by denying "the permanence of the fundamental problems."[109] The "tentative" and "experimental" return to classical political thought is necessary as a means of recovering this "natural horizon" (the world of the political association itself, of commonsense insights into political life). Not Heidegger but the classical political philosophers return us "to the things themselves."[110] The return to the cave, to the world of the commonsense understanding of political things, is the necessary prelude to the ascent to truth. According to Strauss, the world of commonsense experience—of "authoritative opinions"—can serve as the basis for this ascent because it, unlike scientific or historical knowledge, reflects a "natural articulation" of the whole, albeit in clouded, fragmentary form.[111]

Arendt and Strauss's vastly different responses to the provocation of Heidegger seem to create an abyss between the two thinkers. On the one hand, we have Arendt, the phenomenologist of the public realm, wary of the appeal to extrapolitical foundations or absolutes, anxious to abandon what she views as a distorting philosophical standpoint; on the other, we have Strauss, with his unyielding desire to reopen the possibility of philosophical wisdom of the "human things." From Arendt's perspective Strauss's quest for the "true standards" cannot help but appear as authoritarian in the worst Platonist sense. It seeks to impose an absolute upon the realm of human affairs, the better to reduce the role of human plurality and the diversity of opinion in political life. This, in her view, was the motive behind Plato's conversion in the *Republic* of the "ideas" from "that which shines forth most, the beautiful" to "yardsticks" for the political sphere, and indeed behind every attempt—philosophical, religious, or ideological—to ground political power on something transpolitical and supposedly absolute. While Strauss might respond that his interpretation of Plato's "ideas" in the *Republic* expressly questions the supposition that these were intended to provide generally applicable standards for the realm of human affairs (Strauss calls the interpretation of the ideas as self-subsisting metaphysical certainties "incredible, . . . not to say fantastic"[112],) the authoritarian charge retains a certain plausibility. This is true despite Strauss's Aristotelian insistence on the importance of the "commonsense" understanding of political things and the priority of prudence (practical wisdom, *phronesis*) over theoretical science in the realm of politics.[113]

As Arendt argued in her 1956 essay "What Is Authority?," Aristotle's abandonment of the Platonic ideas did not prevent his own political philosophy from being "authoritarian," centering as it did on the "natural" hierarchy of age in order to split ostensibly equal citizens along generational lines—as teachers and taught, rulers and ruled.[114] This educational metaphor—viewed by Arendt as both antidemocratic and antipolitical—lies at the heart of Strauss's own view of political philosophy, statesmanship, and politics rightly construed, namely, as an "education in virtue" carried out differently by various types of political regimes.[115] For Strauss, as opposed to Arendt, Socrates is emphatically a *teacher*, not a "citizen-philosopher,"[116] and a teacher who knows the first political lesson, namely, that philosophers must address different *types* of people differently.[117] Moreover, Strauss's Socrates (a very Platonic Socrates) "converses only with people who are not common people, who in one way or another belong to an elite. . . ."[118] Philosophical wisdom, properly packaged for its audience, contributes to the "gentleman's" education in virtue. The gentlemen, in turn, will help sustain a suitable civic virtue for the otherwise hopelessly selfish *hoi polloi*.[119]

Strauss is vehement in his insistence that the virtue of the philosopher is qualitatively different—and higher—than that of the "gentleman." Likewise, he insists that the virtue of the gentleman is of a different order than the (merely political) virtue of the average citizen.[120] This leads him to stress what he calls "the fundamental disproportion between philosophy and the city" and to declare that "the philosophers and the non-philosophers cannot have genuinely common deliberations."[121] When we combine this denial of the very possibility of an egalitarian public sphere with his insistence that "political life derives its dignity from something which transcends political life" (whether philosophy, faith, or natural right), we seem to have all the evidence we need to convict Strauss of being "authoritarian" in Arendt's sense. There can be no "philosopher-citizens" because philosophers, as lovers of wisdom, stand above the city (even as they depend upon it), and "citizens"—whether of the upper or lower class—are enveloped by a limited, particularistic (but politically necessary) moral horizon. Philosophy, it turns out, requires that "the many" be good and unquestioning patriots so that "the few" can continue to pursue the *vita contemplativa*. Within this Platonic schema, the worst thing that can happen is that "the many" become infected with the spirit of dissolvent rationality, for this would lead to an inversion of the "natural" order of the noble and the base, the high and the low.[122]

We seem, oddly enough, to be back to the young Nietzsche's insistence upon a protective horizon of moral myth as the sine qua non of a "healthy" culture or political society. This, at any rate, is how Stephen Holmes reads Strauss in his take-no-prisoners critique.[123] Strauss, the champion of the philosophical life as *the* good life (the "life according to nature") defends the myths of religion, patriotism, and tradition the better to keep the unphilosophical masses docile, tranquilized, and accepting of social hierarchy and the exclusionary nature of culture—all of which are necessary conditions for the pursuit of wisdom.[124] Even the idea of "natural law" (*not* to be confused with the hierarchical "natural right" of the classics) is, according to Holmes, no more than a "benign myth" foisted upon the many so that political society might be made safe for philosophy.

But, I would suggest, there is another Strauss behind the Platonic/Nietzschean exterior, a far less dogmatic (that is, more genuinely Socratic) Strauss. This is the skeptical Strauss, who insists that genuine philosophy demands a Socratic awareness that one does not know; that "human wisdom is knowledge of ignorance"; that there is no knowledge of the whole but only partial knowledge of the parts; that, as a result, there can be "no unqualified transcending, even by the wisest man as such, of the sphere of opinion."[125] This Strauss does not offer philosophy as a form of foundationalism but rather as the severest challenge to authority in *all* its forms.[126] The "discovery of nature" may be the task of philosophy, but nature turns out to be (at least in moral and political affairs) no more than a kind of "regulative ideal," a symbol not of ready-to-hand yardsticks or standards but of the desire to avoid the identification of the moral with the conventional, an identification which most historicism (truth be told) clearly facilitates.[127]

This Strauss can be seen as the enemy of all dogmatism, of all moral-political positions that base themselves on a supposedly secure possession of truth. Strauss himself identifies such certainty with "political idealism," that is, with movements which attempt to use theory as a blueprint for political practice, social reform, or societal transformation. Like Burke, Oakeshott, and Arendt, Strauss wants to alert us to the dangers of positing a "technical" relation between theory and practice.[128] Unlike them, he sees the warning against the deduction of just political action from abstract theoretical premises as most forcefully articulated in Plato's *Republic*. The argument of the *Republic* is precisely one designed to make us realize that a fully just polity is neither possible nor desirable; hence it liberates us "from the charms of what we would now call political idealism."[129]

In rejecting both conventionalism and an activist "theoreticism," Strauss's thought opens up a space for judgment—a space he sees endangered by both historicism and "idealist" or ideological thinking. His fear is similar to one we find in Arendt: judgment has become increasingly "automatic," the mere reflection of social norms and conventions, the unthinking application of customary rules. Like her, Strauss turns to Socrates (at least in part) to reclaim judgment's specific autonomy. Their primary difference, in this regard, less concerns their aims than their respective diagnoses of the chief threat to judgment as an independent faculty. For Arendt the primary threat comes from the reduction of morality to rules and mere mores; for Strauss the danger resides in the historicist relativization of moral codes. The broader point is that neither Arendt nor Strauss sees any advantage in cultivating an unthinking relationship to rule-bound morality or, indeed, to an uncritical patriotism. If their experience as Jews in Germany during the thirties taught them anything,

it was a certain suspicion of the morality of "my station and its duties."[130] (Whether this suspicion went deep enough is another question, one particularly relevant in the case of Strauss.)

Thinking—whether Socratic in Arendt's sense or philosophical
in Strauss's—is absolutely essential for the liberation of judgment.
But thinking, as both Arendt and Strauss emphasize, is dissolvent in
character: the Socratic dialogues are aporetic and lead to no firm
ground.[131] The essential difference between Strauss and Arendt concerns their attitudes toward the political implications of such thinking in the *public* sphere. For Arendt the potentially nihilistic consequences of Socratic thinking are offset by the value of the "stop and
think," which throws the everyday derivation of moral judgment
and conclusions "out of gear." For Strauss the situation is more pre-
carious. Aside from the usual doubts about the ordinary person's
capacity for thoughtfulness, he worries about the conclusions such
an individual might draw if exposed to a dissolvent (or endlessly
critical) rationality. A thinking which takes place in the agora, which
is truly open to everyone, will be corrupting to those whose character is insufficiently virtuous to withstand the disorientation caused
by Socratic negativity.

This, it seems, is Strauss's primary response to the Arendtian attempt to partially harmonize philosophy and politics through the
figure of Socrates. His clear preference for the Socrates of the *Republic* and the *Gorgias* over the philosopher-citizen of the *Apology* flows
from this fear. His intense concern with the relation of philosophy
to both poetry and rhetoric mirrors his conviction that philosophical
insight will not draw the truth out of the citizen's *doxa* but rather
be transformed into the most dangerous form of untruth. In this
regard, it is no exaggeration to state that the prospect of an Arendtian Socrates—the Socrates of "Philosophy and Politics"—fills him
with horror. No good can come of the attempt to make the *demos*
philosophical: the very project is an oxymoron. Judgment must be
liberated (from the *doxa* of historicism/relativism), but, in the case
of the average citizen, it can never do without leading strings. Here
Strauss stands not only against Arendt but also against Kant. His
distrust of the many makes him confine the prospect of independent
judgment to the few, while hoping for a more edifying (in not necessarily more truthful) *doxa* for the many.[132] Thus, while there is a
strong Socratic dimension to his thinking and conception of philos-

ophy, Strauss remains resolutely Platonist in his view of politics and the nature of citizenship. The *demos* is, by nature, a beast immune to the "charms of philosophy."[133]

Does this mean that the "skeptical" or Socratic Strauss is overshadowed by the Platonic Strauss, one who believes in a set of eternal moral standards revealed by the classical philosophers? The answer is yes and no. Yes because Strauss, like the young Nietzsche, is frightened by the corrosive effects "Socratism" might have on culture at large and upon the morality of the masses in particular. No because Strauss turns out to be quite far from the brand of moral objectivism (and philosophical domination) his rhetoric seems to encourage. Insofar as philosophy can successfully "ascend" from the cave to the universal, its "discoveries" turn out to be largely irrelevant to the life of the city and the citizen. By nature the "best regime" cannot be realized in the realm of becoming, nor should any attempt in this direction be made.[134] The "fundamental disproportion" between philosophy and the city refers not just to the tension between philosophy and citizenship as ways of life but to *the kind of wisdom* the philosophical life reveals, one which is more existential than moral, which reveals the "best regime"—the object of classical political philosophy's quest—to be something of a chimera (at least from the point of view of any feasible politics). There *is* a best way of life (namely, the philosopher's), but the "just city" is merely a mirror image of his self-sufficient, temperate soul and, as such is unrealizable in *this* world.[135]

Strauss, then, is far from being a philosophical authoritarian bent on imposing universal (and supposedly "natural") norms upon the political realm. This is made clear by his counterintuitive reading of the *Republic* as a critique of political idealism. It is also made clear in a passage from *Natural Right and History*, where Strauss (discussing Aquinas's and Averroës's interpretations of Aristotelian natural right) emphasizes the *mutability* of what is "right by nature," going so far as to frame all "correct" action as context-dependent. He delivers a startling summary of the wisdom contained in the classical "natural right" teaching (flexible, attentive to circumstance). "There is," Strauss writes, "a universally valid hierarchy of ends [or ways of life], but there are no universally valid rules of action."[136] The range of action considered in a given set of circumstances depends upon the urgency of the situation, prudential considerations, and an imaginative sense of the "inventiveness of evil." These take precedence over the political actor's knowledge of "what is noble." We can try to bring these factors together through the "inspirational" quality of the latter, but a large and ultimately unbridgeable gap remains: "It is our duty to make the highest activity, as much as we can, the most urgent or the most needful thing. And the maximum of effort which can be expected necessarily varies from individual to individual. *The only universally valid standard is the hierarchy of ends*. This standard is sufficient for passing judgment on the level of nobility of individuals and groups and of actions and institutions. But it is insufficient for guiding our actions."[137]

No actions, in other words, are intrinsically just or unjust, nor are there any rules (certainly not those of everyday morality or common decency) which are sufficient to guide our actions in the treacherous realm of politics. There are, in short, no moral facts, only interpretations (preferably, to be made, by a "statesman" of character).[138] The "hierarchy of ends"—the standard which enables us to articulate a "rank order" of individuals and *bioi* according to their nobility or baseness—is, in fact, the only thing that is really "right by nature." Everything else—political or moral—is a matter of prudence.

With this interpretation of the political import of "natural right," Strauss winds up creating a space for judgment which is at once too large and too small: too large because it puts everything up for grabs without the kind of moral restrictions built into either Socrates' or Mill's conception; too small because it confines the activity of independent judgment to supposed virtuosos of practical wisdom.

Strauss's rhetoric—of timeless absolutes versus historical horizons, of truth versus opinion—conceals this, his actual or "esoteric" teaching. Yet, as the previously cited passage indicates, he often cannot help giving his secret away, even to his less elite readers. His skepticism toward the egalitarian *doxa* of *our* day leads him to endorse the classical view of Plato and Aristotle, namely, that there is and must be a natural hierarchy of activities and lives, with the philosopher on top, the "gentlemen" somewhat below, and the masses at the bottom. The most disturbing idiosyncrasy on Strauss's part, however, is not that he uses "natural right" to argue for inequality and a limited defense of particularism. Rather, it is that he subjects so many of the moral presuppositions of liberalism (such as respect for the individual's moral capacities) to corrosive assault, only to regard as being in bad taste a similarly skeptical view of the hierarchical doctrine he identifies with the "natural right" of the classics.[139]

This would be forgivable, perhaps, if Strauss really carried through on his promise of a "tentative" and "experimental" return to the ancients. Such a return would help us take a large step back from the *doxai* that make up the moral world of liberalism and enable us to see that world—for better or worse—in sharper outline. But there is ultimately nothing tentative or experimental about Strauss's "return." He is essentially a seeker of secrets who thinks he has un- covered the forbidden truth—the right of the higher over the lower, of wisdom over consent—which modern egalitarianism has assidu- ously covered up. Unlike Socrates, he is not a "gadfly" who wants to wake us up to the injustice of much of what we take for granted. Rather, he wants most of us to remain in our moral slumber, reflex- ively loyal to God and to country.[140] In other words, he wants to restrict enlightenment and the escape from avoidable illusion to the smallest possible number, those whose character and "natural" tal- ent for moderation make them suitable candidates for a life of ques- tioning. For the rest, a largely unquestioned reliance upon authority is, or ought to be, the order of the day. In this way intellectual integ- rity is effectively severed from moral integrity, at least when it comes to the merely political virtue of the *hoi polloi*. The morality of "my station and its duties," it turns out, is basically good enough for the masses.[141]

In the end, the classical figure who looms largest in Strauss's writ- ing is not Socrates or even Plato but Aristotle. For it is the latter who supplies Strauss with his conception of a hierarchically articulated "natural" whole, as well as the notion of degrees of virtue—less full or real the lower one goes—attainable by different "types" of men.[142] And it is Aristotle who suggests that the better sort of polity will exclude those in "banausic" occupations (such as shopkeeping and manual crafts) from genuine citizenship and participation in "judg- ment and authority."[143] Finally, it is Aristotle who supplies Strauss with the idea that political society is, first and foremost, a "school" for virtue, one whose job is not to embody "pure" justice (à la Plato's *Republic*) but to inculcate the beliefs, norms, and practices which undergird any stable hierarchy.[144] The many must learn to defer to the wisdom and judgment of the "gentlemen," to those experienced in the realm of public/political affairs. In Strauss's view both public morality and political stability are at stake. Hence his preference for a political regime in which "the gentry" (or their contemporary equivalent) have the greatest possible influence.

It would be hard to imagine a conception more at odds with the ideal of Socratic citizenship I sketched in chapter 1. There I argued that the Socratic idea that intellectual integrity is central to moral integrity has the power to radically revise our idea of what "good citizenship" is or ought to be, distancing it considerably from the civic republican conception which continues to dominate our tradition. Arendt draws our attention to this Socratic revision by underscoring the "dissolvent" character of thinking he practiced in the agora. However, she restricts the political relevance of such thinking, relying on it only in "emergency situations." Strauss can be said to go much further. His tantalizing suggestions about a more philosophical form of citizenship aside, in the end his greatest energies are devoted to keeping philosophy and citizenship separate and distinct.

He does this, I think, for two main reasons. First, Strauss wants to protect the "best life" from the misunderstanding (and resentment) of the nonphilosophers. (In this regard, he fully agrees with Arendt's characterization of the significance Socrates' trial had for the Western philosophical tradition.) Second, he wants nothing to interfere with the continued inculcation of civic and moral virtues necessary to preserve a "moderate" regime, one which can plausibly be seen as dedicated to "noble" rather than base ends. As a result, his challenge to liberal democracy—and, in particular, to its idea of citizenship—is curiously foreshortened. Beyond the call for a more aristocratic "liberal education" (for elites), it leaves everything pretty much as it is.[145] Indeed, when it comes to citizenship, Strauss is content to rely on well-worn nostrums about the need for civic virtue, an ethos of self-sacrifice, and the need for public concern over the formation of character.[146] His relative indifference to the topic is explained by the fact that, while cognizant of citizenship's real world importance, he simply could not take the life of the (democratic) citizen that seriously. Arendt to the contrary, it did not strike Strauss as a fully or "distinctively human" activity.[147] Indeed, from the point of view of classical political rationalism, "the man who is merely just or moral without being a philosopher appears as a mutilated human being."[148]

One could read this as an implicit endorsement of the Socratic suggestion that moral integrity demands intellectual integrity: only when the two go together do we have a non-"mutilated" being and a form of citizenship worthy of respect. But Strauss did not regard civic life—the realm of "merely political or vulgar virtue"—as the appropriate arena for the exercise of intellectual integrity. The great mistake of modern political philosophers like Hobbes, he thought, was to stipulate a potential harmony between philosophy and the people, and to believe that a strategy of disenchantment could lead to greater political stability. On the contrary, among the many, disillusionment led only to the formation of new (and usually more dangerous) dogmas. "Statesmanship" held greater interest for Strauss, but even this was ultimately a means to an end.[149] Whatever dignity politics has is derived from something "higher" than itself, something "transpolitical." For the many, that something might plausibly be "virtue," whether civic or moral. But for the few—for those capable of *genuine* virtue—it could only be philosophy, the life of the mind, the life of understanding.[150]

Strauss's reasons for insisting upon the utter superiority of the philosophical life remain somewhat obscure. We can read his preference as simply a product of his deference to the authority of the classics, or as the expression of his unembarrassed—and much-deplored—elitism. Complicating this mix, however, is the search for ideals in a "disenchanted" world, as well as the need for a post-Auschwitz theodicy. We see this latter aspect—the redemptive power of philosophy—emerge in a curiously elegiac passage from his essay "What Is Liberal Education?":

> We have no other comfort than that inherent in this activity. . . . This experience is entirely independent of whether what we understand primarily is pleasing or displeasing, fair or ugly. It leads us to realize that all evils are in a sense necessary if there is to be understanding. It enables us to accept all evils which befall us and which may break our hearts in the spirit of good citizens of the City of God. By becoming aware of the dignity of the human mind, we realize the true ground of the dignity of man, and therewith the goodness of the world . . . which is the home of man because it is the home of the mind of man.[151]

It is not the polis—the "space of men's free deeds and living words"—that reconciles us with mortality but the wisdom of philosophy.[152] For the few who can find their way out of the cave to an understanding of the whole, it has the power to redeem existence. It is this largely unargued conviction concerning the existential significance of philosophy, I would suggest, that guides Strauss's entire enterprise. It accounts for his love of hierarchy, his condescension toward "citizen morality," and his unwillingness to make intellectual integrity even peripherally important to "merely political" virtue.[153] The many need the cave to reconcile them to reality; the few need philosophy.

We come back, then, to Strauss's insistence that there is a "fundamental disproportion" between philosophy and the city. This disproportion flows not from phenomenological differences between acting and thinking as activities (Arendt's point of departure) but rather from the fact that (as Strauss puts it) "the city as a whole is characterized by a specific recalcitrance to reason." The timeless lesson of the trial and death of Socrates is that the *demos* are all but immune to rational persuasion. This is something both Plato and Aristotle recognized, and made central to their political philosophies. In dealing with the *demos*, persuasion is not enough: laws had to be backed up by ancestral opinions, myths, and even civil theology.[154] The limits of persuasion point to the irreducible need for coercion, myth, habit and custom in political affairs.

Intellectual honesty, then, is an austere virtue—too austere for the *hoi polloi*. Hence the many must be left to their (traditional) illusions—even encouraged in them. The modern idea that there is or could be a "harmony between philosophy and the people" is, in Strauss's view, an absurd assumption which has produced endless suffering, on the one hand, and the banality of "commodious living," on the other.[155] Regardless of enlightenment's intent, dogma will necessarily win out. The only question is *what kind of dogma* it will be. Will it be the certainties of custom and tradition, leavened by the reason of the more moderate and educated of their society (the "gentlemen") or will it be a destructive "doctrinaire-ism" born of the attempt to destroy "superstition" and appeal solely to people's reason?

Regardless of the answer, we see why the skeptical or "Socratic" Strauss must inevitably give way to the Platonic or Aristotelian Strauss. It is not so much a matter of keeping the unphilosophical masses docile and tranquilized (as Holmes suggests) as it is of recognizing the limits of rational discourse and persuasion. Like Nietzsche, Strauss thinks of homo sapiens as the dogmatic animal par excellence. And, like Nietzsche, he thinks that the sovereign individual, "autonomous and supra-moral," is the rarest of rare exceptions. This means that the appeal to reason—the overcoming of creedal morality—will always founder when addressed to the wrong audience.

Intellectual and moral integrity can be linked for the philosopher, that is, for the spirit that has risen above the dogmatic temper. But the "will to the unconditional" that animates most people converts every appeal to reason—or every critique of reason—into a new dogma.[156] This, more than anything else, accounts for the radical divergence of the path of the philosopher and that of the citizen. In response to this divergence, Strauss's rhetorical strategy is to imply that the philosopher's path leads not to uncertainties but to wisdom and timeless absolutes: to "genuine knowledge" of the "true standards."[157] As rhetor, he offers nonphilosophers (a category which includes "the gentlemen") what they always and everywhere desire, namely, a way of making a certain idea of morality, a certain idea of virtue, appear unquestionable. In a word, he offers them reason not as disillusioning force but as the *authority* which sets the seal of "nature" on a specific interpretation of virtue. In this way, doubts of the nonphilosopher are quelled and the "loyal members of society" shielded from the supposedly pervasive skepticism of the modern age.[158]

One can read Arendt and Strauss as offering valuable clues to the nature and character of philosophic citizenship. At their best, they offer us the choice between a Socratic form of citizenship (Arendt) and a philosophical, skeptical or chastened view of politics (Strauss). The problem, however, is that they both took the "war" between politics and philosophy—born of Socrates' trial and condemnation—so seriously that they felt compelled to take up arms on opposing sides. Thus, they wind up undermining their shared (but often merely implied) suggestion that the tension between philosophy and politics generates a new kind of citizenship: one that reserves a central place for the "intellectual conscience"; one dead set against the pieties of patriotism, on the one hand, and narrow self-interest of a demotic materialism, on the other. The disappointing and unsatisfying choice they ultimately offer is the traditional one between the distracted worldliness of the *bios politikos* and the solitary withdrawal of the *bios theoretikos*.

Why this retreat, this failure to go beyond the inherited categories of the tradition? I don't think it is a question of simple bad faith or even the blindness born of partisanship. Arendt and Strauss were both struggling against the Weberian image of an age of bureaucracy, an image which left little room for either citizenship or philosophy. Their intense involvement in the "war" between philosophy and politics thus took place in a world in which this struggle had (evidently) been rendered irrelevant. Though coming from opposite directions, their efforts bore fruit in reminding us that political power is not simply the enforcement of one's will; that political action is more than a means to an end; that judgment is no mere deduction from a rule or absolute; and that the "unity of theory and practice" is a dangerous and often misunderstood ideal, one capable of generating moral horror. Arendt's polemics against the modern "instrumental" account of action, like Strauss's polemics against positivist social science and political idealism, reveal a space for action and moral judgment in a world where technocratic ideology and institutional organization apparently render both activities superfluous. The ideals Arendt and Strauss pose may be somewhat hoary, but they will be relevant as long as humans remain acting and thinking beings.

Moreover, we should not underestimate the degree to which human beings really do have what Strauss called a "fundamentally divided nature." As I suggested in chapter 1, it is rather pointless (and probably false) to posit an original harmony between thought and action in the distant past and then to suggest that we somehow try to recover it. It is even more pointless to suggest that the figure of Socrates embodies this original harmony, and that the "war" between philosophy and politics is simply the result of misunderstanding and mutual suspicion, both of which can be set aside by individuals acting in good faith. Thinking and acting—the life of the mind and the life of the citizen—*really are* in tension, if not necessary, unending, and deadly conflict. Whatever reconciliation is possible between them will necessarily be episodic and individual in character. Insofar as neither Arendt nor Strauss lets us forget this tension, we should view them as doing us a service by contributing to the cause of intellectual honesty.

It becomes harder to praise Arendt and Strauss, however, when we give due weight to their perfectionist accounts of the range of human activities. Both Arendt and Strauss are convinced that there is, in fact, a "best life," one which is intrinsically superior to other types of activities and ways of life. For Arendt it is the life of the citizen, engaged in sharing words and deeds in the public realm; for Strauss it is the life of the philosopher, making the ascent from opinion to knowledge or wisdom. Each of these hierarchies (derived, ironically enough, from Aristotle) represents a self-conscious break with the "common sense" of a modern liberal society in which consumerism and a materialistic individualism reign.

In itself, this desire to challenge the dominant ethos is perfectly legitimate. The problem resides in Arendt's and Strauss's inability to appreciate the moral pluralism that characterizes such a society, to see it as anything other than an inverted (and perverted) hierarchy which represents an obstacle to the attainment of the good (or fully human) life. Thus, while Arendt emphasizes human plurality and difference of opinion, she anxiously insists on a common public realm—and a shared "common sense"—as their proper horizon and referent. Thus, Strauss attacks the "relativism" he detects in both Weber and Isaiah Berlin but is unwilling (or unable) to see their fundamental point, namely, that value conflict and moral disagreement are part of what constitutes us as both moderns and moral beings.[159] As a result, he is reduced to insisting upon the mere *logical possibility* of a comprehensive, value-ranking reason in the modern age, one which will do away with the *appearance* of conflict. His refusal to acknowledge what John Rawls has called the "absolute depth of that irreconcilable latent conflict" between controversial views of the good or best life makes his calls to excellence and nobility ring hollow.[160]

This failure to sufficiently plumb the depths of moral disagreement in contemporary society invariably affects our assessment of Arendt's and Strauss's attempt to go beyond Weber. Insofar as neither of them takes moral pluralism seriously (not even the pluralism that exists *within* a particular political society), we are compelled to note a fundamental deficiency in their thought. Like the young Nietzsche, Arendt and Strauss were far too inclined to view political societies as self-contained moral worlds, enclosed within an encompassing horizon.[161] The result is, on the one hand, the identification of the moral life with a dominant ethos or group and, on the other, the marginalization of individual conscience and intellectual integrity. This tendency is manifest in Arendt's restriction of the political importance of thinking and individual conscience to "emergency situations," in which a relatively homogenous moral world is perverted or turned upside down (as in the case of Nazi Germany). It is also evident in Strauss's restriction of the powers of moral doubt and skepticism to a philosophical elite, who pursue intellectual honesty among themselves while simultaneously propping up the metaphysical/religious dimensions of popular moral culture (as so many "noble lies" needed for the edification of the masses and the stability of society).

Neither Arendt nor Strauss is willing to put respect for individual's moral and rational capacities at the center of their thought, *despite* their praise for agonistic or philosophical individualism. This is because neither of them is really willing to take moral disagreement seriously, that is, as setting the frame for all contemporary discussions of citizenship. Where "plurality" is securely inscribed within the "common sense" of a "shared public world" or where philosophy sees its primary duty not as the illumination of value conflict but its *elimination* through the restoration of an ordered hierarchy—there political philosophy has failed to seriously engage the moral world of modernity.

This is a world in which there are *many* conflicting answers to the question of what constitutes genuine civic or moral virtue; a world, moreover, in which any *critical* alternative view will appear arbitrary and dogmatic so long as it pretends that the responsibility for choosing (and giving an account of) a particular scale of values resides anywhere than with the individual. Socrates can be seen, without too much violence, as the first figure in the Western philosophical tradition to insist on this "existentialist" point. Insofar as the "Socratisms" of Arendt and Strauss obscure this point, encouraging us to orient ourselves morally and politically in terms of the *sensus communis* or a "natural" ranking of values, they diminish both the weight and the seriousness of the moral task confronting every individual in a "disenchanted" age. Weber may have been unjustifiably pessimistic about the prospects for citizenship and moral argument in the late modern age, but he was right to insist on this oft-forgotten Socratic lesson.

Conclusion

ARENDT'S AND STRAUSS'S return to the *topos* of philosophy versus citizenship obscures the most radical suggestion contained in the *Apology of Socrates*, namely, the idea that *everyone* can potentially lead the life of a thinking citizen. Of course, Arendt and Strauss can hardly be held responsible for burying this ideal. For more than two thousand years the Western philosophical tradition has insisted upon the Platonic distinction between the philosopher and the citizen, elevating a *tension* to the status of an ontological difference. In the relatively few free republics and democracies that arose during the same period, citizens have generally preferred the verities of God and country over a more skeptical or critical form of membership.

Today, as in the past, the phrase "good citizen" has a fundamentally anti-Socratic resonance. It brings to mind people who fully engage the obligations of membership, as defined by the community or institution they happen to find themselves a part of. "Good citizens" channel their energy into loyal service to their company, church, schools, and political associations. That the ends pursued and means employed by these groups and organizations are at times morally questionable is something that rarely, if ever, engages their attention. For the most part, "good citizens" fulfill their obligations loyally and without criticism. "Conscientiousness" means attentiveness to duty and nothing more.

From a Socratic point of view, this is—and will always be—a travesty. It is especially so with respect to *political* membership, since the injustices committed by the state—*any* state—have the force of policy or law and are thereby vested with a bogus legitimacy. It is certainly not the duty of the "Socratic" citizen perpetually to be at war with his political association, nor to take on the role of avenging moral zealot. Rather, the duty of a "Socratic" citizen consists in paying critical attention to the moral consequences of the actions, policies, and beliefs of his or her political community and fellow citizens. Where these depart from the claims of morality or procedural fairness, the thinking citizen will point this out, ignoring the immediate consequences for him- or herself. *All* polities are "large, lazy horses" in need of a gadfly. This is especially the case in polities characterized by a high degree of energy and common purpose, like democratic Athens. Where activity is the norm, skepticism and thinking about what one is doing are obviously the exception.

But what about *us*? In contemporary America skepticism and a moderate alienation from political life hardly seem the proper prescription. Indeed, from the standpoint of many critics on both left and right, our problem is a pervasive civic *disengagement*. Shocked by the lowest voter participation rate of the advanced industrial democracies, anxious about the decline of voluntary associations and the "social capital" they engender, and morally repulsed by a culture of materialistic egoism, a growing chorus of critics urges community involvement in any form. Some even recommend mandated national service as a way of jump-starting declining civic energies. The "nation of joiners" Tocqueville described in *Democracy in America* seems to have turned into a nation of alienated individuals, disinclined to live up to the obligations of citizenship or the responsibilities of self-government.

Hence the remarkable contemporary consensus among political theorists and social analysts. What is mainly needed, we are told, is *more engagement with one's community and with public concerns*. Put in so general a form, it is hard to disagree. The question remains: What *kind* of engagement do we want? What sort of citizenship should we try to encourage? The impression one gets from the critics is that engagement *as such* is good, regardless of its form or tonality. This, I would suggest, is profoundly untrue, especially when "engagement" takes the form of voluntary associations such as bowling leagues, church choirs, or business and professional associations. These forms of association may indeed help reproduce important "social capital" and strengthen important networks of social trust. They may even provide their members with richer, happier, more connected lives. But they do little, if anything, to encourage morally serious, thoughtful citizenship.

A similar objection can be lodged against radical democratic critics of liberal society. They typically point out that for "joining" to yield a *critical* form of citizenship, what must be joined is a political *struggle*, not a community association or charitable organization. While the latter provide valuable services, their rigorously nonpolitical orientation offers little encouragement to engaged, critical citizenship. "Joining" is politically relevant when it takes the form of enlistment in a struggle, preferably for social justice. Political activ-

300

ists of the old and new left thus made engagement in this struggle the sine qua non of critical citizenship. But while struggle is an essential part of politics, it by no means provides a reliable standard for morally serious citizenship. Indeed, enlistment has the invariable tendency of immunizing the "cause" against criticism, blinding the enlistee to the inconsistencies and implicit injustices of the adhered to position.

The "postideological" idiom of contemporary politics may well make one nostalgic for ideologically denser times, and for the sharply defined commitments that "movement" politics makes possible. The problem, of course, is that every politics of struggle or contestation is predicated on a leap of faith of the kind Weber masterfully analyzed in "Science as a Vocation." One *chooses* one's god (nationalism, capitalism, technology, the environment, property rights, multiculturalism, etc.) and then one *fights*. The hard part, as Weber recognized, is keeping even the semblance of "intellectual conscience" alive after one has made the leap. The tragedy of the European and American "old left" was that it gave the value of solidarity an unquestioned (and unquestionable) priority over the demands of the intellectual conscience. This tragedy is now being replayed (often as farce) on countless smaller stages of "identity politics."

This is not to deny that there are political and moral situations where one is indeed forced to choose, and where the failure to choose may facilitate evil. But such "tragic" conflicts—as opposed to the more routine moral dilemmas of everyday life and politics—are rarer than many advocates of moral pluralism are wont to assume. In any event, it is absurd to try to turn such choices into the normative model of "engaged" citizenship. Anyone who has lived through an authentically tragic situation would hardly be anxious to turn that moment into a way of life. *Antigone* cannot provide us with a viable model of citizenship any more than can the *Illiad*. But can the *Apology*?

It has been the burden of this study to suggest that it can. Socrates' insistence that the only morally praiseworthy brand of citizenship is thoughtful and conscientious clashed with the Athenian assumption that active citizenship is a good in itself. Today it clashes with the neo-Tocquevillian idea of the citizen-joiner, as well as with the radical democratic idea of the "agonistic" or solidaristic citizen. Both ideals radically foreshorten the philosophical and deliberative dimensions of citizenship, the better to enlist citizens in the "cause" of the nation, the community, or a particular struggle. The fact that contemporary prescriptions for civic "reengagement" reinstate precisely the "division of labor" Socrates devoted a lifetime to combating—the division between the claims of thinking and those of acting, between philosophy and citizenship—reveals a great deal about how little value is attached to the claims of intellectual conscience in contemporary politics and the culture at large. We hear a great deal about the need to cultivate civic virtue and a heightened sense of obligation, but rarely—if ever—are skepticism, conscientiousness, and intellectual honesty included among the list of virtues presented by those who would renew public life. It is as if civic engagement required a moral-intellectual lobotomy, the better to overcome doubts about the inherent goodness of the community, the moral worth of a given group identity, or the value of specific ideological commitment. The intellectually conscientious "I" must be silenced in order to serve the self-righteous (or morally complacent) "we."

The marginalization of the "intellectual conscience" in contemporary discussions of citizenship is hardly a break with the past. Socrates' attempt to introduce its claims met with fierce and sustained resistance from a *demos* proud of its power and way of life. This resistance has been echoed and amplified by politicians, priests, and moralizers down through the ages, but it has also emanated from our tradition of political and philosophical thought. Intellectual honesty has repeatedly been separated from moral virtue. Elitists (like Plato and Strauss) do this to preserve "genuine" virtue—that of the philosopher—from the "merely moral" virtue of the *hoi polloi*; egalitarians (like Rousseau and Kant) do it to ensure that the moral life is within reach of every feeling or rational person. The mistake of both sides is to assume that thoughtfulness and intellectual honesty are virtues reserved only for "professional thinkers" and not ordinary people. This is something Socrates felt to be profoundly untrue. Thoughtfulness and intellectual integrity are not the property of any group; they are qualities *all* human beings can cultivate, so long as their moral sense has not been permanently stunted or deformed by the "common sense" of their group, creed, or nation.

The true oddity, though, is not the broad consensus in the Western philosophical tradition that intellectual and moral integrity have little to do with one another (and that neither forms an integral part of civic virtue). Rather, it is the ambivalence of thinkers sensitive to their interrelationship that is most surprising. As we have seen, even thinkers deeply influenced by Socratic ideals have a tendency to restrict their importance to the *cultural* realm while promoting more traditional civic virtues in the political sphere. Thus, whereas the Mill of *On Liberty* proposes a "socialized" form of *elenchus* to promote recognition of the partiality of all views—noting that the true beneficiary of a diversity of views is the spectator of, rather than the participant in, robust moral and political debate—the Mill of *Representative Government* insists that participation is the key to political education and the moral core of citizenship. In similar fashion, Nietzsche and Weber make intellectual integrity the moral center of their thought while restricting its provenance to a "spiritual aristocracy" of one sort or another. Finally, Arendt and Strauss recognize the absolute importance of Socrates' dissolvent rationality, but they both set severe restrictions on its employment—Arendt to preserve the "common sense" of the political community and Strauss to promote the role that authority (in the form of religion, patriotism, and tradition) plays in the life of the average citizen.

Why do all these thinkers restrict or ultimately betray the Socratic dimensions of their thought? I would suggest the answer is intimately related to the role the idea of "the masses" plays in their thought. The story of nineteenth- and early twentieth-century politics is, to be sure, that of the "rise of the masses." The trauma as well as the promise of this event is profoundly inscribed in the work of the theorists I have considered. This is clearly evident in elitists like Nietzsche and Strauss; but it is no less true of Mill and Arendt (their respective commitments to representative democracy and a self-organizing "people" notwithstanding). The entry of vast numbers of poor and uneducated people into "the bright light of the public realm" seemed to carry with it an enormous potential for disaster, one that cannot easily be shrugged off when considering the political history of the twentieth century. What had remained largely a premonition for Mill and Nietzsche became a stark reality for Weber, Arendt, and Strauss. The result was an overly rigid identification of modern politics with *mass* politics, and a corresponding inability to consider average citizens as (potential or actual) thinking individuals.

Of course, modern politics is, to a large extent, mass politics. The devolution of politics into advertising—something pioneered by totalitarianism and perfected by Madison Avenue—makes Nietzsche's comment about the "great frescoes of stupidity" required by party politics seem unduly restrained. Yet it is wrong to assume (as Nietzsche did) that these frescoes are the inevitable result of the "mob" beginning to reason, just as it is wrong to assume (as Strauss did) that only philosophers can question without disaster ensuing. Moral and intellectual immaturity are not an ineradicable constant of the human condition, no matter how much support they receive from political ideologies and the usual agencies of social life. We remain prisoners in the cave—part of a "mass"—only so long as we lazily allow the frescoes on the wall to define who we are as political and moral beings. The moment we begin to think, to question the moral adequacy of socially available creeds and ideologies, we gradually slip the bonds that Plato assumed would always hold the vast majority of humankind captive.

The fact that there is no definitively disillusioned perspective—that there is no "unqualified transcending," as Strauss would say, of the realm of *doxa* and ideology—hardly renders the moral need for a disillusioning intelligence less pressing, especially when it comes to politics. Again, one must return to the Socrates of the *Apology* to fully appreciate this lesson. Socratic citizenship is not a matter of opposing truth to mere opinion or genuine moral knowledge to pretended wisdom. Rather, Socrates' "human wisdom"—the recognition that human beings do not possess any craftlike knowledge when it comes to the "most important things"—defines itself in contrast to the rhetorical stance of the "moral expert." It is against the claims of such "experts"—and the odd combination of hubris and complacency they represent—that Socrates directs the deflationary powers of *elenchus*. The claim of statesmen and citizens alike to moral expertise is repeatedly revealed as fiction.

Does this make Socrates—or the Socratic citizen—*simply* a skeptic? Obviously not. Socrates' "human wisdom" allows for nonexpert moral knowledge of the abstentionist sort outlined in chapter 1, a knowledge of widely recognized forms of injustice. We cannot begin to understand Socrates' "care for the soul" unless we see that it is animated, above all, by the desire to avoid the performance of, or complicity with, such injustice. Socrates uses *elenchus* to attack the claim to moral expertise precisely because he sees this claim as a sure route to injustice.

If the history of the West has taught us anything, it is that moral disasters do indeed occur whenever reason or faith lay claim to such expertise. Sometimes the disasters are spectacular and horrific (the wars of religion in Europe during the sixteenth and seventeenth centuries; Soviet communism) and result from a claimed monopoly on moral truth. At other times they are more "everyday" in nature and result from the particularist predisposition to see *our* policies and actions as necessarily just and those of our enemies as necessarily evil. The hubris involved in the latter case is not that of reason or faith but the reflexive patriotism that believes one's nation, community, or group stands in a privileged relation to virtue or truth. Under the influence of this type of hubris, one forgets that every nation—and virtually every community and group—has, morally speaking, *much* to be ashamed of.

This is why it is so important for Socrates to urge all he meets to "care for their souls," that is, to take up the project and the burden of their own moral self-formation. They must "think for themselves"—a phrase often used with little appreciation of the energy necessary to overcome the presumption of one's own moral expertise. First, thinking for oneself demands the recognition of one's ignorance on this score, the realization that one *does not have* a firm grasp of what virtue is. Only through the knowledge of such ignorance do moral matters become, as Nietzsche says, "thought-provoking." Second, thinking for oneself requires a continuous effort; the dialogue, whether internal or external, must be recommenced on an almost daily basis. Hence Socrates' constant questioning and cross-examination about the meaning of virtue and the nature of ethical knowledge. If "the unexamined life is not worth living," this is doubly true of the life of unexamined citizenship. Indeed, it was precisely *this* mode of the unexamined life that led Socrates to take up his "mission" in the first place.

For us, the life of citizenship is unexamined not because it is lived too intensely, but because it is barely lived at all. Many exhort us to become citizens (in the strong, normative sense) once again, but few, if any, see the examination of self and others as an essential component of that role. In a politically apathetic society, moral attention tends to be confused with moralizing and polemic. *Anything* that gets a rise out of people—from the hoariest of "elating clichés" to self-conscious efforts at "subverting" the established order—is hailed, if only because it creates the *illusion* of wakefulness. The fact that many pay minimal, somnolent attention to politics and government policies has led more than a few political theorists to praise conflict and contestation as such—as if these and thinking attention were the same thing. They are not, and it is self-deluding to think that a more "agonistic" politics necessarily wakes people up to such attention. The dynamism and conflict of democratic Athens did not prevent it from being (morally speaking) a large and lazy horse (*Ap.* 30e–31).

It might be objected that Socratic citizenship, as I have described it, differs hardly at all from the ideal of a critical, moderately alienated citizen familiar from the liberal tradition. Indeed, as I tried to show in chapter 2, the affinities with a certain strand of Millian liberalism run quite deep. But it would be wrong to suggest that "Socratic citizenship" offers us nothing that we might not gain from a reading, say, of Constant, Berlin, or Rawls. What is missing from these three highly influential liberal writers is the focus on the moral uses of dissolvent rationality we find in the Socratic dialogues (as well as in Mill and the antiliberal Nietzsche).

The relative inattention to a disabusing or philosophic brand of citizenship in Constant, Berlin, and Rawls indicates that we cannot simply assume the presence of a strong Socratic dimension in liberal thought about citizenship. Indeed, a curious phenomenon has accompanied the growing acceptance of the fact of pluralism (Berlin) and the resulting need to strictly delimit the "domain of the political" (Rawls). That is the idea that beliefs and practices protected by constitutional government and the doctrine of rights require not just toleration but *affirmation*. The various traditions, religious beliefs, and comprehensive philosophical doctrines that animate individuals and groups are increasingly seen as sacrosanct—as, in a real sense, beyond criticism. Nothing is more common today than the individual who makes his or her identity, religious beliefs, or group affiliation the moral basis of political activity but who cries "foul" when the moral substance of these beliefs or their suitability as public norms of a liberal democracy are questioned.

Ironically, moral pluralism—or, to be more precise, popular misinterpretation of its implications—has restricted rather than extended the range of Socratic criticism. The Athenians accused Socrates of impiety and corrupting the youth. Today it is likely that he would be accused of giving gratuitous offense by daring to suggest that any closely held belief was inconsistent, morally parochial, or unsound. The current reigning ideology, I fear, is that the "encumbered self" has an absolute right to be left secure in its wrappings.

Respect and toleration—essential to any liberal society—have been wrongly equated with the rigorous avoidance of criticism that cuts too close to the bone or makes anyone uncomfortable.

This is a curious situation for a liberal society to find itself in. Of course, Rawls is correct in maintaining that *public authority* must observe a strict neutrality vis-à-vis controversial conceptions of the good life. But it is extremely odd that a society which values free speech should increasingly endorse a conception of "dialogue" which is stripped of all critical-elenchic potential. Today most people assume that the universe of moral-political discourse is exhausted by homiletics, ideological polemics, or empathetic attempts at "conversation." A Socratic insistence upon the integral relationship between moral and intellectual integrity is, as a result, as unwelcome in our society as it was in fifth-century Athens—perhaps more so.

I should note that this hostility to dissolvent rationality is not (or not merely) a function of demotic antiintellectualism. The past thirty years has witnessed a remarkable growth in the antiphilosophical temper among intellectuals as well. Across the political spectrum we find an emerging consensus that worthwhile criticism must be of the connected or "immanent" sort. Granted, there is a minimal sense in which this idea of criticism is probably true: the notion of a "view from nowhere," while praiseworthy as an ideal, tends to be self-deluding. And it must be acknowledged that Socratic *elenchus* proceeds by pointing out the gap between an interlocutor's strongly held beliefs and his acceptance of other, widely shared moral propositions. But "connected criticism"—one which stays within the ambit of a preexisting moral world or tradition—all too easily bestows praise or moral approbation where none is warranted. Here we must recognize that any appeal to "shared meanings" given by local, national, or religious traditions has the effect of endowing these same traditions with a fundamental rightness. The critic never fundamentally questions these *doxai*, let alone dissolves or destroys in a Socratic manner. He or she only draws out, in hermeneutic fashion, what they already contain.

I have previously indicated some of my doubts concerning this approach. It is indeed true that political and moral criticism may well have to be contextual to be rhetorically effective. But the price of such effectiveness is that no real challenge to reigning orthodoxies occurs, nor can genuine moral progress be made. The "connected critic" is limited to reminding his community of the higher moral possibilities inscribed in its tradition or culture. His audience is chastened and made to feel good about itself at the same time. We may not be living up to our best selves, but are "we" not the children of a rich and morally praiseworthy tradition? Doesn't "our" tradition contain all the necessary material for moral progress and renewal? Are not higher moral possibilities already a part of who "we" are? Isn't moral progress simply a matter of teasing out something contained in our inheritance rather than striving to transcend a constricting (and morally blinding) parochialism?

To be sure, national and cultural traditions contain many possibilities, some of which are good and some bad. But the idea that one need only turn to the forgotten wisdom of one's tradition, creed, or nation is a recipe for moral stultification, complacency, and, ultimately, injustice. We can acknowledge the fact that, sociologically speaking, we are "encumbered" selves without turning it into a cause for celebration, let alone the effective horizon for moral and political criticism.

The recent celebration of context and the "situated" self has undermined the nondogmatic form of moral aspiration we have come to identify with Socrates and Mill. The remedy for this is not (*pace* Strauss) to return to the standard of what is "right by nature." Rather, it is, to recover the moral-political potential of the knowledge of ignorance, the partiality of truth, and the horizon-expanding power of perspectivism as an intellectual discipline or "method" for thinking. This potential, I have argued, is implicit in the practice of Socratic negativity. It becomes fully explicit in Mill and is given its most sophisticated (albeit internally contradictory) philosophical articulation by Nietzsche. Socratic *elenchus*, Millian "discussion," and Nietzschean perspectivism are ideas which enable us to draw a very different lesson from the basic point of the contextualists, namely, that there is and can be no unqualified transcending of the realm of *doxa* and convention.

The ideas of these thinkers remind us that there are two very different responses to human situatedness and the limits of human wisdom. One can either accept and even glorify cultural or social embeddedness, seeing tradition or convention as a rich source of materials for the critical moralist, *or* one can attempt a partial, never fully realized transcendence, not luxuriating in custom and convention but straining against it. The latter course demands a never-ending practice of critical disillusionment, coupled with a healthy sense of the intrinsic moral inadequacy of all "local" forms. It also outlines a new conception of citizenship, one which does not demand the *sacrifizio dell'intelletto* and in which moral and intellectual integrity finally take their rightful place as important *civic* virtues. By transforming the idea of moral subjectivity—by inventing the intellectually awake, conscientious "I"—Socrates also transformed the idea of citizenship. Twenty-four hundred years later, we have yet to catch up with the revolution in citizenship implicit in the great ironist's thought and practice.

Notes

CHAPTER ONE
WHAT IS SOCRATIC CITIZENSHIP?

1. Judith Shklar, *American Citizenship: The Quest for Inclusion* (Cambridge, Mass.: Harvard University Press, 1991), p. 1.

2. See Hannah Arendt, "The Public and the Private," *The Human Condition* (Chicago: University of Chicago Press, 1958), pp. 22–78.

3. The phrase "moderately alienated" is from George Kateb, *The Inner Ocean* (Ithaca: Cornell University Press, 1994).

4. I should state at the outset that I am persuaded by Gregory Vlastos's delineation of a genuinely "Socratic" Socrates in Plato's early dialogues (the "elenctic" dialogues including the *Apology, Charmides, Crito, Euthyphro, Gorgias, Protagoras,* and *Republic* 1) and a "Platonic" Socrates in the dialogues of Plato's middle period (including the *Cratylus, Phaedo, Symposium, Republic* 2–10, *Phaedrus, Parmenides,* and *Theaetetus*). See Gregory Vlastos, *Socrates: Ironist and Moral Philosopher* (Ithaca: Cornell University Press, 1991), esp. chap. 2 and 3. For a detailed critique of this partitioning of the Platonic dialogues and a powerful argument for viewing them as a unified artistic and philosophical whole, see Charles H. Kahn, *Plato and the Socratic Dialogue: The Philosophical Use of a Literary Form* (New York: Cambridge University Press, 1996).

5. See C. D. C. Reeve, *Socrates in the Apology: An Essay on Plato's "Apology of Socrates"* (Indianapolis: Hackett, 1989), p. xii.

6. Hannah Arendt, "Thinking and Moral Considerations," *Social Research* 51, no. 3 (Spring-Summer 1984), 23.

7. Michael Walzer, *The Company of Critics* (New York: Basic Books, 1988), pp. 14–15. As I will argue, there are important senses in which Socrates both is and is not a "connected" critic. In some places he calls the Athenians to live up to their best selves; elsewhere he proposes notions (such as nonretaliation) which are entirely revolutionary in their moral implications.

8. Vlastos, *Socrates*, p. 14.

9. Ibid., p. 4. Cf. Terence Irwin's discussion in "Socrates' Method," *Plato's Ethics* (New York: Oxford University Press, 1995), pp. 17–30.

10. See George Kateb's essay, "Socratic Integrity" in *Nomos*, vol. 40, "Integrity and Conscience," ed. Ian Shapiro (New York: New York University Press, 1998), pp. 97–98.

11. I will develop this suggestion in the next two chapters on Mill and Nietzsche, respectively.

12. It seems to me that F. M. Cornford is simply wrong when he states that Socrates, like Plato, accepts a doctrine of the "art of living" which is "comparable to the special crafts in which trained intelligence creates some product." See *The Republic of Plato*, ed. and trans. F. M. Cornford (New York: Oxford University Press, 1945), p. 30. On this reading, virtue depends on a specialized knowledge of the ends of human life, which Socrates supposedly has. The conflict between this interpretation and Socrates' self-understanding in the *Apology* is quite pronounced.

13. Alexander Nehamas, *The Art of Living: Socratic Reflections from Plato to Foucault* (Berkeley: University of California Press, 1998), p. 96.

14. Plato, *Gorgias*, 515a4–7.

15. Arendt, "Thinking and Moral Considerations," p. 36.

16. Thucydides, *History of the Peloponnesian War*, trans. Rex Warner (New York: Penguin, 1972), pp. 75–76.

17. Victor Ehrenberg, *From Solon to Socrates* (New York: Routledge, 1991), pp. 382–83.

18. Hannah Arendt, "Tradition and the Modern Age" in Arendt, *Between Past and Future* (New York: Penguin, 1968), pp. 17–40.

19. Arendt is hardly alone when it comes to the basic elements of this narrative. One finds similar accounts in the work of Leo Strauss and Eric Voegelin. Cf. F. M. Cornford's *The Unwritten Philosophy* (New York: Cambridge University Press, 1950), which states that the death of Pericles and the Peloponnesian War mark "the moment when men of thought and men of action began to take different paths, destined to diverge more and more widely. . . ."

20. See J. Peter Euben, "Creatures of a Day: Thought and Action in Thucydides," in *Political Theory and Praxis: New Perspectives*, ed. Terence Ball (Minneapolis: University of Minnesota Press, 1977), pp. 28–56.

21. Thucydides, *History*, p. 147.

22. Ibid., p. 214.

23. Ibid., p. 242.

24. Even worse than this repudiation of speech and public debate as vehicles of intelligent policy is the self-conception revealed by the Athenian spokesmen in the Melian dialogue, where they justify their alternatives of coerced obedience or genocide for the Melians by claiming that they, as an imperial power, have no choice as to how they are to act in such situations: "Our opinion is that it is a general and necessary law of nature to rule whatever one can. This is not a law we made ourselves, nor were we the first to act upon it when it was made. . . . We are merely acting in accordance with it. . . ." (*History*, p. 405). As Euben notes, "To the degree the Athenians regard themselves as mere executors of natural laws and assimilate their actions to a "natural" causal chain, they deny the possibility of human agency" ("Creatures," p. 48).

25. Thucydides, *History*, p. 122.

26. See Nicole Loraux's magisterial study entitled *The Invention of Athens*, trans. Alan Sheridan (Cambridge, Mass.: Harvard University Press, 1989).

27. Thucydides, *History*, p. 149.

28. Ibid., p. 145.

29. My use of "public" and "private" here is no doubt somewhat anachronistic and ignores the fact—emphasized by Arendt in *The Human Condition*—that the "private realm" for the Greeks was the *oikos* or household, the scene of activities related to subsistence.

30. Thucydides, *History*, p. 147.

31. Ibid., pp. 147–48.

32. Ibid., p. 147.

33. Thus, Pericles states that "in my opinion each single one of our citizens, in all the manifold aspects of life, is able to show himself the rightful lord and owner of his own person, and do this, moreover, with exceptional grace and exceptional versatility" (*History*, pp. 147–48). This formulation of the self as a work of art is echoed in Hegel's characterization of Pericles (and Socrates) as "great plastic natures consistent through and through": "Such are not made, but have formed themselves into what they are; they have become what they have wished to be, and are true to this" (G.W.F. Hegel, *Lectures on the History of Philosophy*, trans. E. S. Haldane [Lincoln: University of Nebraska Press, 1995], 1:393). It is echoed more famously in Nietzsche's *Gay Science*, sec. 290.

34. Thucydides, *History*, p. 148.

35. Euben, "Creatures," p. 45.

36. Friedrich Nietzsche, *On the Genealogy of Morals*, trans. Walter Kaufmann (New York: Random House, 1969), 1:11.

37. Thucydides, *History*, p. 161.

38. As Thoreau notes, "Statesmen and legislators, standing so completely within the institution, never distinctly and nakedly behold it." See Henry David Thoreau, *Political Writings*, ed. Nancy Rosenblum (New York: Cambridge University Press, 1996), pp. 18–19.

39. Indeed, from a certain perspective the "weary realism" of the Athenians at Melos is to be preferred to the heights scaled by Pericles' rhetoric, if only because their disillusioned perspective no longer drapes the business of domination in euphemisms of any type.

40. Thucydides, *History*, p. 217.

41. See Leo Strauss, *The City and Man* (Chicago: University of Chicago Press, 1964), p. 209. I should note Strauss's tremendous sympathy for the traditionally virtuous Nicias; indeed, Strauss reads the *History* as a fable about the ultimate moral and political superiority of Spartan traditionalism to Athenian daring and innovation. See, for example, page 146, where the Spartan regime is praised as the embodiment of moderation.

42. Thucydides, *History*, pp. 404–5.

43. Ibid., p. 402.

44. For an exemplary account of Alcibiades' many exploits and maneuverings, see chapters 3–7 in Mark Munn, *The School of History: Athens in the Age of Socrates* (Berkeley: University of California Press, 2000).

45. See *Ap.* 21d.

46. See Alcibiades' comments on Athenian democracy to the Spartans in Thucydides, *History*, p. 467.

47. Gregory Vlastos, "The Historical Socrates and Athenian Democracy," in *Socratic Studies*, ed. Miles Burnyeat (New York: Cambridge University Press, 1994), pp. 87–108.

48. See Eli Sagen, *The Honey and the Hemlock* (Princeton: Princeton University Press, 1994).

49. So does the parallel scholarly perception in this century. See, for example, Ernest Barker, *The Political Thought of Plato and Aristotle* (New York: Dover, 1959), pp. 51–52; W. K. C. Guthrie, *Socrates* (New York: Cambridge University Press, 1971), pp. 89–90; and Ellen M. Wood and Neal Wood, *Class Ideology and Ancient Political Theory: Socrates, Plato, and Aristotle in Social Context* (New York: Oxford University Press, 1978).

50. Hannah Arendt, "Philosophy and Politics," *Social Research* 57, no. 1 (Spring 1990), 73.

51. Peter Euben, *The Tragedy of Political Theory: The Road Not Taken* (Princeton: Princeton University Press, 1990), p. 204.

52. Hegel, *Lectures on the History of Philosophy*, 1:407.

53. See Richard Kraut, *Socrates and the State* (Princeton: Princeton University Press, 1984), pp. 196–99.

54. This argument of the *Gorgias* is given more colorful treatment in book 6 of the *Republic*, where Plato compares the people to a "great strong beast" whose desires are catered to by sophists and politicians but which never receives proper training.

55. "Organized democracy" is the translation of the Greek *plethora*, which can also mean any multitude or large group or crowd.

56. Thucydides, *History*, p. 220.

57. Cf. *Ap.* 23, where Socrates cites his reputation as a "professor of wisdom" as a "malicious suggestion," and *Ap.* 33b, where he emphatically states: "I have never promised or imparted any teaching to anybody."

58. Obviously, the distinction between the kind of *knowledge* of the most important things claimed by the sophists and Socrates' largely negative "human wisdom" is central to the interpretation of the *Apology* and Socrates' philosophical activity. See Reeve, *Socrates in the Apology*, p. 13.

59. This almost proto-Kantian emphasis by Socrates on the finitude of human knowledge is nicely brought out by Lazlo Versenyi in his *Socratic Humanism* (New Haven: Yale University Press, 1963).

60. I agree here with the interpretation of Socratic ignorance given by Thomas Brickhouse and Nicolas Smith in their book *Plato's Socrates* (New York: Oxford University Press, 1995), p. 34. Reeve's interpretation (in his *Socrates in the Apology*, p. 58) stresses that Socrates only disclaims *expert* knowledge of virtue—a stance which enables him to lay claim to a certain "nonexpert" knowledge without contradiction. Reeve's point is important, since it is clearly wrong to state that Socrates is a radical skeptic who denies the possibility of *any* form of moral knowledge (such as ordinary knowledge of injustice or warranted belief). However, I think Reeve's emphasis on the expert/nonexpert contrast has the effect of foreshortening the skeptical dimension of Socratic thought, making it appear that Socrates is only concerned with epistemic hubris and not with everyday thoughtlessness in moral affairs.

61. Kraut, *Socrates and the State*, pp. 200–203, 218–28.

62. Arendt, "Thinking and Moral Considerations," p. 23.

63. Ibid.

64. Ibid., p. 24.

65. The *Euthyphro* is a good example of the implicitly endless, and inevitably circular, nature of Socratic questioning. When, at the end of the dialogue, Socrates cheerfully proposes to start again, Euthyphro begs off, claiming a late appointment.

66. There is an important irony here, for Kraut criticizes Karl Popper's interpretation of Socrates as being too akin to J. S. Mill (*Socrates and the State*, p. 204). Kraut's broad characterization of Socratic testing and examination of propositions is that it operates by ridding us of false moral beliefs, thus enabling us to approach nearer to knowledge of true moral propositions (pp. 220–21). But this, of course, is the basic argument given by Mill in chapter 2 of *On Liberty* (on freedom of thought and discussion).

67. Kraut, *Socrates and the State*, p. 221.

68. Arendt, "Thinking and Moral Considerations," p. 25.

69. Hence the well-known Socratic paradox that no one does evil knowingly, that evil is a function of ignorance whereas virtue is a form of knowledge.

70. Arendt, "Thinking and Moral Considerations," p. 7.

71. Ibid., p. 8. As Arendt points out in her *Eichmann in Jerusalem* ([New York: Harcourt Brace, 1963], pp. 146ff.), Eichmann's thoughtless conflation of legality with morality led him to perform his duties with a genuine conscientiousness until the very end. To not carry out Hitler's order—which had the force of law—was, in his mind, tantamount to the most unprincipled behavior.

72. Ibid., p. 36.

73. Ibid.

74. I treat Thoreau's essay "Civil Disobedience" later in this chapter. One should, however, bear in mind Shklar's repeated point that, prior to the abolition of slavery, one is not morally entitled to call the United States a liberal democracy. See Judith Shklar, "The Liberalism of Fear" in *Liberalism and the Moral Life*, ed. Nancy Rosenblum (Cambridge, Mass.: Harvard University Press, 1989), p. 22.

75. See *Gorgias*, 457d–458b.

76. See Michael Sandel, *Liberalism and the Limits of Justice* (New York: Cambridge University Press, 1982), pp. 58–59.

77. This is not to deny that there are *degrees* of examination and reflection, and that liberal education can certainly encourage both activities. It is the nature of Socrates' claim, however, to rob us all of the comfort that derives from thinking a little episodic self-reflection (performed, say, during one's undergraduate years or one's midlife crisis) approximates an examined life.

78. See Kraut, *Socrates and the State*, pp. 211, 219.

79. Kateb, "Socratic Integrity," pp. 79–80.

80. For an account of this incident, and the legal/political questions involved, see Munn, *The School of History*, pp. 181–87.

81. My argument in the preceding two paragraphs is greatly indebted to Kateb. It raises the question of why we are prone to assume that a notion of injustice, no matter how widely recognized, must rest on one of justice which is not merely antecedent but "thick" rather than "thin." Part of the reason, I think, has to do with habits of thought instilled not only by Plato and Aristotle but by the early Christian theological tradition as well—notably Augustine's influential argument that evil and injustice are ontologically deficient in contrast to the "fullness" of God and the good. See Augustine, *City of God*, bk. 12, chaps. 5–6.

82. I borrow the notion of "non-expert knowledge" from Reeve; see his *Socrates in the Apology*, pp. 53–58.

83. See Kraut, *Socrates and the State*, pp. 207–15. This reasoning leads Kraut to attribute to Socrates a kind of Churchillian defense of democracy (the "worst form of government, except for all the others"). For until moral expertise is actually attained, radical political reform or changes of regime will produce minimal benefits hardly commensurate with the heavy human costs.

84. Compare Plato, *Rep.* 494a: "Philosophy, then, the love of wisdom, is impossible for the multitude."

85. See Vlastos, "The Historical Socrates and Athenian Democracy," esp. pp. 102–5.

86. These are the only options, it seems to me, that Kraut's interpretation allows.

87. This is no small task, given the degree to which the continuity between ethics and politics was taken for granted by the Greeks. See Barker, *The Political Thought of Plato and Aristotle*, pp. 282–83.

88. See, for example, Aristotle, *The Politics*, bk. 1, chap. 2, and bk. 7, chap. 14 (1252b and 1333b, resp.).

89. The coercive nature of Plato's scheme is too well known to emphasize here. However, we should not forget Aristotle's approval of highly coercive means for the inculcation of virtue as stated in the *Nicomachean Ethics*, 1179b–1180a.

90. Arendt's endorsement of what she calls "representative thinking" as *the* form of political thought par excellence has led many of her commentators to attribute

to her either a dialogical conception of political judgment or a doctrine of the unity of theory and practice in the form of political judgment. See Arendt, *Between Past and Future* (New York: Penguin, 1968), p. 240.

91. Euben, *The Tragedy of Political Theory*, p. 209.

92. Ibid., pp. 204–5. Euben stresses that the "failed relationship" between philosophy and politics symbolized by the trial and condemnation of Socrates is tragic, the premature snuffing out of a healthy dialectical relationship which impoverishes Athenian civic life. This is not incorrect, as far as it goes. Where I disagree is on the issue of whether Socrates' philosophical activity consisted in what Euben calls "the attempt to reintegrate civic and individual life by reestablishing the preconditions for political deliberation and moral discourse" (p. 205). If it is wrong to say that Socrates offers us the choice between citizenship and the soul, it is equally wrong to say that he offers us a way of removing the tension between the two. As I understand it, "philosophical citizenship" largely consists of this tension and is animated by a moral distrust of political power and popular passion.

93. Kateb opts for the first alternative; Brickhouse and Smith for the second.

94. See Ehrenberg, *From Solon to Socrates*, p. 350.

95. See Peter Euben, "Democracy and Political Theory: A Reading of Plato's *Gorgias*" in *Athenian Political Thought and the Reconstruction of American Democracy*, ed. Peter Euben, John Wallach, and Joshua Ober (Ithaca: Cornell University Press, 1994), p. 208. The ease with which we condemn the fascination of the Athenian demos with absolute power is belied by our own proud self-description as the "world's only superpower."

96. See *Gorgias*, 474b; cf. *Ap.* 17d.

97. Euben, *The Tragedy of Political Theory*, p. 208.

98. Cf. Nehamas, *The Art of Living*, p. 89. The pathos of this failure is underlined by the fact that, while the "wild" Alcibiades was Pericles' ward, he was also one of Socrates' closest associates. The failure to tame him was a joint one.

99. Vlastos, "Socrates and Vietnam," in *Socratic Studies*, ed. Burnyeat, pp. 127–33.

100. Hannah Arendt, *Lectures on Kant's Political Philosophy* (Chicago: University of Chicago Press, 1982), p. 37.

101. As the argument of the *Protagoras* makes clear, Socrates is more than a little skeptical of the idea that virtue can be "taught" at all, let alone by political or social means.

102. The only thing worse than a nation or state convinced of its greatness is a nation or state convinced that its *greatness* is a function of its (presumed) morality. The moralization of the idea of national greatness is the distinctively American disease.

103. For the "immanent" character of elenchic argument, see Reeve, *Socrates in the Apology*, pp. 45–48.

104. Euben, *The Tragedy of Political Theory*, p. 203. Cf. Walzer, *The Company of Critics*, p. 4.

105. Euben, *The Tragedy of Political Theory*, p. 206.

106. This formulation suggests a kinship between Socrates' critique of Periclean democracy and Augustine's critique of republican and imperial Rome in *The City of God*. Like Socrates, Augustine wants to put the accepted interpretation of the virtues in question; unlike him, he wants to replace "false" virtues with "true" ones. This fact creates a gap between two otherwise similar dissolutions of the reigning tables of virtue.

107. Following Arendt, I have altered Woodhead's translation of this passage.

108. See Thomas Hobbes, *Leviathan*, ed. C. B. Macpherson (New York: Penguin, 1988), p. 270.

109. Michael Walzer, "Political Action: The Problem of Dirty Hands," in *Philosophy and Public Affairs* 2, no. 2 (1972), 160–80.

110. Brickhouse and Smith, *Plato's Socrates*, pp. 144ff. Cf. Thomas C. Brickhouse and Nicolas D. Smith, *Socrates on Trial* (Princeton: Princeton University Press, 1989), pp. 137–53.

111. Brickhouse and Smith, *Plato's Socrates*, p. 152. Cf. p. 153: "In our view, Socrates can consistently require that the citizen never act unjustly and never disobey the law even when the law itself is unjust and even where the citizen's actions in accordance with the law will produce injustice. The reason for this is that the responsible agent of injustice in such cases is the state, and not the citizen acting as the states' 'offspring' or 'slave'." I should point out that the general pattern for this position was set by Luther.

112. Brickhouse and Smith are quite aware of this implication of their argument and attempt to defend the "I was only following orders" excuse on page 154 of their study.

113. See Arendt, *Eichmann in Jerusalem*, pp. 148–49.

114. Kraut, *Socrates and the State*, pp. 13–22.

115. Ibid., p. 24.

116. Ibid., pp. 55–56.

117. Ibid., p. 59.

118. Ibid., pp. 58–69.

119. Ibid., pp. 59–60.

120. Cf. Rousseau, *On the Social Contract*, bk. 2, chap. 4: "Their [the citizens'] life itself, which they have devoted to the state, is continually protected by it; and when they risk their lives for its defense, what are they then doing but returning to the state what they received from it?"

121. Kateb, "Socratic Integrity," p. 93.

122. Kraut, *Socrates and the State*, pp. 59, 72.

123. I should note that, while I think the tension between the *Apology* and the *Crito* is irreducible, I do not think they are simply contradictory. On the contrary, we cannot understand Socrates' choice to forgo escape in the *Crito* without the *Apology*, in which he makes clear that he would rather die than face exile or a life without philosophy. To escape, as Crito recommends, would show that he didn't really stand behind his words in the *Apology*. See, in this regard, N. A. Greenberg,

"Socrates' Choice in the *Crito*," *Harvard Studies in Classical Philology* 70, no. 1 (1965), 45–82.

124. See Vlastos's interpretation of some of the same passages in his essay "The Historical Socrates and Athenian Democracy," pp. 91–92.

125. Cf. Plato, *Republic*, bk. 8, 557a–562a.

126. Sophocles, *Antigone*, trans. David Grene (Chicago: University of Chicago Press, 1991), pp. 188–190.

127. Martha C. Nussbaum, *The Fragility of Goodness* (New York: Cambridge University Press, 1991), pp. 58–61.

128. It seems forced to argue, as Warren J. Lane and Ann M. Lane have, that Antigone is "the exemplary human being who weaves the civic oath of fidelity to city, customs, and gods into the texture of daily life." Such a reading dissolves the tragic conflict of values in *Antigone*, turning the play into a tragedy of misrecognition (Antigone representing the true integration of family, law, and polis, while Creon represents a tyrannical corruption). See their essay "The Politics of *Antigone*" in *Greek Tragedy and Political Theory*, ed. J. Peter Euben (Berkeley: University of California Press, 1986), p. 164.

129. The fact that a woman has usurped the manly prerogative of action is a persistent theme of the play and, from Creon's point of view, the most annoying aspect of Antigone's challenge to his authority. See Sophocles, *Antigone*, p. 187.

130. Hannah Arendt, "Civil Disobedience" in Arendt, *Crises of the Republic* (New York: Harcourt Brace Jovanovich, 1972), p. 65.

131. G. W. F. Hegel, *The Phenomenology of Spirit*, trans. A. V. Miller (New York: Oxford University Press, 1979), p. 400.

132. Arendt, "Civil Disobedience," pp. 67–68.

133. Thoreau, as quoted in Arendt, "Civil Disobedience," p. 61. See Thoreau, *Political Writings*, p. 5.

134. Thoreau, "Resistance to Civil Government," *Political Writings*, p. 4.

135. Ibid., p. 8.

136. Ibid., p. 11.

137. For the import of this distinction, see George Kateb, *Hannah Arendt: Politics, Conscience, Evil* (Totowa, N.J.: Rowman & Allanheld, 1984), p. 85.

138. See chapter 4 of the present study.

139. See Arendt's analysis of the Jacobins' revolutionary compassion in chapter 2 of her *On Revolution* (New York: Penguin, 1990).

140. Rousseau, *On the Social Contract*, bk. 4, chaps. 7 and 8.

141. For a sophisticated version of this argument, see Ronald Beiner, *What's the Matter with Liberalism?* (Berkeley: University of California Press, 1992).

142. For the classical expression of this position, see Aristotle, *The Politics*, 1280b12–1281a9.

143. Plato's moral psychology in the *Republic* has yet to be surpassed as an analysis of *this* dimension of social life.

144. See, for example, Alisdair MacIntyre, *After Virtue* (South Bend: Notre Dame University Press, 1980); Daniel Bell, *The Cultural Contradictions of Capitalism* (New York: Basic Books, 1978), chapter 4; and William Galston, *Liberal Purposes* (New York: Cambridge University Press, 1991), who writes: "The greatest threat to children in modern liberal society is not that they will believe in something too deeply, but that they will believe in nothing very deeply at all" (p. 255).

145. Aristotle, *The Politics*, bk. 1, 1252a1.

CHAPTER TWO
JOHN STUART MILL

1. The idea that independent thought or diversity of opinion could be "ends in themselves" is obviously in tension with Mill's utilitarian stance, in which the only thing that truly qualifies as an end in itself is happiness. This is one strand of the controversy which has plagued *On Liberty* virtually since its publication, and which has been much remarked upon in the scholarly literature. Most commentators have detected a basic incoherence in Mill's project, finding his Principle of Liberty to be an arbitrary and contradictory abridgement of his Principle of Utility (or "Greatest Happiness Principle"). Since Mill is officially committed to the Principle of Utility—the idea that "actions are right in proportion as they tend to promote happiness and wrong as they tend to promote the reverse of happiness"—his insistence in *On Liberty* that liberty ought never be abridged unless such abridgement prevents harm to others seems to create a set of a priori limits to policies promoting the general welfare. That is, it seems to place liberty above utility, and without much attempt at an explanation, let alone a reconciliation, of the two principles. For an ingenious attempt to save Mill from the charge of incoherence, see John Gray, *Mill on Liberty: A Defense* (New York: Routledge, 1996).

2. Alan Ryan, introduction to Mill, *Texts and Commentaries* (New York: Norton, 1997), p. xxxv.

3. John Stuart Mill, *On Liberty*, in Mill, *Texts and Commentaries*, ed. Alan Ryan, pp. 78–79.

4. See John Stuart Mill, "Bentham," in Mill, *Essays on Politics and Culture*, ed. Gertrude Himmelfarb (Gloucester, Mass.: Peter Smith, 1973), esp. pp. 92–96.

5. See Mill, "Coleridge," *Essays*, pp. 153–166.

6. Mill, *On Liberty*, pp. 54–76.

7. In this regard I should note that Mill, while writing with a Victorian audience in mind, would have been just as critical of the pose of immaculate suspended judgment popular in the contemporary American academy. For Mill moral judgment was unavoidable and the thing which makes us human. The problem was not how to avoid it but rather how to avoid the habits of mind which predisposed judgment to become a predictable exercise in the expression of group prejudice, creedal belief, or ideology.

8. Mill, *On Liberty*, p. 54.

9. For an illuminating discussion of Plato's reformulation of the idea of authority in the Greek context, see Hannah Arendt's essay "What Is Authority?" in Arendt, *Between Past and Future* (New York: Penguin, 1968), pp. 104–15.

10. See Karl R. Popper, *The Open Society and Its Enemies*, vol. 1, *The Spell of Plato* (Princeton: Princeton University Press, 1966).

11. Mill, "The Spirit of the Age," *Essays*, pp. 8–9.

12. Ibid., p. 9.

13. Ibid., pp. 11, 17, 18.

14. Mill, *On Liberty*, pp. 91–92. As I discuss later, when this quote is placed in context, its "elitism" is significantly qualified.

15. John Stuart Mill, *Considerations on Representative Government*, in Mill, *Utilitarianism, On Liberty*, and *Considerations on Representative Government*, ed. H. B. Acton (London: Dent, 1984), p. 198; hereafter cited as *CRG*.

16. Mill, "Tocqueville on Democracy in America (Vol. 1)," in *Essays*, p. 175; hereafter cited as "Tocqueville (Vol. 1)."

17. Ibid., pp. 182–83.

18. Alexis de Tocqueville, introduction to vol. 1 of *Democracy in America*, quoted in Mill, "Tocqueville (Vol. 1)," p. 177.

19. Mill, "Tocqueville (Vol. 1)," p. 195.

20. Ibid., p. 204.

21. Ibid., pp. 196–97 (Mill's n. 8).

22. Ibid., pp. 203–4.

23. Ibid., p. 204.

24. Tocqueville quoted in Mill, "Tocqueville (Vol. 1)," p. 206.

25. Mill, "Tocqueville (Vol. 1)," p. 207.

26. Tocqueville, quoted in Mill, "Tocqueville (Vol. 1)," p. 206.

27. See Jürgen Habermas, *The Structural Transformation of the Public Sphere*, trans. Thomas Burger (Cambridge, Mass.: MIT Press, 1989), pp. 132–35.

28. Tocqueville quoted in Mill, "Tocqueville (Vol. 2)," p. 242.

29. Mill, "Tocqueville (Vol. 1)," p. 210.

30. John Stuart Mill, *Autobiography*, ed. John M. Robson (New York: Penguin, 1989), p. 150.

31. Mill, "Tocqueville on Democracy in America (Vol. 2)," in *Essays*, p. 229, hereafter cited as "Tocqueville (Vol. 2)."

32. Ibid., pp. 230–31.

33. See Aristotle, *The Politics*, trans. T. A. Sinclair (New York: Penguin, 1981), 1277b33–1278b5; 1275a22. The quoted phrase is the famous definition of citizenship which Aristotle gives in the first section of book 3 of *The Politics*, one which lies at the root of the republican tradition in Western political thought.

34. Mill, "Tocqueville (Vol. 2)" p. 232.

35. The ties between this new emphasis on the self-formation of citizens, the doctrine of self-education in *On Liberty*, and Mill's own experience (brought on by his mental crisis in 1826) are close indeed. In each instance the individual's

responsibility to actively form him- or herself appears in reaction to a model of character formation in which the "student" figures as so much helpless clay, to be molded in accordance with "enlightened views," middle-class values, or the dictates of a philosophical theory (Benthamite utilitarianism).

36. Mill, "Tocqueville (Vol. 2)," p. 242.

37. Ibid., p. 261.

38. Ibid., p. 264.

39. Ibid., p. 266.

40. Cf. Mill's discussion of Grote's interpretation of the *Protagoras* in his review of the latter's *Plato and Other Companions of Socrates*, in Mill, *Collected Works*, ed. J. M. Robson (Toronto: University of Toronto Press, 1978), 11:402–3: "The enemy against whom Plato [and Socrates] really fought . . . was not Sophistry . . . but Commonplace. It was the acceptance of traditional opinions and current sentiments as an ultimate fact. . . ."

41. For a sophisticated historical account of the practice and culture of dissent in Athens, see Josiah Ober, *Political Dissent in Democratic Athens: Intellectual Critics of Popular Rule* (Princeton: Princeton University Press, 1998).

42. Mill, "Bentham," p. 79.

43. Ibid., p. 80.

44. Mill, *Autobiography*, pp. 38–39 (his account of the influence of *elenchus* as a mode of investigation on his young mind), 54–55, 99. Mill's translations of Plato and his notes on the dialogues may be found in the *Collected Works*, vol. 11, *Essays on Philosophy and the Classics*. See F. E. Sparshott's introduction, pp. xviii–xxi.

45. Mill, *On Liberty*, pp. 59–60.

46. Ibid., p. 48. Mill continues: "He cannot rightfully be compelled to do or forbear because it will be better for him to do so, because it will make him happier, because, in the opinions of others, to do so would be wise, or even right. These are good reasons for remonstrating with him, or reasoning with him, or persuading him, or entreating him, but not for compelling him, or visiting him with any evil in case he do otherwise. . . . The only part of the conduct of any one, for which he is amenable to society, is that which concerns others. In the part which merely concerns himself, his independence is, of right, absolute. Over himself, over his own body and mind, the individual is sovereign."

47. Ibid., p. 43.

48. Ibid., p. 44.

49. Ibid.

50. Ibid., p. 47.

51. For a good general discussion of Nietzsche's concept of genealogy and how it applies to the historical study of morals, see Alexander Nehamas, *Nietzsche: Life as Literature* (Cambridge, Mass.: Harvard University Press, 1985), pp. 106–14.

52. Oddly, the Nietzschean conclusion is drawn by the liberal Isaiah Berlin, his protests that there are objective "human values" notwithstanding. The hallmark of Berlin's much-discussed pluralism is that there are multiple (historically and cultur-

ally specific) tables of values, and that these conflict not only with one another but internally as well. For Berlin, as for Nietzsche, there can be no overarching rational standard which can decide among warring ultimate values, nor is there any way of rendering specific values (e.g., equality and liberty) commensurable with one another.

53. "Liberty, as a principle, has no application to any state of things anterior to the time when mankind have become capable of being improved by free and equal discussion" (*On Liberty*, p. 49).

54. Ibid., p. 52.

55. Ibid., p. 76.

56. Papal infallibility became a doctrine of the Catholic church in 1870, some years after Mill wrote *On Liberty*.

57. Mill, *On Liberty*, p. 54.

58. See chapter 1 of the present study.

59. Mill, *On Liberty*, pp. 56–57.

60. Ibid.

61. Alan Ryan invokes Kuhn, as well as the history of art, in order to show that most talk about political or moral progress is highly problematic, assuming as it does some relatively permanent, transepochal and transcultural standard of assessment. See his essay "A Political Assessment of Progress" in *Progress: Fact or Illusion*, ed. Leo Marx and Bruce Mazlish (Ann Arbor: University of Michigan Press, 1998), pp. 97–98.

62. This appreciation of "revolutionary" figures is much in evidence in chapter 3 of *On Liberty*, which I discuss later.

63. Mill, *On Liberty*, p. 66.

64. Ibid.

65. Of course, the teaching of Jesus became the basis for the most successful creed of all, and for the most persistent attempt to root out heretics everywhere. I will defer consideration of this until my discussion of the "second division" of Mill's argument.

66. Mill, *On Liberty*, p. 67.

67. Ibid., p. 68. Cf. Mill's estimation of what we owe to ancient Athens in his review of Grote's *History of Greece*, in *Collected Works*, 11:321, in which he goes so far as to excuse, in a manner reminiscent of Hegel, Athenian imperialism as "most beneficial to the world." What Mill loves about Periclean Athens is what he loves about the three periods enumerated in *On Liberty*, namely, its "undiminished spirit and energy," its relative freedom from the dead hand of custom and authority.

68. Mill, *On Liberty*, p. 74.

69. Ibid., p. 75.

70. Ibid., p. 68.

71. Ibid., p. 69.

72. Ibid. See Mill's description of the Athenian *demos* in his review of Grote's *History of Greece*, 11:316, 324.

73. Mill, *On Liberty*, p. 71.

74. Ibid.

75. Ibid., p. 73.

76. Ibid., pp. 74–75.

77. Ibid., p. 75.

78. For a good contrast of Mill's and Comte's respective approaches to history, see Maurice Mandelbaum's *History, Man, & Reason: A Study in Nineteenth-Century Thought* (Baltimore: Johns Hopkins University Press, 1974), pp. 163–74.

79. Isaiah Berlin, "John Stuart Mill and the Ends of Life," in his *Four Essays on Liberty* (New York: Oxford University Press, 1969) pp. 181, 184.

80. Ibid., pp. 189–90. See Mill, *On Liberty*, pp. 97–98.

81. The tension between diversity of opinion and truth is more a function of Berlin's analysis than Mill's. For Berlin "truth" signifies what it has meant for the Western rationalist tradition, stretching (in his reading) from Socrates to the present: a single set of harmonious answers to the fundamental questions of life. Only if there is such a set of answers does the philosophical quest for the best life for man make any sense. For Mill, on the other hand, the many-sidedness of truth dovetails with diversity of opinion and a perspectivist outlook, enabling him to maintain a commitment to moral truth (as many-sided) and diversity of opinion.

82. See Berlin, "Two Concepts of Liberty," in *Four Essays on Liberty*, esp. pp. 154–66.

83. Berlin, "John Stuart Mill," p. 189.

84. Mill, *On Liberty*, p. 81.

85. Ibid., p. 76.

86. See Isaiah Berlin, "The Originality of Machiavelli," in his *Against the Current* (New York: Penguin, 1982), pp. 45–48.

87. Mill, *On Liberty*, pp. 76–77 (my emphasis).

88. Ibid., p. 77.

89. Ibid., p. 78.

90. Ibid.

91. Mill's endorsement of what has come to be called an "agonistic" position may be seen quite clearly in his depiction of the nature of debate and deliberation in the Athenian assembly. See his review of Grote's *History of Greece*, 11:316–17, where Mill praises the energy and "mobility" of the Athenian people in debate. I should note that Mill's position is oft misunderstood as a kind of interest-group pluralism. For example, in his *Structural Transformation of the Public Sphere*, Habermas argues that Mill's view that diversity of opinion is essential to giving "fair play to all sides of the truth" signals a resignation before "the inability to resolve rationally the competition of interests in the public sphere," a resignation Mill attempts to cover up with a "perspectivist epistemology" (p. 135). Habermas's critique of Mill rests on the assumption that critical reason can provide "the objective guarantee of a concordance of interests existing in society [through] the rational demonstrability of a universal interest as such" (ibid.). I have criticized the a priori

character of this assumption in my book *Arendt and Heidegger* (Princeton: Princeton University Press, 1996), pp. 70–71. Suffice it to say here that the "universal interest" is many-sided and subject to numerous (not necessarily ideological) interpretations. As such it is neither reducible to the sum of individual interests (as Bentham and the elder Mill thought) nor identifiable simply by virtue of its opposition to particular interests (as Rousseau and, to some degree, Habermas contend).

92. I do not mean to imply that this "spectator" will *not* act when confronted by injustice. His appreciation of the complexity—and sometimes the simplicity—of moral-political issues hardly prevents his episodic intervention.

93. Cf. Mill, *Utilitarianism*, ed. Acton, pp.17–18.

94. Mill, *On Liberty*, pp. 80–81.

95. Saying this does not, of course, prevent us from appealing to the Socratic injunction to avoid injustice, or to the Golden Rule of Jesus (as Mill does in *Utilitarianism*), as the essence of any minimally acceptable conception of morality. However, as the history of the Western conception of who is worthy of humane treatment indicates, even the full unfolding of the maxims of a minimalist morality depends, in large part, on a complicated history of interpretation, reformulation, and expansion.

96. Berlin, "John Stuart Mill," p. 192.

97. Liberal sensitivity on this score—namely, that liberal "pluralism" is merely a mask for the endorsement of what is, in fact, a controversial conception of the Good Life—has resulted in both affirmation and retreat on the part of liberal theorists. For the affirmation, see Stephen Macedo, *Liberal Virtues* (Oxford: Clarendon Press, 1990); for the retreat, see John Rawls's, *Political Liberalism* (New York: Columbia University Press, 1993). Rawls's political liberalism attempts to bracket the entire question of specifically liberal virtues beyond those absolutely necessary to the maintenance of a "well-ordered [pluralist] society" (e.g., tolerance).

98. Mill, *On Liberty*, pp. 85–86.

99. This summary may appear to create too close a parallel between Mill and the negative or skeptical Socrates depicted in chapter 1. It is helpful, in this regard, to recall Mill's characterization of Socrates' "method" in his *Autobiography*: "The Socratic method . . . is unsurpassed as a discipline for correcting the errors, and clearing up the confusions incident to the *intellectus sibi permissus*, the understanding which has made up all its bundles of associations under the guidance of popular phraseology. The close, searching *elenchus* by which the man of vague generalities is constrained either to express his meaning to himself in definite terms, or to confess that he does not know what he is talking about; the perpetual testing of all general statements by particular instances; the siege in form which is laid to to the meaning of large abstract terms . . . all this, as an education for precise thinking, is inestimable. . . ." (pp. 38–39). One should also refer to Mill's discussion of *elenchus* as the chief weapon of Socrates (and Plato) in the war against the customary or "commonplace." See Mill's emphasis on the negative character of Socrates' philosophical practice in his review of Grote's *Plato and Other Companions of Socrates* in

Collected Works, 11:403–5. Cf. his critique of the "dogmatic" (or positive, dialectic-eschewing) Plato: "The dogmatic Plato seems a different person from the elenctic Plato" pp. 413–14.

100. Mill, *On Liberty*, p. 89.

101. Mill, *CRG*, pp. 202, 230.

102. I take it as too obvious for further comment that Mill, like Weber, is "Orientalist" in Edward Said's sense. When Mill wants an image of what Western civilization will look like as a mass society, he invokes China, whereas Weber writes of the "Egyptianization" of society. Their point is to convey what European society will look like if the last remnants of Renaissance humanism and liberal individualism go by the board, leaving us with a centrally administered ant heap. For a critique of Mill's Eurocentrism, see John Gray, "Postscript" to his *Mill on Liberty: A Defense*, pp. 130–58.

103. Mill, *On Liberty*, pp. 92–93.

104. As with much else in Mill, there is an unexpected parallel here with Heidegger's *Being and Time* and its notion of "authentic following."

105. Mill, *CRG*, p. 210.

106. See Bonnie Honig, *Political Theory and the Displacement of Politics* (Ithaca: Cornell University Press, 1993), pp. 2–3.

107. Mill, *On Liberty*, p. 84.

108. Ibid., p. 87.

109. The parallel with section 290 of Nietzsche's *Gay Science* is striking. See my discussion in chapter 3 of this book.

110. Mill, *On Liberty*, pp. 87–88.

111. Mill, *On Liberty*, p. 88.

112. When we add in political correctness (of the left and right) and the hysteria bred of the American middle class's "fear of falling," we see that the forces encouraging conformism and docility have not exactly abated. Our surface may be far more varied than that of Mill's England, but our depths are surprisingly uniform.

113. Mill, *On Liberty*, p. 88 (my emphasis).

114. Ibid., pp. 92–93.

115. Ibid., pp. 91, 93.

116. Ibid., p. 93.

117. One needs to bear in mind how, in the *Crito*, the Laws of Athens remind Socrates that he prefers them to all others. That freedom of speech was one reason why Socrates preferred Athens to other, "more disciplined" cities is clear from both the speech of the Laws and Socrates' description of his philosophical activity in the *Apology*.

118. Mill, *On Liberty*, p. 93.

119. Mill, *CRG*, pp. 211, 201.

120. Ibid., pp. 202; 207–9.

121. Ibid., p. 202. Cf. Mill, review of Grote's *History of Greece*, 11:313–14.

122. Ibid., p. 190.

NOTES TO CHAPTER TWO

123. Ibid., pp. 205, 207.

124. Ibid., pp. 233–34. See also pp. 301–2 for Mill's characterization of what participation in public discussion contributes to the civic formation of "the manual laborer."

125. Ibid., p. 234.

126. For a discussion of the affinities and differences between Mill and Rousseau on the educative value of political participation, see Dennis Thompson, *John Stuart Mill and Representative Government* (Princeton: Princeton University Press, 1976), pp. 36–53.

127. Jean-Jacques Rousseau, "On the Social Contract" in Rousseau, *The Basic Political Writings*, ed. and trans. Donald Cress (Indianapolis: Hackett, 1987), bk. 1, chap. 8, p. 151.

128. Rousseau, "Discourse on the Sciences and the Arts," in Rousseau, *The Basic Political Writings*, pp. 8–9. Rousseau enlists Socrates, perversely enough, in the cause of virtuous ignorance. This is taking "knowing that one doesn't know" in a self-serving and strikingly literal, sense.

129. Rousseau, "On the Social Contract," bk. 2, chap. 3.

130. Mill wrote two review essays (1846 and 1853) of Grote's eight-volume work, both entitled "Grote's *History of Greece*." It is in the 1853 essay that we find his surprisingly laudatory assessment of the Athenian love of talk, participation, and deliberation. See Mill, *Collected Works*, 11:316–20. Mill goes so far as to quote (approvingly) a substantial section of Pericles' Funeral Oration, the better to depict the unique Athenian combination of public-spiritedness and individualism. Indeed, he encourages us to be seduced by Pericles' idealized description and to see Socrates as, in many respects, the quintessential Athenian.

131. Mill, *Representative Government*, p. 233.

132. Thompson, *John Stuart Mill*, p. 49.

133. Leo Strauss, *"What Is Political Philosophy?" and Other Studies* (Chicago: University of Chicago Press, 1988), p. 17. See my discussion of Strauss in chapter 5 of this study.

134. Mill, *Representative Government*, p. 220.

135. Ibid., p. 224.

136. Ibid., p. 249. Cf. Aristotle, *The Politics*, 1281a39–1282b13.

137. Mill, *Representative Government*, pp. 259–60.

138. Ibid. p. 290. Cf. Machiavelli, *The Discourses*, bk. 1, chap. 4. This stance is not as far as it might seem from Madison's argument in *The Federalist Papers*, number 10, about the causes and containment of faction. Suffice it to note here that Madison was concerned with conflicting interests and the possibility—indeed, likelihood—of a class interest becoming hegemonic unless such conflicts were multiplied and dispersed across the social body. See Thompson's discussion in *John Stuart Mill*, pp. 70–71. I disagree with Thompson on the extent to which Mill's invocation of the "general interest" signaled a desire for and expectation of consensus (something neither Machiavelli nor Madison thought likely or desirable).

139. Mill, *Representative Government*, p. 290.

140. Ibid., p. 306. Cf. pp. 307–8: "Every one has a right to feel insulted by being made a nobody, and stamped as of no account at all. No one but a fool, and only a fool of a peculiar description, feels offended by the acknowledgment that there are others whose opinion, and even whose wish, is entitled to a greater amount of consideration than his."

141. Ibid., p. 299.

142. I will deal with the "Platonic" side of Mill's argument in the next section of this chapter.

143. Mill, *CRG*, p. 302.

144. Ibid., p. 326.

145. Rousseau, of course, makes an emphatic distinction between the "general will" and the "will of all"—that is, a majority will which expresses not a true universal interest, but the mere coincidence of particular wills. For Mill the general will, if not exactly a fiction, is nevertheless utterly elusive as a practical reality. The temptation of democracy, as Tocqueville pointed out, is to assume that the majority will and the general will coincide.

146. Mill, *CRG*, p. 327. I borrow from Thompson (p. 55) the distinction between "instrumental" competence (the ability to seek out the most efficient means to achieve a given end) and moral competence (the ability to distinguish and rank ends in light of the common good).

147. Mill, *CRG*, pp. 262–63.

148. Thompson, *John Stuart Mill*, p. 85.

149. Mill, "Bentham," p. 112.

150. Mill, *CRG*, p. 290. Cf. Mill, "Bentham," pp. 111–12.

151. Mill, "Bentham," p. 113.

152. In his review of Grote's *Plato*, Mill cites approvingly the Platonic idea that government is a "skilled employment" which ought to be carried out by those of superior wisdom and virtue. See Mill, *Collected Works*, 11:436.

153. See G. W. F. Hegel, *The Philosophy of Right*, trans. T. M. Knox (Oxford: Oxford University Press, 1949), and Karl Mannheim, *Ideology and Utopia* (New York: Harcourt, Brace and World, 1936).

154. Of course, I am not maintaining that formal education excludes or necessarily diminishes such skeptical intelligence. Rather, my point is that Mill more or less abandons his focus on such intelligence when he considers the function of the "educated class."

155. Mill, *CRG*, pp. 306–307 (my emphasis).

156. Mill was to have his own doubts about this assumption, but these doubts were based on practical considerations, not principle. See Thompson's discussion, *John Stuart Mill*, pp. 100–101.

157. Mill, *CRG*, pp. 378, 382.

158. Ibid., p. 390.

159. Ibid., p. 313.

160. This is a reversion to the stance taken in his review of the second volume of Tocqueville's *Democracy in America*. See the discussion in the first section of this chapter.

161. Mill, *Autobiography*, p. 38. Cf. Mill, "Grote's Plato," in *Collected Works*, 11:405.

162. Mill, "Grote's *Plato*," 11:382–83.

163. This is the name Grote, following Plato, gives to the "commonsense" precepts governing Greek moral, political, and social life. See George Grote, *Plato and Other Companions of Socrates* (London: 1875), 1:253, and Plato, *Gorgias*, 484b. Mill cites the relevant passage from Grote in his review (11:390). Mill's own characterization of the tyranny of "King Nomos" and the persecution of the philosophical spirit (399–403) is one of the most moving and revealing in his entire oeuvre.

164. Mill, *CRG*, p. 291.

165. This characterization is offered by Graeme Duncan in his *Marx and Mill: Two Views of Social Conflict and Social Harmony* (Cambridge: Cambridge University Press, 1973), p. 261.

166. Mill, *The Later Letters, 1849 to 1873*, in *Collected Works*, 15:550. (Mill's original is in French.)

167. See Mill, *Collected Works*, 11:400–405.

168. Mill, *Collected Works*, 11:436. Mill attributes this insight to Plato, describing it as "a truth of transcendent importance and universal application."

169. It also clashes with Mill's (and Grote's) extraordinarily positive depiction of Athenian democratic institutions and, indeed, of the *demos* itself. See Mill, "Grote's *History of Greece*," 11:324–25. One way of explaining Mill's shift away from the project of attempting to combine the best of Periclean democracy and Socratic skepticism to the emphasis on expertise is in terms of the enormous difference he saw between the competence and broad-mindedness of the average Athenian citizen and the relative incompetence of his contemporaries. Where citizens are competent—as Mill thinks they undoubtedly were in Athens—the additional element of Socratic skepticism and moral integrity is enough; where they are not competent, "science" is needed to supplement *elenchus*.

CHAPTER THREE
FRIEDRICH NIETZSCHE

1. Friedrich Nietzsche, *Beyond Good and Evil*, trans. Walter Kaufmann (New York: Vintage, 1986), sec. 241; hereafter cited as *BGE*.

2. Friedrich Nietzsche, "The Problem of Socrates," *Twilight of the Idols*, in *Twilight of the Idols/The Anti-Christ*, trans. R. J. Hollingdale (New York: Penguin, 1990), sec. 2, 5, 6, 10; hereafter cited as *TI* and *AC*, resp.

3. See my discussion in chapter 4 of this study.

4. This phrase was coined by the Danish philosopher Georg Brandes, who used it in a series of essays on Nietzsche he wrote at the end of the nineteenth and

beginning of the twentieth century. See Georg Brandes, *Friedrich Nietzsche*, trans. A. G. Chater (London: Heineman, 1914). In a letter to Brandes dated December 2, 1887, Nietzsche writes, "The expression 'aristocratic radicalism,' which you use is very good. That is, if I may say so, the shrewdest remark that I have read about myself till now." In *Selected Letters of Friedrich Nietzsche*, ed. and trans. Christopher Middleton (Indianapolis: Hackett, 1996), pp. 278–280. Of course, this still leaves us with the problem of what, exactly, "aristocratic radicalism" is and whether it is intended as a *political* doctrine at all.

5. This, of course, raises the question of the relation between Nietzsche's philosophy and his political thought, a relationship which is murky given Nietzsche's conception of the (genuine) philosopher as a cultural physician, one who diagnoses the diseases of an age and suggests a "cure." Nietzsche's absurd and repellant political views are often offered as the "cure" for the bottomless decadence of the West, and thus seem to be the more than logical outcome of his cultural diagnosis. But this way of reading Nietzsche invests his texts with a teleological momentum, turning what is in fact the least interesting (and least persuasive) dimension of his thought into its crowning moment, in whose shadow the rest of his philosophy must be read.

6. Nietzsche, *Human, All Too Human*, trans. R. J. Hollingdale (New York: Cambridge University Press, 1996), sec. 438; hereafter cited as *HATH*.

7. See Nietzsche's remarks on the "desert" in *"On the Genealogy of Morals"* and *"Ecce Homo,"* trans. Walter Kaufmann (New York: Vintage, 1989), bk. 3, sec. 8 (hereafter cited as *GM* and *EH*, resp.). But cf. Plato, "Apology of Socrates," 32e–33a.

8. Nietzsche, *GM*, essay 3, sec. 11.

9. Hence Nietzsche's boast (sec. 7, "Why I Am a Destiny") in *Ecce Homo* that "what defines me, what sets me apart from the whole rest of humanity, is that I *uncovered* Christian morality" (*EH*, p. 332).

10. See Nietzsche, *GM*, essay 2, sec. 24; *BGE*, sec. 208. For Nietzsche's misanthropy, see Judith Shklar, "Putting Cruelty First," in her *Ordinary Vices* (Cambridge, Mass.: Harvard University Press, 1984), pp. 7–44.

11. Writers influenced by Leo Strauss have been particularly prominent in this category. See Werner Dannhauser, *Nietzsche's View of Socrates* (Ithaca: Cornell University Press, 1974); Bruce Detwiler, *Nietzsche and the Politics of Aristocratic Radicalism* (Chicago: University of Chicago Press, 1990); and Peter Berkowitz, *Nietzsche: The Ethics of an Immoralist* (Cambridge, Mass.: Harvard University Press, 1995).

12. See Walter Kaufmann, *Nietzsche: Philosopher, Psychologist, Antichrist* (Princeton: Princeton University Press, 1974); Alexander Nehamas, *Nietzsche: Life as Literature* (Cambridge, Mass.: Harvard University Press, 1985).

13. See, for example, Keith Ansell-Pearson, *An Introduction to Nietzsche and Politics* (Cambridge: Cambridge University Press, 1996); Bonnie Honig, *Political Theory and the Displacement of Politics* (Ithaca: Cornell University Press, 1993); and David Owen, *Nietzsche, Politics, and Modernity* (Thousand Oaks, Calif.: Sage Publications, 1995).

14. See, for example, Nehamas, *Nietzsche: Life as Literature*. That Nietzsche has an inclusive conception of morality can be seen in the preface to *GM*, sec. 6. For a good discussion of the issues involved, see Maudmarie Clark, "Nietzsche's Immoralism and the Concept of Morality" in *Nietzsche, Genealogy, Morality: Essays on Nietzsche's* "On the Genealogy of Morals," ed. Richard Schacht (Berkeley: University of California Press, 1994).

15. Nietzsche was quite self-conscious of how his own exercises in unmasking derived from the "ascetic ideal." See esp. *GM*, essay 3, sec. 24.

16. See, for example, Nietzsche, *AC*, secs. 9 and 12, where Nietzsche frames the "theologian instinct" to idealize (and falsify) the world as his target, and where he condemns most philosophers, excepting some sceptics, as "ignorant of the first requirements of intellectual integrity." See also Nietzsche, *BGE*, sec. 230, where he places the term "honesty" in the class of "moral word tinsel."

17. See, for example, Dannhauser, *Nietzsche's View of Socrates*, p. 124.

18. See Nietzsche, preface, *GM*, secs. 2, 3. For Nietzsche's relation to Kant on the problem of critique, see Gilles Deleuze, *Nietzsche and Philosophy*, trans. Hugh Tomlinson (New York: Columbia University Press, 1982), pp. 88–94. For philosophy as "radical questioning" and Socrates' role in inventing it, see Martin Heidegger, *What Is Called Thinking?*, trans. J. Glenn Gray (New York: Harper and Row, 1968). For Nietzsche's basic view of Plato, see Nietzsche, preface, *BGE*. Here Nietzsche attacks Plato as the inventor of philosophical dogmatism, albeit one inspired by Socrates. See my later discussion in the section entitled "Perspective, Self-Fashioning and Independent Judgment."

19. As Plato famously put it in *The Republic*, the *demos* is a beast immune to the charms of philosophy (493b).

20. Nietzsche, *BGE*, sec. 202.

21. See Nietzsche, *GM*, essay 1, sec. 16.

22. Nietzsche, *BGE*, sec. 199.

23. Nietzsche, *TI*, p. 103.

24. As has often been noted, *On the Genealogy of Morals* is an expansion of thoughts Nietzsche first expresses in section 260 of *Beyond Good and Evil*.

25. Nietzsche, *GM*, bk. 2, sec. 2.

26. Immanuel Kant, *Groundwork of the Metaphysics of Morals*, trans. H. J. Paton (New York: Harper and Row, 1956). Cf. Nietzsche, *AC*, sec. 11: " 'Virtue,' 'duty,' 'good in itself,' impersonal and universal—phantoms, expressions of decline, of the final exhaustion of life, of Königsburgian Chinadom. The profoundest laws of preservation and growth demand the reverse of this: that each one of us should devise *his own* virtue, *his own* categorical imperative. A people perishes if it mistakes *its own* duty for the concept of duty in general." Note how easily Nietzsche shifts from an autonomous individual to an autonomous *people* in this passage.

27. Nietzsche, "The 'Improvers' of Mankind," *TI*, secs. 1, 2. For Nietzsche's general conception of morality as the means by which individuals are rendered "useful" to the herd, see *The Gay Science*, trans. Kaufmann (New York: Vintage,

1974) sec. 116 (hereafter referred to as *GS*). For his conception of the morality of mores and "tradition" as a "higher authority" which one obeys simply because it *commands*, see *Daybreak*, trans. R. J. Hollingdale (Cambridge: Cambridge University Press, 1997), sec. 9.

28. Nietzsche, "The 'Improvers' of Mankind," *TI*, sec. 5.

29. One should also include Hegel.

30. Nietzsche, preface, *Daybreak*, sec. 3.

31. Nietzsche, *GS*, sec. 2.

32. Nietzsche, *BGE*, sec. 199.

33. Plato, *Gorgias*, 482c.

34. In preface, *GM*, sec. 6, Nietzsche describes how his skeptical approach to the morality of pity led to a more general, and radical project: "Whoever sticks with it and *learns* how to ask questions here will experience what I experienced—a tremendous new prospect opens up for him, a new possibility comes over him like a vertigo, every kind of mistrust, suspicion, fear leaps up, his belief in morality, in all morality, falters. . . ." As one critic has pointed out, it would be shortsighted, given passages like this, to claim that when Nietzsche writes of a critique of moral values, he simply has a *particular* (Christian) morality in mind (see Clark, "Nietzsche's Immoralism and the Concept of Morality"). On the other hand, nothing prevents us from claiming that Nietzsche's usage equates "morality" with a set of particular cultural and historical *moralities*, which are themselves variations on "ascetic ideals," different iterations of the table of values that flow from the "good/ evil" binary as Nietzsche characterizes it in essay 1 of the *Genealogy*. Thus, not all tables of values are *moral* values in Nietzsche's restricted sense since some (such as the "noble") fail to promote ascetic ideals. *We* would prefer to call such non- or antiascetic values *moral* values, but Nietzsche prefers to label them "extramoral." There is, as a result, an inevitable slippage between our use of "morality" to refer to moral values in general, and Nietzsche's more determinate critical usage.

35. Nietzsche, *GM*, essay 2, secs. 19 and 24.

36. See Nehamas, *Nietzsche: Life as Literature*, p. 122.

37. Nietzsche, *GM*, essay 2, sec. 17.

38. Nietzsche, *BGE*, sec. 36.

39. Nietzsche, *GM*, essay 2, sec. 16.

40. Ibid.

41. Ibid., sec. 18: "This entire *active* 'bad conscience'—you will have guessed it—as the womb of all ideal and imaginative phenomena, also brought to light an abundance of strange new beauty and affirmation, and perhaps beauty itself."

42. See Nietzsche, *GS*, sec. 290. See also Nehamas, *Nietzsche: Life as Literature*, p. 121.

43. It needs to be emphasized here that "bad conscience" in its most primordial sense—as the "internalization" of man—is not identical with the "bad conscience" of the "mediocre men" who make up the majority of any society. The latter case is an offshoot of the more fundamental phenomenon. Thus, when Nietzsche refers to man as "the sick animal" (*GM*, essay 3, sec. 14), he uses this phrase in two distinct

senses: first, to denote the primordial self-division born of enclosure in society (something that affects "masters" as well as "slaves"); second, to denote the self-destructive form of this sickness which afflicts those incapable of distinction. It is the moralization of the latter's feelings of self-division and existential discomfort which the ascetic priest performs. For a good discussion of these issues, see Aaron Ridley, *Nietzsche's Conscience: Six Character Studies from the "Genealogy"* (Ithaca: Cornell University Press, 1999), pp. 21–22.

44. Nietzsche, *GM*, essay 3, sec. 11.

45. Ibid., sec. 15.

46. Ibid., sec. 20.

47. Ibid., sec. 15.

48. Ibid., sec. 16.

49. Ibid., sec. 20.

50. Ibid., sec. 13.

51. Ibid., sec. 15.

52. Ibid., essay 1, sec. 2.

53. Ibid., sec. 10.

54. Nietzsche, *BGE*, sec. 260.

55. For a summary of Nietzsche's views on these matters, see Arthur Danto "Perspectivism," in his *Nietzsche as Philosopher* (New York: Columbia University Press, 1965), pp. 68–99.

56. See Nietzsche, *BGE*, sec. 260.

57. See Tracy Strong, *Nietzsche and the Politics of Transfiguration* (Berkeley: University of California Press, 1975), pp. 63–64. See also Nietzsche, *BGE*, sec. 17.

58. Nietzsche, *GM*, essay 1, sec. 13.

59. Nietzsche, "The Problem of Socrates," *TI*, sec. 5. Cf. Nietzsche, *Daybreak*, sec. 41.

60. Nietzsche, "The Problem of Socrates," sec. 10.

61. Nietzsche, *GM*, essay 1, sec. 11; and "What I Owe to the Ancients," *TI*, sec. 2.

62. Nietzsche, *BGE*, sec. 4.

63. For doubts about the Nietzschean story concerning agency and the Greeks (at least in its overly literal form), see Bernard Williams, *Shame and Necessity* (Berkeley: University of California Press, 1994).

64. Friedrich Nietzsche, "On the Utility and Liability of History for Life," in Nietzsche, *Unfashionable Observations*, trans. Richard T. Grey (Stanford: Stanford University Press, 1995), p. 90.

65. Nietzsche, *BGE*, sec. 257.

66. Cf. Hannah Arendt, *The Human Condition* (Chicago: University of Chicago Press, 1958).

67. Nietzsche, *BGE*, sec. 203.

68. Nietzsche, *GM*, essay 1, sec. 9.

69. Nietzsche, *BGE*, secs. 203, 211. Cf. *BGE*, sec. 208.

70. Cf. Max Weber, "Science as a Vocation," in *From Max Weber*, ed. H. Gerth and C. W. Mills (New York: Oxford University Press, 1958), where he discusses

how "the grandiose moral fervor" of Christian ethics blinded Western civilization to this possibility "for a thousand years" (p. 149).

71. See Nehamas, *Nietzsche: Life as Literature*, p. 126.

72. Nietzsche, *GM*, essay 1, sec. 14; and *BGE*, sec. 199.

73. Nietzsche, *BGE*, secs. 202, 203.

74. Nietzsche, "The Wanderer and His Shadow," in *HATH*, sec. 275.

75. See Karl Marx, "Contribution to the Critique of Hegel's *Philosophy of Right*" in *The Marx-Engels Reader*, ed. Robert Tucker (New York: Norton, 1978), pp. 19–20.

76. Nietzsche, "Expeditions of an Untimely Man," *TI*, sec. 43.

77. See especially, in this regard, Nietzsche, *GM*, essay 2, sec. 12.

78. This distinction between institutions and the spirit which animates them is essentially anti-Platonic, as is Nietzsche's distinction between *culture*, on the one hand, and the *state* and politics, on the other. See Nietzsche, "What the Germans Lack," *TI*, sec. 4. Cf. Nietzche, *HATH*, sec. 474.

79. See, for example, Detwiler, *Nietzsche*, pp. 15–16, where these "favorable" mentions of democracy are characterized as aberrations. However, as Maudmarie Clark has pointed out, there is no place in Nietzsche's "mature" work where he repudiates his earlier views. See her, "Nietzsche's Antidemocratic Rhetoric," *Southern Journal of Philosophy* 38 (1999), pp. 119–41. This is not to say that Nietzsche, ultimately, was prodemocratic in anything approaching a straightforward sense (as Lawrence Hatab argues in his *A Nietzschean Defense of Democracy* [Chicago: Open Court, 1995]). Rather, it is simply to say that the surface in Nietzsche is always somewhat deceptive, and that apparent contradictions always tempt the commentator to marginalize certain remarks while highlighting others. Detwiler, anxious to show that Nietzsche was, in fact, a proto-Nazi and protofascist (albeit not a "simple" one), more or less brackets the "middle" period Nietzsche while highlighting the early (1872) unpublished essay fragment on "The Greek State" as authentically Nietzschean.

80. See Bernard Yack, "Nietzsche and Cultural Revolution," *The Longing for Total Revolution* (Berkeley: University of California Press, 1992), pp. 310–64; Detwiler, *Nietzsche and the Politics of Aristocratic Radicalism*, pp. 8, 12–13.

81. Friedrich Nietzsche, "Der griechische Staat" *Nietzsche Werke: Kritische Gesamtausgabe*, ed. Giorgio Colli and Mazzino Monatinari (Berlin: Walter de Gruyter, 1973), 3:258–71.

82. Although even here the force of his comments is open to dispute.

83. Nietzsche, "The 'Improvers' of Mankind," *TI*, sec. 5.

84. Friedrich Nietzsche, "On the New Idol," *Thus Spoke Zarathustra* in *The Portable Nietzsche*, ed. Walter Kaufmann (New York: Penguin, 1982), p. 160.

85. It will be objected that, given Nietzsche's view of life as exploitation and will to power (*BGE*, sec. 259), it is simply wrong to state that he has any real objection to cruelty, whether physical or psychic. Such a critic will see Nietzsche simply as performing a one-dimensionalizing naturalization of human phenomenon similar

to that performed by Sade in "Yet Another Effort, Frenchmen, If You Would Be Truly Free," in Sade's *Philosophy in the Bedroom*). See Max Horkheimer and Theodor Adorno, "*Juliette*, or Morality and Enlightenment," *Dialectic of Enlightenment*, trans. John Cumming (New York: Seabury Press, 1972), pp. 81–119. Such interpretations presume that Nietzsche engages in a simple celebration of power and cruelty, a reading which simply cannot be sustained given Nietzsche's frequent critical comments about surplus (willed) suffering in the world.

86. See Nietzsche, "Expeditions," *TI*, sec. 38. Here Nietzsche expresses his preference for a "positive," active, and quasi-republican conception of freedom, as opposed to the "reactive" negative conception favored by liberals (like Mill). See also sec. 41.

87. See Mill, *On Liberty*, in *Texts and Commentaries*, ed. Alan Ryan (New York: Norton 1997), 48–49.

88. Nietzsche, *BGE*, sec. 242; *GM*, essay 3, sec. 20, where "orgies of feeling" takes on a prescient cast for the coming century.

89. Nietzsche, "Expeditions," secs. 37, 39.

90. Ibid., sec. 38. Hannah Arendt—and many others in the civic republican tradition, broadly defined—would agree. See her *On Revolution* (New York: Penguin, 1968).

91. Nietzsche, *BGE*, sec. 199.

92. Ibid., sec. 253.

93. See Alexander Nehamas's essay "Who Are the 'Philosophers of the Future'?: A Reading of *Beyond Good and Evil*," in *Reading Nietzsche*, ed. Robert C. Solomon and Kathleen M. Higgins (New York: Oxford University Press, 1988).

94. See Hannah Arendt's gloss in her introduction to *The Life of the Mind* (New York: Harcourt Brace Jovanovich, 1978), p. 10.

95. Nietzsche, *GS*, sec. 343. Cf. *GS*, sec. 125, entitled "The Madman."

96. Nietzsche, "Expeditions," sec. 5.

97. Nietzsche, *GS*, sec. 290.

98. Nietzsche, *BGE*, sec. 199.

99. See Nietzsche, preface, *Daybreak*, sec. 3.

100. See Alasdair MacIntyre, *After Virtue: A Study in Moral Theory* (Notre Dame: Notre Dame University Press, 1981), p. 107.

101. Cf. Friedrich Nietzsche, *The Will to Power*, trans. Walter Kaufmann and R. J. Hollingdale (New York: Vintage, 1968): "Ultimately, the individual derives the values of his acts from himself; because he has to interpret in a quite individual way even the words he has inherited. His interpretation of a formula at least is personal, even if he does not create a formula: as an interpreter he is still creative" (sec. 767); hereafter cited as *WP*.

102. Nietzsche, *BGE*, sec. 210.

103. Ibid., sec. 212.

104. Cf. Nietzsche's characterizations of Goethe in *WP*, secs. 95, 1014; and "Expeditions," *TI*, sec. 49.

105. Nietzsche, "Why I Am a Destiny," 1.

106. Nietzsche, preface, *BGE*.

107. Ibid.

108. Nietzsche, "The Problem of Socrates," *TI*, sec. 7. Cf. Nietzsche, *BGE*, sec. 190.

109. Nietzsche, preface, *BGE*.

110. Plato, *Apology of Socrates*, 31a.

111. See, for example, the essay "On Truth and Lie in a Nonmoral Sense," in Friedrich Nietzsche, *Philosophy and Truth*, ed. and trans. Donald Breazeale (Atlantic Highlands, N.J.: Humanities Press, 1979), pp. 79–97.

112. See Clark, "Perspectivism," *Nietzsche on Truth and Philosophy*, pp. 127–58; and Nehamas, *Nietzsche: Life as Literature*, chap. 2.

113. See the famous section "How the Real World Became a Fable" in Nietzsche, *TI*.

114. See esp. Nietzsche, *WP*, secs. 566–69.

115. Nehamas, *Nietzsche: Life as Literature*, pp. 49, 52.

116. The phrase in quotation marks is a paraphrase of Nietzsche, *WP*, sec. 493. See also *BGE*, sec. 34.

117. Nietzsche, *BGE*, sec. 24.

118. Nietzsche, *GM*, essay 1, sec. 11.

119. Nietzsche, "On the Utility and Liability of History for Life," p. 90.

120. Nietzsche, *GS*, sec. 374.

121. Nietzsche, *GM*, essay 3, sec. 12.

122. See Nietzsche, *WP*, sec. 12.

123. See Immanuel Kant, "An Answer to the Question: What Is Enlightenment?," in Kant, *Political Writings*, ed. Hans Reiss (New York: Cambridge University Press, 1971), pp. 54–60.

124. Nietzsche, preface, *HATH*, sec. 3.

125. Ibid., sec. 4.

126. Nietzsche, *BGE*, sec. 44. A good example of such a *Freidenker* is the character Settembrini in Thomas Mann's novel *The Magic Mountain*.

127. Nietzsche, *BGE*, sec. 44.

128. Nietzsche, *GM*, essay 3, sec. 12.

129. Nietzsche, *BGE*, sec. 29; cf. also sec. 41.

130. Danto, *Nietzsche as Philosopher*, p. 78.

131. Strong, *Nietzsche and the Politics of Transfiguration*, p. 72.

132. Ibid., p. 49.

133. Ibid., p. 74. As Strong points out, it is because of this "materialist" understanding of language's role in pulling together a world that Nietzsche rejects the Enlightenment/Marxian model of the reformation of consciousness.

134. Nietzsche, *BGE*, sec.188.

135. Ibid.

136. Ibid., sec. 57.

137. Ibid., secs. 41, 44.

138. Cf. Richard Rorty's description of the figure of the "ironist" in his *Contingency, Irony, and Solidarity* (New York: Cambridge University Press, 1989), pp. 73–75.

139. Much of Nietzsche's contempt for the "herd" flows from its lack of Socratic modesty, its complacent assumption of moral knowledge or expertise. Cf. *BGE*: "Here exactly lies our novel insight. We have found that in all major moral judgments Europe is now of one mind. . . . [P]lainly, one now *knows* in Europe what Socrates thought he did not know and what that famous old serpent once promised to teach—today one 'knows' what is good and evil" (sec. 202).

140. Nietzsche, *BGE*, sec. 260.

141. Thus, in *Ecce Homo* Nietzsche describes himself as both *decadent* and aristocrat, as mixing both the "highest and lowest" rungs on the "ladder of life." Moreover, he traces his capacity for psychological insight and for reversing perspectives precisely to this "dual descent."

142. See Deleuze, "The Overman: Against the Dialectic," *Nietzsche and Philosophy*, pp. 156–64. Strong, *Friedrich Nietzsche and the Politics of Transfiguration*, pp. 29–30.

143. Cf. Freud's metaphor of the psyche as built up on "archaeological" strata in a manner similar to that of the city of Rome, in *Civilization and Its Discontents*, trans. James Strachey (New York: Norton, 1961), pp. 16–17.

144. Nietzsche, *GS*, sec. 347.

145. In the preface to *Daybreak* Nietzsche explains the internal connection between his brand of conscience and "the German piety and integrity of millennia" (sec. 4). It is not, in other words, a question of "overcoming" conscience but of making something different, more independent, out of it.

146. I take issue here with Alexander Nehamas's otherwise persuasive interpretation of Nietzsche.

147. Nietzsche, *GS*, sec. 270. I have opted for Nehamas's translation over Kaufmann's, since it is closer to the original German. See Nehamas, *Nietzsche: Life as Literature*, p. 171.

148. I place "goal" in quotes because, as Nehamas emphasizes, there is a strong antiteleological cast to Nietzsche's conception of self-fashioning. One does not, as in Aristotle, form one's character in one's youth, the better to enjoy the fruits of "virtue in action" in adulthood. For Nietzsche a fundamental open-endedness and uncertainty attend the project of becoming an individual, which banish all complacency on this score. See Nehamas, *Nietzsche: Life as Literature*, p. 189.

149. Nietzsche, "Schopenhauer as Educator," in *Unfashionable Observations*, p. 172.

150. I would not charge Nehamas with making this error, as have some critics. Nehamas's study is quite sensitive, on the whole, to the intertwining of the moral and the aesthetic in Nietzsche and in life. He seems anxious, however, to play up the aesthetic side (the formation of character being like the creation of a literary

character) in order to escape the charge of a neoexistentialism. My own position is that there is no need for anxiety on this count.

151. Nietzsche, *HATH*, sec. 263.

152. Nietzsche, *BGE*, sec. 21.

153. Nietzsche, "Expeditions," *TI*, sec. 38.

154. Nietzsche, *BGE*, sec. 43.

155. See Hannah Arendt, "The Crisis in Culture" in Arendt, *Between Past and Future* (New York: Penguin, 1965), p. 220.

156. See Kant, *Critique of Judgment*, trans. Werner S. Pluhar (Indianapolis: Hackett, 1987) sec. 40.

157. Hence Hegel's famous critique of the categorical imperative's formal test. As Hegel pointed out, the weak spot of this test is that the universality of a maxim of action hinges (fatally) upon the *formulation* of the maxim itself.

158. See Leo Strauss, "Note on the Plan of *Beyond Good and Evil*," in *Studies in Platonic Political Philosophy* (Chicago: University of Chicago Press, 1983), pp. 174–191. Also Detwiler, "Genealogy, Politics, and the Revaluation of all Values," in *Nietzsche and the Politics of Aristocratic Radicalism*, pp. 115–43.

159. See, especially, Nietzsche, *BGE*, secs. 208–10.

160. This is the primary theme of Peter Berkowitz's *Nietzsche: The Ethics of an Immoralist*.

161. See Richard Rorty, "Private Irony and Liberal Hope," in his *Contingency, Irony, and Solidarity*, pp. 73–95; Nehamas, "How One Becomes What One Is," *Nietzsche: Life as Literature*, pp. 170–99.

162. Nietzsche, "On the Utility and Liability of History for Life," p. 90.

163. Weber picks up on this theme with merciless consistency in his lecture "Science as a Vocation" (see my discussion in chapter 4 of this book). Horkheimer and Adorno definitively (if opaquely) addressed the issue of the "corrosive" character of rationality in the first essay ("The Concept of Enlightenment") of their *Dialectic of Enlightenment*, pp. 3–42.

164. Nietzsche, *WP*, sec. 1.

165. Ibid., sec. 2.

166. See chapter 1, note 144, in the present study. However, cf. Nietzsche's statement in, *HATH*: "Ethics of truth: convictions are more dangerous enemies of truth than are lies" (sec. 483).

CHAPTER FOUR
MAX WEBER

1. Max Weber, " 'Objectivity' in Social Science" in Weber, *The Methodology of the Social Sciences*, ed. and trans. by Edward A. Shils and Henry A. Finch (New York: The Free Press, 1949), p. 57.

2. Ibid.

3. Aristotle, *The Politics*, 1275a22.

4. As Weber writes: "In a modern state the actual ruler is necessarily and unavoidably the bureaucracy, since power is exercised neither through parliamentary speeches nor through monarchical enunciations, but through the routines of administration." Weber, "Parliament and Government in a Reconstructed Germany," in *Economy and Society*, ed. Guenther Roth and Claus Wittich (Berkeley: University of California Press, 1978), vol. 2, app. 2, p. 1393, hereafter cited as *ES*.

5. Max Weber, "Politics as a Vocation" in *From Max Weber: Essays in Sociology*, ed. and trans., and with an introduction by H. H. Gerth and C. Wright Mills (New York: Oxford University Press, 1958), p. 113; hereafter cited as *FMW*.

6. Ibid., pp. 107, 125.

7. Weber, "Parliament and Government," p. 1399; Weber, "Politics as a Vocation," p. 119.

8. See Harvey Goldman, *Politics, Death, and the Devil: Self and Power in Max Weber and Thomas Mann* (Berkeley: University of California Press, 1992), p.163.

9. Weber, "Parliament and Government," p. 1393.

10. The phrase "spiritual aristocracy" is taken from Max Weber, *The Protestant Ethic and the Spirit of Capitalism* (New York: Routledge, 1996), p. 121.

11. See the essays in *Max Weber and His Contemporaries*, ed. Wolfgang J. Mommsen and Jürgen Osterhammel (London: Unwin Hyman, 1987).

12. Karl Jaspers, "Max Weber: A Commemorative Address," in Jaspers, *On Max Weber*, ed. John Dreijmanis (New York: Paragon House, 1989), p. 16.

13. Weber, "Science as a Vocation," *FMW*, p. 155.

14. Ibid., p. 143.

15. Ibid., p. 140.

16. Ibid., p. 155.

17. Ibid.

18. Of course, Socrates was every bit as dubious of the public argument of the assembly as Weber is of the deliberative potential of electoral politics. See chapter 1 of this study.

19. Weber, "Parliament and Government," p. 1399.

20. Weber, "Politics as a Vocation," p. 78.

21. Weber, "Parliament and Government," p. 1403.

22. Weber, "Science as a Vocation," p. 149.

23. Ibid., pp. 148–49.

24. Ibid., p. 148.

25. Weber, "Parliament and Government," p. 1402. Cf. Weber, "On the Situation of Constitutional Democracy in Russia" in Weber, *Political Writings* ed. Peter Lassman and Ronald Spiers (Cambridge: Cambridge University Press, 1994), p. 68, where he speaks of the "housing for the new serfdom" which is "ready everywhere."

26. This article was first published in 1892 in the *Verein für Sozialpolitik*.

27. Weber, "The Nation State and Economic Policy," *Political Writings*, p. 2.

28. Ibid., p. 9.

29. Ibid., pp. 8, 10.

30. Ibid., p. 14.

31. Ibid., p. 19.

32. Ibid., pp. 15, 16.

33. Ibid., p. 16.

34. Ibid., p. 15.

35. Ibid., p. 20.

36. For an overview of Weber's relations to his own class, see Tracy Strong, "Weber and the Bourgeoisie," in *The Barbarism of Reason: Max Weber and the Twilight of Enlightenment*, ed. Asher Horowitz and Terry Maley (Toronto: University of Toronto Press, 1994). For a more biographical account, see Arthur Mitzman, *The Iron Cage: An Historical Interpretation of Max Weber* (New York: Knopf, 1970), pp. 15–163.

37. Weber, "The Nation State and Economic Policy," p. 26.

38. Ibid., pp. 25, 26.

39. Ibid.

40. Ibid, pp. 26–27.

41. Ibid, p. 27.

42. Weber, quoted in introduction to *FMW*, p. 11.

43. Weber, "The Nation State and Economic Policy," p. 17.

44. This is not to deny its importance as a piece of ideological persuasion at a crucial juncture in German history. See Wolfgang Mommsen, *Max Weber and German Politics, 1890–1920* (Chicago: University of Chicago Press, 1984), pp. 68–72. Mommsen argues that Weber's liberal imperialist rhetoric played a crucial role in converting Friedrich Naumann, editor of *Die Hilfe*, and Hans Delbrück, editor of the *Preussische Jahrbücher*, to the cause of imperialism. Their respective journals soon became organs of liberal imperialist ideology, contributing greatly to making imperialism "socially acceptable" in Germany.

45. For an excellent reconstruction of the cultural moment (and its generational tensions) in which Weber made these remarks, see Lawrence Scaff "Epigones of a Great Age," in *Fleeing the Iron Cage: Culture, Politics, and Modernity in the Thought of Max Weber* (Berkeley: University of California Press, 1989), pp. 11–33.

46. This is not to deny that the mature Weber tended to view all "domestic" political reforms in light of their potential contribution to Germany's power position in the world. However, he came to view the international arena with a certain amount of fatalism, an attitude he never really held with regard to the struggles within German politics.

47. Weber, "Between Two Laws," *Political Writings*, p. 76.

48. Ibid., pp. 75, 76.

49. Ibid.

50. Weber, "The Meaning of 'Ethical Neutrality' in Sociology and Economics," in *The Methodology of the Social Sciences*, pp. 26–27.

51. See Machiavelli, *Discourses on the First Ten Books of Titus Livy*, bk. 1, chap. 4.

52. Weber, "Parliament and Government," p. 1403.

53. Ibid., p. 1417.

54. See Peter Breiner's account in his *Max Weber and Democratic Politics* (Ithaca: Cornell University Press, 1996), p. 164.

55. See Wolfgang Mommsen, *The Political and Social Theory of Max Weber* (Chicago: University of Chicago Press, 1989), pp. 32–35.

56. See Weber, *ES*, vol. 1, p. 292.

57. Mommsen, *The Political and Social Theory of Max Weber*, p. 32.

58. See Weber, "Politics as a Vocation," pp. 103, 125.

59. Weber, "Parliament and Government," p. 1392.

60. Ibid., p. 1396.

61. Weber, "Politics as a Vocation," p. 107.

62. Weber to Michels, August 4, 1908; quoted in Mommsen, *Political and Social Theory of Max Weber*, p. 31.

63. Weber, "Parliament and Government," p. 1393.

64. Ibid, pp. 1395, 1407.

65. Ibid., p. 1417.

66. Ibid., p. 1414.

67. Weber, "Politics as a Vocation," p. 107; "Parliament and Government," pp. 1449–50.

68. Weber, "Parliament and Government," p. 1450.

69. Thucydides, *History*, bk. 3, para., 37–41. Fortunately, the Athenians had second thoughts and the order was revoked, albeit without a moment to spare. It is striking that Weber reminds the audience of "Politics as a Vocation" that it was not Cleon but Pericles who "was the first to bear the name of demagogue" (p. 96).

70. Weber, "Parliament and Government," p. 1420.

71. Ibid.

72. Weber, "Politics as a Vocation," p. 106; cf. "Parliament and Government," p. 1459.

73. Weber, "Parliament and Government," p. 1409.

74. Weber, "Politics as a Vocation," p. 125.

75. See Habermas's remarks at the 1964 Heidelberg Conference on Max Weber in *Max Weber and Sociology Today*, ed. Otto Stammer (New York: Oxford University Press, 1971), p. 66.

76. Breiner, *Max Weber and Democratic Politics*, p. 164.

77. Weber, "Parliament and Government," pp. 1391–92.

78. Ibid., p. 1403.

79. See Jürgen Habermas, "Reason and the Rationalization of Society," *The Theory of Communicative Action*, trans. Thomas McCarthy (Boston: Beacon Press, 1984), 1:247–54.

80. Leo Strauss also makes this charge. See his *Natural Right and History* (Chicago: University of Chicago Press, 1953), p. 44. For the distinction between subjective and objective forms of moral pluralism, see Charles Larmore, "Pluralism and

Reasonable Disagreement," in his book *The Morals of Modernity* (New York: Cambridge University Press, 1996), pp. 154–58.

81. It is on this issue that Habermas's program of an ethics derived from the very structure of communicative action itself diverges most noticeably from parallel liberal accounts of the political consequences of moral disagreement, such as that of Rawls or (more radically) Berlin. Habermas does not hold out the prospect of moral consensus in a pluralistic political society; however, he does hold out the possibility of agreement (under ideal conditions of argument) as to where the "force of the better argument" does, in fact, reside in "practical discourses." See Jürgen Habermas, "Discourse Ethics: Notes on a Program of Philosophical Justification," in his *Moral Consciousness and Communicative Action*, trans. Christian Lenhardt and Shierry Weber Nicholson (Cambridge: MIT Press, 1990), pp. 43–115.

82. This charge is also made by Strauss, *National Right and History*, p. 40, and by Sheldon Wolin in his essay "Max Weber: Legitimation, Method, and the Politics of Theory" in *The Barbarism of Reason*, pp. 298–99.

83. This tendency has hardly been eradicated. In the form of sociobiology, it is in many respects as strong as ever.

84. See Weber, "Science as a Vocation," pp. 140–43.

85. Ibid., p. 143.

86. Ibid., p. 144.

87. See Strauss, *National Right and History*, p. 48; Wolin, "Max Weber," p. 291.

88. "Science as a Vocation," p. 147.

89. For a good summary of the Weber/Nietzsche connection in terms of the problem of power and reason, see Mark Warren, "Nietzsche and Weber: When Does Reason Become Power?," in *The Barborism of Reason*, ed. Horowitz and Maley, esp. pp. 76–78.

90. See Max Weber's, introduction to *The Protestant Ethic*, pp. 13–31. See also Habermas's discussion in *The Theory of Communicative Action*, I:157–85.

91. Plato, *Protagoras*, 356d–358a.

92. Weber, "Science as a Vocation," p. 152.

93. Ibid., p. 141.

94. The greatest example of this strain of Nietzsche's influence is Martin Heidegger's metahistory of Western philosophy. See "The End of Philosophy and the Task for Thinking," in Heidegger, *Basic Writings*, ed. David Farrell Krell (New York: Harper and Row, 1977), pp. 372–92. Unlike Weber, however, Heidegger specifically exempted Socrates from the category of "philosophy," understood as a metaphysical "science of grounds." For Heidegger Socrates remained "the purest *thinker* of the West," one committed to radical questioning.

95. See Weber, "Science as a Vocation," pp. 139–43, on the "disenchantment" of science and the slow death of the belief that analysis of the world will reveal its meaning.

96. Weber, "Parliament and Government," p. 1403.

97. Weber uses the term "spiritual aristocracy" in reference to the Puritan "saints." See *The Protestant Ethic*, p. 121.

98. Goldman, *Politics, Death, and the Devil*, p. 55.

99. Cf. J. G. A. Pocock, *The Machiavellian Moment* (Princeton: Princeton University Press, 1975), p. 201.

100. Goldman, *Politics, Death, and the Devil*, p. 84.

101. This characterization is roughly the one Goldman gives in his superbly argued study.

102. Weber, "Politics as a Vocation," p. 114.

103. Ibid.

104. Ibid., p. 77.

105. Ibid., p.113.

106. Ibid., p. 103.

107. Thus, Weber goes out of his way to draw his audience's attention to the continuities between revolutionary, communist politics and more everyday forms, the lesson being that political struggle has a way of accentuating self-interest even when the politics in question repudiates the very idea of self-interest.

108. "Politics as a Vocation," p. 117.

109. Ibid., p. 113.

110. As Weber puts it, blind obedience is the price paid for "guidance by leaders." Ibid.

111. Ibid., p. 115.

112. Ibid., pp. 115–16.

113. Ibid., p. 115.

114. Weber, *The Protestant Ethnic*, pp. 113–19.

115. See Goldman's discussion in *Politics, Death, and the Devil*, pp. 178–84. See also Jeffrey Alexander's essay "The Dialectic of Individuation and Domination: Weber's Rationalization Theory and Beyond," in *Max Weber: Rationality and Modernity*, ed. Sam Whimster and Scott Lash (London: Allen and Unwin, 1987), pp. 185–206.

116. Weber, "Politics as a Vocation," p. 115.

117. Ibid., p. 116.

118. Cf. Weber, *The Protestant Ethnic*, pp. 118–19.

119. Weber, "Politics as a Vocation," p. 117 (my emphasis).

120. Ibid., p. 116.

121. See Gregory Vlastos's consideration in chapter 6 of his *Socrates: Ironist and Moral Philosopher* (Ithaca: Cornell University Press, 1991), pp. 157–78. As Vlastos argues, piety for Socrates is "doing god's work to benefit human beings—work such as Socrates' kind of god would wish done on his behalf, in service to him" (p. 176). Socrates' "kind of god" is one from which all magic has been purged; he is, moreover, a god who is powerless to effect the moral self-examination which Socrates tries to induce. Hence his need for a helper. Thus, "piety" for Socrates means obeying the only kind of divinity worth obeying, namely, one that rejects as superstition reigning religious belief and the believers' conception of what moral health consists

in. This is, as Vlastos laconically puts it, a "revolutionary" conception of piety, one which would not be recognized by the conventionally pious since they are its primary target.

122. I cite from the Tredennick translation of the *Apology* in Plato, *Collected Dialogues*, ed. Edith Hamilton and Huntington Cairns (Princeton: Princeton University Press, 1982).

123. Weber, "Politics as a Vocation," pp. 118–19.

124. Ibid., p. 118.

125. Isaiah Berlin, *Against the Current*, p. 56.

126. See, in this regard, Sheldon Wolin's discussion of the parallel idea in Machiavelli in chapter 7 of his *Politics and Vision* (Boston: Little, Brown, 1960), pp. 220–28.

127. Weber, "Politics as a Vocation," pp. 119–20.

128. Ibid., p. 119.

129. Ibid.

130. Ibid.

131. See, in this regard, Goldman's illuminating discussion concerning the curiously "Christian," demonizing character of Weber's "polytheism" in his *Politics, Death, and the Devil*, pp. 76–78.

132. See chapter 1 of this study.

133. Weber, "Politics as a Vocation," p. 117.

134. Ibid., p. 126.

135. Ibid., p. 121.

136. Ibid. p. 126.

137. Cf. Michael Walzer's discussion in "Political Action: The Problem of Dirty Hands," *Philosophy and Public Affairs*, 2, no. 2 (1972).

138. Weber, "Politics as a Vocation," p. 127 (my emphases).

139. See Goldman, *Politics, Death, and the Devil*, pp. 66, 78.

140. See the second section of this chapter.

141. Strauss, for example, dismissively states that "we cannot take seriously this belated insistence on responsibility and sanity, this inconsistent concern with consistency, this irrational praise of rationality." See Strauss, *National Right and History*, p. 47.

142. See the chapter "Democratizing the Agon: On the Agonistic Tendency in Recent Political Theory" in my *Politics, Philosophy, Terror* (Princeton: Princeton University Press, 1999), pp. 107–27.

143. Weber, "Politics as a Vocation," p. 128. To be fair to Weber, one must remember that the turn to "responsible" leading politicians is primarily a reaction to the erasure of responsibility under bureaucratic forms of domination. See John Patrick Diggins, *Max Weber: Politics and the Spirit of Tragedy* (New York: Basic Books, 1996), p. 208.

144. Mommsen, *The Political and Social Theory of Max Weber*, p. 28.

145. Weber, "Politics as a Vocation," p. 113.

146. Weber, "Science as a Vocation," pp. 134–35.

147. Ibid., p. 136.

148. Ibid., pp. 138–39.

149. Ibid., p. 141.

150. Ibid., p. 142.

151. Ibid., p. 143.

152. Ibid. (my emphasis)

153. This paragraph summarizes the logic of Weber's argument on pp. 143–45.

154. Ibid., p. 145.

155. Immanuel Kant, *Political Writings*, ed. Hans Reiss (New York: Cambridge University Press, 1970), p. 54.

156. Weber, "Science as a Vocation," p. 146.

157. Ibid., p. 149.

158. Ibid., p. 147.

159. Ibid.

160. Ibid., p. 148.

161. Ibid., p. 151.

162. Ibid., pp. 151–52.

163. This may strike some readers as too easy an example. Consider, however, the rarity of a figure like Alexander Herzen in the history of Western socialism. Herzen believed in both individual liberty and greater social equality yet was honest enough (unlike the far more doctrinaire Marx) to realize that the pursuit of the latter would involve the sacrifice of many of the things he held dear. He nevertheless remained loyal to the cause of revolutionary social change in Russia. See Isaiah Berlin's introduction to Herzen, *My Past and Thoughts*, trans. Constance Garnett (Berkeley: University of California Press, 1999), p. xl.

164. Goldman, *Politics, Death, and the Devil*, p. 79. Cf. Strauss's comments on "clarification" in *Natural Right and History*, pp. 72–73.

165. Weber, "Science as a Vocation," p. 153.

166. Ibid.

167. Ibid., p. 155.

168. For a very different reading of "Science as a Vocation," one which frames Weber's lecture as a response to Nietzsche and the vulgar Nietzscheanism popular with German youth at the time, see chapter 5 in Robert Eden, *Political Leadership and Nihilism* (Gainesville: University Presses of Florida, 1983), pp. 134–73.

169. Weber, "Science as a Vocation," p. 156.

170. Weber, "Politics as a Vocation," p. 128.

CHAPTER FIVE
HANNAH ARENDT AND LEO STRAUSS

1. I am simply referring to the ideals of the *bios politikos* and the *bios theoretikos*. Of course, Arendt and Strauss were hardly "traditionalists" in the usual sense of

the word, and both devoted a good deal of thought and ink to illuminating why any "recovery" of traditional ideals in the current epoch would also necessitate their reinvention. See, in this regard, Arendt's preface to *Between Past and Future* (New York: Penguin, 1968), pp. 3–15, as well as her essay "Tradition and the Modern Age" in the same volume. The theme of the "break in the tradition" is common to both, as I shall argue.

2. Of course, there are significant differences between these two works, which are both centrally concerned with the public realm and the nature of political action. *On Revolution* addresses political action in the modern age, specifically the initiatory action manifest in the revolutionary founding of new forms of government. It differs chiefly from *The Human Condition* not because Arendt abandons the model of the polis, but rather because she focuses so intently on the constitution of a new public realm made possible by human promising and agreement. This is a new and distinctly modern phenomenon, one unknown to the Greeks.

3. The origins of this particular either/or go back, of course, to Plato's *Protagoras*.

4. See, for example, Aristotle, *The Politics*, 1253a7; cf. Arendt, *The Human Condition* (Chicago: University of Chicago Press, 1958), p. 176, hereafter cited as *HC*.

5. Arendt, *HC*, p. 176. For a critical view of this stance, see Hauke Brunkhorst, "Equality and Elitism in Hannah Arendt," in *The Cambridge Companion to Hannah Arendt*, ed. Dana Villa (Cambridge: Cambridge University Press, 2000).

6. Ibid.

7. See Hannah Arendt, *On Revolution* (New York: Penguin, 1968), pp. 32–33; hereafter cited as *OR*.

8. See Aristotle, *Nicomachean Ethics*, bks. 10; cf. Arendt, *HC*, esp. the third and fifth chapters.

9. For the *locus classicus*, see Adam Smith, *The Wealth of Nations* (New York: Random House, 1994), p. 315. In *The Human Condition*, Arendt cites Smith and Karl Marx as *the* thinkers of modernity who "invert" the hierarchy of activities which make up the *vita activa*, or active life: labor, work, and action.

10. I deal with the issue of public self-fashioning at length in the chapter "Theatricality and the Public Realm," in my *Politics, Philosophy, Terror: Essays on the Thought of Hannah Arendt* (Princeton: Princeton University Press, 1999), pp. 128–54.

11. For Arendt's discussion of "principles" as the inspiration of free political action, see her essay "What Is Freedom?," in Arendt, *Between Past and Future*, pp. 152–53; hereafter cited as *BPF*. For her discussion of the role of masks and personae in the creation of a public self, see Arendt, *OR*, pp. 106–8.

12. Arendt, *HC*, pp. 179–80.

13. For the indebtedness of this conception to Heidegger's position in *Being and Time*, see my discussion in chapter 4 of *Arendt and Heidegger: The Fate of the Political* (Princeton: Princeton University Press, 1996), pp. 113–43.

14. Arendt, *HC*, p. 57. cf. p. 199.

15. Ibid., p. 58.

16. On this point, see Margaret Canovan's essay "Politics as Culture: Hannah Arendt and the Public Realm," *History of Political Thought* 6, no. 3 (1985), 617–42.

17. Arendt, "The Crisis in Culture," in *BPF*, p. 214. Rex Warner's English translation of these lines runs: "Our love of what is beautiful does not lead to extravagance; our love of things of the mind does not make us soft" Thucydides, *History of the Peloponnesian War* (New York: Penguin, 1972), 40.

18. Thucydides, *History*, 40.

19. See my discussion of Pericles' "monumental aestheticism" in chapter 1 of this study, as well as my essay "Arendt and Socrates," *Revue Internationale de Philosophie*, no. 206 (June 1999), 241–57.

20. Arendt, *HC*, p. 205.

21. See, for example, Seyla Benhabib, *The Reluctant Modernism of Hannah Arendt* (Thousand Oaks, Ca.: Sage, 1996), pp. 123–30; Maurizio Passerin d'Entrèves, *The Political Philosophy of Hannah Arendt* (New York: Routledge, 1994), pp. 83–85.

22. For these distinctions, see her essay "On Violence," in Arendt, *CR*, pp. 143–146.

23. Arendt, *HC*, p. 229.

24. See my essay "Theatricality and the Public Realm."

25. Mill, review of Grote's *History of Greece*, in Mill, *Collected Works* vol. 11, p. 324.

26. See chapter 7 of Munn, *The School of History: Athens in the Age of Socrates* (Berkeley: University of California Press, 2000) pp. 175–94. Both Mark Munn and Peter Euben (*The Tragedy of Political Theory: The Road Not Taken* [Princeton: Princeton University Press, 1990]) point out how the public performance of tragedy held up a critical mirror to Athenian political practice. This fact, however, does not detract from my main point, which is that it is the nature of an agonistic or deliberative public sphere to set rather firm limits to moral reflection.

27. For the truly remarkable extent to which the prospects of Athenian democracy were tied up with Alcibiades' quest for individual greatness, see chapters 4–7 of Munn, *The School of History*.

28. Arendt, *OR*, p. 229.

29. Plato, *Gorgias*, 485b.

30. See Jeremy Waldron, "Arendt's Constitutional Politics," in *The Cambridge Companion to Hannah Arendt*, pp. 201–19. Waldron argues that there is a substantial divide between Arendt's "Greek" model and the "constitutional politics" of *On Revolution*. There is certainly more than a little truth to this claim; however, one can doubt whether this difference signifies as much as Waldron would like, particularly from the standpoint of philosophical citizenship.

31. See chaper 4 of Arendt, *OR*.

32. Arendt, *OR*, pp. 130–31.

33. Ibid., p. 135.

34. Ibid., pp. 136–39.

35. Ibid., p. 269.

36. This essay originally formed part of a lecture series she gave at Notre Dame University entitled "The Problem of Thought and Action after the French Revolution."

37. Arendt, "Philosophy and Politics," p. 73.

38. This, of course, is the essential theme of Plato's *Republic*.

39. Arendt, "Philosophy and Politics," p. 80.

40. Ibid., p. 81.

41. Ibid (my emphasis).

42. Ibid., p. 82.

43. Ibid., p. 87.

44. Ibid., p. 85.

45. It is noteworthy that Arendt, the political thinker, should make this claim, while the philosopher Stuart Hampshire should take the opposite approach, reading our intellectual virtues as internalizations of social practices. See his *Justice as Conflict* (Princeton: Princeton University Press, 1999).

46. Arendt, "Philosophy and Politics," p. 89.

47. Arendt, "Civil Disobedience" in Arendt, *Crises of the Republic* (New York: Harcourt, Brace, Jovanovich, 1972), pp. 63–64.

48. Arendt, "Thinking and Moral Considerations," *Social Research* 51, no. 1–2 (Spring-Summer 1984), 8.

49. Ibid., p. 17.

50. Ibid., pp. 17–18.

51. Ibid., pp. 22–23.

52. Ibid., p. 23.

53. Ibid. The Plato reference is to *Sophist* 258.

54. For Arendt's typical usage, see *On Revolution*, p. 227.

55. Arendt, "Thinking and Moral Considerations," pp. 23–24.

56. Ibid., p. 24.

57. Ibid.

58. Ibid., p. 25.

59. Ibid., p. 26.

60. Ibid., p. 25. For the extended formulation of this point, see Arendt, "Tradition and the Modern Age" in Arendt, *Between Past and Future*, pp. 17–40.

61. Arendt, "Thinking and Moral Considerations," p. 26.

62. Ibid., p. 27.

63. Callicles is the spokesman for the former thesis, Thrasymachus for the latter.

64. Arendt, "Thinking and Moral Considerations," p. 35.

65. Ibid.

66. Arendt, "Philosophy and Politics," p. 88.

67. The parallel with Heidegger's *Being and Time* is all too clear.

68. Arendt, "Thinking and Moral Considerations," p. 36 (my emphasis).

69. Ibid.

70. Ibid. One is reminded here of Arendt's earlier description of ideological "thinking" in the essay "Ideology and Terror," which became the last chapter of later editions of *The Origins of Totalitarianism*. She located the nerve center of ideology in the tyranny of logicality, that is, in the insistence that all judgment could be reduced to the simple operation of subsuming diverse particulars under a few incessantly invoked universals. Hence, world history could be subsumed under the idea of class struggle (Marxism), or a Darwinian struggle among the races for hegemony (National Socialism). *All* facts could be made to fit such highly elastic schema, and this is precisely what the totalitarians did with their privileging of ideological fictions.

71. Arendt, "Thinking and Moral Considerations," p. 37.

72. Ibid., p. 36 (my emphasis).

73. Arendt, "Truth and Politics" in *Between Past and Future*, p. 241.

74. Nietzsche, "*On the Genealogy of Morals*" and "*ECCE Homo,*" trans. Walter Kaufmann (New York: Vintage, 1989), essay 3, sec. 12.

75. Hannah Arendt, preface to *Men in Dark Times* (New York: Harcourt, Brace & World, 1968), p. ix.

76. See, for example, Arendt, *HC*, p. 58.

77. On the importance of distance to judgment, see Arendt, *Lectures on Kant's Political Philosophy* (Chicago: University of Chicago Press, 1982), pp. 54–55.

78. For a critical reading of Arendt on this score, see George Kateb, "The Judgment of Arendt" *Revue Internationale de Philosophie*, no. 208 (June 1999), 133–54.

79. For an analysis of how Arendt reads the tradition on this score, see my discussion in *Arendt and Heidegger*, pp. 86–87.

80. See my discussion in chapter 3 of this study.

81. Arendt, *Lectures on Kant's Political Philosophy*, p. 75. Admittedly, Arendt is glossing Kant here. Her next sentence reads: "But in the last analysis, one is a member of a world community by the sheer fact of being human; that is one's 'cosmopolitan existence.' " This nod to Kantian universalism should not distract us from the fact that it is the previous sentence which best captures Arendt's own sense of the relation between judgment and "communitysense," a relation clearly expressed in the effort of the Kant lectures to read moral and political judgments as judgments of *taste*.

82. See Michael Ignatieff, "The Myth of Citizenship," in *Theorizing Citizenship*, ed. R. Beiner (Albany: State University of New York Press, 1995), pp. 53–78.

83. See Arendt, "Philosophy and Politics," pp. 96–103.

84. Leo Strauss, "On Aristotle's Politics," *The City and Man* (Chicago: University of Chicago Press, 1964), pp. 20–21, hereafter cited as *CM*.

85. Arendt, *HC*, p. 20. For the import of the *physis/nomos* distinction, see Leo Strauss, "Natural Right and the Historical Approach" in *Natural Right and History* (Chicago: University of Chicago Press, 1953), hereafter cited as *NRH*.

86. Strauss, "On Aristotle's Politics," pp. 20, 29.

87. Ibid.

88. Strauss, "Classic Natural Right," p. 124.

89. Strauss, *"What Is Political Philosophy?"* and Other Studies (Chicago: University of Chicago Press, 1988), pp. 11–12 (my emphasis); hereafter cited as *WIPP*. Cf., however, the formulation Strauss gives in *NRH*, p. 162. I discuss this contrast later in this chapter.

90. Strauss, "What Is Political Philosophy?," *WIPP*, p. 12.

91. Strauss, "On Classical Political Philosophy," in *WIPP*, pp. 84, 81.

92. Strauss, "What Is Political Philosophy?," pp. 15–16.

93. Ibid., p. 17.

94. Strauss, "Introduction," *CM*, p. 3; cf. Nietzsche, *The Will to Power*, bk. 1, sec. 2. Of course, Strauss does not agree with Nietzsche as to *why* the highest values "devaluate themselves," nor does he share Nietzsche's sense that the only way out is to create new, post-Christian, postrationalist values. On the contrary, for Strauss the solution to the nihilistic loss of purpose and goal is a return to the forgotten wisdom of Nietzsche's great enemies: Socrates and Plato. For the Nietzsche/Strauss connection, see Lawrence Lampert, *Leo Strauss and Friedrich Nietzsche* (Chicago: University of Chicago Press, 1997).

95. See "Natural Right and the Distinction Between Facts and Values," *NRH*, also "What Is Political Philosophy?," where he states that Weber "postulated the insolubility of all [*sic*] value conflicts, because his soul craved a universe in which failure, that bastard of forceful sinning accompanied by still more forceful faith . . . was to be the mark of human nobility" (p. 23).

96. In his "edifying" mode, however, he often pretends otherwise. See, for example, *NRH*, p. 29, where he criticizes historicism by stating that as a doctrine it "stands or falls by the denial of the solubility of the fundamental riddles" (p. 29). Natural rights doctrines, conversely, "claim that the fundamentals of justice are, in principle, accessible to man as man" (p. 28). Natural right, thus understood, eschews Socrates' epistemological modesty and claims *wisdom* of the most fundamental things.

97. Strauss, "What Is Political Philosophy?," pp. 26–27. Cf. Strauss, "Natural Right and the Historical Approach," pp. 26–32.

98. Strauss, "What Is Political Philosophy?," p. 27.

99. Strauss, p. 11.

100. Strauss, "Natural Right and the Historical Approach," p. 12.

101. Leo Strauss, "An Introduction to Heideggerian Existentialism," in Strauss, *The Rebirth of Classical Political Rationalism*, ed. Thomas L. Pangle (Chicago: University of Chicago Press, 1989), p. 37; hereafter cited as *RCPR*.

102. Cf. Strauss, "Introduction," *CM*: "We cannot reasonably expect that a fresh understanding of classical political philosophy will supply us with recipes for today's use" (p. 11).

103. As chapter 3 of *NRH* makes clear, it is not that Strauss utterly disowned the "dissolvent" character of reason, whether in its Socratic or other forms. It is the nature of philosophy to undercut the traditional, the ancestral, the local—in short,

to dissolve the moral horizons of traditional forms of life. Yet Strauss would like to prevent reason from becoming its own target, from undergoing the "dialectic of enlightenment" which reveals the pretensions of substantive rationality to be baseless. He would evidently like to put certain "discoveries" of reason beyond question—at least for "the many." (See my discussion toward the end of this chapter.)

104. See Hannah Arendt, "What Is Authority?" in Arendt, *Between Past and Future*, esp. pp. 104–15.

105. Hannah Arendt, introduction to *The Life of the Mind* (New York: Harcourt Brace Jovanovich, 1977), p. 10.

106. Ibid. Cf. Strauss, "Introduction," *CM*, p. 9.

107. Hannah Arendt, "The Concern for Politics in Recent European Philosophy," in Arendt, *Essays in Understanding, 1930–1954*, ed. Jerome Kohn (New York: Harcourt Brace, 1994), pp. 432–33.

108. Ibid.

109. Strauss, "On Collingwood's Philosophy of History," quoted by Jürgen Gebhardt in "Leo Strauss: The Quest for Truth," in *Hannah Arendt and Leo Strauss: German Emigrés and American Political Thought After World War II*, ed. Peter G. Kielmansegg, Horst Mewes, and Elisabeth Glaser-Schmidt (New York: Cambridge University Press, 1995), p. 100.

110. Strauss, "Introduction," *CM*, pp. 11–12.

111. Strauss, "Classic Natural Right," p. 124.

112. Strauss, pp. 119–20; "Classic Natural Right," pp. 122–23. See Thomas Pangle's remarks on Strauss's "new interpretation of the Ideas" in his Introduction to Leo Strauss, *Studies in Platonic Political Philosophy* (Chicago: University of Chicago Press, 1983), pp. 2–5. Emphasizing Strauss's incredulity at the notion that Plato's ideas are "self-subsisting, being at home as it were in an entirely different place from human beings" (p. 119), Pangle argues that Strauss nevertheless took the ideas seriously "insofar as it appears to provide a sound way of converting our experience of the nature of things." So viewed, the doctrine of ideas is merely the extension of the logic of the "class character" presumed by Socrates' "what is?" questions. It expresses the attempt of Socratic dialectic to "ascend from the many local and temporary particulars to their universal and lasting (transhistorical, though not necessarily eternal) class characteristics. . . ." (p. 3). Cf. Arendt's interpretation of the ideas in her essay "What Is Authority?" in Arendt, *BPF*, pp. 104–15.

113. See Strauss, "The Crisis of Modern Natural Right,"*NRH*, pp. 295–323.

114. Arendt, "What Is Authority," pp. 116–20.

115. Strauss, "What Is Political Philosophy?" p. 34. Here Strauss defines "regime" in terms of the dominance of one particular type of character (for example, democratic, aristocratic, tyrannical) and describes classical political philosophy as the quest for the best regime—a quest which has been given up by the moderns. The notion that political society is, first and foremost, a "school" for virtue or character is readily apparent in "Liberal Education and Responsibility," in Strauss, *Liberalism Ancient and Modern* (Chicago: University of Chicago Press, 1995), pp. 20–21 (here-

after cited as *LAM*), and in his essays on Aristotle and Plato in *CM* (see esp. pp. 25–27, 33–34, 38–41). See also Strauss, "Classic Natural Right," pp. 153–56.

116. Strauss, pp. 139, 150–54.

117. Strauss, p. 152; p. 51.

118. Strauss, "The Problem of Socrates," p. 154; "Liberal Education and Responsibility," pp. 6–7; *Studies in Platonic Political Philosophy*, p. 47; "On Plato's Republic," pp. 53–54. Strauss views Socrates' statement in the *Apology*—that he converses with everyone, regardless of class, sex, or social position—as an obvious rhetorical strategy which plays to the *demos*, one deployed in the context of his trial for "corrupting the youth." See "On Plato's Republic," p. 57. The contrast with Vlastos's position (see chapter 1 of this study) is clear.

119. Strauss, "The Problem of Socrates," p. 163. For the relation between civic and *genuine* (philosophical) virtue, see p. 133. See also pp. 25–28, and "Classic Natural Right," pp. 138–43. For the relation between the virtue of the gentleman and that of the "vulgar," see "Liberal Education and Responsibility," pp. 11–14, 16.

120. Strauss, "Liberal Education and Responsibility," pp. 13–14. See also the discussion of "citizen morality" in "Classic Natural Right," pp. 149–51, which makes clear why the *hoi polloi* must be fed a careful diet of "noble lies" if they are to fulfill the duties (such as military self-sacrifice) the polity demands of them.

121. Strauss, "Liberal Education and Responsibility," p. 14. See Ronald Beiner's discussion in "Hannah Arendt and Leo Strauss: The Uncommenced Dialogue," *Political Theory* 18, no. 2 (1990): 247–49.

122. It is precisely such an inversion that Strauss sees *modern* political philosophy and practice as performing. See chapters 5 and 6 in *NRH*.

123. Stephen Holmes, "Strauss: Truths for Philosophers Alone," in Holmes, *The Anatomy of Antiliberalism* (Cambridge, Mass.: Harvard University Press, 1993), pp. 61–87.

124. Ibid., pp. 68–71.

125. Strauss, p. 20. Cf. "What Is Political Philosophy?," p. 11. See Steven B. Smith's illuminating essay "*Destruktion* or Recovery? Leo Strauss's Critique of Heidegger," *Review of Metaphysics* 51, no. 2 (1997): 345–77. Smith makes a powerful argument for what I call the "skeptical" Strauss.

126. See Strauss, "Crisis of Modern Natural Right," pp. 270, 278. Cf. "Liberal Education and Responsibility," p. 14.

127. See Strauss, "Crisis of Modern Natural Right," pp. 284–85, where he warns of the possibility—indeed the likelihood—that the "natural-right teacher" will identify natural right with "those notions of justice that are cherished by his own society." Cf. the obviously more "pious" statements found in the Introduction to the same work (notably p. 5): "The contemporary rejection of natural right leads to nihilism—nay, it is identical with nihilism." With regard to historicism's encouragement of the reduction of morality to local convention, see *WIPP*, p. 71.

128. See, in this regard, the chapter on Burke in *NRH*, pp. 294–311.

129. Strauss, p. 127; "The Problem of Socrates," pp. 160, 162.

130. One could say that the most perverse part of Strauss is his seeming endorsement of the Platonic version of such a morality. See *CM*, pp. 94–96.

131. It should be noted that Strauss has an unfortunate tendency to intimate that such open-endedness is a function of Socrates' "irony," which he interprets as the attempt to dissimulate his wisdom from his inferiors. See, pp. 51–53.

132. Strauss, "The Problem of Socrates," p. 171; pp. 54–55; "Introduction," *NRH*, pp. 1–2; "Liberal Education and Responsibility," pp. 16–17. See Holmes's discussion in *Anatomy of Antiliberalism*, pp. 63–66. Cf. Arendt, *Lectures on Kant's Political Philosophy*, pp. 35–36.

133. Strauss, "Classic Natural Right," p. 143; "On Aristotle's Politics," p. 37. Cf. Plato, *Republic*, 493b–494a.

134. See Strauss, "The Problem of Socrates," p. 161. Cf. Plato, *Republic*, 592b. In this regard, Strauss's claim that philosophical knowledge of "natural right" needs to be "diluted" by popular consent before it is applied in a political setting ("Classic Natural Right," p. 152) significantly understates the case.

135. Strauss, "On Plato's Republic," p. 127. Strauss here is referring to the "just city" of Plato's *Republic*, which he describes as "impossible" and "against nature." He makes a point, however, of stating that the "best regime" is "according to nature" and "possible on earth," although "extremely improbable" ("Classic Natural Right," p. 139). I would suggest that the implied distinction here—between the perfectly just city and the "best regime"—ultimately makes little difference from the point of view of practical politics once Strauss's various qualifications concerning the feasibility of the latter are taken into account.

136. Strauss, "Classic Natural Right," p. 162.

137. Ibid., p. 163 (my emphasis). I am grateful to George Kateb for underscoring the importance of this passage to me.

138. Strauss's defenders would no doubt say that he is merely questioning the inflexibility of Thomistic natural law in certain (extraordinary) situations, where force and fraud are necessary. He is not commending force and fraud as standard operating procedure (as Machiavelli supposedly does). See "Classic Natural Right," p. 160, where he refers to "extreme situations" which call for altering "the normally valid rules of natural right," as well as his insistence that the statesman "in the Aristotelian sense . . . reluctantly deviates from what is normally right." Yet Strauss moves from exception to broad generalization, namely, "There is a universally valid hierarchy of ends, but there are no universally valid rules of action" (both p. 162). Even when duly qualified, Strauss's basic stance (like Plato's in the *Statesman* or Carl Schmitt's) denigrates the limits imposed by constitutional law and ordinary morality, and gives enormous, virtually unrestricted prerogative to the "statesman."

139. For Strauss's summary of why the classics were not egalitarians, see "Classic Natural Right," pp. 134–35. Since Strauss fully shares the perfectionism of Plato and Aristotle, as well as their view that "not all men are naturally equipped by nature for progress towards perfection," there can be little doubt that he saw no *intrinsic* moral worth to the doctrine of rights-based individualism that underlies

353

modern liberalism. His various qualified statements of support of this "regime" as the best or most practical, given the circumstances, are another matter.

140. Thus, in "Liberal Education and Responsibility"—in many respects his response to Weber's "Vocation" lectures—Strauss states that "our present predicament appears to be caused by the decay of religious education of the people and the decay of liberal education of the representatives of the people" (*LAM*, p. 18).

141. This seems yet another point on which Strauss simply accepted Plato's doctrine in the *Republic*.

142. Strauss, "On Aristotle's Politics," p. 38.

143. See Aristotle, *Politics*, 1277b33.

144. Strauss, "On Aristotle's Politics," pp. 45–47.

145. Strauss, "Liberal Education and Responsibility," p. 5.

146. See, for example, his criticism of Hobbes's "lowering" of the standard of virtue in "Modern Natural Right," p. 187.

147. See Strauss, "On Artisotle's Politics," p. 27.

148. Strauss, "Classic Natural Right," p. 151.

149. See the discussion in Strauss, "On Artisotle's Politics,"pp. 28–29.

150. Strauss, "What Is Political Philosophy?," p. 35.

151. Strauss, "Liberal Education and Responsibility," p. 8

152. See Arendt, *On Revolution*, p. 281.

153. Strauss, "Classic Natural Right," p. 149.

154. Strauss, "On Artisotle's Politics," p. 22.

155. Ibid., p. 39.

156. Strauss is a master at showing how every critique of "dogmatic metaphysics" converts itself into a new dogma. See esp. chap. 1–2 of *NRH*.

157. Strauss, "What Is Political Philosophy?," p. 12. Cf. Strauss, "Introduction," *NRH*, pp. 1–2.

158. Strauss, "Introduction," *NRH*, p. 6.

159. See Strauss's critique of Weber in chapter 2 of *NRH* and his critique of Berlin in "Relativism," in *RCPR*, pp. 13–18.

160. John Rawls, *Political Liberalism* (New York: Columbia University Press, 1993), pp. xxiv–xxv.

161. See, for example, Strauss's idea of the "regime" in "What Is Political Philosophy?," p. 34.

Index

"absolute ethic of the Gospel," 225–26
abstentionist morality, 128, 181, 231
action: Antigone's usurpation of manly,
319n.129; Arendt's rescue from devaluation of political, 278–79; breaking harmony of thought and, 30; comparing
Antigone with Socratic, 51–52; conscience
saying no to, 270–71; danger of applying
private to public, 225; estrangement of
thought and political, 6, 14, 302; harmony between thinking and, 296; Hegel's
maxim of, 338n.157; Mill on stimulating,
99; political "dirty hands," 43; political
vs. moral, 39; self-protection motive for
liberty, 75–76; social movements and political, 259; statesmanship and unjust,
230–31; taking responsibility for political,
227–29; Thoreau's conception of, 54–56;
value found in utility, 173; virtue of abstention from, 142; Weber's definition of
political, 206, 221. *See also* dissent;
speech/deed integration; thinking/
thought
active character, 107–8
Aesthetics (Hegel), 52
agonistic politics, 275–76, 306, 347n.26
Alcibiades, 12, 220, 268
alienation: "new infinite" born of, 170–71;
Nietzsche on philosophical, 126–27, 131
American character, 119–20
American Constitution, 255, 257–58
American Political Science Association, 293
The Anti-Christ (Nietzsche), 151, 153
Antigone (*Antigone* character): as disobedience model, 6; political values of, 51,
319n.128; as usurping manly action,
319n.129
Antigone (Sophocles): civil disobedience
model of, 43; Socratic disobedience vs.
model of, 50–52

Antrittsrede (Weber), 203
Anytus, 16, 43
Apology (Plato): appeal to inner voice/con-
science in, 41; Athenian democracy presented in, 13–30; comparing *Crito* to,
243–44, 318n.123; depiction of Socrates
in, 1; disobedience conflict of *Crito* and,
44–46; rational conscience articulated in,
40–41; Socrates' defense of self in, 221–
22; "stinging fly" simile of, 3, 20, 165; on
universal potential of thinking citizen,
299; Weber's "Vocation" lectures as response to, 125–26, 191, 194, 213, 215
Arendt, Hannah: adaptation of perspectivism by, 252–53, 255–56, 274–75; applying
Socratic thinking to evil-doing, 21–23,
259–70; on civil disobedience/conscience,
52, 53–54; comparing Mill to, 276–77;
comparing Strauss to, 283–86, 287–89;
comparing Weber to Strauss and, 247–
49; influence of Socratic ideal on, 59,
126; inspired by political action, 57; on
nature of conscience, 270–72; on philosophic citizenship, 295–98; on philoso-
phy/politics gap, 14; on politics/philoso-
phy gulf, 14, 259–61, 278–79; promotes
return to traditional values, 247; rescue of
political action from devaluation, 278–79;
response to "death of God," 283; Socrates as depicted by, 262–63, 264–65, 277–
78; on Socratic philosophical activity, 19,
20; on Socratic rationality, 2–3; on Socratic thinking, 38, 39; on vulnerability
due to conventionalism, 269–70
arete (virtue). *See* virtue
aristocratic radicalism, 329n.4
aristocratic values: association of good with,
139–43; attack against dogmatic conduct
based on, 160; created for institutions, 154,
184; enhancement of man through, 146; superiority of, 145–47, 152. *See also* elites

Aristotle: approval of coercive virtue, 316n.89; citizenship as defined by, 321n.33; defense of "good" slavery by, 146; good man vs. good citizen of, 45; influence on Strauss by, 291–92; practical wisdom of, 1

"art of living" doctrine, 312n.12

ascetic priest figure: described, 138–39; Socrates viewed as, 139, 143–44

Athenian citizenship: debate and decision process of, 7; *Gorgias* criticisms of, 15; nature of, 251; offered in Socrates' *Apology*, 13–30; Periclean civic greatness of, 10–12; practiced by Socrates, 5. See also citizenship

Athens: comparing 19th century England to, 100; contributions to Western culture by, 323n.67; democratic institutions of, 329n.169; Pericles on beauty of, 255; repudiation of speech/public debate in, 312n.24; Socrates' preference for, 49–50. See also Laws of Athens

authority: boundaries of private/public, 106–7; civic participation balanced by, 119; contributions of dissent against, 85–99; discredited philosophical, 235; justifying coerced obedience to, 312n.24; meaning equated with, 234; morality as obedience to, 134–39; of natural vs. transitional ages, 64–65; neutrality of public, 307; *Ordnungsmensch* adherence to, 213–14; Platonic dialogues on decline in, 64; public opinion as form of, 71–72; secularization and crisis of, 283; Socratic dissent against unjust, 25–27, 41; Socratic refusal to dissent against, 42; of specialized knowledge, 117; Strauss on reason as, 295; struggle between liberty and, 76; unquestioned creed as false, 238

Autobiography (Mill), 75

avoidance of injustice: disobedience and, 46–51; greatness through, 40; as moral life basic, 106; self-agreement and, 41; Socrates on, 24–26, 27–28; Weber rejection of, 227. See also justice

bad conscience, 231, 332nn. 41, 43

Bäumer, Gertrud, 200

Bentham, Jeremy, 60, 74, 89

Berlin, Isaiah, 90, 92, 97, 224, 297, 306

best/good life, 97–98, 250, 296–97, 325n.97

"Between Two Laws" (Weber), 200

Beyond Good and Evil (Nietzsche): on authentic conscience, 159; as critique of democratic/demotic culture, 149–51; *elenchus* radicalized in, 171; on greatness, 162–63; on herd animal morality, 130–36, 144–45; on philosophers of the future, 146, 153–55, 161–62, 179; revaluation of values called for by, 151; on superiority of aristocratic values, 145–47, 152; on will, 178–79

bios politikos, 6

bios theoretikos, 6

The Birth of Tragedy (Nietzsche), 144, 183

Bismarck, Otto von, 197–98

Bloch, Ernst, 189

bourgeois/working class struggle, 197–99. See also politics of struggle

Brickhouse, Thomas, 44, 45

Burckhardt, Jacob, 10, 104

bureaucracy: English Parliament authority over, 204; Weber on freedom in age of, 217–18; Weber on nature of, 193–94, 339n.4

Burke, Edmond, 287

Callicles, 16, 32, 33, 34, 35, 39, 52, 222, 223, 226

calling (*Beruf*): of politics, 213, 215, 217–19, 222, 226, 230; of science, 232–33, 240

"care for one's soul," 222–23, 305

Carlyle, Thomas, 104

cave parable (*The Republic*), 171, 282

Chaerephon, 18

character: aesthetics of, 101–2; elements of active, 107–8; impact of institutions on U.S., 119–20; political economy from population, 196; of sovereign individual, 176–77; Weber on political leader, 218, 230–31. See also moral integrity

charismatic leader, 188, 205, 231–32, 241

Charmides, 13

Christ. *See* Jesus Christ

Christianity: as breeding morality, 153; conversion of truth in, 88–89; democracy as heir to, 132, 149, 176; Nietzsche indictment of, 130–32, 156; as partial truth, 96; politics/ethics relationship under, 224; as successful creed, 323n.65. *See also* Jesus Christ

Cimon, 15

citizens: Arendt on Socrates as great, 264–65; best life for, 250, 296–97; civic involvement benefits to, 108–9; deferring to elite, 122–23; duty to justice by, 47–56, 95–96; failure of statesmen to improve, 36, 37–38; government role in promoting virtue in, 100; humanity of politically equal, 249–50; inability of free spirit to be, 171–72; injustice responsibility of state vs., 318n.111; "joiner," 300–302; Laws-as-parents to, 47–48; shared political faith/values of, 56–57; standard for responsible, 257; thinking/acting conflict of, 296; universal potential of thinking, 299; Weber on intellectual proletarianization of, 231–32; Weber's indifference to ethics of, 188–89

citizenship: Arendt on life benefits of, 253–54; Arendt's conception of, 249–50; Aristotelian definition of, 186; Aristotle's definition of, 321n.33; comparison of Funeral Oration and Socratic, 11–12; debate over Western, 1; engaged, 300–302; exclusion of working class from, 70; Mill on individuality and, 99–115; need for virtue in, 56–57; Nietzsche on philosophers and, 126, 185; Nietzsche's rejection of philosophical, 129, 130–31; Platonic conception of, 148, 149; *Representative Government* concept of, 97; Socrates on dissident, 41–56, 73–74; unexamined state of, 305–6; *via negativa* and, 56–58. *See also* Athenian citizenship; philosophical citizenship; Socratic citizenship

civic greatness (Periclean), 10–12

civic involvement. *See* political participation

civic virtue vision, 56–57. *See also* virtue

Civil Disobedience (Arendt), 52, 264

civil disobedience models: avoiding injustice criterion of, 46–51; comparing *Antigone* to Socratic, 43, 50–52; comparing Thoreau and Socratic, 54–56; conflict of *Apology/Crito*, 44–46; *Crito*, 47–58; examination of alternative, 6. *See also* dissent

Cleon, 7, 12, 17

code of conduct. *See* moral integrity

Coleridge, Samuel Taylor, 61, 100, 103

common good: civic education promoting, 116; controversial nature of, 111; distinction between interests and, 116; opinion pluralism and, 277; Socratic use of, 279; Strauss on nature of, 111

commonsense: conscience manifestation over monstrous, 273; dogmatism of, 72–75; governing Greek life, 329n.163; knowledge of, 172–73; social class prejudices as, 79–80; Strauss on function of, 284

Comte, Auguste, 89, 91

"The Conditions of the Agricultural Workers in the East Elbian regions of Germany" (Weber), 194

conflict: ability to choose during, 301; *Crito* and *Apology* disobedience, 44–46; of disenchanted world values, 194–95; leading to liberty, 202; as part of social life, 201; Strauss on reason doing away with, 297; Weber on freedom gained through, 206–7; Weber on politics of struggle and, 187–88, 191–99, 216–17; Weber on social class, 197–99. *See also* violence

conformism, 253, 326n.112

"connected critic," 3, 307–8, 311n.7

conscience: Arendt on nature of, 270–72; emergency situations in society and, 272–73, 297; formal vs. authentic, 159; Nietzsche's intellectual, 135–39, 155, 158–59, 170; Protestantism privilege of, 120; reality of "bad," 231, 332nn. 41, 43; Socratic rational, 40–41, 52–54; solitude, thinking, citizenship and, 263–65; Thoreau's concept of, 55. *See also* "examined life" consensus, 342n.81

Considerations on Representative Government (Mill), 60, 61, 62, 65; authority vs. participation debate in, 118–24, 303; citizenship concept in, 97; tutorial state vision in, 107; virtues ascribed to groups in, 117–18

Constant, Benjamin, 306

Contribution to the Critique of Hegel's "Philosophy of Right" (Marx), 148

Corcyrean civil war, 7

creed: equality as false, 120; false authority of unquestioned, 238; morality presented as, 96; Nietzsche on paradigm of ethical, 96; thinking as dangerous to, 269. *See also* Christianity; dogma

Creon (*Antigone* character), 50–51

Critias, 13, 268

Critique of Pure Reason (Kant), 166, 186

Crito (Plato): comparing *Gorgias* and *Apology* to, 243–44; disobedience argument in, 47–58; disobedience conflict of *Apology* and, 44–46, 318n.123; on dissent, 42–43; Laws of Athens speech in, 48–49, 326n.117; "persuade or obey" formula of, 50, 52; on political obligation, 45–46

cross-examination (*elenchus*) method, 2, 3

cultural space, 154

culture: Arendt on politics as form of, 254; Athens' contribution to Western, 323n.67; based on illusion, 182–83; creating new values for, 184; "God is dead" reference to end of, 155, 156, 157, 185; impact of philosophers of the future on, 154–55; moral myth as sign of healthy, 286; morality as conceived by Western, 325n.95; Nietzsche's criticisms of democratic, 146–47, 149–51; Nietzsche's distinction of politics and, 148, 182; nihilism phenomenon and, 183–84, 190; secularization of Western, 192

Danto, Arthur, 172

Darwin, Charles, 154

Daybreak (Nietzsche), 134

Declaration of Independence, 258

deed. *See* action; speech/deed integration

democracy: dangers of marginalization in, 113–15; education in, 66, 69, 70–71; as heir to Christianity, 132, 149, 176; Mill's rational conception of, 67; Nietzsche's conception of modern, 144–45, 146, 148–50; Tocqueville's examination of, 65–66; tyranny of the majority in, 62, 67–68, 76–77, 113–15; values articulated by Pericles, 5; Weber on German, 201–3; Weber on political machine leadership in, 217–18

Democracy in America (Tocqueville), 65–66, 71, 300

democratic constitution, 244

democratic culture, 146–47

democratic imperialism credo, 34

demos: flattering of the, 27, 36; as immune to philosophy, 289; law against philosophizing the, 44; Mill on the, 117, 129; nature of Athenian, 251; paradox of civic education for, 119; rhetoric used on, 37; Weber's deemphasis on role of, 203

Derrida, Jacques, 282

dialectics, 280. *See also* philosophy

Diodotus, 17, 38

Discourses on The First Ten Books of Titus Livey (Machiavelli), 113, 202, 224

disenchantment. *See* ethos of disenchantment

disillusion, 175, 181, 183, 185, 229

dissent: against unjust authority, 25–27, 41; *Apology* on Socrates' political, 43–44; comparing *Antigone* to Socratic, 50–52; *Crito* on Socrates and, 42–43; Mill on institutionalization of, 63; moral truth revealed through, 78–99; pluralism revealed through, 62; Socrates' philosophical invention of, 41–56, 73–74. *See also* civil disobedience models

diversity of opinion, 88–91, 92–97. *See also* pluralism

dogma: of commonsense, 72–75; Strauss on conversion of, 354n.156; as threat to sovereign individual, 150. *See also* creed

doxa (opinion), 121, 260–61, 279, 280, 288. *See also* public opinion

Ehrenberg, Victor, 5

Eichmann, Adolf, 21–22, 23, 45, 265, 270, 315n.71

elenchus (cross-examination): Arendt on thinking as quality of, 273; connected criticism using, 307; Mill's praise of, 120–21, 325n.99; *On Liberty* (Mill) expansion of, 89–90, 303; reformulated into perspectivism, 128, 165–66, 171; skeptical intelligence fostered by, 117; Socratic use of, 2, 3, 18, 19, 34, 261, 267–68, 304

elites: average citizens deferring to, 122–23; balancing participation/authority of, 119–24; plural voting scheme protecting, 113–15, 118; superior civic education/participation by, 122–23. *See also* aristocratic values; social classes

Elliot, George, 155

"emergency situations," 272–73, 297

engaged citizenship, 300–302

England (19th century): comparing Athens to, 100; morality prejudice of, 102–3; working-class suffrage of, 70

Enlightenment, 84, 174, 189, 234

episteme, 121

equality: Arendt on freedom/humanity and, 249–50; as false creed, 120

ethic of responsibility (*Verantwortungsethik*), 189; See also responsibility

"ethic of ultimate ends," 228–29

ethical substance (*Sittlichkeit*), 57

ethics: Weber on "absolute ethic of the Gospel," 225–26; Weber/Machiavelli on politics and, 223–29. *See also* morality

ethos of disenchantment: abstentionist morality and, 128, 181, 231; comparing Weber and Socratic, 231; conflict of values in world of, 194–95; over parliamentary democracy, 204; over science/rationality, 209–11; scientific progress in age of, 233–34

ethos of disillusion, 175, 181, 183, 185, 229

Euben, Peter, 40, 317n.92

evil-doing: applying Socratic thinking to, 21–23, 265–70; failure of statesmen as,

37–38; *Gorgias* on injustice of, 32–33; political struggle against, 226; Thoreau's demand to abolish, 55–56

"examined life": irreconcilable with encumbered self, 23; Mill on value of, 75, 106; nature of authentic, 316n.77; Nietzsche's contributions to, 128, 157–59. *See also* conscience

Die Frau journal, 200

"free spirit" (intellectual honesty), 170–72, 175. *See also* intellectual integrity

freedom: Arendt on political equality linked to, 249–50; Arendt on public realm and, 247–48, 251–52, 256–59; Arendt on public vs. political, 258; distinction between moral and intellectual, 123–24; importance of dissent to protecting, 78–99; importance of institutions promoting, 69; lack of action as slave's, 142; Nietzsche on function of, 178–79; open discussion model promoting, 80–85, 92–93, 98–99; threatened by market self-interest, 69–70; Weber on bureaucracy and, 217–18; Weber on political struggle to gain, 206–7. *See also* liberty

"gadfly" simile, 3, 20, 165, 244, 261

The Gay Science (Nietzsche), 135, 155, 157, 158, 168–69, 177

The Genealogy of Morals (Nietzsche): on code of conduct, 10; on human being as animals, 176; on importance of historicity, 77; on morality of mores, 132–35; noble/non-noble good-evil couplet of, 139–43; on physical and psychic cruelty, 152; responsible and sovereign individuals, 133, 134

Germany: economic struggle for power in, 197–99; Goethian/Fichtean period of, 84; *Machtstaat* mentality of, 200–201; *Ordnungsmensch* of, 213–14; Weber on democratic, 201–3; Weber' influence on history of, 340n.44; Weber on peasants of, 195–96; Weber on political economy of, 194–95; Weber on post-war state of,

Germany (*Cont.*)
  199–201; Weber's promotion of political
  education in, 203–4, 206–7
Gettysburg Address (Lincoln), 8
"God is dead": Arendt response to, 283;
  Nietzsche's use of, 155, 156, 157, 185;
  Weber's use of, 212
Goethian/Fichtean period (Germany), 84
Goldman, Harvey, 215, 230, 240
Good Life, 97–98, 250, 296–97, 325n.97.
  See also life spheres
Gorgias (Plato): Athenian democracy criticisms in, 13; on caring for one's soul,
  222–23, 305; characterization of Socrates
  in, 5, 6, 31–32; comparing *Crito* to, 243–
  44; comparing rhetoric and philosophy,
  236; as dialogue on rhetoric, 32, 35–39;
  on harmony with conscience, 271; on
  moral knowledge, 15–16; on oligarchical
  idea, 243; on political artist, 28; on pursuit of philosophy, 34–36; rational conscience articulated by, 40–41; statesmanship claims in, 15, 27; transvaluation of
  values in, 32, 39–40
government: active character and, 107–8;
  bureaucracy controlled by parliamentary,
  204; Mill's early support of elite, 116–17;
  political talents recruited by parliamentary, 204–5; struggle for power in parliamentary, 205–6; virtue promoting role by,
  100. *See also* representative government;
  state
"The Greek State" (Nietzsche), 151
Grote, George, 46, 110, 121, 129, 251
The Groundwork of the Metaphysics of Morals
  (Kant), 152

Habermas, Jürgen, 180, 208, 342n.81
Hare, Thomas, 122
harmony: between thinking and action, 296;
  breaking apart of, 30; Periclean, 6–12;
  postwar ruin of societal, 6
Hegel, Georg, 3, 10, 15, 52, 92, 117, 186
Heidegger, Martin, 24, 104, 241, 275, 282,
  283, 284, 342n.94

herd mentality: morality of, 130–36, 144–
  45; Nietzsche on ascendance of, 168,
  337n.139; virtues tailored to, 146
heretical dissident: Mill on importance of,
  82–83, 84; Socrates and Jesus as, 81, 82,
  83. *See also* dissent
Herzen, Alexander, 345n.163
hierarchy of ends standard, 290
historicity (*Geschichtlichkeit*) [Heidegger],
  283, 284
History of Greece (Grote), 129, 251
History (Thucydides), 7, 8, 11, 14
Hobbes, Thomas, 1, 6, 42, 111, 293
Holmes, Stephen, 286
Human, All Too Human (Nietzsche), 126,
  146, 150, 178
The Human Condition (Arendt), 247–48,
  249–50, 251, 255–56, 274, 275, 279,
  346n.2
Hume, David, 74

ideological thinking, 349n.70
illusion: evidence of Weber's, 189–90, 208;
  Nietzsche on, 182–83; Weber on politics
  and, 229, 243–45, 247; Weber on science
  and, 234–35
imperialism: credo of, 34; Weber on, 194–
  95, 340n.44
"The 'Improvers' of Mankind" (Nietzsche),
  151
individual: freedom as function of disciplined, 178–79; Nietzsche's celebration
  of creative, 160–61, 335n.101;
  Nietzsche's responsible, 133. *See also* sovereign individual
individualism: Arendt on conditions for,
  251–52, 274; balance of civil involvement
  and, 9–10; Mill on citizenship and, 99–
  115; moral integrity and genuine, 177;
  Nietzsche on Socrates,' 163; Thoreau on
  conscientious, 54–56; "true political art"
  vs., 16. *See also* moral individualism
injustice: assumptions regarding, 316n.81;
  disobedience and avoidance of, 46–51;
  Gorgias on evil of, 32–33; greatness
  through avoiding, 40; impact of democratic constitution on, 244; moral life

through avoidance of, 106; natural justice doctrine and, 33–34; self-agreement to avoid, 41; Socratic avoidance of, 24–26, 27–28, 304; state vs. citizen as responsible for, 318n.111; statesmanship and actions of, 230–31, 244; Weber rejection of avoidance of, 227

institutions: Athenian democratic, 329n.169; dissent expressed through, 63; elements of legitimate, 108; impact on national character of U.S., 119–20; importance to freedom promoting, 69; replacing aristocratic for democratic, 154, 184

integrity. *See* intellectual integrity; moral integrity

intellect: Athenian democratic faith in, 7–8; Mill's emphasis on authority and, 117; Pericles on love of, 9–10; values created through, 160

intellectual conscience: illusions denounced through, 155; marginalization of, 302–3; Nietzsche's examination of, 158–59, 170; process toward, 136–39; of the sovereign individual, 135–36

intellectual integrity: attempts to separate from moral virtue, 302–3; as civic virtue, 309; connected to moral integrity, 159, 175, 180–81, 292–93, 295, 302–3; *hoi polloi* and, 294, 302; Nietzsche's definition of, 129; Socratic vision of universal, 302–3; Weber on duty of, 241–42

interest. *See* political interest; self-interest

Introduction to Metphysics? (Heidegger), 104

Irwin, Terence, 3

Ismene (*Antigone* character), 50

Jaspers, Karl, 190

Jefferson, Thomas, 258

Jesus Christ: as heretic dissident, 81, 82, 83; Mill on teachings of, 96; trial and condemnation of, 259. *See also* Christianity

"John Stuart Mill and the Ends of Life" (Berlin), 90

"joining" activities, 300–301. *See also* political action

judgment: hierarchy of ends standard for, 290; Mill on unavoidable, 320n.7;

Nietzsche on lack of self-knowledge and, 158–59; Nietzsche on power of, 179–80; thinking and liberation of, 288; tyranny of logicality regarding, 349n.70

justice: citizen duty to, 47–56, 95–96; doctrine of natural, 33–34. *See also* avoidance of injustice

Kant, Immanual, 31, 65, 95, 152, 170, 179, 236, 271, 331n.26

Kateb, George, 24

Kaufmann, Walter, 127

Kierkegaard, Søren, 3

"King Nomos," 121, 122, 123, 130, 329n.163

knowing/doing separation, 6, 14, 302. *See also* speech/deed integration

knowledge. *See* moral truth/knowledge; truth

Knox, John, 99

Kraut, Richard, 20, 24, 26, 45, 46, 47, 48, 90

Kuhn, Thomas, 82

lamb/bird of prey parable (Nietzsche), 140–41, 142

Laws of Athens: *Crito* speech on, 48–49, 326n.117; disobedience to, 46–51; either/or obedience choice and, 46–47; as parents to citizens, 47–48; Socrates' agreement with, 46. *See also* Athens

Laws-as-parents metaphor (*Crito*), 47–48

Lebensphilosphie rhetoric of life, 144

Lectures on Kant's Political Philosophy (Arendt), 277

Leon of Salamis, 26

Leonardo da Vinci, 234

liberty: conflicts within republic leading to, 202; importance of dissent to protecting, 78–99; struggle between authority and, 76; tyranny of the majority and, 62, 67–68, 76–77, 113–14. *See also* freedom

The Life of the Mind (Arendt), 283

life spheres: contributions of science to practical, 238–39; danger of denying pluralism of, 223–24; natural hierarchy of "good," 250; pursuit of happiness in,

life spheres (*cont.*)
257–58. *See also* Good Life; private life; public life
Locke, John, 1, 41
London and Westminster Review, 66
Lukács, Georg, 189
Lycon, 16

Machiavelli, Niccolò: citizen-soldier of, 1; comparing Weber to, 223–26; on unavoidable political sin, 43; values held by, 224; Weber's updating of, 188, 214
Machtstaat, 200–201
Mannheim, Karl, 117
Marx, Karl, 6
Mayflower Compact, 257
meaning: of action/will by political actor, 220; equated with authority, 234; given to scientific progress, 233–34; role of struggle in, 243
"The Meaning of 'Ethical Neutrality' in Sociology and Economics" (Weber), 201
mediocrity, 103–5
Meletus, 16
Melian Dialogue, 12
Meno, 19
Michels, Roberto, 204
Mill, James, 60
Mill, John Stuart: Berlin's essay on views of, 90; on citizenship and individualism, 99–115; comparing Arendt to, 276–77; comparing Nietzsche's themes and, 77, 150, 153, 154, 168, 169–70; comparing Rousseau's themes to, 109–11; comparing Socratic thought to, 99; on dogmatism of commonsense, 72–75; on *elenchus*, 89–90, 120–21, 303, 325n.99; focus on political education by, 70–71, 107–9, 130; influence of Socratic ideal on, 59–60; mediocrity argument posed by, 103–5; moral individualism commitment by, 60, 65, 101, 105–9, 115; open discussion model of, 80–85, 92–93, 98–99; philosophical beliefs of, 60–63; plural voting scheme supported by, 113–15, 118, 122; on political art of representative government, 115–

24; on political participation and social class, 70, 72–73, 129–30; on public opinion, 61–62, 68–69, 78–99, 320n.1, 324n.91; Socratic method described by, 325n.99; on transitional ages, 64–65; utilitarianism modifications by, 74–75
Miltiades, 15
minority representation, Mill's discussion on, 113–15
Montaigne, Michel de, 82
moral individualism: as existential possibility, 41; influence of Socratic, 59; *On Liberty* (Mill) commitment to, 60, 65, 101, 105–9, 115; political participation and progress of, 109; shared beliefs/convictions of, 57; Socrates' introduction of, 2; Thoreau's vision of, 54–55. *See also* individualism
moral integrity: based on self-agreement, 263; calling as form of, 213, 215, 217–19, 222, 226; as civic virtue, 309; consistency/steadfastness as part of, 226; genuine individuality linked to, 177; importance of multiple perspectivism to, 168; intellectual integrity and, 159, 175, 180–81, 292–93, 295, 302–3; Socratic vision of universal, 302–3; Weber on political actor's, 215, 216–17, 226–29. *See also* character
moral pluralism, 147
moral truth/knowledge: avoiding injustice as, 24–26, 27–28; diversity of opinion revelation of, 88–91; enlarged thought and, 95; *Gorgias* passage on, 15–16; perversion of, 77–78; positive vs. negative, 18; revealed through dissent, 78–99; science as serving, 232; shared by citizens, 56–57; Socratic, 3–4, 29–30. *See also* perspectival knowledge; truth
morality: abstentionist, 128, 181, 231; avoidance of injustice as basic to, 106; creed presentation of, 96; Nietzsche on herd mentality of, 130–36, 144–45; Nietzsche on breeding of, 151–54; Nietzsche on mores of, 132–35, 136, 332n.34; Nietzsche on slave, 140–41, 142–43, 147;

as obedience to authority, 134–39; political actors as experts on, 230–31, 244; prejudges of Victorian, 102–3; rational grounding for, 174; Supreme Goodness of, 96–97; Weber's indifference to citizen, 188–89; Western conception of, 325n.95. *See also* values; virtue
morality of abstention, 128
morality of mores, 132–35, 136
Mouffe, Chantal, 245
Mytilenian debate, 17

namos, 121
"narrow test," 24, 26–27, 39
"The Nation State and Economic Policy" (Weber), 194
nations: as carriers of ideals, 197; convinced of moral greatness, 317n.102; impact of class struggle on, 198–99; Weber on struggle between/within, 193–94, 196–97. *See also* state
natural justice doctrine, 33–34
natural morality, 15
natural right argument, 290–91, 352n.134
Natural Right and History (Strauss), 280, 282, 289
natural-right teacher, 352n.127
Nehamas, Alexander, 4, 184
"new infinite," 168–69, 170–71
Nicias, 12
Nietzsche, Friedrich: ascetic priest ideal type of, 138–39; attacks against Socrates by, 183, 185; call for revaluation of values by, 151, 155–61, 181, 184, 350n.94; on Christ, 82; compared to Socrates or Thoreau, 180; comparing Mill's themes to, 77, 150, 153, 154, 168, 169–70; comparing Strauss to, 294–95; on dogmatist's error on truth, 164–65, 183–85; *elenchus* adapted by, 128; endorsing multiple perspectival knowledge, 167–81; on ethical creed paradigm, 96; examining code of conducts, 10–11; "God is dead" statement by, 155, 156, 157, 185; on herd mentality, 130, 132–36, 145–46, 168, 337n.139; importance of language to,

173–74; indictment of Christianity by, 130–32, 156, 183–84; influence of Socratic ideal on, 59; intellectual integrity defined by, 129; inversion of theory/practice by, 6; lamb/bird of prey parable by, 140–41, 142; on morality of breeding, 151–54; on nature of morality, 130, 132–39, 332n.34; philosophy and political thought of, 330n.5, 334nn.79, 85; self-betrayal of, 184–85; uncovering the real, 127–29
nihilism phenomenon, 183–84, 190, 281, 282–83
noble types: aristocratic values of, 139–47, 152, 154, 160, 184; mixture of morality within, 175–76
non-noble bad value, 139–43
noncontradiction principle, 41
Nussbaum, Martha, 50

Oakeshott, Michael, 287
obedience: conscience development prevented by, 159–60; justification of coerced, 312n.24; morality through, 134–39
"Of Individuality" (Mill), 100, 101
"On the Duty of Civil Disobedience" (Thoreau), 54
On the Genealogy of Morals (Nietzsche), 126
On Liberty (Mill): on Calvinist virtues, 96; *elenchus* expansion in, 89–90, 303; intellectual progress model in, 61; moral individualism commitment in, 60, 65, 101, 105–9, 115; primary work of, 63, 74–76, 97; on private/public authority boundaries, 106–7; on public opinion and dissent, 61–62, 78–99, 320n.1; regarding liberty vs. authority struggle, 76; Socratic culture envisioned in, 124; on vulnerability due to conventionalism, 269
On Revolution (Arendt), 247–48, 255, 256–57, 264, 346n.2
"On the Utility and Liability of History for Life" (Nietzsche), 168
one-sidedness of opinion, 95–97
open discussion model (Mill), 80–85, 92–93, 98–99

opinion. *See* public opinion
Ordnungsmensch, 213–14
The Origins of Totalitarianism (Arendt), 275
Ortega y Gasset,, 104

Paris Commune, 257
"Parliament and Government in a Reconstructed Germany" (Weber), 191, 194,
   201–2, 203, 207
parliamentary government: bureaucracy
   controlled by, 204; political talents recruited by, 204–5; struggle for power
   within, 205–6
Peloponnesian War (432 B.C.), 4
Periclean civic greatness, 10–12
Periclean Funeral Oration: aesthetic monumentalism of, 6–12; historical significance
   of, 8–9; on nature of Athenian democracy, 251; on political debate/decision, 7;
   political values presented in, 5, 39; Socratic citizenship compared to vision of,
   11–12; on speech/deed integration, 8
Pericles: on beauty of Athens, 255; comparing Alcibiades and, 220; "false political
   art" by, 27; *Gorgias* criticisms of, 15; on
   ownership of self, 313n.33; political values presented by, 5; on public-spiritedness, 254; represented in Thucydides'
   History, 7; Socrates criticism of, 122
perspective knowledge: Arendt's adaptation
   of, 252–53, 255–56, 274–75; commonsense vs. mere, 172–73; communicative rationality of, 180; *elenchus* reformulated
   into, 128, 165–66, 171; importance of language to, 173–74; limitations of, 166–67;
   Nietzsche's endorsement of multiple,
   167–81; Nietzsche's opposition to, 164–
   65; as practiced by Nietzsche, 179–80.
   See also moral truth/knowledge
"persuade or obey" formula (*Crito*), 50, 52
Phaedo, 37
Phenomenology of Spirit (Hegel), 52
philosopher-citizens, 286
philosopher-kings, 153, 184, 246
philosophers: contribution to representative
   government by, 275–78; of the future,
146, 153–55, 161–63, 179; Socrates' activities as, 13–30, 73–74, 162; Socrates on
   duty of, 222; Strauss' defense of life of,
   126; Strauss on virtue of gentleman vs.,
   285–86
"philosophers of the future," 146, 153–55,
   161–63, 179
philosophical activity: character of Socrates', 13–30, 162, 267–69, 317n.92; philosophy vs., 260; Strauss's belief in superiority of, 293
philosophical alienation, 126–27, 257–58,
   259
philosophical citizenship: alienation characteristic of, 126–27, 257–58, 259; Arendt
   and Strauss on nature of, 295–98; Arendt's thoughts on nature of, 259, 273;
   conscience, thinking, solitude and, 263–
   65; Nietzsche's rejection of, 129, 130–31,
   165; Socrates' dissenting, 41–56, 73–74;
   Weber as obstacle to, 186–91. *See also* citizenship
philosophical duty, 222
philosophy: Arendt on gulf between politics
   and, 14, 259–61, 278–79; comparing
   Nietzsche's thought and, 330n.5,
   334nn.79, 85; *demos* as immune to, 289;
   Gorgias on rhetoric vs., 236; Nietzsche on
   citizenship and, 126, 185; Strauss on conflict of politics and, 279–83; Strauss' definition of political, 280, 281–82; Weber
   on Socrates' activities of, 212, 213; Weber's views of, 211–12
"Philosophy and Politics" (Arendt): comparing "Thinking and Moral Considerations" to, 267; on gulf between philoso-
   phy/politics, 14, 259–61, 278–79; on
   philosophical citizenship, 259; on solitude, thinking, conscience, and citizenship, 263–65
Plato: *Apology* depiction of Socrates by, 1–2;
   cave parable by, 171; comparing Arendt's
   and Strauss' views on, 285; on philosophy
   vs. philosophical activity, 260
Plato and Other Companions of Socrates
   (Grote), 121, 124, 129
Platonic conception, 148, 149

Platonic dialogues: on decline in authority, 64; Mill's study of, 75, 120–21; overview of, 311n.4; See also *Apology* (Plato); *Gorgias* (Plato)

Plato's philosopher-kings, 153, 184, 246

plural voting scheme, 113–15, 118, 122

pluralism: common good basis of opinion, 277; consensus prospect in, 342n.81; danger of denying life sphere, 223–24; of *doxa* (opinion), 121, 260–61, 279, 280, 288; as mask for Good Life conception, 325n.97; Mill's promotion of, 61–62; moral, 147; political improvements through, 111–15; revealed through dissent, 62; single truth vs., 260–61; Socratic criticism restricted by moral, 306–7; truth revealed through diversity of, 89–91, 92–97; value attached to, 92; Weber's, 212, 214

political action: Arendt's rescue from devaluation of, 278–79; estrangement of thought and, 14; moral vs., 39; Periclean conception of, 57; Pericles on integration of speech and, 8; social movements and, 259; taking responsibility for, 227–29; Weber's definition of, 206, 221

political actor/leader: calling by, 213, 215, 217–19, 222, 226, 230; charismatic, 188, 205, 231–32, 241; "firm taming of the soul" and, 219–20; meaning of action by, 220; as moral expert, 230–31, 244; political thinker compared to, 281; public-political self of, 252–53; with responsibility, 218, 344n.143; responsible use of violence by, 224–25; struggle as means of selecting, 207; talents required of, 204–5; Weber on moral integrity of, 215, 216–17, 226–29; Weber on vocation/character of, 218–21, 230–31, 244; Weber's self-denying, 246. See also statesmanship

political art: Athens and practice of true, 50; false, 27; knowledge/experienced judgment elements of, 67; philosophical nature of, 32, 36; in representative government, 115–24; understanding of true, 37, 38–39

political economy: character basis of, 196; Weber on Germany's, 194–95

political education: comparing Rousseau and Mill on, 111; Mill's focus on, 70–71, 107–9, 130; promoting common good, 116; Strauss on decline of, 354n.140; Tocqueville's promotion of, 66, 69; Weber's focus on, 203–4, 206–7

political interest: comparing Machiavelli and Madison on, 327n.138; impact of despotism on, 111–12; pluralism and expression of, 111–15. See also self-interest

political life: harmony of Periclean Athens, 6–12; Mill's promotion of pluralism in, 61–62; morality and private/public, 29–30; narrow test of, 24, 26–27, 39; postwar ruin of, 6; self-loss marking, 4; Socrates' view of, 4–5; thoughtlessness secreted by, 22–24

political machine, 217–18

political obligation: *Crito's* doctrine of, 45–46; Mill on social class and, 70, 72–73; of Socratic citizenship, 43

political participation: balance of self-cultivation and, 9–10; balanced by authority, 119; benefits to citizen of, 108–9; *Crito* on obligation of, 45–46; Mill on social classes and, 70, 72–73, 129–30. See also political education

political philosophy, 280, 281–82

politics: agonistic, 275–76, 306, 347n.26; Arendt on gulf between philosophy and, 14, 259–61, 278–79; Arendt's conception of, 249, 250–51, 254; impact on thought by mass, 303–4; Nietzsche's distinction of culture and, 148, 182; postideological idiom of, 301; Strauss on conflict of philosophy and, 279–83; Weber on calling/cause of, 213, 215, 217–19, 222, 226, 230; Weber on conflict/violence in, 187–88, 191–99, 216–17; Weber on illusions of, 229, 243–45, 247; Weber on professionalism of, 187; Weber on two deadly sins of, 218; Weber/Machiavelli on ethics and, 223–29; Weber's vision of modern, 246–47

The Politics (book 1) [Aristotle], 146

The Politics (book 3) [Aristotle], 69–70
"Politics and Government in a Reconstructed Germany" (Weber), 199
politics of struggle: accentuating self-interest, 343n.107; against evil-doing, 226; evolution of Weber's, 207–8; faith foundation of, 301; freedom gained through, 206–7; Weber on conflict and, 187–88, 191–99; Weber on social class conflict and, 197–99; Weber's prediction on German, 191–92
"Politics as a Vocation" (Weber): on "calling" for politics, 188; on charismatic leader, 188, 205, 231–32, 241; on freedom in age of bureaucracy, 217–18; on illusion of politics, 229; on immaturity of student idealist, 219; on mixing public and private spheres, 223–25; Platonic self-deception in, 244; on political actor's moral integrity, 215–16; political responsibility defined in, 187, 227–29
Polus, 32, 33, 34, 39
Polyneices (*Antigone* character), 50
Popper, Karl, 64
power: mediocrity as, 103–4; Mill's rejection of political, 61; parliamentary struggle for, 205–6; rhetoric as key to political, 32–33; U.S. Constitution and development of, 258; Weber on economic struggle in terms of, 197–99; Weber on necessity of, 187–88; Weber on political leaders pursuing, 218
practical life contributions, 238–39
practice (*praxis*), 6
prejudices: communicative rationality of, 180; social class commonsense, 79–80
The Prince (Machiavelli), 188, 202, 224
principle of noncontradiction, 41
private judgement, 120
private life: transvaluation of values to public from, 32, 39–40, 128, 184; Weber/Machiavelli on mixing public and, 223–24
"The Problem of Socrates" (Nietzsche), 143
Protagoras, 119, 209

The Protestant Ethic and the Spirit of Capitalism (Weber), 219
public happiness, 257–58
public life: Arendt on freedom through, 247–48, 251–52, 256–59; performing self in political, 252–53; pursuit of happiness in, 258; transvaluation of values from private to, 32, 39–40, 128, 184; Weber/Machiavelli on applying private action to, 223–25
public opinion: commonsense basis of pluralistic, 277; distinction between knowledge and, 280–81; dogmatism of commonsense and, 72–75; as form of authority, 71–72; "King Nomos" of, 121, 122, 123, 130, 329n.163; knowing grounds of, 86, 87; leveling effect of mass, 104–5; Mill's concerns with, 61–62, 68–69, 78–99, 320n.1, 324n.91; one-sidedness of, 95–97; open discussion model and, 80–85, 92–93, 98–99; partiality of truth in, 93–94; tension between truth and, 324n.81; truth revealed during dissent from, 78–99; truth revealed through pluralism of, 89–91, 92–97, 324n.91; tyranny of the majority, 62, 67–68, 76–77, 113–15; tyranny of the truth solution for, 260–61; warranted belief in, 86–87; See also *doxa* (opinion)
public-spirited aestheticism, 254

rational conscience. *See* Socratic rational conscience
rationalism: doing away with appearance of conflict, 297; politics/ethics relationship under, 224; Strauss use of, 248, 295, 344n.141, 350n.103; Weber on disenchantment with, 209–11; Weber on value of, 208–9; Western cultural secularization and, 192. *See also* secularization
Rawls, John, 306, 307
Reformation, 84, 234
religion. *See* Christianity; creed
religious communal life, 91
Renaissance science, 234

representative government: philosopher contribution to, 275–78; pluralism and expression of, 111–15; political art in, 115–24; self-cultivation promoted by, 114–15; See also *Considerations on Representative Government* (Mill); government

representative thinking, 316n.90

Republic (Plato), 6, 16, 28, 171, 219, 285, 287, 289

responsibility: ethic of, 189; for political action consequences, 227–29; political leaders with, 218, 344n.143

responsible individual, 133

revaluation of values, 151, 155–61, 181

rhetoric: contrast of dialectic with, 38; used to flatter *demos*, 37; *Gorgias* dialogue on, 32, 35–39, 236; as key to political power, 32–33; *Lebensphilosophie*, 144

Rorty, Richard, 184, 282

Rousseau, Jean-Jacques, 1, 56, 109, 109–11

Russian revolutions (1905, 1917), 257

Ryan, Alan, 60

Sartre, Jean-Paul, 24

Schmitt, Carl, 201, 245

"Science as a Vocation" (Weber): on clarifications, 239, 240–41; on defining science, 235–36; Edomite watchman's song cited in, 242; on intellectual integrity duty, 241–42; on new polytheism, 192–93; on pretensions of faith and science, 208–9, 301; on selfless devotion to task, 232; on struggle over ultimate values, 211

science (*Wissenschaft*): as calling, 232–33, 240; clarifications through, 239, 240–41; contributions to practical life by, 238–39; giving meaning to progress of, 233–34; Weber on disenchantment with, 209–11; Weber on value of, 208–9; Weber's defining of, 235–36

secularization: crisis in authority due to, 283; impact of modern, 57; of Western culture, 192. *See also* rationalism

self: examined life irreconcilable with encumbered, 23; Mill's model for cultivation of, 99–100, 102–3, 114–15; Pericles on ownership of, 313n.33

self-agreement, 263

self-interest: distinction between common good and, 116; freedom threatened by market, 69–70; as liberty action motive, 75–76; morality untainted by, 174; political struggle and, 343n.107. *See also* political interest

Shklar, Judith, 1

Simonians, Saint, 89, 119

Sittlichkeit (ethical substance), 57

slave morality, 140–41, 142–43, 147

Smith, Nicolas, 44, 45

"so-called authority," 133, 134

social classes: commonsense prejudices of, 79–80; Mill's skepticism regarding state of, 74; political participation and, 70, 72–73, 129–30; Weber on economic struggle between, 197–99. *See also* elites

The Social Contract (Rousseau), 109

social life: harmony of Periclean Athens, 6–12; postwar ruin of, 6; self-loss marking, 4; Socrates' view of, 4–5; thoughtlessness secreted by, 22–24; Weber on conflict in, 201

society: "connected critic" of, 307–8; conscience and emergency situations in, 272–73, 297; dissent challenge to infallibility of, 78–99; examining application of liberty by, 76; fearing conformism of mass, 253, 326n.112; impact of moral pluralism on, 306–7; impact of transitional ages on, 64–65; influence of bureaucracy on, 194; Mill's indictment of own, 102–3; Nietzsche's rank order of, 126; perceived as tyrant of the majority, 76–77

Socrates: Arendt's depiction as great citizen, 262–63, 264–65, 277–78; as ascetic priest, 139, 143–44; Athenian citizenship practiced by, 5; commitment to avoiding injustice, 24–26, 27–28; comparing Nietzsche or Thoreau to, 180; comparing Weber to, 186–89; as "connected critic," 3, 307–8, 311n.7; defense of self against charges by, 221–22; individualism of, 163; Nietzsche's attacks against, 183, 185; Periclean ethos transformed by, 5; philosophical activity by, 13–30, 162, 267–69, 317n.92;

Socrates (*cont.*)
philosophical invention of dissent by, 73–74; piety for, 343n.121; Plato's *Apology* depiction of, 1–2; preference to Athens by, 49–50; "stinging fish" likening of, 19–20, 268; "stinging gadfly" simile and, 3, 20, 165, 244, 261; "strangeness" of, 23; Strauss' depiction of, 285, 288–89, 352n.119; trial/condemnation for dissent, 13, 81, 82, 83, 259, 317n.92; virtue concept of, 2, 27, 58; on withdrawal from public life, 16–17

Socratic citizenship: *Apology* description of, 13–30, 25–26; *Apology* on universal potential of, 299; Arendt's description of, 19–20; comparison of Funeral Oration and, 11–12; duty to justice by, 47–56; ideal type of, 301–2; "persuade or obey" formula and, 50; political obligation of, 43, 45–46; Strauss opposition to, 292–93. *See also* citizenship; thinking/thought

Socratic integrity, 40

Socratic method, 325n.99. *See also elenchus* (cross-examination)

Socratic moral truth, 3–4, 29–30

Socratic rational conscience: described, 40–41; objection to, 52–54

Socratic thinking: Arendt's application to evil-doing, 21–23, 265–70; common good used in, 279; comparing Mill to, 99; "paralysis of thought," 268; true political art through, 38–39. *See also* thinking/thought

sovereign individual: dogmatism as threat to, 150; examples of, 161; Mill's conception of, 322n.46; Nietzsche's conception of, 134, 135–36, 144, 154, 160, 176–77; process cultivating, 178

speech/deed integration: breaking apart of, 30; Pericles on, 8; pluralism impact on expression of, 112–15. *See also* action; thinking/thought

Spencer, Herbert, 154

"The Spirit of the Age" (Mill), 64, 65

Staatsraison (reason of state), 199

state: "bad conscience" from, 136–37; bureaucracies of the, 193–94, 204, 217–18, 339n.4; convinced of moral greatness,

317n.102; *Crito* on life as gift by, 48; *Representative Government* tutorial, 107; as responsible for injustice, 318n.111; Strauss on best regime for, 351n.115, 353n.139; Weber on compulsory association nature of, 216; Weber on struggle between/within, 193–94, 196–97; Weber's focus on internal affairs, 200–201. *See also* government; nations

Statesman (Plato), 16

statesmanship: false vs. true political art as, 27–28; Socratic claims regarding, 15, 27; Socratic criticism of, 36; Strauss' interest in, 293; unjust actions and, 230–31, 244. *See also* political actor/leader

"stinging fish" simile, 19–20, 268

"stinging gadlfy" simile, 3, 20, 165

Strauss, Leo: Aristotle's influence on, 291–92; on the common good, 111; comparing Arendt to, 283–86, 287–89; comparing Nietzsche to, 294–95; comparing Weber to Arendt and, 247–49; on conflict of philosophy and politics, 279–83; on decline of religious/political education, 354n.140; defense of the philosophical life by, 126; as enemy of all dogmatism, 287; influence of Socratic ideal on, 59, 351n.112; on nature of philosophic citizenship, 295–98; opposition to Socratic citizenship by, 292–93; philosophical quest by, 289–95; promotes return to traditional values, 247; questioning Thomistic natural law, 353n.138; on rationalism/reason, 248, 295, 344n.141, 350n.103; on search for best regime, 351n.115, 353n.139; Socrates as depicted by, 285, 288–89, 352n.119

Strong, Tracy, 173

struggle. *See* politics of struggle

suffering: ascetic priest role in, 138–39; Nietzsche on development of, 137–38

Supreme Goodness, 96–97

teachers: contrast of demagogue with honest, 243; different between political leaders and, 242; primary task of, 238–39; self-restraint of, 232, 236, 237; Strauss on natural-right, 352n.127; Strauss on Socrates' role as, 285

techne (science), 121

Themistocles, 15

theory (*theoria*), practice vs., 6

"Thinking and Moral Considerations" (Arendt), 19, 265, 267, 268, 270, 271, 272–73

thinking/thought: Arendt's promotion of representative, 316n.90; comparing Mill's to Socratic, 99; comparing Nietzsche's philosophy and, 330n.5, 334nn.79, 85; conscience, solitude, citizenship and, 263–65; as dangerous to creed, 269; as essential for judgment liberation, 288; estrangement of political action and, 14; evil-doing and application of Socratic, 21–23, 265–70; harmony between action and, 296; ideological, 349n.70; impact of mass politics on, 303–4; "paralysis of," 268; as quality of *elenchus*, 273; separation of doing/action from knowing and, 6, 14, 302; true political art through Socratic, 38–39. *See also* Socratic thinking

Thirty Tyrants (Athens), 13, 26

Thompson, Dennis, 110

Thoreau, Henry David, 2, 6, 23, 54–56, 180

Thucydides, 7, 17, 255

Tocqueville, Alexis de: desire to educate democracy by, 66, 69; influence on Mill by, 65–66; "moral slavery" warning by, 77; on nation of joiners, 300; on public opinion as authority, 71–72; tyranny of the majority theme by, 62, 67–68, 76–77, 113–15

Tolstoy, Leo, 234, 235, 240

"Tradition and the Modern Age" (Arendt), 6

"transitional" ages: declining authority of, 64; natural vs., 64–65

transvaluation of values, 32, 39–40, 128, 151, 155–61, 181, 184, 350n.94

true political art: possible in Athens, 50; understanding of, 37, 38–39

truth: Christianity as partial, 96; of the commonplace, 94–95; conversion of Christian, 88–89; "more disinterested bystander" of, 95; multiple (doxa), 121,

260–61, 279, 280, 288; Nietzsche on dogmatist's error on, 164–65, 183–85; opinion and partiality of, 93–94; representative political expression of, 112–15; revealed through dissent, 78–99; revealed through diversity of opinion, 89–91, 92–97, 324n.91; tension between opinion and, 324n.81; tyranny of the, 260–61; warranted belief in, 86–87. *See also* moral truth/knowledge

"Truth and Politics" (Arendt), 274

Twilight of the Idols (Nietzsche), 143, 151, 155, 183

tyranny of the majority: fears of, 62, 67–68, 76–77; plural voting scheme to avoid, 113–15, 118, 122. *See also* public opinion

"tyranny of the truth," 260–61

universalizability test, 180

Untimely Meditations (Nietzsche), 144, 168

values: Antigone's political, 51, 319n.128; aristocratic, 139–43, 145–47, 152, 154, 160, 184; created through intellect, 160; culture and creating new, 184; of Machiavelli, 224; noble/non-noble good-evil couplet, 139–43; objective human, 322n.52; provided by ascetic priest, 138–39; transvaluation of, 32, 39–40, 128, 151, 155–61, 181, 184, 350n.94; Weber on disaggregation of, 192–93

Villari, Pasquale, 123

violence: responsible use of, 224–25; Weber on politics and, 187–88, 191–99, 216–17. *See also* conflict

virtue: Aristotle approval of coercive, 316n.89; ascribed to groups, 117–18; Calvinist reduction of, 96; citizen sharing of common, 56–57; created by philosophers of the future, 146, 153–55, 161–63; democracy built on translated Christian, 132; function of government to instill, 100; herd mentality, 146; intellectual examination of, 160; Kant on creating personal, 331n.26; moral/intellectual integrity as civic, 309; moralities of, 97;

virtue (*cont.*)

  narrow test of, 24, 26–27, 39; Nietzsche's collection of, 140; Periclean Funeral Oration presented, 5, 39; political education as, 70–71; separating intellectual integrity from, 302–3; Socrates' view of, 2, 27, 58; specialized knowledge needed for, 312n.12; Strauss on philospher's vs. gentleman's, 285–86. *See also* morality

Vlastos, Gregory, 3, 13, 37

"Vocation" lectures (Weber), 125–26, 191, 194, 213, 215. *See also* "Politics as a Vocation" (Weber); "Science as a Vocation" (Weber)

Walzer, Michael, 43

The Wanderer and His Shadow (Nietzsche), 125, 146, 148, 163, 164

warranted belief, 86–87

Weber, Max: changed views of mature, 199–200; compared to other political thinkers, 214; comparing Socrates to, 186–89, 214; ethical paradoxes awareness of, 229; influence on German history by, 340n.44; influence of Socratic ideal on, 59; on life spheres, 223–25; as obstacle to philosophical citizenship, 186–91; on politics of struggle, 187–88, 191–213; on politics as a vocation, 213–31; on science as vocation, 192–93, 208–9, 211, 235–42, 301; "Vocation" lectures of, 125–26, 191, 194, 213, 215

"What Is Authority?" (Arendt), 285

"What Is Liberal Education?" (Strauss), 293

"What Is Political Philosophy?" (Strauss), 280

will: comparing "general" and "of all," 328n.145; described, 178–79; meaning through imposing one's, 220; political actor's qualities of, 205; stopping weakening of the, 184; to truth/meaning, 185

The Will to Power (Nietzsche), 155, 281

wisdom: responding to limits of human, 308–9; Socrates' definition of human, 304; Socrates' negative, 57n.315. *See also* moral truth/knowledge; truth

Wissenschaft. See science (*Wissenschaft*)

working class: economic struggle of bourgeois and, 197–99; Mill's rejection of suffrage for, 70

Zarathustra (Nietzsche), 190